COMPLIMENTARY TALES

DAVID STRAW

http://storiesbydavidstraw.com

ISBN: 978-1-948928-06-9 (sc)
ISBN: 978-1-948928-07-6 (hc)
ISBN: 978-1-948928-08-3 (e)

Sincerest gratitude to
Sherry Galbraith & Donna London,
who will never buy their
own coffee again.

CONTENTS

FOREWORD

Eastern Airlines was once known as Pitcairn Aviation. It originally flew mail, not people, between the cities of Atlanta and New York. The name was changed in 1930. In 1938 it was owned by General Motors when Eddie Rickenbacker bought the airline. Eastern Airlines grew under the leadership of the former World War I flying ace.

The airline's headquarters was Miami, Florida, while Atlanta, New York, Charlotte, and San Juan were main hubs. Those driving in Miami to and from Key Biscayne might see an Eastern flight take off, or if a cold front came through, coast in for a landing, while driving on Rickenbacker Causeway.

The once proud airline was able to claim several "firsts" in aviation. They were one of the first major airlines not to paint their planes, as the white paint could add up to 100 pounds to its weight. In 1960, it was the first airline to fly the Boeing 727 jet. Then in 1983, they were the first to fly the new Boeing 757. Eastern was also the first U.S. airline to fly the European-based Airbus A-300. And it was the original "official" airline of Walt Disney World, when it opened in 1971.

Eastern flew people and families to half the United States, London (Gatwick), and to Central and South America in almost every type of airplane: DC-8, DC-9, 727, 757, L-1011, A-300, and even a few 747's, thanks to Pan Am.

And it was fun. Really fun.

Yes, that's right, believe it or not, there was a time when flying was a joyful experience. Everything, from strolling in with your luggage, checking in, getting onto the plane, and flying at over 30,000 feet, was as exciting as the possible port of call. The vacation started when you got to the departure terminal, not when you arrived at your destination.

You could walk out to the gate, even if you weren't flying, to greet family and friends as they stepped right off the plane. No one needed a phone or the internet to pass the time while waiting for a plane. There was something called excitement. Giant windows at the gates provided the best views of real, close up airplanes.

Security consisted of an x-ray machine that resembled an Apple IIe computer and took two to three minutes. That's if there was a line. You could take anything you wanted on the plane, in as many bags as you needed. Your gate and seat numbers were written in marker.

Once someone was traveling from Miami to Chicago. They had been lobster fishing while vacationing in the Keys. They approached the gate with a dozen lobsters in a styrofoam cooler filled with ice. The lid was mostly on. They got to the gate and asked to take the cooler on the plane with them, not put it below in baggage. Then once on board, they asked the stewardesses if they could keep it in front of them at their seat. Take a minute to think about that…

Of course, it was not a problem. After 20 minutes with no legroom and being uncomfortable, the crew offered to put it up front with them in the galley. Can you image that happening today?

The airlines took pride in what they did, seeing how much the public enjoyed it. Stewardesses, sorry flight attendants today, would remember those who traveled on repeated flights and routes, and refer to them by name. Men traveling for business would have to catch them up on their lives. Seeing a passenger pull out their wallet and thumb through family photos for a stewardess was as common as the bag of peanuts.

Movies were played, shown on the cabin walls on what today would be called a widescreen or flat screen. The movies weren't tacky, cheesy movies you'd see at two in the morning on some obscure cable channel, but blockbusters straight out of the theater. The actors probably had some Oscars in their trailer. It was a new generation's drive-in.

There were meals on planes. On longer flights, one could actually choose between a couple options: from steak, to chicken, to fish, or to pasta. Was it wonderful? No, but it was a real meal. Drinks and alcohol flowed. A deck of playing cards, matches, cigarettes, blankets, or pens were given out without a care. Not loaned, but given. Kids got airline wings to pin to their shirt, even a toy plane sometimes. You could move around and sit without being interrogated. While walking off the plane, the pilot and co-pilot would stand outside the cockpit and thank you for flying with them. Kids were then allowed to see inside the cockpit, sometimes even during the flight. If someone asked to see the cockpit today, they would be tasered.

When you stepped on board, you immediately took the persona of your idol, favorite actor, or historical figure. It felt as if your plane was the only one taking off. It was a party. Every flight, Pulitzer material was recycled throughout the plane. Flying coach was like flying first class and flying first class was like flying private. Don't believe me? Then why was everyone dressed up.

It wasn't just Eastern. Continental, TWA, Braniff, National, American, Piedmont, United, Delta, and Pan Am, were just some of the airlines that fostered smiles and memories as thick as the clouds they visited. Most of those airlines are gone today.

So is the joy.

PART I

Interstellar
Guardians of the Galaxy
Gone Girl
The Imitation Game
The Grand Budapest Hotel

CHAPTER ONE

A picture can't do it justice.

Misty was positive they dyed the ocean. They just had to, it can't be this color. Dane thought it was fake; part of some secret, massive aquarium the size of Liechtenstein. It was too aqua. It was too clear. It was way too perfect. The white caps were even elegant. Splotches of white foam cresting and popping up sporadically over the ocean like camera flashes, pushed by a cleansing wind. There seemed to be no horizon. The ocean just spilled over the edge of the flat earth like an infinity pool.

The oval island had restaurants, bars, a library, tennis courts, shops, a pool, spa, dive shop, a Turkish coffee house, and reception area. Finally, the beach villas, framed most of the island with unobstructed views of the ocean and your own private sand a few feet away. They were on that island for all of 12 minutes just to check in and they haven't been back since. They were 90 yards away. 90 glorious paces off it.

The honeymoon travelers arrived in the Maldives Monday night on tired, tight legs. The wooden dock was lit like a runway leading out to the ocean villas. Hundreds of tiny night lights casting down from the pilings, leading you out to your dream world. The kind of dock and walk that made stiff legs and joints loosen with every board. Their's was the fourth villa from the end, perched up on stilts. Even strolling out at night, they had the feeling it was something special. They could just make out shapes in glimpses. What they couldn't see, they heard. The sounds were there, in teasing notes swirling from everywhere. It was an amazing unwrapped present, but annoyingly hiding behind the tree through branches, tinsel, and ornaments. No matter what you did, you just couldn't see it.

They awoke in the morning as if on another planet.

It was now Thursday and after all her worries about packing; Misty had worn a total of four things up until now: her bikini, a robe, negligee, and a watch. The silk robe wasn't even from her bag, it was hanging in the closet with the resort symbol on it. She was now in the square pool sticking off their deck, wearing the watch. Misty glanced down at that body, wavering below the surface. She wondered if something other than the robe or bikini would cover it today. She gazed off at the infinite ocean, and closed her eyes to just listen to it. The waves were hushes.

To someone swimming or sailing by, they would see her head with slicked back blond hair and arms resting on the edge. From above, it was a cover for *Playboy.*

Dane woke up and stepped out to the teak deck, stretching. Prickles grew on his arms from the breeze, or was it the trillions of waves rolling past, or the equator's sun, or was it her naked body? Probably all four. Low puffy clouds marched across the sky, appearing to inflate as they approached. The bright tennis ball of a sun would hide behind one of them for a few seconds at a time. He inhaled the air of their week-long setting, as if a drug.

Misty looked up. "Hey sleepy."

"Hey beautiful. When did you get up?"

"I think 9:30ish? You may have to make more coffee, it's probably cold by now."

Dane turned for inside.

There was no kitchen, just a counter with a coffee maker, cutting board, small sink, and bowl with fruit. Under the counter was a small refrigerator. Guests ate on the island, unless you had one of the butlers that served the villas bring out your meals. It sure sounded good to Dane and Misty.

Four minutes later the small 4-cup Braun stopped gurgling. They picked up a bag of ground coffee at the general store in the reception building. It was an arabica coffee from Sumatra. They both agreed that first morning; it was the greatest coffee they had ever tasted. Dane wondered if they brewed it at home or in the office, would they think the same thing. He pulled out two mugs from the sink and looked over his shoulder at his naked wife, in a pool 15 feet away, in the middle of this atoll. He shook his head. He knew the answer.

"Want some?"

"Why not."

He came over and placed the mug down beside Misty's head. Next to the pool were steps to the ocean water below. On the other side of the steps was a net, like a flat hammock that hung over the water. Dane bounced a couple of times as he sat down. He laid back crossing his legs, the steaming mug behind him.

Like the last three mornings, they said nothing for the first seven to eight sips. With their sense of taste finally getting some attention, their other senses continued to soak in and digest everything. They just stared at the ocean. That's what you did here. Stare.

Her mug then found its spot again on her giant teak coaster. Then her eyes found her new husband.

"You coming in or what?"

A grin blossomed. "Eventually." He turned to her. "Nice watch." He stood up, swaying a little at first.

Her watch had stayed on more than her rings. She didn't wear them in the ocean. The water may be as clear as the vodka inside their hut, but finding both an engagement and wedding ring on the bottom, would be like finding that bottle in recycling. She was petrified of losing them. At least the tan lines were there.

It was the one thing she frowned upon about San Francisco. The lack of constant sun. Texas and four years in Los Angeles had spoiled her. If Misty wasn't in class, she was laying out in the sun with a book. At UCLA, she and two friends convinced a dorm worker to give them access to the roof. It was quiet and more peaceful. After a week, they no longer felt afraid of getting stuck up there. After two weeks, she left her book and extra sunglasses hidden in the shade of a huge air conditioning vent. After a month, she didn't bother hiding them anymore.

She found it funny that in less than two years, even in the Bay Area's unpredictable and sporadic sunshine, a thin tan line blossomed on her finger. It was like her skin's own ring. She first saw it while at the doctor's office after sliding it off. Now, in just three full days of the sun, directly overhead, the band of white was a smidgen wider already.

The watch stayed on, even in bed. Dane gave her a look that first night, but Misty said she wasn't taking it off until going to bed back home. Now three days from doing just that, she extended her fingers, stretching them out flat, and looked at her hand. The diamond glowed. The watch sparkled. The sun was bringing them to life. She looked upon both as a pair now. One she wanted to die with. The other she would hand down hopefully to a daughter. On the flight into the Maldives, a bouncy swaying flight with 'lawn mower blades on the wings' according to Dane, she came up with the beginning of the speech she'd give her daughter someday. As for the rest of the speech, that would come after several watch battery replacements and possibly a few nicks. Each nick coming with its own fantastic story.

Her arm plopped back down on the edge. "That's what you notice? Really?" She tilted her head back, peering up at him. Dane's eyes found her face, then slid down her body, a little slower at some parts. He eventually stopped at her painted toenails near the opposite corner of the small pool.

"Well uh, not from this angle."

"Welcome to Colton & Anderson." The man was leaning down locking a jewelry case with a twist of his wrist. He stood up and slid the key chain into his pants. It was second nature to him. "How may we help you today?"

The jewelry boutique was small when compared to bigger, more nationally known stores. Dane was excited about that. The carpet was burgundy, rich with paisley, and you felt ashamed for stepping on it. It was like walking across a giant tapestry from some 14th century castle. Banker's lamps glowed green on dark wood tables. Teak, maybe off the Honey Fitz itself, wrapped around everyone. Dane and Ryan moved around the closest jewelry case, crystal clear and squeaky clean. It felt like the store could be off in the corner of a large library, maybe a vast study in an English manor house, or down in a basement of an office building in Zurich, that only eight people know exists.

The man walked out from behind his display case, right arm extended despite being a lefty. "Allen Anderson."

"Dane Carmichael." He smiled.

Ryan was two steps behind. "Ryan." They all shook hands.

"Mr. Anderson, I'm looking for a woman's watch."

"Ah yes, is there a specific watch maker you're interested in. And please, call me Allen."

Dane nodded. "Omega."

Allen smiled. "Very nice choice." He held out his hand to his right, palm up. "This way Dane, let's see what we have for you."

Dane glanced at Ryan. He was thrilled that the word Omega didn't turn Allen into a nice guy. He seemed nice when the alarm dinged back at the front door.

"The watch is a gift, I'm assuming?"

"Yes. For my," there was a pause, "wife." It would take some getting used to.

Ryan nudged him in the shoulder. "I guess you don't believe in jinxing things."

Dane glanced at his own watch, then over to Ryan. "I think we're going to make it."

Allen clasped his hands in front of him, as if he was ready to begin a journey. "Is there a certain type you had in mind or an occasion?" Anderson's bow tie was perfectly level and even.

The store was not like most where there was a definite dividing line between worker and customer. The owner was not sandwiched between the wall and display case, with the customers out in the middle. Here, the cases were at angles with the tables between. There was a sense of openness that fostered smiles and conversations while leaning towards each other, maybe even rubbing shoulders.

"Something she can wear every day, rain or shine. Forever."

Allen smiled and peered into the case full of women's watches, while slipping on a glove. This case was of higher-end watches. Dane's eyes swept over two IWC and three Baume & Mercier watches before settling on Allen's gloved fingers plucking out a silver Omega. He brought out three more and delicately laid them on a burgundy velvet mat, with *C&A* in gold calligraphy across it.

Dane and Ryan bent down looking at them. Allen then noticed the watch encircling Dane's tan wrist. It was an Omega, slightly older, with a black leather band. Allen cocked his head to his left eyeing it with pleasure, like a framed painting he'd only seen in textbooks. He hoped there was a caption with it. A middle-aged woman came over smiling and shook hands as well. Her name was Beverly. She took the role of the mother everyone wishes they had. It seemed she was interested in simply watching it all.

As Dane reached to touch the second one from the left, Allen was studying his timepiece painting.

"Dane, you must be an Omega fan?"

Dane looked up from the thin women's watch, noticing Allen's eyes leaving his own. "Oh, well I wouldn't go that far. I don't make this a habit."

"May I?" Allen nodded at Dane's watch.

"Of course." He undid the band's butterfly clasp and handed it to Allen. Allen slid his fingers through it and brought it up closer. The fact that Allen didn't say anything for a while brought Beverly closer, leaning over to look.

"Is that a GMT?" She brought up glasses hanging down over her blouse. They were propped on the end of her nose now.

Allen nodded. "Dane, this is a lovely watch. I've never seen one from Omega in person." He looked up with curious eyes. "May I ask where you got this?"

Beverly took off her glasses and looked at Dane.

The Kia Optima pulled out of the parking garage and turned into traffic. Dane grimaced while looking away and flipped down his sun visor, greeted by the noon sun. Ryan just slipped on his sunglasses. The rental began keeping pace with traffic and sped on.

"So where is this place?" Ryan shifted in his seat while switching hands on the wheel.

"Drive straight for two miles and turn left on Hines. It's called C&A Jewelers."

"Have you been there before?"

Dane looked out his window to the skyscrapers of downtown Dallas, peeking between trees and buildings, way off in the distance.

"No. The concierge claims this is the place to go though. I'm going to trust him." He turned to Ryan. "He just told one of Misty's bridesmaids which hotel bar the visiting hockey teams tend to go to and don't order a white wine if you see any players."

Ryan laughed and checked the lane over his shoulder. "So with four hours before walking down the aisle, you just now think about buying her something? And a watch?"

Dane started tapping his finger on his knee to the beat of "Mr. Brightside" by *The Killers.*

"Yeah, I know. I guess with everything going on I kind of lost track of time. I realized on my flight Thursday, I hadn't gotten her one."

Ryan glanced over at Dane's wrist resting on his jeans. "I've known you for 16 years and never knew you had that thing." He looked up at Dane.

"Well we've never flown together."

Ryan nodded and looked back out front as traffic came to a stop.

"Alright, I'm ready. Let me have it." He slapped the steering wheel.

Dane's finger stopped tapping. "Growing up my father was real good friends with this guy. Wyatt, Wyatt Cavanaugh. They were members at the St. Francis too. They sailed together for years and he and his wife had known me since I could walk. He was a pilot, flew for United when I knew him but was with someone else before. I can't remember?" He looked out his window in thought, but couldn't see the airline, so he looked back out front again.

"Anyways, we're sitting in his boat one evening talking about his flights. I wanted to be a pilot and he knew it. He would tell me all about the traveling, the airports, runways, flight plans, everything. I was a sponge."

Ryan narrowed his eyes and slowly turned to Dane. He was a little confused, but listened. He then began pulling through the light.

"So there we are, I'm 12 or 13, and he's telling me about his new flights to Europe. He shows me his watch. I may have asked about it, I can't remember, but he takes it off and shows me."

Dane looked over at Ryan. "I'll never forget how heavy it felt at the time. I don't know why I remember that." He looks past Ryan out the driver's side window as if seeing Wyatt's reflection. He then turned his wrist a little and looked at the watch. He saw Wyatt's thick finger pointing to the 24-hour hand and then twisting the bezel. He continues, speaking slowly, deliberately like carefully reading an ancient scroll or text.

"He tells me it's a pilot's GMT watch, for telling time in two different places at once. Pan Am went to Rolex back in the day about making a watch for their pilots. They were the first to make one, but he didn't want a Rolex. So he found this Omega. He showed me how the hands and bezel work in reading the 24-hour time in two different time zones. It was with him on all his flights."

Dane shook his head. "Next thing I know he's handing me the watch. He tells me, 'I want you to have it. I know you'll use it and take care of it, flying all over the world someday'. I was speechless. I refused, but he would have none of it." Ryan glanced over and turned the music off. Dane continued.

"My parents didn't even know until last night at our hotel, before going to the rehearsal dinner." He stopped shaking his head. He remembers just then looking up, rocking up and down in Wyatt's Island Packet, at a fat 747 taking off out of San Francisco International. It soared off over the bay. Then over the Golden Gate, and off to the west. They were so big he wondered how they could get off the ground, let alone fly. He always felt they floated rather than flew. It was dusk and its blinking, pulsing lights slowly seemed to melt away into the purple night sky. He watched it go, envisioning being in the cockpit one day.

Ryan, again, slowly looked over at his best friend. This time saying what was on his mind since the last red light.

"Uh, one problem I see in this Hallmark story. You hate to fly?"

Dane bit his lip and then shut his eyes, not because it was too bright, but too embarrassed.

"Yeah, life is ironic huh." He opened them and shot a glance over at Ryan. "I didn't hate flying till I was older." He shook his head.

"Does he know you grew a fear of flying?"

"No, thank god." Dane swallowed hard. "The thing is, turns out he had less than a year to live. He knew it when he gave the watch to me. Even my father didn't know he was sick until the very end. He died a little over ten months later.

"He had no children. I'm not sure why, I never asked, but there was something to it, something going on in the background. So, he gave it to me."

Ryan let that soak in a little and could tell he had probably never told that story before, or maybe just once. He then glanced over at him. "So you think he's rolling over in his grave?"

Dane laughed. "God I hope not. If he's looking down, which he has to be, where else would pilots go, I'm sure he's smiling." He peered down at it and twisted the bezel until the 10 was in front of the 24-hour hand.

"Now I only wear it when I fly, which thanks to work is about eight to ten times a year. It makes me feel comfortable. I feel safe when I wear it, like nothing can happen to the plane as long as I'm wearing this watch. No matter what, we're going to make it wherever we're flying to."

Ryan missed the turn.

Dane licked his lips and looked at the watch in Allen's palm.

"It was passed down with great care for even a better reason. I appreciate it."

Allen was still looking at Dane. "But it's a long story. Isn't it?"

Dane's eyes shot up at Allen's and he smiled while nodding.

"Well let's start a new one shall we." Allen handed it back to Dane and they looked at the four watches in front of them. One was gold and the other three were silver. Dane liked the second from the left and Ryan agreed with a nod. It was a simple silver watch with a dark face. He now needed an arm, and his was too big.

"I need a wrist."

He held the watch and looked at Beverly standing next to Allen, sizing up her wrist. Nope. Narrow like his grandmother. He then turned to the other side of the store. Two woman were sitting at a table, one worked at the store and the other was a customer. He placed the watch back down and walked over to their table smiling. He looked at the customer first, who was feeling a bracelet with her fingers as if a flower petal. Her arm was too thick as well. He then looked at the other girl, younger, probably in her mid-20's. She eyed Dane the minute he headed over towards them. She was leaning on the table towards the customer, but now sat back and put her hands in her lap.

"Hi, what's your name?"

"Jourdin." She smiled up at him.

"Dane." They shook hands and he didn't let go. "Jourdin I need a wrist and I like yours." He smiled at her and nodded at her arm. "May I borrow yours for a second?" Dane may being saying 'I do' in four hours, but he still liked to flirt, and always would. It was as far as he would go. And this girl was worth flirting with.

"Of course." She laughed, slid some hair over her ear, as Dane twisted her arm a little inspecting her wrist. Beverly came over to switch places as

Allen waved Jourdin over. Dane followed. Jourdin had straight black hair past her shoulders and an olive complexion. There was either some part Greek or Middle Eastern in her parents' past. She was very attractive in her white blouse and tight black shirt to her knees.

Allen slid the watch onto her arm and clasped it closed. It dangled on her slender wrist and Allen pinched the loose part. It tightened and he moved her arm to Dane. Dane smiled and reached for her wrist twisting it around, admiring the watch and wrist. From the elbow down, it was Misty.

Dane nodded, "Yeah I like it." He glanced up at Jourdin, then Allen. The watch made Dane's eyes sparkle, but so did trying to picture Misty's face when she first sees it.

"Does that size look about right?" Allen had pulled out his glasses and was about to put them on. The glasses and glove earlier seemed to come out of nowhere. Ryan wondered how he did that.

"Maybe," he bent down closer for another look, "maybe one link loose."

Allen reached for her wrist and the watch, checking the links. Dane smiled and looked at Jourdin.

"Are we about to twist your arm off?"

Everyone laughed and she shook her head. "No, no I'm fine." Her eyes hadn't left Dane since he came over. Ryan noticed and shook his head.

Allen took the watch off and checked the tiny tag. He then disappeared to the back of the store through a door. He came back two minutes later with a small white box.

Inside the white box was a smaller red one made of leather, with the omega symbol on it. The new watch was inside this. Then there was a small book, like a Bible, that was the owner's manual in 20 different languages. Finally, there was a cardholder with plastic cards slid into slots, like credit cards. One was the registration and another was the international warranty card. Allen would write a date on both in sharpie. The third had a bar code along the back and Allen swiped it through a machine.

Allen took the new watch behind a counter near the back to take out some links, and start filling out the paperwork and cards inside. Jourdin moved back to her customer and Beverly came over. She looked at Ryan and then Dane.

"I think your wife will love the watch. Very tasteful, yet classy. Is there anything else we can do for you this afternoon?" She looked down at his hand. "Perhaps a new wedding band?" She gave him a look with a grin.

Dane looked at her with tight eyes, then got it. "Oh, no thank you." He held up his bare hand. "I'm getting that in a couple hours actually."

Ryan smiled, making eye contact with Beverly and nodded.

A shocked Beverly looked at him. "Oh my goodness, you're getting married this afternoon?" She covered her chest with her hand.

Dane smiled.

"Well congratulations Dane. That's wonderful." It was sincere. Beverly was called to the back to talk to someone on the phone. Allen arrived a couple minutes later with the box and the bill. Dane handed him his credit card.

"If it's okay, I'd like to add a tip for Jourdin. She was a nice wrist model."

Allen smiled. "That's very considerate of you. I know she would appreciate it." He looked up and called Jourdin over one more time. He put the new watch on her wrist and showed Dane to make sure he got it right.

Dane tilted his head to the right. "Perfect." Jourdin held up her arm and Allen started taking it off to put it back in the box.

"Thank you Jourdin." Dane smiled at her and she returned it.

"No problem and congratulations." They laughed a little and she moved back around to the tables. She only meant the first part. Dane was another guy she was too late for.

Allen handed him the box in a brown bag with handles. "Dane, it was a pleasure serving you today. If it needs adjustment, do not hesitate to bring it back. My card is inside."

Dane reached up and they shook hands. "I will. Thank you."

Allen pulled off his glasses with his other hand.

"And congratulations as well. May this start another long story."

Dane smiled and let go of his hand. He glided out of the store with anticipation pushing him along.

Two minutes later, they were headed back to the hotel.

"What's our time frame?" Dane asked while flipping through the owner's manual for fun. He was in the Japanese section.

"We should get you to the church in an hour. We also need to hit the liquor store."

"Definitely."

"So how much did you tip her?"

"$200. She was kind of hot too. Exotic looking."

Ryan gave him a quick glance. "Kind of? She was real hot."

Three blocks later, Dane was flipping through the Swedish section.

"Armbandsur." Dane looked over at Ryan, then back down in the book, saying it like at a spelling bee. He thinks it meant watch.

"Does Misty know you're getting her that?"

"No." Dane closed the small, thick manual and looked out Ryan's window at Dallas in the distance. "I'll give it to her tomorrow before our flight."

"You got a book or something for the flights?"

"Yeah. I'm sure we'll pick up some magazines. We need to get some playing cards."

Ryan nodded. Then quickly looked over his left shoulder and changed lanes.

"Here we go." The rental veered into the liquor store parking lot.

That first time you wake up to your wife only happens once. Unlike yesterday, Dane was determined to slow down and enjoy it. He was told by everyone for the last month, the wedding would go by in a flash. He's pretty sure he was at the pool in the morning, the suit was barely dry when he packed it. He's got Misty's watch to prove he and Ryan were at the jeweler's. There is a ring on his finger from the church and a slight headache behind his eyes from the reception. Yeah, it happened. He's pretty sure there is going to be a video of the wedding. He can always watch that. There is no video of this morning.

He took a deep breath and turned his head to the right. His chin nudged the top of Misty's head as she burrowed it in farther between his shoulder and neck. His left hand escaped the sheet and began stroking her blond hair over her ear. He opened his eyes and watched her strands of blond hair slip through his fingers. Dane then rolled over on his side facing her as his stroking now moved to her cheek.

"Wake up Mrs. Carmichael."

A moan.

He smiled as his fingers continued stroking, attempting to get her eyes open through her cheek. It finally worked.

Her eyes were the same. Her hair, even messy, was the same. The way she hooks her leg between his and caresses his hip and side is the same. His desire was the same. Even the side of the bed she's on hasn't changed. But it still felt like night and day. His insides were different. He prayed that never changed.

While kissing her forehead, she tilted her head up and slid her hand to his chest. Two fingers tapped his chest and a smile warmed the room.

"Say that again."

"Wake up Mrs. Carmichael."

The room got even warmer.

Misty's eyes peered around half the room before returning to his. She scooted up a bit and played with his hair.

"So this all wasn't a dream?"

"Nope." Dane laughed to himself at the resemblance. Like a dream, he couldn't remember everything. "Although it did go by fairly fast."

"I remember everything." She was now touching his face. "Go brush your teeth."

Dane rolled his eyes, "No, no Mrs. Carmichael, we're married now. I don't have to do that anymore." He was impressed he said it without laughing.

She started pushing him, rolling him over towards his end of the bed like a fallen log, with a slight grunt. "Well if Mr. Carmichael wants to make love to his wife, he needs to go brush his teeth."

As if giving in, but thrilled to do it, a "fine" wafted up to the angled ceiling above them. He sat up on the edge of the bed and rubbed his face. He noticed the clock by the phone read 10:04. *Slowly, slowly, go slow.*

He brushed his teeth and splashed some water on his face. He came out and stood in the bathroom doorway. He leaned into it. The *Governor's Suite* was actually in the attic of the old bed & breakfast. There wasn't a flat, level part of the ceiling anywhere. The peaked, Victorian style roof and spires above enforced its will on the room directly under it. Even the door in the corner wasn't a rectangle, with the top edge slanting down. *Trapezoid or rhombus?* Dane couldn't remember his third grade math. The girl in bed kept erasing the mental whiteboard. The wife in bed, that is.

He glanced at the clock again. 10:06. He took a slow deep breath, the kind that signals peace and assurance. He was afraid it would read 10:12 or 10:15 already. He wanted to keep the wedding-day clock, the fast one, in the past. Their everyday life-clock was ticking now, and he wants it to be much slower.

He of course remembers a lot from yesterday. There was the ceremonial drink of scotch, carefully placed behind a book in the church library thanks to Ryan, with his groomsmen. Most of whom haven't seen one another in a year or two. There was Misty emerging from open doors with her father making his chest thump. Then those brown eyes in a pool of tears as she somehow managed to squeak out, 'I do'. Their first dance was INXS's *Never Tear Us Apart,* and he remembers simply looking at each other mouthing one lyric together, as if preplanned though it wasn't.

I was standing. You were there. Two worlds collided. And they could never tear us apart. He never saw the faces of the wedding party and old classmates that smiled and nodded their heads at the beautiful irony.

"That's them, you know." Jill, a bridesmaid, leaned over to her date touching his arm. "They met in line while getting beers at halftime of the UCLA - USC game."

Finally the cake and speeches, along with the morning pool visit, that bookended a speedy, glorious day. Maybe so glorious it's supposed to be fast? One thing wasn't fast, but slow. The attic. And it started downstairs.

They arrived at the Corinthian Bed & Breakfast around 11:15 in a daze. Dane thinks it was the furniture and lace. Misty the carpet and wallpaper. But the Victorian style inn took them back in time to an English estate. As the clock hands rotated counter, they got stuck. To their relief, the newlyweds were trapped in time.

Of all the suites sandwiched between that peak roof and wrap around porch of white, this room was them. As lovely as the ones below are, they are all the same in a way, like the ones across town and the ones in San Francisco and Denver and Boston and Charleston and so on. Everyone's wedding night tends to be in the same setting. The suite in the attic was their escape.

It was as if they ran out of the church on a whim after being announced and left everyone behind, confused yet celebrating. Then, holding hands while she held her flowers, they stood on the sidewalk and looked around the block for someplace to run to before anyone came out. Then they snuck in the closest house and hurried upstairs to the attic room to hide. Alone. Together finally.

From the head down, the room was like most in the B&B. It was from the head up that it was different and unique. The attic ceiling angled down on all sides with a pocket over the window between the eaves. He remembers hitting his head after leaning down to look out at the back gardens.

They were given a picnic basket with food, champagne, and cake from the wedding. They changed into silk robes, almost signaling the wedding was unofficially over. They sat on the floor with their basket and finally enjoyed some food, drink, and each other.

"Was this on the table?" Misty asked while holding up an appetizer.

"I guess? Did you even eat?"

She laughed, "Not really. Oh, what is that?"

"I don't know," he started chewing, "but it's good."

She sipped her champagne and laid down on her stomach facing him. "My dad got hammered."

Dane laughed. "I know, my mom too. Did you see them dancing together?"

"I thought it was cute." She took another sip. "Was Ryan trying to hook up with Colette?"

"They were? I didn't notice. That would be interesting."

"Yeah. I'll call her tomorrow and see what happened."

Dane started shifting items around in the basket, searching for unknown treats.

"I met Miss Vasner." He pulled out some strawberries, "She's taller than I imagined."

"Oh my god you did? I'm so happy she was there, I hadn't seen her in years." Misty twirled some of her hair thinking of Veronica Vasner. "She was my first ballet instructor when I was four."

They realized sitting and lying there, that after all the planning over the last 15 months and events the last three days, a simple picnic alone in an attic was all they desired. It would almost be what they would remember the most. Eventually she would pick up her head inviting a kiss, which would lead to them undoing their robes half way. Then making love as husband and wife for the first time. The sitting area was off to the side with a sofa and coffee table. The sofa was up against the wall, or was it technically the ceiling, coming down at 45 degrees? Who cares? They took the half empty, or maybe half full is a better thought, bottle of champagne to the coffee table. With their robes open, they sat on the sofa for more passion, she reaching up and pressing her hands into that sloping ceiling for leverage on top of him. They don't remember getting to the bed or falling asleep.

So at 10:06am, his head turns to that bed at the blond vision rumpling the sheets in curves. The 25 year old turns her head, resting her chin on her left shoulder. With an outstretched arm reaching across the bed, tiny fingers begin curling up calling him over. The husband seems to float to her, slowly, to make love to his wife. In a bed, for the first time.

"Did you sign the guest book?"

Dane was at the desk sorting things in his wallet. "Yeah, before taking everything out to the car."

Misty's heels clicked on the parquet floor after stepping down from the carpeted stairs. She held her small purse to her side as she touched his back and looked over his shoulder at what he was doing. The newlyweds were up before most of the bed & breakfast.

"You ready?"

"Yeah, just about. I love those jeans on you."

She smiled, "I know."

Sitting on a plane for a couple long flights is not Dane's idea of a pleasing time. With Misty sitting next to him in those jeans and heels, that he also loved, she would be a little distracting and make the flights go faster. She knew this as well. It all stems from their first flight together two years ago to this very city.

During her junior, and his senior year at UCLA, they flew to Dallas for a childhood friend's wedding. Misty was excited about Kristen's wedding, seeing maybe 11 or 12 other ex-ballet dancers, and bringing Dane home with her. It was their first big trip together after dating for over a year. She knew people were looking forward to meeting him and she was thrilled to surprise those who didn't know.

They were at LAX sitting in *Cole's* in Terminal 4, waiting for their American Airlines flight to Dallas-Fort Worth. He was already on his third drink.

"So is your plan to just pass out on takeoff and for me to wake you at the gate?"

"Works for me."

Misty sipped her weak gin & tonic. "You're not going to like, flip out all psycho on me, are you?"

He laughed, "no I'm not that bad. Just, I don't know, just tense and stressed."

"Why don't you read?"

"I try, but sometimes I can't relax enough to concentrate."

She reached across and grabbed his hand. "It'll be fine. Weather looks good all the way." She picked some lint or something off his sleeve and flicked it to the ground before grabbing her drink again.

"Besides, it's different now, you're flying with me." She finished her tonic drink. "I'll keep you company."

Out at the gate, they were sitting waiting to board their flight. His left arm was on the chair rest between them as he grabbed her hand. She was staring off to her left when a smile bubbled up on her face. Tingles began simmering, as she loved when he held her hand in public. He grabbed her whole hand, covering it like a shell. She looked down and twisted her hand to interlock their fingers. That's when she noticed the watch.

Misty's lips parted slightly and she cocked her head to the left at the shiny watch peeking out from his sleeve. She wouldn't dare unlock fingers, so with her left hand, she reached over and pulled back the sleeve completely.

"Hey, when did you get this?" She looked up at him with eyes as perplexed and bright as the coaxial escapement inside the Swiss timepiece. "It's…an Omega?"

Dane glanced down at it, then up to her. "I only wear it when I have to fly."

She gave him a look that finally allowed Dane to tell his story of his pilot's watch. It was the first time he ever told anyone. Ever. Misty could tell in his pauses and eyes this wasn't rehearsed, but fresh. It seemed fitting he was doing it at an airport, with a Boeing 767 at the end of the jet way. Wyatt would be pleased.

As Dane shared the story, with each page of the memory flipping for her, Misty grabbed his hand harder. By the time he mentioned he wore it to feel safe, that the plane was 'indestructible' as long as he had it on, she was gripping his hand so tight he would have to shake away the redness.

When he was done, he looked up at her as if shy. Her eyes were almost teary as she touched his cheek. She leaned over pulling his face closer and kissed him. "I love you." She pulled away just in front of him and stared at him. *I'm going to marry you,* she thought to herself.

Over 16 months, they went to four 'special' dinners, either birthdays or anniversaries. They went up to Napa for a long weekend for their first overnight trip together. They dressed up with 45,000 other students for a homecoming weekend and game against Cal senior year. He never had it on, never mentioned it, never thought of impressing her with a $6,000 watch. Most girls would be awed by seeing a watch like this. Misty was now in awe, by not seeing it.

She brought up her right hand, which brought up his left as well, and looked at it. She rotated the bezel and listened to it click. She then put their arms down, still squeezing the blood out of his hand.

"I want you to wear this all the time," her eyes left the crown of the watch and looked at him, with a pretend crown on his head. "Not just when flying or with me."

Dane moved some of her hair over her ear. He loved when he could bring Misty to the verge of tears. He told himself that's where her name came from.

"You do?"

She nodded. "You're my guardian angel. Nothing can happen to you and if this watch will do that, then you have to wear it. Always."

Dane could do nothing but nod and smile. It was the greatest flight of his life, not once was he nervous or fidgety. As she fell asleep, resting her head on his right shoulder somewhere over New Mexico, he thought about getting her a watch. She would need protection too.

Dane slipped his wallet into his inner jacket pocket and reached down for his small duffle bag. He grabbed her hand with the other and turned towards the back of the bottom floor. At the other end of the B&B, facing the gardens, was a bright room in the corner with lace curtains on both sides. A white wicker sofa with cushions sat under a window, with fake ferns sprouting out on either side. He pulled Misty over in that direction and she tilted her head to get a look at him.

"Did you forget something?"

"Not exactly." They sat on the sofa cushions, with a print that matched the large round rug in the middle of the room. He quickly looked over at an imaginary Wyatt sitting in the wooden chair in the opposite corner, or was it a seat cousin on a sailboat, or was it the cockpit seat? He couldn't tell. What he did know was Wyatt nodded at him. *Go ahead, give it to her.*

He unzipped his bag and pulled out a plain white box. Their knees were touching as he handed it to her.

"I want to give you something. It's been on my mind for a while now."

She took the box while looking at him with a face that was a few seconds ago curious, now overcome with emotion. Something told her this was special. She placed it in her lap as her chest began swelling. She licked her lips. She swore the air conditioner had just kicked on. She glanced at her new husband quickly before reaching for the lid. She pulled off the top. Her hand immediately came up covering her mouth and took a huge breath. The red, leather box with Omega on the top greeted her eyes. And heart.

Misty would be naive to say the brand didn't excite her. What brought out the tears was the long story that would make Mr. Anderson proud.

"Now you'll be safe, always." Misty looked up at him with her hand still glued over her mouth and began crying. She nodded as if saying yes, and let go of her mouth to hug him.

She pulled away 20 seconds later and wiped her eyes. She looked down at the box realizing she hadn't even seen the watch yet.

"My dad is going to be pissed." She sniffled. "He bought me this for my sweet sixteen." A little laugh escaped those sniffles as she started unclasping her Seiko tank watch. Dane smiled and took it as she tilted open the Omega box.

She brought it up closer. "It's beautiful." She shook her head in disbelief. She pulled it out and off the holder. She slipped her hand through the metal band and snapped it shut around her wrist. The whole time Dane looked on like a kid gawking at a plump stocking over a fireplace.

"How does it fit?" He was so nervous that it would fit okay, more so than the rings fitting.

"It's perfect."

Dane closed his eyes for a second. *Thank you Jourdin.*

CHAPTER TWO

The bathroom is one of only two rooms in the villa, with the bedroom next to it. The stand-alone terrazzo bathtub is in the middle of the bathroom, far enough in for privacy, but close enough to the deck for the view. It was part leather wingback chair, part waterbed, all in front of a real life IMAX screen of the Indian Ocean. At some point, they each had taken an hour-long nap in it without meaning to. It was better than NyQuil.

Dane was leaning back against Misty, as her fingers made little circles on his chest, just above the bath water. As customary the last four days, their ears were perked. There was a constant lapping sound coming from the water under the hut, as the numerous pilings played radio antenna. Instead of grabbing the frequencies from above, pulling them down the metal wand to your ears, this radio tuned in sounds from below. It siphoned them upwards, resonating through the teak floor, to swirl around you and be absorbed in the thatched roof. It was constant, encompassing, and marvelous.

"God I just want to record this so we can wake up to it every day."

Dane grinned in agreement. "When did we sign up for the dive trip?"

"Tomorrow. I can't wait to try out the underwater camera." Misty closed her eyes so she could listen better.

"Oh yeah, almost forgot. So should we actually go to the island today?"

"Ugh, it's so far."

Dane loved when she gets sarcastic. "You should check out the spa, I'm sure it's really good."

"I hope their gin & tonics are better than the airports." She said it while sliding her hand under the water to his stomach.

"No, they rob you. Something tells me they will be stronger here. When do you want to go?"

She closed her eyes and let her head fall to the side. "Not right now. We should finish off that last bottle of wine before we go. We can get more there." Her knee poked up from below the surface and rested against the side of the tub, carelessly.

He peered over into the bedroom at a small table, where four empty bottles and one-half full one sat. The butler brought those after they finished off the first three, plus two champagne bottles. His esophagus was basically a grape vine at this point.

Five minutes later, Misty had nearly fallen asleep. Her eyes popped open a couple of times startled. She sighed and sat up a little, which was hard with him on top of her. The last thing she wanted to do here was nap.

"Hey let's play cards and finish the bottle. We haven't played in a while. I need to wake up."

"I didn't know you brought some?" He pressed his hands onto the edges, and stood up making it rain in the tub. He stepped out and grabbed a towel.

"I didn't. There's some in the drawer."

"Oh." He wrapped the towel around his waist and headed over.

"I noticed them yesterday." Misty twisted looking behind her. "No the other one."

He shut one and pulled open the other. He reached in and shifted some things around. There was a knife, bottle opener, matches, small flashlight, a pen, and the playing cards.

Dane picked them up and held them in front of him. "Where the hell did these come from?" He could tell they were old. They were in a dark blue box with *Eastern* written in white at the top, and the bottom upside down. He flipped them over, then squinted his eyes.

"These aren't from here."

Misty twisted in the tub and looked back. "Someone must have left them?" She stood up and pointed to the towel rack. "Hey can you hand me one."

Dane looked up from the cards and eyed her glistening slick body up and down.

"Not really."

"Ugh." She rolled her eyes and got out. Dane found he adored looking at Misty with little to no clothes on even more now. He thinks it's just knowing she's his wife now and he's the only one who ever will.

They put on the robes and moved to the reclining chairs just out from the tub and in front of the hammock. He brought the cards, she the bottle. They couldn't find the glasses, which were probably dirty anyway, so they just drank from the bottle.

After five minutes, Dane couldn't take his eyes off the empty box or draw pile. *Eastern*. It continued to blink in his eyes like a film reel, looking for it back in time. Dane shook his head and drew a card.

Misty smiled and thumbed her cards with a rippling sound. She came from a family of card players, her grandfather was known around Dallas back in the day. She took pride in beating Dane.

"Already in trouble huh?"

He glared up at her. "No." He picked up the box. "Does Eastern mean anything to you?" He discarded an eight of hearts and held up the box to her.

She looked at it shaking her head, then up to him. "Some company I guess. Why what is it?" She pulled a card from the pile.

"I don't know, there's something about it. I've seen or heard it somewhere, I just know it."

She discarded and lifted the bottle up. "From the U.S.? California?" She tilted back a sip and handed him the bottle.

"Not sure." He took it and drank. "It's familiar though." He put the bottle down and took her nine of spades discard.

She shrugged her shoulders and looked at her hand, then tilted her head eyeing his hand, knowing he had spades and clubs. *Eastern* was staring back at her. After his discard, she picked up the four of diamonds. She froze, staring at the card.

"Oh." She turned it around showing Dane. "Look what's written on this one."

Dane leaned forward, squinting. "Huh."

The number 358 50 555 75 22 was written along the side in blue ink. Along the other edge was *Barnstation*, written in the same ink.

"Kind of weird."

She turned it back around to her. "Is that a phone number or code?"

Dane shook his head. "Not sure. I wonder what *Barnstation* is?"

Misty stacked it in the discard pile. Dane picked up from the draw pile next to it.

"Knocking three."

"What?" She looked down, mouth open.

He grinned, took another sip of Pomerol, and offered her the bottle. For a brief second, it was the milk jug from the Indianapolis 500.

She tossed her cards down knowing what she had, shaking off the bottle.

"Come on, let's hit the island." He sat back stretching.

"Oh hell no we're going now." She scooped up the cards and began shuffling. He finished the bottle grinning at her.

Two hands later, she redeemed herself and the Palmer name. She put on real clothing for the first time, a peach summer dress, and they walked hand in hand back down that runway. In daylight this time.

Misty made an appointment at the spa for 3:00. They had lunch and ordered more wine and champagne to be delivered to their villa. They walked around the island taking it all in. It didn't take long. They were at a bar overlooking the other side of the island as the winds picked up. Misty's small ponytail was almost a windsock.

"How's that G&T?" Dane leaned on the table towards her, the candle under his chin.

Misty swallowed. "Oh my god, so good." She sat it down and matched his lean. "Mostly gin."

"Told you."

"Two more of these and I'm going to be stumbling." Misty held up her face to the freshening breeze blowing through. She sighed softly and shut her eyes feeling it caress her cheeks. Moby's "Porcelain" was playing, and seemed to coming from everywhere from hidden speakers.

"Let's get three." He turned looking for the waiter.

"No. I've got the spa in 20 minutes." She reached over grabbing his arm. "I can't be drunk there."

"Why not? That would be funny."

She gave him a look. Then looked down at his arm in front of her and his watch.

"What time is it back home?"

He twisted his wrist. "9:00pm, last night."

She nodded. "So when we go back, will we gain a day, go back in time?"

"Yeah, we fly over the international date line, so we'll go back to the previous day."

She was resting her chin in her palm. "So coming out here we went ahead in time."

Dane grinned, "Uh I guess you could say that."

"My god, we have the flux capacitor."

"The flux capacitor?" Dane grinned.

Misty started laughing and sat back. "Yeah, you know."

Dane laughed and signed the villa number to the bill. He finished his drink. She noticed "Porcelain" was still playing, on repeat. Ordinarily it would be annoying to hear the same song over and over, but it seemed to fit. Hearing the song years later, like the breeze against her cheeks at the table, would immediately smack Misty's senses with visions of this place.

"What will you do?"

"Maybe go the library. Head back, we'll see." He leaned over farther. "Have fun."

She met him for a kiss, then reached up and held him there longer. Eventually she pulled away.

"I'll have your G&T's waiting for you," he smiled.

"Good." She walked away quickly towards the spa, holding down the dress in the wind.

Dane decided to check out the library, then head back out to their villa. The sky was clear, but the growing wind was rolling up black clouds on the horizon and pushing them this way. He figured he had an hour at the library before he should get to the villa.

While on the way to find book, he gazed up at the sky while it was still clear. Parallel lines of chalk streaked across the sky, probably flights heading to Malaysia or maybe the Philippines. A new one was being drawn by a minuscule silver spec, zooming east. The chalk line was sharp and definite at first, then thinned out and puffy.

Dane took a breath of satisfaction knowing he didn't have to get on a plane for a couple more days. Although the last time wasn't that bad. Even the airport experience, that is awful and actually getting worse, wasn't too bad either.

He kept it a secret for five months. He didn't tell anyone, not even his parents. With possibly a little more than 200 people attending the wedding, someone was bound to find out where the honeymoon was. All Misty knew was it was warm, there was plenty of water, and it was not close.

Dane figured he's only getting married once and felt blessed to have found his new wife. The long flight would be a sacrifice he'd deal with. It was hard keeping it from Misty with all her questions about packing. After a week, she just kept asking, thinking it would break him. She even used her body. Nothing worked.

How warm does it get there…are the nights cool…it's a beach right…are we on the beach or near it…I don't need a passport do I…will we go out a lot…how many dresses do I need…flip flops too?...how many bathing suits… do I need one for diving…are we hiking…do I need a hat…what kind of jacket should I bring…can I do shopping there…you're bringing your camera right…I'm assuming they have hairdryers?

Questions about the flight were just as lengthy. All he said was it was far and he would make sure her clothes for the flight were okay that morning. While standing in her closet two weeks earlier, she picked up her fashionable boots and held them up to him. Dane rolled over on the bed.

"Nope". She was surprised; she knew he liked them with her jeans tucked in. "Heels." He rolled back over on his back. "You can take them off easily. And they're sexy."

A week later, they left the Corinthian B&B in Dallas and drove the agonizing long 26 miles to the airport. They parked in long-term and took the shuttle. They each pulled their suitcase and he held a duffle they would take on the plane. As they approached the ticket counter on the curb, Misty was bouncing in her heels. The wonder was killing her. Her mind was running to possibilities she couldn't keep up with.

Dane knew she would most likely figure it out before taking off, he just wanted to prolong it as much as he could. If they went to the airline counter inside, it would narrow down the marathon route in her head. What he was about to hand the lady, would give enough away.

They heaved their bags down on the metal scale next to the counter. He brought up the duffle. The lady waited for a bus to pass and a plane roaring off in the background over the roof.

"Destination and airline?"

Dane smiled and pulled out two passports.

"Wait, we need passports?" She stared at them in shock as he handed them over. "And how'd you know where mine was?"

Dane just smiled, his eyes gave nothing away. Misty's were roaming the earth, from in front of her to a globe in a classroom. She glanced down at her bag thinking what's in there, then his, then the sky above. *Oh my god, we're leaving the country? Bye bye Hawaii.*

The lady behind the counter showed the patience of someone 20 minutes away from finishing an eight-hour shift in noisy, curbside conditions. Her backdrop was traffic and engine exhaust. She took a deep breath and tried again. Firmer.

"Destination and..." Then she saw the sticky note fluttering on one of the passports. She grabbed the passports and read it. The note allowed his secret to continue. The woman's eyes softened and her jaw relaxed. She glanced at Misty first with a slight smile. If seven hours earlier, it would have been more than that.

She looked over at Dane. "How many bags will you be checking?"

"Two please."

Misty was still staring at him. "Do they speak English?"

"Yes Mrs. Carmichael. Don't worry." He pulled away from whispering in her ear and smiled. She dragged her teeth over her lip and narrowed her eyes on him. Another American flight took off and banked right, disappearing into the clouds. She watched it go, taking her away to other options. *Bahamas, Caribbean, Bermuda?*

Dane took back the passports and handed the lady a $20 bill, mostly paying for her silence, with a smile. They had their boarding passes and could eventually just go right to the gate. They stopped at a newsstand first. They stepped up to the checkout counter when she tossed some breath mints on the five magazines they grabbed. She then peered at Dane, knowing his sense of humor.

"Hold on. Let me guess, we're going to like, El Paso aren't we? God damn Corpus Christi."

Dane immediately closed his eyes and started laughing. He was bending over slightly.

She tilted her head more looking at him. "The passports were just a ploy weren't they?" She gently slapped his shoulder. She knew he would do something like that, but for the honeymoon?

"That's awesome. You so know me."

"Exactly!"

Dane handed the lady a debit card. He shook his head, now suppressing the laugh.

Her eyebrows scrunched, "I didn't think so…"

Eventually they found a bar out on their terminal. Misty checked the airlines on the sign they passed under and a lot were some she had never heard of and/or were foreign. Of course, American was also out there. They were on their second drink as the table continued getting weak from her leaning on it. Misty was swaying slightly as she stared at him.

"So what does 'far' constitute? Four hours? Fourteen hours?"

Dane took a sip and held his glass in front of him. He shrugged. "Don't remember."

"Which compass directions are we going?"

"It's a cardinal direction. No wait, an intermediate direction. Or is it both?"

She then kicked him under the table. "Come on already!"

He reached down and rubbed his shin. "Jesus, okay okay." He sat back up. People nearby shot glances over at them. He took a deep breath.

"We have two stops on the way. Going west."

"West?" She wasn't expecting that, head tilting down a little. *There goes Bermuda, the Caribbean, and the Adriatic.*

Dane tried changing the subject. "Look at these people." He nodded over the railing next to their table at the bustling concourse. "No one dresses up anymore. Half of them look like they walked out of their hotel room searching for the ice machine."

She didn't bite. "Do we fly due west, or head west, but fly over the poles to get somewhere west? Like a shortcut."

Dane turned back to her. He was half-serious about the dress code thing. He then decided to give in a little. He was no CIA operative, that's for sure. The interrogators wouldn't need pliers or a water board, just Misty's helpless gaze and pouty eyes.

"We fly into San Francisco, then Singapore, and finally a smaller plane to the last stop."

God dammit, where's Bora Bora? Is that west or south? It started to sink in. It was the Far East and exotic. Her chest starting bouncing her necklace off of it.

Dane was glancing off noticing the dress code again. "We have a bit of a wait in San Francisco."

"Is the last stop an island?" She sat back as if bracing herself.

Dane didn't say anything, but failed to hide the smirk. He reached down to take a long sip, but it was too late.

A switch was thrown and her face glowed.

"It's a tiny island, isn't it? Are we taking one of those little propeller planes to it that you are going to be a basket case on?" Her tone sounded like she had discovered oil.

Now it was his turn to bite his lip and lean on the table. "Probably."

Her mouth sprang open and covered it with her hand. She looked off to the bar. This dream was continuing. And she was awake.

She dropped her hand and the vulnerable tone, as her face changed to confidence.

"I knew it."

"Right." He nodded.

Half an hour later they were at the gate, where Singapore Airlines flight #517 was about ready to start boarding for the Bay area, with continuing service across the vast Pacific. Misty was looking down at her watch while thinking about the island and beach that they would spend the next week at, and have in their minds and heart until she stopped breathing someday. She almost didn't care to know the exact location; it was an isolated beach with stunning water somewhere. The trump card Dane still had to play was folded up in his jeans pocket. He would show her eventually the picture of where they were staying. He still had a surprise in store.

Dane was looking down the terminal, people watching, when a reoccurring theme was playing out like a theater show. It was Act 14, or maybe 16, scene 12 at least by now. It was played over and over. He tilted his head studying a family walking from the far end towards them. Misty looked up from her watch at him and noticed the look on his face. The play wasn't a comedy.

He was already holding her hand in his lap, when he squeezed it and pointed with his chin. "Misty look at these families."

She looked off searching.

"Look at them, with the two kids and the stroller."

It started sinking in. She looked at Dane again before finding the young couple, now 15 feet away.

"Look at them. They're miserable, defeated. They're lives are over." He looked at his new wife and was deadly serious. "We can't get that way. We just can't." He stared back at them, now passing by. The man was rolling his eyes and she was tugging at something in the stroller.

"I know it's tiring and mindlessly exhausting, I know it will be, I get that, but we can't let it dull us. I won't live that way. I haven't seen one set of parents smile in the last 10 minutes or look remotely happy."

She brought his hand over into her lap and squeezed it. "Flying sucks these days you know."

Dane shook his head. "I guarantee if this were Disney or SeaWorld, they'd look the same." He took a breath.

"Wyatt told me that night on his boat, you have to live your life. I didn't pay much attention at the time, hell I was 12 or 13. But when he died, I thought about it. I understood it." Dane didn't think any of these people had a Wyatt to help them in their pasts.

He looked at her. "We're not going to end up like Richard and Karen."

Misty blinked a couple times. She then thought back to yesterday's toast she made with several childhood friends. A toast to someone not on this earth anymore, maybe with Wyatt some place, looking down on a special few.

She swallowed hard and looked at him. She simply nodded and touched his face. She then leaned on him, looking past him out the window at the fins of airplanes, like sharks, moving left and right.

She used to go to the airport to see her father off for his monthly flights. She remembers not being impressed with the smaller planes; they never flew anywhere extravagant or romantic. It was those bigger fins, belonging to the planes that crossed seas and time zones that stamped her visions like a passport page. She remembers pressing her face against the giant windows at the gate, leaving tiny smudges, watching his plane push back and roll away with the others.

Now she looked around the gate for any kids, specifically young girls to possess or bewitch for a second. She wanted to take over their body as if her own at that age. She would tell that little dreamer, that at the age of just 25, not only would she be a professional ballet dancer, but married and getting on two of those big planes with her new angel. Her real one, not the one she played dress up with and sipped tea with when she was six in her room. The best part was she was looking forward to stepping on one of those "trivial" small planes, as it would take them to their own little aqua postcard of refreshing trade winds.

His childhood hometown was behind them and Singapore was 7,300 nautical miles away. After that, the resort in the Maldives another hour or so farther. Now they would gladly take wedding day-like clock hands. Misty's heels were off and her hair was up in a makeshift knot. She leaned into Dane's right shoulder with her legs curled up in her seat. They were going to try to get some sleep. The whine of the engine out their window lessened, and the 767 slowly began to level.

She was playing with his watch, as he played with her hair. He was fidgeting more after this take off than before in Dallas. She needed to distract him until they slept, and had a really good idea, but knew they would get kicked off the plane. They also forgot to get playing cards at the airport gift shop, but assumed the airlines would have some. Not anymore. On to plan C.

"Show me the watch. How does it work?" She unclasped it and slid it off his wrist. "It's heavy."

Dane peered down at her with a smile, the smile of that 12 or 13 year old in the Island Packet. He took it, messed with the bezel, and turned the knob for a couple minutes. He then held it in front of her. He pointed to the normal hour hand just past the 10.

"So it's 10:15 here, pacific time. Singapore is 15 hours ahead of us." Dane pointed to a fourth hand with a triangle at the end, like an arrow. It was pointing just past the 13 on the outer bezel.

"There, it is 1:15 in the afternoon tomorrow."

"13 is 1? That's army time right?"

"Exactly."

"That's cool. Why didn't you buy me one like this?"

Just as he looked down at her, her sly grin greeted him. "I'm kidding." She patted his chest and then held the watch for a second, before putting it back on him. She pulled over the sleeve covering it and nestled up closer into him.

"Do you want a blanket?" His hand went back to running though her hair.

"I have what I want." She shot a glance up at him quickly, then held it as his eyes were skittering all over the window and seat in front of him. His hands were calm, enjoying her hair, but his thoughts were turbulent. Misty then looked past him out the window. There were no clouds. There was no moon. Just blackness. They could have been inside a submarine as far as they knew.

"Tell me some Wyatt Cavanaugh stories."

Dane talked for about 20 minutes, his memories smothering the bumps and rolls of the plane. He felt them, but were no longer turbulence, but waves gently rocking the Island Packet or his parent's Catalina 385 up and down.

He kissed the top of her head as he noticed she had fallen asleep. Her hand slid down from his chest to his stomach. He peered out his window, then down at his sleeve knowing what was under it. The bumps in his seat, or was it the rocking of the boat he still pictured, took its toll on his eyelids. The stories and his visions were his lullaby, weighing them down. A minute later, Dane Carmichael fell asleep on an airplane, for the first time.

Watching rain was even fun here.

He thought it must be the unique noise it made splattering into the ocean. The world's kettledrums were tapping across the vastness. It almost sounded like a waterfall. That, or watching it drill into it with millions of plops exploding up. Either way, he left the library earlier than he thought with two things: eagerness and *Treasure Island.*

He grabbed one of his favorite books. Misty reads more than him, but there are a few he loves and rereads. Maybe it was the title, but he didn't want to start it in the library. He felt he needed to get out to the villa and appreciate what they had.

Dane got to page 33 when he shut his book. His senses kept getting in the way of Stevenson's lines. He was sitting at the small table he had moved in front of the bed, just under the overhang. The noise and sight of the rain, even in grayness, was relaxing. He was gazing out at the 360-degree postcard and holding the deck of cards, twirling it like dice. He was hoping it would spin his memory in his favor.

Misty's two G&T's were sitting on the bedside table, as solitaire was the game of the moment. It was now just a steady rain, supposed to last until tomorrow around noon before clearing up. Dane was just looking forward to Misty getting back and going for a swim.

The cards weren't cooperating, in color and in memories. As his thumb pushed over every three cards, he seemed to always flip over a black, when he needed red. He needed a red jack and red seven. He shook his head as he started scooping up all the cards. The four of diamonds slid over and he looked down at the number.

It was either a code or international phone number. For fun, he thought about trying to call it when they got back home. He was definitely taking the cards back home with him. At the reception building there is a business center with computers. He typed "barnstation" in google, but nothing came back. The weird thing was not only did it say nothing found, but it didn't even show alternate options or hits that were close. The search page was blank. He'd never seen a search page blank without even websites with parts of the name. He didn't even get a hit for barns.

Two hands later it was now red that always turned up. *Go figure.* He moaned to no one but teak and the trillions of exploding plops. He stacked up the cards and held them, looking at *Eastern* again, rubbing his thumb over it back and forth. He was trying to wipe away the film or filter not letting his memory in, or its memory out. He then dropped the cards and closed his eyes. He spoke again, more to himself this time.

"God you're an idiot!" He laughed as it just hit him. He could have tried Eastern in google.

He stood up to go when he heard thumping footsteps out their door approaching. She didn't bother with an umbrella, as the wet plastered sundress made things easier for what was on her mind. Her body was still tingling and muscles loose from 90 minutes at the spa, and her body wanted something else even more. Dane was more than happy to satisfy the urge. With Mother Nature's real shower head above, they were climbing in the pool again. The dress actually stayed on for some of it, before he peeled it off eventually. He would never look at that dress the same way again.

Thirty minutes later, they were in bathing suits swimming off their villa. After a while, they didn't even feel the rain on their heads. Watching rain from below the ocean surface, was like looking up at a flexible mirror. It sounded like applause, a theater crowd roaring its approval above. At one point a kayaker paddled by, sending a crack spreading across that mirror above.

Dinner was brought out, to the great relief of Misty, who after those two G&T's foreign to an airport, needed something in her stomach. She and Dane were now at the table, playing cards and starting on another bottle of champagne with their shrimp cocktail. They were reliving the wedding reception. They were remembering things the other didn't recall, and piecing together the evening from their ends. They met in the middle at the cake and speeches.

After a game of Gin, they laughed as they decided to play War, a step up from Go Fish. Misty hoped her grandfather was not looking down from above.

Misty was shuffling as Dane then remembered something from two weddings, their's and Kristen's. He poured more champagne as he finally got around to asking.

"So what was with the toast you and your friends did just after we cut the cake? I'm pretty sure you did the same at Kristen's wedding? Was it a ballet thing?"

Dane was reaching down to put the bottle on the floor, as there was no room on the little table, when he noticed a pause in her dealing. A door creaked open in her head. A door to a dark place. By the time he sat back up, she took a deep breath and continued dealing until all the cards were out. Her face was different. She piled her cards up in a single stack and started fanning them out in her hands. She looked up at him. Dane found himself wishing he hadn't asked after all. He got the sense it was like asking a cancer survivor how the chemo was. Something was wrong.

Misty stared down at her thumb, brushing over the two of hearts. She pulled it up and slid it in over on the other side by the three of hearts.

"That was for Miss Cobb." She tilted her head to the left, still staring at the red heart. "Riley Cobb. She was my ballet instructor when I was nine years old. She finished college and moved to Dallas to teach at the company. We moved up from Miss Vasner's group and she taught us. She was the kindest person I ever met. That's not a cliché." She looked at Dane whose eyes and mouth were still stuck open. "She belonged on a Disney painting or something."

She glanced off. "We use to all joke that she'd never make it as a top dance teacher because you have to be strict, mean sometimes, and we didn't think she had it in her. She did. We all loved her like a big sister. She left to go back to North Carolina where she was from, when I was 15 or 16 I think. She started teaching at the Raleigh School of Ballet, which is huge. We were sad to see her go, but so so happy for her. She married soon after. She took the name Grace. Riley Grace. We all thought it was so appropriate."

Riley Grace. Dane nodded, thinking the name even sounded like a Disney character.

Up till now, she was actually smiling a little, as her story would be the caption under that painting hanging on Cinderella's castle wall. She then closed her eyes and ran her hands through her hair looking off to her left. She looked back at Dane with eyes completely different. It was like she couldn't continue.

She pushed back from the table and moved around to Dane. He instinctively slid back and she sat in his lap, her knees together off to the side. He reached up touching her cheek, coaxing more out. She grabbed his hand looking at it, and let it fall to their laps.

"It was just a common weekday and she was walking out of a mall. She was mugged at her car." Dane could hear her gulping a swallow. "They shot her. Took her purse and drove off with the car." She blinked a couple times, but it was too late. She then closed her eyes, which pushed out two drops down each cheek. She opened her eyes and gave Dane a look, *oh you haven't heard anything yet…*

"She was pregnant."

She glanced past Dane to the ocean of rain. The sky was even crying.

"She was almost eight months. She was just there fixing something on her registry. She died in the ambulance ride going to the hospital."

Dane had a glazed look on his face, as if suffering from amnesia. "What happened to…did the unborn baby live?"

She shook her head.

"They got the baby out, but only survived two days." She took a deep breath and blew out.

Dane almost didn't believe her. It had to be a rumor or something. Stuff like that doesn't really happen.

"Jesus Christ."

Misty shrugged, as it was the type of story that not only brings up doubts, but bangs the gavel.

Dane played with her hair. "What about the husband?"

Misty wiped the tear on her cheek, wiping away that part of the story. "I don't know." Her eyes roamed around Dane's face and damp hair. "I forget his name, it was a different name."

Dane needed a drink, and reached for his. "I think I'd kill myself." He chugged his glass and looked at Misty. "Seriously."

She was staring off in a trance. Dane knew the card game was over. He picked her up and carried her to bed. They shed their clothes and finished the champagne while lying in bed whispering. Dane could tell Misty was lost, drowning in a rolling sea of memories. He tossed her a life vest.

"Tell me some Riley Cobb stories."

Misty bit her lip and rested her head on his chest as they looked over the end of the bed at the ocean, now just sprinkled with raindrops. She told stories of the Riley in Dallas for 25 minutes until she just stopped talking. Dane tilted his head down and saw she had fallen asleep. He then stoked her hair and watched her sleep, before drifting off himself to the sounds of the Indian Ocean.

A warning gibbous rising out of their private aquarium greeted them on their last night. It projected a soft glow down on the sleeping postcard. Just as they were afraid, the week went by fast. Despite relishing every breath, gust, sip, plunge, kiss, and sunrise, they were all part of memories beginning to blur. Cutting the cake and making love in the hammock at midnight under than moon, seemed to happen on the same day.

Armed with watches and rings, and speculating how long their rapture would tick on, they were ready to begin a new life on Monday. At some point during that last day, each thought back to the families they saw while sitting in the Dallas gate, waiting for their flight. An ocean breeze building up from somewhere with nothing to stop it, would blow through and swipe that memory away seconds later. Come Monday, there would be no unobstructed gust to carry that thought away. No sound of lapping water that could drown out the memory. They would do their best to make sure this week on another planet, would not get lost in their future together.

Dane and Misty would leave the Maldives brainwashed, with sights, sounds, and feels. A week ago they strolled down that dock to enter a dream. Now they treaded down it to leave that dream, and enter the real world. They also left the villa with some shells from the Indian Ocean floor, tans, half a bag of arabica coffee, and a deck of old airline playing cards.

The honeymoon was definitely over. It didn't take long. Apparently the flux capacitor broke.

Dane and Misty looked at each other at the gate shaking their heads. They were at least able to laugh about it. After all, they both felt like they had gone to another world in the Maldives. So when reality hit, and the real world came calling, it would make a good story someday. Someday.

A small, faraway earthquake sent out a tsunami warning, which turned out to be false, but delayed their arrival into Singapore. 30 years ago, the pilot would have waved everyone on the rocking seaplane until there was no room, without a thought of the fine print of regulations and guidelines. He would then slide away in the choppy water until lifting off into the air, with drops of water spiraling off the twin pontoons. Not today.

Getting into Singapore late, they missed their flight at Changi International. Then thanks to overbooking, they watched their Airbus A320 push back from the gate and roll off towards a far runway. Eight hours later, they boarded a smaller Airbus to Rome, heading west not east, towards home.

From Rome the next morning, it was west again to America, but the wrong side, 2,500 miles away from the Golden Gate. The silver lining was

Singapore, Rome, and New York were good airports to be stuck in. Plenty to do or have at your disposal. They just needed to get off the airplane.

They sat. And sat. They were on the tarmac for three hours with no gate to nudge up against. The amazing, wonderful thing they had going for them was they didn't have to buckle up. That's as good as it got. 30 years ago the stewardesses would have passed out champagne, drinks, and played trivia over the intercom for treats, while mingling with the passengers, all kneeling in the seats to talk to the people behind them. Again, not today.

Terminal 4 at JFK was busy. The PA system seemed to never shut off. It was a wonder the ground didn't shake with the constant, sporadic movement. There was also whispers and talk of Ebola, that like the virus, seem to float and swirl among the crowds. JFK started screening certain passengers and flights that month.

Misty was now napping in his lap, while Dane stroked her hair as he gazed down the concourse. It was Wednesday and they hadn't changed clothes since Sunday. Dane wondered if they had gone to some ordinary place for their honeymoon, would they have gotten home normally, not cursed? Misty had joked earlier. "See, and you thought I was joking about going to god damn Corpus Christi."

Seats were hard to come by; it was musical chairs with the PA system. If you were within 50 feet of your gate, you were doing well. A guy was on his second lap through their gate. Dane looked down at Misty and realized his bag was in the seat next to him. He felt bad and pulled it down to his feet. The guy came down towards him and Dane motioned next to him.

"Thanks," he plopped down and blew out a satisfying breath.

"Yeah, no problem."

He pulled out his phone, thumbed it for a while, and dropped it into a bag. He rubbed the back of his neck, squinting his eyes.

"Where you headed?" Dane was playing with Misty's hair, then turned to him for a second. He was wearing khaki corduroy pants, that Dane always thought were comfortable, and a quarter-zip fleece sweater with the Notre Dame insignia on the left side.

"Boston. My god-daughter is graduating high school." He looked over at Dane then down to Misty. "How about you guys?"

"Trying to get home. San Francisco." He looked up from her hair and didn't really want to get into their adventure home, but the guy seemed okay. Dane thought anyone wearing cords and saddle oxford shoes had to be pretty cool.

"We've been in airports since Sunday."

The guy looked up from Misty to Dane. "Are you kidding?"

"I wish." He looked back down to Misty's hair. "Maldives Sunday, Singapore, Rome, to here."

The guy shook his head. "Damn I'm sorry. What took you to the Indian Ocean? I've always wanted to go there."

"Honeymoon." Dane noticed his hands were the smoothest he'd ever seen. It was the skin of a five year old's hands. He found himself glancing down at them a couple times in the next 15 minutes.

"Oh wow." he looked back down at Misty, then up to Dane, "Well congrats." He reached over to shake hands.

Dane grabbed it. "Thanks. I'm Dane." He nodded down in his lap. "She's Misty."

"Zachary. Nice to meet you even if like this."

"Ahh, it's no big deal I guess. It'll make a good story someday."

"That's true." Zachary eyed the gate. "Well enjoy each other Dane," he glanced over at him, "because it will go by in a flash." He shook his head and returned to eyeing the gate. Dane nodded at the theme of the week, but seemed to take it in differently from Zachary. He looked over at him as if he had heard it for the first time.

"I swear last week we were at church for Samantha's christening, and yesterday for her recital." He looked off, as if picturing it all.

"Now she has a tassel on her hat."

Dane didn't say anything for a while, letting him relive it.

"So do all Notre Dame alum live in Boston?" Dane eventually asked, smiling.

Zachary looked over grinning too. "That's funny, seems like it. They live there. We live here in the city. My wife and kids are already over there, I couldn't get away until today. He and I went to school together in South Bend."

"How many kids do you have Zach?"

"Three," he turned towards Dane, "seven up to fourteen."

They continued to chat until Zachary's flight to Boston began boarding. Eventually the newlywed's were herded onto their flight three hours later. They finally arrived in San Francisco late that night. Their bed was flower petals. Their shower felt like rain from the Garden of Eden.

Their worldwide airport adventure was so marvelous; it brought out a representative from the airline the next afternoon. He waddled up to their front door with two of their three bags. *Well, they found two of them at least,* Dane thought as they walked up to ring the doorbell. After the last four days, they didn't care.

Back at Kennedy, Alex Ortega flung the American Tourister into his trunk. It was heavy, hopefully full of goods. He and his partner, Sean, checked for flag cities or types of luggage. The exotic ports of call or expensive luggage would get their attention. Not that a suitcase from Latvia or Uruguay couldn't have expensive items inside, but statistics are important when pressed for time. Places like Paris, Dubai, Tokyo, and Macau rarely let them down.

Alex and Rick had two other partners as well. One owned a pawnshop and consignment store in Queens. The other worked part-time at an antique store in Manhattan. There was a reason the baggage handler was able to afford $4,000 rims on is 2008 Hyundai Sonata.

He pulled out of the JFK employee parking lot 8, and headed north on the 678 to Queens. After two stops, the Carmichael's clothing, camera, and phone charger got sorted out. Alex then took the subway into Manhattan. The Eastern playing cards and Swiss Army knife would join other items pulled all week. He or Rick made weekly trips to Queens, but only crossed the East River monthly. He knew Lucas would be working this afternoon.

With a month's worth of items in the usual suitcase, Alex took the Flushing Line to Grand Central. Then he picked up the Lexington Avenue Express south. With his distaste for the city and its fortunate, he moved quickly down the block and into the store with one shoulder slightly lower. He passed a wall of fancy teapots on shelves wallpapering his right. The swinging pendulums of four grandfather clocks ushered him down the aisle on his left. He found the middle of the store, glass cases squaring off two workers, and nodded at one of them who reached for a walkie-talkie.

Two minutes later, Alex peered up as Lucas twisted his way down a spiral staircase to the first floor. They shook hands just to pretend to be formal.

It took 10 minutes to go through the suitcase and for Alex to get his pay. Nine minutes too long as far as he was concerned. 55 minutes later he was in his car heading home to Brooklyn.

From October 13-22, 2014……

4 games of Gin
3 games of Klondike Solitaire
1 game of War

PART II

World's Tallest Building Opens, the Burj Khalifa, Dubai
Apple iPad Introduced
Jessica Watson, Youngest to Sail Solo Around the World
Second Successful SpaceX Dragon Launch and Recovery
Self-Replicating Life with Synthetic DNA Created

CHAPTER THREE

There is just something about a moving coastline.

From 200 yards, the shore slid by like a filmstrip. Cafés, streetlights, the corner store, benches, and buildings…all just played out like a show. Syler leaned on the port side railing of the main deck, watching like an audience member from balcony seats. He then glanced down at the water. The mirror-like lake was doubling the movie scene above. Slowly the ripples and wake from the ferry's bow turned the reflection into a blur of rolling colors and shapes.

The lake was dark glass, reflecting its frame near the edges. The frame to the south was jagged mountains with a dusting of snow still too high to melt. The frame to the north and northeast was soft, rolling green hills and farmland. A tartan of fields and vineyards. He turned, looking past the bow flag flapping towards him. The lake opened up in front of him as the ferry aimed east. Gray clouds hung low over the lake. It covered the tips of the mountains like dirty cotton. The white triangle of a sail in the distance was all that was out there. His long stare was interrupted by the boat's horn. He blinked a couple times and turned back to the shoreline.

Four miles out of town, buildings gave way to houses now, dotting the hills and parks along the sidewalks. He was relaxed and let the soft rumble of the engines fill his head. Syler thrust his hands into the warmth of his peacoat pockets. One more glance over the bow to the horizon and he turned towards the warmth of the stern. He no longer needed to see out front, for he knew where it would lead.

Syler walked towards the stern railing, across a deck of teak in rows of perfectly straight planks. He reached the railing, with the giant Swiss flag flapping casually. Lausanne was off in the shrinking horizon. The dock now just a sliver of gray, like a mirage on the water. His dark eyes peered down at the backwash from the twin screws underneath and followed the ferry's wake. The turbulent water of white smoothed and eased eventually as it stretched back to that dock. The wake seemed to connect the ferry to Lausanne, connecting Syler to Lausanne. To his past. To his pain.

Twenty minutes later the lake smothered that wake and connection. The smoothness disconnecting the ferry from port. There was no trace of where he'd come from, no trace to what he'd done, and who he'd met. There was just the occasional pop of the flag, the rumble of the engines, and the lifeless lake swallowing up a connected past.

His destination has been in his mind for decades. For as long as he can remember, he always looked forward, never to the past. It didn't concern him. He had no time to dwell on it. He of course remembered everything: names, places, faces, crowds; a lifetime of mental snap shots were stored away in his mind that he could recall when necessary. His life may depend on it. For he was finally done. That chapter in his life was closed and a new one was opening today. *No, not a new chapter*, he thought, *a new book.*

The boat was not crowded, as was custom this time of year. He found a chair up against the railing on the starboard side and got comfortable. There didn't seem to be a sky, just cloudy grayness hanging off the two yardarms. He stretched out his legs and crossed them at the ankles, keeping his hands in his pockets. He was wrapped in warmth, half from wool and half from a released career. Syler looked aft at the giant Swiss flag off the stern pole waving good-bye to Lausanne. Waving good-bye to a past. He had waited years for this moment. He inhaled the crisp air. He exhaled a waiting future.

The boat would help take him to an isolated cabin in Austria, a short hike from the Italian border. A cabin his grandfather built and a sanctuary where he had spent his childhood vacations. He chose not to remember much from his childhood and the people around him. The one constant for a while, was his grandfather and the cabin far from home. In the winters, he learned to ski, build fires, and hunt. In the summers, he learned to dive, climb, and build and fix things. In all the childhood days between, he began composing the epilogue to his book of life. He would figure out how to get there later. He had a whole life for those parts of the book.

The epilogue was beginning as a mother and her small boy approached him, one shoelace dragging. With one hand holding his mother's, the other held a toy camera. The blond child aimed it down at something on the deck and clicked. A buzzer sounded and a pretend flash popped up. Syler thinks he had one of those as a small child, most kids do. They made their way past his chair and the boy's curious eyes found Syler. The boy pointed the plastic lens at him and clicked. Then he smiled, saying something, and continued to be dragged off by his mother. Syler would have maybe dealt with that situation if it felt odd, but it seemed innocent enough. *That's the way I'd like to go, a brilliant move with childlike freedom.*

Maybe he didn't care anymore. Between the view, the cool air in his nostrils, and the play of a child, he was asleep within four minutes. At 9:27am on a cold Thursday in March, on a ferry sailing across Lake Genéva, a $7 Fisher-Price toy camera clicked one of the three most dangerous men in the world.

"What is it?" Mia covered up the sugar and began stirring her coffee. She glanced down at the small whirlpool in her cup and then back up to his face. A face that changed expressions too quickly. A horn honked around the corner, ricocheting off the curved awnings and window shutters across the street. The dog barked that was tied to the café table just behind them. The waiter brought the extra butter, placing it down next to the croissant. Round iron grate tables fostered discussions like lecterns. The top corner of his newspaper fluttered and dipped, as the taller buildings on either side squeezed a breeze between them. Life moved on at the popular Vienna café.

In his world, everything apparently had stopped a few seconds before. She pulled her spoon out from the coffee and rested it on the saucer. She brought the cup up to her red lips. Her usual Konsul was strong this morning and made with just the right amount of cream; a dash. Perfect, unlike Monday's at Kleine's, where they always add too much. She took another sip while eyeing her husband. It was as if she wasn't there.

"Philip?" She leaned forward. "Honey, what is it?"

He turned towards her, brought out of his trance and looked at her brown eyes trying to will an answer. A strand of blond hair slipped down to his eyebrow.

"I'm sorry dear," he returned to the page as if he still couldn't believe what he had read. He talked into the newspaper. "Daniel Bohm died yesterday."

Her eyes opened much wider as they pulled out more than she wanted. "Died!" Her cup clanked into the saucer. "Wait, how?"

He kept staring at the paper and for a second time blinked and came to. He took a breath and seemed to rejoin the world around him.

"It says he died in his sleep. They found him in his bed at the Hôtel de la Paix."

She brought up her napkin to dab the corner of her mouth.

"Oh my god." She placed it back in her lap. "In Genève?"

He nodded. A second later, he looked up over the newspaper across the street, as if searching for something. It was a blank stare. His blue eyes were doing nothing. It was his mind that was busy.

"Does it say when he died?" Mia was rubbing her forehead. "If it's in the paper now it had to be earlier in the day yesterday. Does he take naps or something? I don't understand?"

She was smart, as well as quick. A trait that appealed to him from the moment they met. She had to be to keep up with him. Philip's eyes left the street and refocused down on the newspaper.

"Just before 9pm." She could see his eyes shifting over a column and down a few paragraphs. She twisted a strand of light brown hair up and over her right ear waiting. Phillip's mouth then matched his eyes as they tracked across the page.

"According to police, Austria's newly appointed Assistant Deputy of Internal Affairs had dinner at Chez Costa around 6:30 that evening. At ten past eight, he walked the two blocks to Hôtel de la Paix and was spotted talking to someone in the lobby before adjourning to his room. Mr. Bohm was found in his bed by a companion who was familiar with the secretary. According to sources inside Austrian security, she arrived in town late and was joining him for the rest of the week. He was pronounced dead at the scene."

With a twist of his right hand, he dipped the corner of the newspaper down to peer over at his wife. Neither said anything. The dog didn't even bark. Now it was her turn to stare for answers, this time off to her left inside the café.

To her, Daniel was a friend. She had known him longer than she knew her husband. They had met socially through one of her coworkers at a party sponsored by her firm. She was impressed that he didn't immediately hit on her and treated her like a lady. He was impressed that she was as bright as she was beautiful.

Daniel was seeing someone at the time, so their first couple of encounters were friendly. The urge to push wasn't there. After he broke up with the woman, they just remained close friends. She often wondered if things would have been different if he hadn't been seeing someone at the time. He often compared his girlfriends to her and she would let him know if she approved of them.

Daniel also played cupid. He introduced her to Philip. She saw Daniel first as she came into the restaurant, shaking her damp umbrella and scanning the room. He was sitting down at a table lighting a cigarette. Daniel's hand disappeared into his pants pocket with the lighter as he inhaled and blew out a stream of smoke. He leaned to his left and saw her, his hand reemerged to give her a beckoning wave and smile. She was two tables away when Philip approached the table from the bar, drinks in both hands. He stopped in stride and locked eyes with her. Their eyes haven't left each other's since.

To Phillip, Daniel was a friend, but there was a business side to it as well. Like the bending lights of a prism, he was trying to form a single thought among the myriad of details going this way and that. The lines of the corporate world, politics, behind the scenes action, and friendship were all crossing each other. He couldn't guide them together yet, towards a single possibility. After 15 seconds his wife broke the silence.

"Camille?" Mia mentioned her name while still staring into the café. Maybe it was the couple on the other side of the cafe's window reading books, but the name suddenly came suddenly came to her. The last time she saw Camille, was at Shakespeare & Company over on Sterngasse where Daniel had introduced them.

"Yeah, I guess." Phillip closed the paper, folded it in one motion, and placed it on the table to the left of the butter plate. He looked back out across the street.

"I couldn't keep up with them for a while there," he turned back to her, "but I think she was the last. Going on…four months?" He looked down at his coffee cup as his fingers gripped the rim and twisted it around on the saucer.

"I don't know." He closed his eyes and rubbed them, almost moving them around.

Mia uncrossed her left leg and stretched it out under the table to touch his. She pointed her high heel and caressed his lower leg. A minute later, she twisted her wrist exposing her Cartier watch. She had 45 minutes to catch her train. She asked if she should stay, to be with Philip, but he said no. There probably wouldn't be anything until the weekend. He reached across the table, grabbed her left hand, and squeezed.

"Go dear. I'll be fine. You've got a big two days coming up that you've worked hard for."

A few minutes later, they left the café holding hands, walking swiftly down Himmelpfortgasse. He made sure to leave the wrinkled newspaper on the table next to the untouched croissant and butter. It was like trying to hide evidence. He had lost his appetite, for food and news.

The walk from the ferry dock to the train station in Montreux was routine. Syler pretended to tie his shoe once as he departed the dock. He studied a bakery window. He looked at his phone. However, thanks to his sunglasses; the shoelace, the pastries, and the phone never entered his field of vision.

Nothing worried him as the six-minute stroll ended at the ticket booth. Syler always thought the only thing better than a ferryboat across Lake Genève was ending it with a train ride heading east. The journey from Montreux, through Gstaad, and to Weismerman, was like traveling in a Christmas forest and the prelude to more striking scenery to the southeast. His ticket would take him due east however, not southerly into the heart of the Alps, but past Interlaken, Luzern, and finally to Zürich. After two days, which would include a good meal at one of his favorite restaurants, some shopping, a visit to the bank, and purchasing an automobile, Syler would meander off to his awaiting cabin in the next country.

The 12:10 train with four stops before Zürich would be on track two in a few minutes. He liked this train station, and most in small cities. They weren't the huge stations of larger cities that rivaled malls and cathedrals. These were quiet and small, not usually crowded, and visually easy on the eyes. There was a small building for purchasing tickets with bathrooms and a café. It was more like a mini chalet, with the customary pretty flowers in the window boxes despite the cold March air. All the thick fern's branches were weighed down with clumps of snow. Some dripping white sweat. Mountains loomed high in the eastern horizon that seemed two miles away, but were actually more like 15.

Syler was among 11 people standing around waiting for the same train. Hands were holding briefcases against their legs, or backpacks over their shoulders. Two girls stood with bags full of skis and equipment. Everyone looked like they belonged. He stood up against a post with a telephone on the other side.

The grey and red train with dark windows appeared around the corner and slowed as it rolled towards the station. The sound of metal and hissing announcing it was about to stop. In unison, everyone began inching forward towards the track. The train doors slid open to a "dinging" sound and only one person got off. Judging by his confused look, he had never been here before.

Five cars were part of the train. He inspected the customary white signs near the door and checked for the destination cities of each car. The last city listed on the final car was Interlaken. That wouldn't do. Zürich was listed last on the first four cars.

Syler waited for everyone to board before deciding where to sit. He twisted back toward his left to a clock hanging on the post he was under. It read 12:08. He then looked at the train judging how long it would take to walk the length inside. Between five cars and the exterior doors between each, he felt he could cover the distance in 80-85 seconds. The one thing he didn't have to estimate was when the train would leave. After all, this was Switzerland.

He stood in the front of the first car and scanned the platform to his right, then turned to his left and did the same. Nothing. He still waited, counting in his head. …24…25…26…*Go.* He stepped up into the car.

He turned left and walked the length of the train. When his hand grabbed the last doorknob, the train began rolling forward. He walked into the last car as the glass door automatically slid closed behind him. He stopped midway in the car and looked at each person inside. All were looking down at a phone, a newspaper, or out the window. One was sleeping. After surveying everyone on the train, he ventured back towards the front and picked the third car.

He grabbed his bag with both hands and pushed it up onto the luggage rack above the seats. He then sat down, picking the window seat facing the front of the train. In front of him were two empty seats facing him. Syler pulled up the silver table under the window and propped it up with the hinge. He placed his phone and sunglasses on it. He wished he could sleep, but he wasn't done yet. He wouldn't be completely satisfied and able to relax until he was leaving Zürich by car, with blond hair and a beard.

The train rocked back and forth, as it snaked through the Swiss countryside. At no point were all five cars and engine in a straight line. The straightest part of the track was in front of the station platform. They dipped into valleys, hugged mountainsides, and whistled through smaller villages. He grabbed a paper resting on the seat across the aisle and flipped through it, unfolding sections and opening others. Like everything he read, he did it carefully and deliberately.

On page two, there was an article that grabbed his eyes. He brought it up closer. It wasn't the name that garnered attention, but the dead man's title that was news worthy. People don't know most foreign names, but they know titles. Syler read it three times and, of course, memorized the journalist. Once in Zürich he would check the internet for any updates. A small smirk creased his lips after reading it. He then let the paper fall to his side and let his head rest back against the cushion. *Almost there.*

He turned his head and looked out his window to the Swiss countryside. The evergreen trees slid by rapidly with creeks and streams winding between the trunks. The mountains and chalets off in the distance were sliding by slower as another movie began.

Syler lifted down his bag and took out a small woman's purse. He reached in and pulled out a deck of playing cards. He shoved the purse back in, zippered the duffle, and heaved it up onto the rack. He flipped open the box of cards and slid them out while glancing outside at his movie. They would help keep him awake. He shuffled the cards in his lap, blue cards arching under his thumbs until flat. He lost track of how many times he had shuffled, thanks to the scenery out his window and the slight hypnotic rocking of the train. He made seven stacks on the small table, next to the empty Eastern box, and passed the time playing Solitaire.

The restaurant was louder than usual for a Wednesday, especially the bar area along the far wall up front. Markus Hofler twisted in his wicker chair to his left and glanced back at the loudness over his shoulder. Every stool at the bar was occupied, not that he could see them due to the crowd that stood two to three people deep. They were all taken an hour before kickoff. Another row of people lined the mirrored wall on the other side allowing for a long, thin gap for those coming and going.

"My god, where is my beer?"

The voice at his table brought Markus back around and facing forward. The restaurant area was just as crowded as the bar, but seemed more civilized. Everyone sat at their four top tables while glancing up at the televisions.

Markus grabbed his tall glass still half-full and raised it in a toast, a tease that made Michael shake his head. Markus gulped down two swallows worth and placed it back on the table with a thud.

"They're a little busy."

Michael glared at Markus not enjoying the sarcasm. He leaned back and looked out across the right side of the room trying to find a server.

"I think they are watching too. Can you imagine if Switzerland made it, we'd never get served?"

It was back in the summer of 2000 and the country, and continent for that matter, had been gripped by the European Championships. The smaller scale World Cup lasts four weeks. Sixteen teams made it representing every citizen, from the suits and ties in the capital, to those in overalls in the smallest village surrounded by farms. Some watched the games on flat screens the size of a billiards table, some on a black & white the size of a cereal box.

The game on the television was the semi-final, the Netherlands & Italy. Holland was host and pre-tournament favorite. A sea of orange filled the stands and 10 orange jerseys flowed on the field in total sync, as if each connected by an invisible cord. The ball seemed to float around from foot to foot, rather than being kicked. The royal blue Italians were chasing as Holland dominated. But like many football games, especially with Italy, possession wasn't everything and the Dutch didn't show it on the scoreboard.

The waitress balanced a large pizza-sized tray full of glasses clinking together, dropped one off at their table, and moved off behind them to another thirsty table. Markus watched the game and the crowd as well, trying to size up everyone there. Where were they four years ago the last time the tournament was held? What were they wearing, doing? Like most dreamers who lived in Europe, soccer was a benchmark in life and time. He remembered things by it: where he lived when Baggio missed that PK, who he liked and wanted to ask out when England lost on home soil to penalties, even back to what toy was his favorite when a West Germany penalty kick won the most boring final ever.

"You do know Italy is going to win, right?" Markus swallowed the rest of his beer and placed the empty glass on the edge of the table. He continued looking past Michael.

"Has Italy even touched the ball in the last ten minutes? Seriously. They can't even get into the Dutch side of the field. Van der Sar is probably sitting down working on his tan." Michael brought up his long awaited full glass and savored it as only someone would that had just reached the drinking age.

Markus refocused on the television in the corner with everyone else.

"Exactly, you know how Italy plays. I guarantee they win 1-0, maybe even 2-0 with an injury time counter-attack." Just then, the voices and noise grew and then died suddenly with gasps, as Bergkamp's shot hit the post. Sighs lifted up to the decorated ceiling and stayed up there. Still no score.

Markus looked over at a man sitting with other well-dressed men. His corduroy jacket fit snug and complemented his jeans well. They were all talking while fixed on the screen, sipping their beers. *Are they all childhood friends? Do they just work together? Are they strangers and just all sat down as comrades*, he wondered? *Where was that guy when Bergkamp didn't hit the post, but found the top corner against Argentina two years ago?*

Michael broke the silence at the table, bringing Markus back from the past.

"They're a machine. Look at them." He held his glass up at the television. "Their movement, with and without the ball, their spacing, touches, is so precise." He looked back to Markus. "They got guys on the bench that would be on most starting 11's, including ours." He then turned his attention back up to the clockwork formation on the screen. "Can you imagine playing for them?"

Markus looked at his friend, then back up to the television. "I wouldn't," he replied shaking his head, "put me on Switzerland's starting 11 any day."

"Sure, and watch these tournaments on television every four years."

"Maybe." Markus's response hung over the table and swirled around for him and Michael to digest. Markus was now standing in front of a classroom, or locker room.

"I mean, you get out there with those guys in orange and you're just another orange uniform, part of their machine doing your part." Markus tilted his head down and rubbed the back of his neck, then scratched it. He glanced back up.

"They're always good, always going to look like that, expected to look like that. Yes, you're part of a team, but-" he looked in the mirror to his right against the wall at himself, himself now and the 16 year old inside, "-I mean, do you think they get excited in Holland when they qualify? No, it's just common place."

He then turned to Michael, making sure this point got to him and not swirling up above.

"On our team, you could be the one. The one guy that brings an entire country out of hibernation. Puts the team on his shoulders, makes everyone for four weeks appear like that well-oiled machine." Markus shakes his head. "That's history. Be a leader. Someone for kids in this country to look up to."

He peered back up at the television. Dutch winger Marc Overmars collected a pass by the touchline. He dribbled slowly. Teasingly slowly, until kicking it out front and taking off in a sprint. Known for blazing speed, Overmars beat a blue shirt Italian to the ball and kicked it one more time out in front. The Italian midfielder was left behind chasing the blades of grass Overmars' Adidas cleats kicked up. He appeared all alone headed down the sideline when out of nowhere, the Italian #3 came into the screen. His angle, as usual, was perfect.

His slide was flawless, swiping the ball away from the winger's feet in stride, never touching his legs. Overmars went flying forward to the ground, as the ball banged off the advertisement board on the sideline. The Italian defender popped up after his slide, and jogged back to the middle of the field. His thick black hair flowing like a model. He did it in such a nonchalant way. The best always made the toughest things look so easy. The best defender in the world saved the day yet again.

Markus smiled at his idol's technique. Paola Maldini was older now, the poster above Markus's bed showed him much younger, wearing the red and black striped shirt of AC Milan. But the veteran made up for it in experience.

"Did you have a Swiss player's poster or picture hanging up on your wall?" He turned to his friend and began shaking his head slowly. "Of course not. It was Gullit, Maradona, Matthäus, Scifo. Even years later we may not make the world cup, but your name would still come up. Can you even grasp the feeling of hanging on some kid's wall? Jesus! People wondering who the next *you* is going to be, where the next *you* is?"

He pointed off to his left, arm extended, doing its best compass heading in the general direction of northeast from the table.

"That little field we played on would become a shrine, a pilgrimage for others. Only 6,000 fans could sit and watch a game there, in splintery, hard wooden benches for seats and a goal box that was nothing but dirt, but it could be the same as De Meer or the San Siro in some eyes and dreams."

Michael didn't reply, but turned his head and looked at his friend. He thought about their differences in life, the way they looked at things. He nodded, *well said buddy.*

The constant Dutch ball control and pressure was finally awarded with a penalty kick. Blue shirt Italians swarmed around the ref like gnats talking with their hands. One lone orange shirt picked up the ball and walked to the spot, 12 yards away from goal. After everyone calmed down and took their respected places around the arch, Patrick Kluivert took a deep breath and waited for the whistle. You could hear a pin drop in the room, as all eyes painted the televisions. The Czech ref pointed to the goal and blew his whistle. Kluivert took four strides to the ball and kicked. He missed. Screams filled the air. Balled up fists were raised up. Hands either covered faces, or slapping tables and foreheads. Still no score.

The game reached halftime and people started mingling and focusing on faces once again. Michael leaned over, took a bite of his *Käsekrainer* sausage and leaned back in his chair bringing up his napkin to his mouth.

"So what time do you have to be there tomorrow?

"9:00."

"You ready?"

Am I ready, Markus thought? He nodded his head and held up his empty glass to the blond waitress.

"Good. You're going to do fine."

Markus was finally going to be able to do something in life. Like his grandfather, be someone noteworthy. He listened to his grandfather's stories from the war. Stories from the underground and behind closed doors. The cloak & dagger stuff was even more romantic than putting on a uniform, grabbing a gun, and taking a position in a trench.

Markus didn't need to advance on a beachhead or hold a weapon, but needed to hold a position of importance. If it was pen and not a sword, then fine. As longs as the ink flowing out of it scribed worthiness. He longed to leave this little city and enter the world, becoming somebody. Tomorrow's exam would open a gate showing Markus the path.

Years earlier, he sat on the bench of Switzerland's U16 team. He sat somewhere and observed from a standpoint not many did, but only dreamed of. It was a privileged spot, but a cruel one at the same time. He watched the games, the players running and shouting. He watched the ball skip across the grass, curl in the air, listened to the sound that a ball full of air makes as it bounces off a head or is volleyed from an instep. Then finally watching a referee blow his whistle and point to the middle circle, then 22 sweaty, tired, dirty players exchange jerseys and would shake hands, despite ill feelings.

It killed him to watch it all. With his elbows on his upper thighs and chin resting in his hands, he would look down at the grass in front of him and slowly peer up to the white chalk of the pitch.

Ten meters.

Just 10 meters to his dream. The steps down the hallway from his room to the bathroom. The length of a train car. There was the path right in front of him, the field and game were right there, but it might as well have been halfway to the moon. He could spit the length of it, see a blade of grass at the other end, but he would never walk it, never get to it.

Of the 14 games he dressed for, he played in one, and only during the last 10 minutes as a "tactical experiment" the manager would call it.

He often wondered, usually at night while staring up at his ceiling in bed, was it worth it? Should he have tanked that last month of games and not even made the final team? What's worse, seeing your dreams right in front of you and the path to get there, but knowing you will never get to it, or not even knowing the path exists?

He had only swapped two jersey his whole life. A Romanian #4 and Portuguese #16, worn by other 15-16 year olds with similar dreams and thoughts. They probably had blocks under the bed and model planes hanging from their ceiling too. He had the jerseys for a month before he couldn't look at them anymore. Not many people in the world could claim to have one, but it was too painful. It didn't remind him of a missed goal, making a slide tackle at just the right time, or shutting down the left side wing. It reminded him of an opponent who sat on the bench too. The jerseys were too clean.

He couldn't see his next path, but knew it was out there. He wanted someone in trouble looking for answers to find him. Maybe they would go on the rest of their lives wondering who he was, that man that rescued them, and saved them.

CHAPTER FOUR

Two hours later the train pulled out of Luzern. The clouds still hung low in the sky between the mountains, like fog confused where to go. About four km out, the beverage cart came wheeling down the aisle. The only knock he had about this route was that the trains typically didn't have a restaurant car. It was the standard grey cart with soda cans, San Pellegrino bottles, sandwiches choked in wrapped cellophane, and of course Swiss chocolates. The hostess was very attractive, and with her smile, Syler could see why she would be good at selling food and drinks to even uninterested passengers. He kept his eyes on her as she leaned forward to give the cart some help in moving. Like most Swiss women, she had beautiful legs. They can't help it with the terrain.

He swiped his way through the deck of cards, three at a time, and got nowhere in his fifth solitaire game. He sighed and leaned back, and began scooping the cards together. He slid them in the box and looked at Eastern on the top. His mentor made three trips to the U.S. when Syler was getting to know him. One flight was on Eastern, from Washington to New York, right before Eastern went bankrupt.

He had thought about Karl often in the past two weeks, knowing he was almost done. He remembers the exhale when Karl walked away after one last coffee at Café Bevar's in Copenhagen, turned the corner onto Nørrebrogade, and vanished forever. Syler just had coffee with a real ghost. He made it, not many do. Not many are able to walk away healthy and die on your own terms somewhere comfortable and quiet. Years later, Syler was almost another ghost.

He rubbed his thumb over Eastern as if waving goodbye to Karl. He placed the cards next to his phone and rested his head back, staring outside. A rich blue lake slowly slid by. Trees whizzed by immediately in front of him as if trying to distract him. Beyond in the distance through the blur of evergreens, was an inviting lake. Pointed trees ringed it. Three piers reached out. He loved the water, lakes especially. It seemed to rest there as if it was first, and everything around it came later, respecting its master.

He had learned many things on water, either in discussions or in experiences. On diving trips, he learned the importance of a solid dive watch and more importantly, attention to detail. That would stick with him every day. Once while sitting in a rowboat, Karl taught Syler that eyes are important. You can tell a lot about someone through their eyes. Truth, nerves, excitement, a person's eyes were as important as a face. You recognize someone by their face, but you read them through their eyes.

This came naturally to him. He just had a knack for it, something that was seen by Karl early on. Years later, through training, he would learn that from a distance, body movements can be seen and registered. Eye movement cannot. This was important, keeping calm on the outside when your insides are a blaze. This was very evident on the 12:10 train to Zürich.

There…

Something at the far end of the car yanked his eyes away from the lake for a split second. His head gave nothing away though. A man came into the car, the door sliding closed behind him, hissing his arrival. He sat down in the first seat on the far side against the window. Syler's eyes saw a lot, always scanning, always registering things, and most of the time dismissing it. This was different. His eyes were only on the man for two-seconds before they were looking back out his window. He had seen enough. Something didn't fit, something wasn't right. Was his book about to reopen?

Thoughts were careening around in his mind: He was well built and solid, filling out his sweatshirt and dark jeans well. Too well. He had a large duffle bag next to him on the seat within reach, not in the luggage rack above. He was good looking. He was no businessman and no tourist. He looked like he could belong in a magazine ad. The last stop was 10 minutes ago, why is he just now sitting down, or moving? Why was he dressed that way?

Fifteen kilometers later, the most troubling thing about it all was he never looked up, never looked around. The occasional passenger would walk through, the beverage cart lady came by again, even when the blond in the short skirt strolled down the aisle, he didn't look, even though other women even gawked at her. All he did was stare out the window. Worse yet, it wasn't his window an arm's length away. He looked across the aisle out the far said window, Syler's side. Syler glanced up through the top of the glass at the low grey clouds, inhaled deeply and exhaled slowly. *Him, this train, at this moment. It's just not right.*

Eventually the train began slowing as it entered the outskirts of the Zürich. The lush greens of the trees and fields soon gave way to the gray of buildings, fences, warehouses, and streets. The track also took the train on a straighter route as the curves of the countryside vanished with those colors. In the country, mountains, hills, and valleys dictated the route. In Zürich, streets and buildings took the train in straight lines through the heart of it.

With his mind shooting scenarios in front of him, Syler unconsciously started damage control. He was too close to lose now, but that didn't mean his discipline stopped. Only three people knew what he had been doing the last three days, and only two knew he was in Lausanne last night. One thing he had learned from Karl, while in a sleeping bag on a February night 300 km north of Helsinki near Varkaus, was plan for a disaster while expecting victory.

Syler looked at the tiny table under the window and decided to use the deck of cards, smiling at Eastern on the box as if smiling at Karl. He thought that maybe he had put those cards in that hotel room, still teaching him in a way. "You never know what you may use later on," Karl preached once. *Damn right.*

Syler pulled out a pen from his bag and opened the box of cards. He slid out the top card and wrote the phone number "358 50 555 75 22" that less than 10 people knew existed, along the side. He then wrote *Barnstation* along the other edge. The four of diamonds just became a lifeboat. If he didn't make it, they would pay.

He slid the card in the box and put them in his pocket. The many tall clock towers of the city skirted by above the buildings as a Swiss voice came over the intercom reminding passengers about belongings and identification. Syler spent the last three minutes narrowing down those scenarios through his head. He knew the central Zürich station well and would use this, and its size, to his advantage. He knew where the locker was. He knew what was out in front of the doors. He knew how to get to the lower levels. He knew where the bathrooms were. He had come too far to lose now. *Plan for a disaster, expect victory.*

The train slowed to a walk as the station's roof covered it in shade. Passengers all started getting up, collecting items and moving out into the aisles to find the closest door. A dinging sound announced the train had stopped. With his left hand, he slid his sunglasses off the little table, then stood up and pulled down his bag. His phone remained on the table under the window.

Out of the corner of his eye, he saw the man, Syler's new mark get up. Instead of turning back and going out the closest door up front, he came to the back of the train car towards Syler. Syler needed to time his next move perfectly. He had rehearsed it in his head since the train entered the Aussersihl district of Zürich. It was time for the real thing.

Three people across the aisle stayed in their seats. Syler let an older couple go ahead of him down the aisle insuring the next person behind him, hopefully about five steps behind, was the mark. Syler moved into the aisle and took three steps towards the train car door. He was just about to turn left and head down the steps off the train, when Syler looked down, put his hand to his pockets, and stopped abruptly.

As he spun around heading back to his seat, he shook his head as if he had forgotten something. He did. He spun around counter-clockwise so his peripheral vision could record more. As he headed back the three paces to his seat for the phone, he had taken in all he needed. It was in a blink of an eye, but it was enough. The mark coming down the aisle was moving quicker than normal once Syler turned to walk off, and was caught off guard by the sudden, unexpected stop of his prey. Syler had seen enough of a pause in his stride to know the man was not just a usual passenger getting off a train, only concerned with himself. He was concerned with Syler and with what Syler was doing. The man was following him.

He grabbed the phone, still shaking his head, and moved back towards the door. With his mind racing, Syler stepped off the train and turned to his left. He moved towards the center of the platform, where some light poles and benches split the platform in two with the occasional phone booth. On the other side was a gleaming white Eurostar with canary yellow stripes. A modern marvel of German engineering that was the newest and fanciest of the high-speed trains on the continent. He walked parallel between both trains. One was smooth and hummed with electricity. The other was full of ridges and edges, sounding more like gears.

The mark had tied his shoe, letting Syler go by. He was now behind Syler and to the left, shadowing Syler's movement. Syler needed to know what he was dealing with. He wanted to get behind the guy. He then decided to use a phone again, but this time he was going to go back in time. Syler was surprised phone booths were still around in 2010.

He approached the next glass telephone booth. He pulled off the red phone surrounded by glass on three sides from the waist up. He inserted a coin and dialed. He noticed the man continue down the left side and keeping the same pace. He was close and would pass soon. Syler called a number he knew from past experience. The conversation would be awkward and there would be a lot of confusion on the line, but the confusion would remain in the metal cord.

"Good evening. Bucherer's. How may we help you?"

"Yes, my phone battery is not keeping a charge and I was hoping I could bring my phone in?"

"I'm sorry sir, this is Bucherer located on Banhhofstrasse. May I help you?"

The man was approaching the telephone booth. Syler began cocking his head this way and that as if not liking what he heard. His right hand gripped the edge of the glass on the phone booth.

"I see. Well I have the, hold on, it's the Nokia 412. I understand it is an older model."

"Sir this is Bucherer, we are a watch store. Is this a phone battery or watch battery you are requesting information about?"

The mark moved by as Syler studied him from behind his sunglasses. The telephone call continued, his mind thinking what his mouth was not.

"Excellent, well I'm going to head over there now. Are you still located next to Kurtz's?"

"Excuse me sir. Burcherer doesn't sell phones, do you understand?"

"Across the street? Okay. And you close at 6pm?" Syler's irrelevant questions came as the man headed off, walked behind a light pole and reemerged on the right side of the platform heading inside.

"What? You have the wrong number and place." A clicking sound ended the phone call that Syler continued.

He nodded his head. "Yes, yes. Thank you." He replaced the receiver and bent down to pick up his bag. He stepped back out around the glass partition and moved to his right to join a steady stream of people walking, along the now departing Eurostar.

Several tracks feed into the roofed station, with white crossbeams and supports above, giving it a modern look. The parallel tracks ended at what looked like the opening of a huge hanger. Half the tracks had trains sitting, humming, waiting to slide out and race across the continent. The hanger is a giant hall. A huge clock in the shape of a child's alphabet block stands in the middle of the entrance, 15 meters high. A round, precise clock and hands are on each of the four sides instead of letters. Just past it, shiny silver escalators, side by side, take up the middle portions, leading down to the lower levels. Syler moved into the hall sticking to the right side. Echoes bounced from everywhere. The stranger was ahead about 20 meters and heading straight towards the lockers. Syler passed the escalators and needed to get more answers.

Ahead on the left, just past long tables of advertisements for hotels, was a coffee stand. Syler slowed, pretending to read a train station map. His head was still. His eyes were on a sugar rush. He sneaked glances at the spaced out round tables. Faces were down in newspapers. Fingers scissored smoldering cigarettes. Someone was tapping a laptop. His eyes flashed over the tables and out towards the lockers. The mark was turning down a locker aisle. Between the lockers and the coffee stand, Syler's eyes noticed an attractive blond in tight jeans and heels. She was spooning sugar into her coffee at the condiments station. She was in the perfect spot. He quickly checked the line. A man just stepped up thumbing his phone's screen. Syler slinked over behind him, bumping him by accident. Two-seconds later, he leaned over his shoulder.

"Sorry about that. I was staring at the blond over there." It was a whisper, no one but him could hear it. Syler nodded to their right, then focused on the blond. The man quickly turned behind him, then matched Syler's stare in that direction. The tall blond then strutted off towards the front of the station. She was between them and the lockers, his mark somewhere off in the distance.

The man raised an eyebrow. "You're forgiven." Both men then returned their attention to the line, moving up a spot. Syler then reached over and slipped his hand in and out of the man's jacket pocket without him knowing. Syler then backed away and headed for the lockers. They were just hotel matches, but might as well have been gold.

Syler was ten paces from the lockers. His eyes then picked up something familiar out to the left. He peered around an ATM stand where backpackers were huddled around it, and found his mark continuing his pace. He was now walking off to the far side of the station, moving faster than those around him. Syler noticed he had a different bag.

The hall opened up to the main room. A train schedule board took up the whole left side wall. Under the black schedule board, the floor disappeared as stairs lead down to the lower levels. The front of the station was nothing but tall narrow windows stretching towards the roof. Glass doors were underneath, leading out to the street.

Syler looked up to the huge schedule board hanging over the main room. European cities were listed down the left with times and track numbers to the right. Every minute or two the letters of the cities would start flipping, from left to right like a loud wave, before new letters emerged and a new city was listed. The whole board, like many around Europe, was a drawing point, the hub of the station. Syler would use it to his advantage.

He headed for the second row of lockers, where his locker had been for 21 years. While passing the first row he noticed a man standing at one. The bag caught his attention, but he moved on. He turned down the next row of lockers and found his. Syler produced a key from his bag and opened his locker. While scanning the area, he pushed in one bag and partially pulled out another. He unzipped it and replaced his smaller concealable Sig for something larger. He shoved it into his pants under his sweater, then stuffed his coat into the locker. He patted his pants pocket, making sure something was there too. He pressed the locker closed and pulled out the key. His hand remained on the metal locker. He stared at it.

He felt the metal on his palm. He felt the tiny slits of the vent on his fingers. He felt his age. He remembers getting this locker two decades ago. A lifetime ago. The person who got it was different, younger. He remembers all nine times he opened it. The nine times he depended on it. Would he look back at his tenth as his last? Syler peeled away his hand treasuring it. He slowly backed away, eyeing it with satisfaction. *I'll never need you again.* He then thought about another door. This one made of oak that he would take off gloves to feel.

Before closing the locker, he checked for the man from the coffee stand. He was just now leaving with his coffee in his hand, replacing the lid. He was heading towards the giant schedule board. So far, no one took an interest in him. He didn't think he was being watched. Worst case, he loses some matches.

He glanced around the lockers at the windows. He noticed two large tourist buses outside parked at the curb. Their doors sprung open as tour groups stepped off. They mingled around the buses, until as one large mass, they began moving towards the station. Just then, Syler took four 'caution slippery signs' that were scattered in front of the men's bathroom. He quickly walked along the doors dropping one in front of each door. Now down to just half the available doors, the Zürich station's late afternoon hour took on an anti-Swiss theme of confusion and ineffectiveness.

Two tour guides were out front leading the herd into the station. With too many people trying to enter and leave through a couple of doors, Syler moved directly into the throng and disappeared. Like a mouse following curves and turns to find the end of a maze, he slithered through without knowing a definitive direction. Even from above, it was difficult to follow him. From down on the ground, it was nearly impossible. Noise and voices grew as well. With the excitement, confusion, and tired eyes and minds after a day of sightseeing and traveling, Syler knew he could walk through and shop.

By the time he was spit out the other end, he was wearing different clothes. He swiped a scarf from one man who spun around in confusion to no avail, and yanked a field coat out of someone's hand. Unnoticed, he moved off to find his mark.

The train schedule began flapping above the floor. København's letters began morphing into Roma. Syler glanced out the far door and noticed a guy with a bag. *That bag!* That's what caught his attention at the lockers; it was the same bag the mark had on the train. That was the switch.

Within five-seconds, a slicing sound came from his left, followed by a thud three-seconds later. Syler's head snapped around in that direction, noticing a commotion. A crowd parted, heads bent over. Syler took his first step towards it when the first scream echoed in the hall. Followed by another. Then like the spreading rings on a pond's surface, screams and shrieking spread across the train station's main hall. Panic ensued.

People took off in every direction, scattering away from the source like an exploding firework in the sky. The man from the coffee stand was left lying on the ground, with legs and arms twisted at odd angles like a dropped marionette. No one saw the entry wound in the back of his head the size of a fingernail. They just saw blood. Red blood flowing from his head on the tile floor, turning into its own pond.

Most took off for the exits. Syler stayed low and needed to find a wife. His true love was the cabin on the slopping hill surrounded by trees. He needed to get to her. No one knew her, not even those who left notes and assignments in drop boxes, safety deposit boxes, or met in person in dark cafes. Not even the people he suspected behind all this, in a twisted backstabbing way. In training, classrooms, background checks, midnight talks with others in similar programs all about to go out on their own, he never spoke of her, bragged about her. Danish cities from his past and Finland came up, but never the cabin. He buried it way too deep.

To get to it, he needed a mistress in a way. A temporary wife here in Zürich and he found her. She was dressed to the hilt, in a power suit covering a tall slender frame raised up on heels. The chocolate brown suit complemented her light brown hair that even in the hysteria and the chaos around her, seemed to flow and sway in slow motion. She was alone most importantly, but it didn't hurt that she reeked of sophistication.

She was moving towards the doors but stopped to help an elderly woman who fell and was being trampled. She knelt down to help the woman up, rubbing her back as she talked to her. Syler stared and wondered was she there for the fallen woman or him? They were both up now on their feet, she holding the other woman's hand and seconds later letting her go, an outstretched arm releasing her. An angel letting her dove fly off. Syler approached her, quickly, being bumped along the way.

"Oh thank god there you are, are you okay? Let me look at you!" He wrapped his arms around her and hugged her. Her world just got even more confusing. She had no chance to respond, not a second to say anything. He continued talking in her ear while they stood as one. This time not in a loud, joyous voice, but a cold, calm serious tone. Cruel Syler arrived. She was now shaking.

"Do as I say and no harm will come to you. If you do not, I will kill you. Do you understand?" He waited two-seconds for that to sink in. He wrapped a strong arm around her, pulling her into his side.

"Look and read your watch to show me you understand and we are clear." They were side by side beginning to move out with everyone. Her dreamy brown eyes danced left and right and her chest heaved up and down under her silk blouse. She shook her head and moved her mouth but nothing came out.

"Are we clear?" As he pulled her in tighter, his left hand pressed a Glock 17 into her ribs. Her eyes stopped dancing and locked onto his. Syler's face was emotionless. Her eyes peered down first, followed by her head, and she looked at her tiny wrist twisting the watch into view. The Cartier watch glimmering.

Her arm came down and she moved with him out towards the doors. She was nearly hyperventilating, climbing her own mountain in Nepal with little to no oxygen. He slipped the gun in his pants waistline, then pulled out the deck of playing cards. Being at the top of the world, she never knew he had slipped them into her purse.

Syler glanced back over his right shoulder behind her head, then back off to his left.

"Elegant watch." He then studied the doors ahead of him. The comment caught her by surprise. Her eyebrows twitched and she glanced at him. She then found two deep breaths as if sucking on oxygen.

"It's from my husband. Anniversary present." The proud way she said it impressed Syler.

"What's his name?"

Her eyes shifted over towards him and then back out front.

"What's his name!" he said through clenched teeth, gripping her shoulder.

"Philip," came quickly.

"Well, I want you to picture Philip right now and remember the time you just read. Decide if it is the time you choose to die or the time you chose you wanted to see him again." They reached the doors, keeping pace with those around them in a panicked jog. "Put your arm around my waist." She did, and soon the 'couple' moved briskly outside, leaving the train station.

They were now in a slow jog as the evening air greeted the fleeing.

Outside the station was a cobblestone plaza area where people would meet, mingle, or just wait in the warm sun before heading inside. Three streets converged and met out front. Sirens were wailing in the backgrounds. Emergency vehicles came from all directions. Vienna seemed to be converging on the station. Blue blinking lights spun everywhere. Trolley cables crisscrossed in the sky above the street. Trolleys were death traps and he didn't bother looking for one. His arm released her shoulder and he reached down grabbing her nearest hand.

"Where are we going?" Her voice was steady even if her insides were flooding. No answer. She looked off to her right at a child crying in her mother's arms, the mother gently stroking the child's cheek. Was she ever going to have a child? Would she ever tell them about this day? She was pulled to her left unexpectedly as she wasn't paying attention to where they were going. She tried again.

"Where are you taking me? Please I..."

"Quiet." His manner and response through gritted teeth worried her. She honestly felt like he didn't know. She was hoping for an answer, assuming he would have a plan so she could have some reassurance. The uncertainty was numbing. Would this end across the street? Would they get in a car and she be left some place? Would this masquerade end hours away in another city, tied to a bedpost to sleep as his hostage until he's safe the next morning? *This isn't happening. This isn't happening. Oh God... Phillip!*

"You're doing good. Keep picturing Philip." He was studying the street, then began looking to his left. "It's almost over, I just..."

He froze still holding her hand and she was yanked back to him. They stood on the cobblestone with people crossing in front and behind them. Syler was fixated on something to his left. Amidst all the people going to and fro, most scattering without definition, there was somebody standing still. It was out of place. *Why isn't he moving?*

His hand obscured the side of his face as he held a phone up to his ear. *A phone?* Syler knew no one in the right mind would stand there and talk on the phone considering what was going on around him. Syler cocked his head to the side and focused on him. A sickening feeling ascended up his throat from his stomach, coating it like a poison. *That's him.*

It was the man at the lockers switching bags. He was about to let go of his mistress and head over in his directions, but it was the eyes. The man's eyes gave something away.

"Take off your heels," he demanded as he continued being a statue and holding her hand. She didn't move.

"Do it!"

Using him to balance, she leaned over and reached down, her legs kicking up at the knee. Syler cocked his head the other way. The man was peered up to the building across the street and then turned to his left and finally moved on. The right hand bringing the cell phone down and into his pocket.

Syler's head shot up and looked up over the street at the building. The office building's windows were dark and the lights of the street and the Hauptbahnhof glared in the windows, leaving reflections. He couldn't see inside any of them. Buildings lined the streets on all sides, most about 4-5 flights high. She stood holding her heels by the straps and was about to ask what's going on. Syler didn't give her a chance.

"Run!"

They took off to their right, he pulling her along. He switched her to his left hand. She was between him and the building. He didn't like doing it, but this was sinister Syler and had been sinister Syler since he hugged her. The smidgen of caring was buried deep down, not to cloud his judgment and not driving him.

They really didn't look out of the ordinary, as confusion and panic still blanketed the country's largest train station. *My god this was an ambush. Who betrayed me? How many are out here? Two or three scattered around?*

She was a fast runner and in shape. She did well keeping up, but he wasn't moving as fast as he'd liked. He planned on letting her go once they crossed the street. She would slow him down. Another 10 seconds and they would be there. He'd no longer be out in the open. Like a concrete jungle, he'd use buildings, awnings, stores, and side streets for cover.

Just then and ambulance veered around the corner and headed towards them. Its lights were off which was very strange. Syler noticed it immediately. The ambulance pulled up and the driver drove onto the curb. The left front tire coming to a screeching stop just up on the sidewalk. It was about five paces in front of them. Syler came to a stop and lurched forward a bit as her momentum carried her on a bit. She was breathing hard and turned to look at him, still holding hands. Syler stood and knew he was stuck out in the open at the moment. *My god, I didn't have a chance.*

Inside the driver shoved the gearshift up as far as it would go. "Damn lights don't work!" He glared at the man seated next to him.

"I'm sorry Markus, I thought I reported it yesterday? I'm sorry, really." He was fiddling with his seatbelt, more nervous than usual under the present cross-examination.

The driver twisted back to his right and ripped off a clipboard hanging on the back wall in the front cab. "Took us forever to get here." He turned back facing forward and pulled out his pen from his chest pocket, glanced at his watch, and scribbled down the time. The pen strokes matched his tight grip. "We should have been here a couple minutes ago." He stopped writing, put it back in his pocket, and stared at him while unlatching his seatbelt.

The driver's door swung opened and Markus got out. He happened to find Syler right in front of them. The back doors of the rescue vehicle flew open banging against the sides. A man hopped out, then turned and reached back inside.

Syler let go of her hand, but held out his arm as if he didn't want to. It appeared he was reaching for her. Her hand dropped and she took two steps back, but didn't run. For some reason, despite what this man just did to her, she didn't run. She followed his stare to the ambulance.

The driver closed his door and stood there, while out of the passenger side another paramedic trotted around the hood. Syler wondered how he got this far, this close only to fail now. Should he have just been another banker? A paramedic like these guys were pretending to be? A Philip?

The man emerged out the back pulling a gurney. He kicked a lever near the bottom and it sprang up. The doors were shut and they lifted the stretcher up onto the sidewalk and they all began moving towards the station.

Syler watched it all happening as if he'd never seen paramedics or an ambulance before. In a way what happened really hadn't happened before. Syler's hunch, instincts, little voice in his head, had been wrong.

The ambulance wasn't pulling up for him. He twisted to his right and watched them race towards the station against the grain of people still flowing out. He should be running, but for some reason he stopped and watched. *Wow, a real ambulance with real paramedics,* he thought. He smirked to himself at the plain, simple coincidence. For the first time in his life, he had thought too much.

She continued to stand there, part in a trance as to what had taken place in the last 5 minutes, but also curious. It hit her that she would be fine. He wasn't going to lift up the gun, aim it at her, and pull the trigger. He wouldn't lay another finger on her, she wouldn't be a hostage. Part of her wanted to say thank you for keeping his word. Part of her wanted to go and hit him for doing this. She stood there watching him stare off.

His eyes left the scene behind and slowly turned to her. After all, that he had done in his life, was this angel sent here for him? He leaned forward a fraction, about to go find that jungle. Just then, a splat sound found his ears and the angelic face he was looking at changed to shock. Then fear. Her brown eyes widened and moved down to his chest. There was a deepening pain like a long needle from a syringe in his chest. He felt light. There was a burning smell. He looked down and saw a small black hole in his sweater. He blew out a long breath, but when he tried to inhale, he couldn't. Her heels fell to the cobblestones as her hands came up in unison to her face. They muffled a high-pitched shriek. He didn't hear it.

He couldn't see the exit wound. She glanced on the other side of him and saw red mush on the pavement.

He fell to his knees and teetered forward and back, then to the side a little. He was a child's top. Syler looked up at the building in front of them. *Why did I watch the ambulance*? He noticed a puff of smoke billowing away from the corner of the building. He knew what had caused it. He then looked to her. Thinking she was an angel a few minutes ago, now a messenger. He managed to point to her purse, but only for a second, before his arm fell limp to his side. Syler looked down at his open hand. He felt the cold metal of a locker, not wood. This was not in his epilogue. Syler was supposed to feel something else.

His thoughts then drifted away to other smoke. This smoke was spiraling out of a chimney, on top of a cabin in a quiet valley. He could see it now, but he would never smell that smoke, never breath in the cold dry air of a winter afternoon, and never hear the crunch of fresh snow on the porch. That same porch sheltering a heavy wood door that will remain closed and untouched. His last thought was of the cabin that he'd never see again. His own little heaven. Maybe it was meant to be.

He accepted that a lifetime ago, knowing he was headed for someplace else. Was she there to send him off to his final destination? Was she there to show him what could have been? Deep down he understood that he was never going to get to heaven, but now, he would never get to the cabin either. Or was it the same? He had called the cabin and the valley heaven many times growing up as young child. Syler would never know. The angel stood before him, wobbly, woozy herself. His eyelids came down darkening his world. Then his book closed.

If only Paolo Maldini had not run into James Bond.

CHAPTER FIVE

Mia Strobl sat in the back of the ambulance wrapped in a blanket; arms crossed, gripping the edges tightly. Secure. She was still shaking, but not from being cold. After Syler leaned forward and plopped down onto the cobblestones, Mia gazed around sucking in air, and did the same. The last five-minutes were just too much on her. Her body gave in, nothing but a bloodstream of tingles, and she fainted.

With two dead bodies, there was no hurry. With one entry wound in the forehead, the second in the chest, neither man had a chance. At least the coffee shop guy never knew what hit him; he died even before the drop of mercury had time to spread. Two heavy, bulky body bags were waiting to be lifted up into a second ambulance. Jens and another man were walking over to grab one of them, as Markus passed them. Jens still couldn't look at Markus out of fright. The only saving grace of the lights not working, was it wouldn't have made a difference looking back now.

Markus walked to the back of his ambulance and stepped up inside. He sat across from Mia and leaned down a little to look up into her eyes. His tiny flashlight bringing her beautiful brown eyes to life.

"How are we doing?" He always hated asking it, knowing what their mind was saying, but it had just became custom, natural. He then stood up and checked the left side of her head. There was a slight bump from her fall, but physically she was fine. There was nothing more he could do, just comfort her. Mentally she was a mess. When she woke up, she couldn't even tell Markus her last name. Now she could, she remembered everything. Mia almost wished she couldn't again. That lapse in memory and her past was warm and soothing, like the blanket.

Mia nodded, still in a daze. Her breathing was almost normal and she was shaking a little less. A man came around to peek in the open doors. Markus turned as he was scribbling something down in his notes.

"Give her a couple minutes please."

The man nodded and began talking into a radio as he moved behind one of the doors.

"Mrs. Strobl is there someone you can call here in Zürich?"

She shook her head, a strand of hair swaying in front of her right eye. "Well yes, but I arrived for business." She took a deep breath. "I really just want to get home. I need to call my husband." She moved it back out of the way.

"I understand. Vienna, correct?"

Mia finally looked at Markus. "Yes."

He nodded. "The police want to ask you some questions." Markus then bit his lip and sneaked a glance out the back of the ambulance, then leaned forward towards her. He whispered.

"If you want, I can say you are not in a condition to remember things and take you to the hospital. Give you some time to relax?" He cocked his head to the left looking at her.

Mia smiled at the gesture. "No, no I'm fine now. Whatever I need to do so I can get out of here and home." Mia's legs were pressed together tight, knees rubbing. Her fingers digging into the ends of the blanket, pulling it snug.

Markus sat back and smiled. He stopped whispering. "Keep the blanket. Watch that bump on your head, ice will help. Otherwise I see nothing physically that concerns me." He put his clipboard to the side and stepped out the back. He reached back in, offering a hand. "I'll walk you up."

Mia stepped out and looked up at the sky. Gray clouds moved in and became the ceiling. With an arm on her upper back, Markus guided her towards the train station.

Just outside the doors, her pace slowed, as if not wanting to go back in. The prologue to her nightmare. Markus sensed it and rubbed her back in little circles.

"It's okay, come on. It's all over." He smiled at her and she looked at him.

It will never be over for me. She nodded and shrugged out of the blanket. "Thank you Markus. You were very kind." She handed him the blanket.

"You take care. Safe travels back home." Markus took it and held the door for her. He watched her go in, almost tip toeing. He nodded and smiled at the policeman posted at the door. The door swung closed and the street side's reflection was displayed again. Just like that she was gone. Another name in the paperwork. Another person he touched. He turned and headed back to the ambulance. Markus looked down at the blanket, rubbing it with his fingers. For a reason he couldn't explain, he knew he would remember her face. She would be one of the few that wasn't just a statistic in his log. *Mia Strobl. From Vienna.*

The Swiss's Federal Crime Police took over the Zürich Hauptbahnhof. The more investigative unit set up stations inside, each with its own purpose and men in charge. The cafe near the lockers became a hold for witnesses. An officer greeted Mia just inside the doors and brought her to a table. His outstretched open palm showed her where to sit.

He pushed in her chair. "May I get you some coffee? Bottled water?"

She wanted a drink for her nerves. "Water would be fine." The officer headed off. Mia looked across the table at the detective. He was scribbling notes down with one hand, holding up the stapled papers out of the way with the other. She moved a loose strand of hair away from her eye. She wished she had kept that blanket. It was like a flexible vault.

The detective's handwriting was that of an architect. His mind was that of a chess player. And his responses mimicked a psychiatrist. He finished the page's notes and let the top page fall. He began slowly twisting on the pen's cap. He screwed it on and placed it parallel next to the notebook, resembling a compass needle. He took a deep breath and looked up at Mia. The wounded baby animal.

"Mrs. Strobl, my name is detective Henrick Brehmre." He began his psychiatry session. He knew almost immediately he wouldn't need to think two or three moves ahead with her.

The police were studying the CCTV from inside and outside the station. They would, until hopefully finding out who pulled the trigger, or triggers. They had no idea how many there were. Mia was the most important witness right now. After studying those images, they did't think she was directly involved, but had plenty of questions and wanted to be 100% sure. After ten minutes, unofficially interrogating her even though it was in a cafe, not a plain room with a one-way mirror, he could tell in her body language and slight trembles she was just in the wrong place at the wrong time. Her answers were truthful.

"Mrs. Strobl, we're almost done. One last thing. Besides what you've already told me, there is nothing else he said to you? No matter how odd? A phrase, even something he said to himself perhaps? Under his breath?"

"No." Mia's body was calmer, but her hands weren't. Her fingers appeared shivering on the water bottle. "Mr. Brehmre, I really need to call my husband." She finally made eye contact with him. The man sticking a Glock in her side told her to picture him in her head. She did then, and he was still there.

Mr. Brehmre stopped writing and looked up. "Has no one contacted him yet?"

She was almost in tears now. "I don't know. I don't think so."

His sat back. "Mrs. Strobl, I'm so sorry." He reached inside his jacket. "Here, please take my phone." He slid it across to her. "I will be right back, please take your time." He scooted back to stand up.

She reached for the phone. "Mr. Brehmre," she tried, but couldn't look him in the eyes, "will you please stay with me." Her eyes got as far as his coffee cup.

He smiled at her. "Of course, I'm going to stand right over here though." He nodded with his head to his left, then looked up at the officer behind her.

"Get her some coffee."

"Yes sir."

Mr. Brehmre stood and moved two paces away and called over two people. They started discussing their notes and findings.

Mia dialed. She slipped the phone under her hair to her ear. At the third beep, she tilted her head down.

"Phillip! It's me."

After hearing his voice, she started crying. She brought her hand up to her face. The officer brought her a coffee and walked away. One man leaned to his right and looked around Brehmre at Mia, then leaned back.

Five-minutes later, she placed the phone on the table, and cleared her hair off her forehead. She took a deep breath looking around the cafe and station. Mr. Brehmre returned and sat back down. He handed her a handkerchief.

"Is he okay?"

"He is now."

He shook his head and leaned towards her on the table, staring at her coffee now.

"My wife was in London during that bus bombing years ago. I remember the panic once I turned the television on. Being unsure, not knowing." He remembers pouring his own coffee back then and never touching it, just staring at it on his desk while his insides brewed. He then left it to pace back and forth. He wonders if Mr. Strobl has an untouched cup of coffee, or maybe a glass of Saint-Emilion after a day's work that he finally got to a minute ago, and was the most glorious swallow of his life. He looked up at her.

"I was helpless for 30 minutes. Seemed like an hour. All my connections, sources, talents, and just had to wait and wait."

Mia tilted her head to the right.

"She was okay?"

He smiled, more to himself, and nodded. "Other side of the city as it turned out. But it doesn't matter does it?" He leaned on the table.

Mia shook her head as they locked eyes. They both squeezed out tiny smiles.

"Mrs. Strobl, you and I are done. Unfortunately, we are not done with all this." He sighed and slid a card across the table. "This is my card. If you think of anything else, anything, no matter how incidental, please call me. My office and cell numbers are there." He leaned back and put his phone inside his jacket. "We will be in contact with you again unfortunately, but as of now, I do not see the need for you to come back to Zürich."

Mia took the card and nodded.

"Mrs. Strobl, after this incident and another in Genéva yesterday, we are looking into possible connections. There may be a correlation. Our borders are closed. All vehicles leaving the country are being stopped at check points. Most flights are grounded until tomorrow. Those trains that are cleared to leave the city, are at a crawl. I will do everything I can to get you home as soon as possible."

Mia closed her eyes and nodded.

"Thank you."

A plane ticket was in her name the next afternoon. Friday saw travel in Switzerland a little easier for some, but still slow. Mia boarded SwissAir flight 1504 at Terminal A of Zürich's probing airport. The Airbus A320 lifted off runway 16 and landed in Vienna 75 minutes later. The longest, worst part was the last three minutes; the walk from the gate to the main terminal where Phillip was waiting. Her brisk walk could be mistaken for a panicked jog.

For that 75-minute flight, she tried filling her head with thoughts of the future. Right now, her past, despite approaching her 34th birthday, consisted of only five minutes. She sat in the window seat, as far over against the bulkhead as possible. As if, Syler was in the seat beside her. She leaned on the armrest, sneaking glances out the window, as if afraid of the reflections she might see. She asked for a blanket, but it never arrived. She missed the ambulance. She missed Markus.

Her initial instinct was to quit work, have children, and allow motherhood to pulse through her veins. She'd spend every breath at Philip's side, as they nurtured a child surrounded by the exposure only a city like Vienna can offer. She would pass down as many physical and mental items as she could to them, to take on a world where a Syler or two are hiding around any corner. This was as the A-320 climbed through the clouds.

But after finally reaching its cruising altitude of 31,000 feet, her thoughts changed with her view. Finally above the clouds, with the grayness and memories below like a stained carpet, a new sun gleamed into the starboard side of the plane. Clouds of white like soft curvy icebergs greeted her. The darker, dangerous unknown was lurking below now. Her confidence grew, blooming like a poppy seed field outside Salzburg. It was bright, and as she pulled down the window shade to block the dazzle to her eyes, the warmth radiated new ideas in her heart and mind. Work, the firm, Phillip, a baby, children, their lives, all spread out in front of her mixing and meshing together in harmony. She could make it all work. She had to. Mia didn't need a magic genie in a bottle for her wishes. She had Syler and an afternoon in a Zürich train station, pushing her to a path that was always there, but now viewed with a purpose. A purpose and drive you only see when given a second chance at life.

110 miles from the airport, the A320's engines started to hum softer, skipping a few revolutions. The Airbus began slowly floating down. The

sky was clear. The icebergs had melted, leaving a sea of green and beige Austrian fields below. The plane's shadow skimming over it all in humps, getting fatter and fatter with every notch the flaps lowered.

After arriving that Friday until Sunday, she didn't leave their Vienna apartment. She was never more than an arm's reach away from Phillip. She rarely left the third and second floor. Surrounded and wrapped up in their sheets, his arms, his body, the roman tub, the clingy bubbles, the new Mia was cleansed and mentally moving forward, heedfully.

They were rarely out of bed. By Sunday afternoon Mia wondered how Phillip had anything left to give.

"What time is the game?" Mia looked down at him, stroking his thick blond hair as they laid in bed. He was resting his head on her rising chest after another session. He looked down at his finger making tiny circles around her belly button.

"3:00. So you think we got something brewing in here?"

She closed her eyes and grinned. "Well you've certainly filled me up."

"I'm running on empty right now." His finger slid over to her hip, pushing down the sheets as it moved down her thigh.

"I think I've squeezed every milliliter out of you." She raised her knee sliding his finger down to her hip again. "So do you ever actually run out?" She opened her eyes and peered down at him.

"I guess not completely. Let's find out in an hour."

She bit her lip and ran her fingers through his hair. "You're on. You coming back at halftime or something?"

"No I'm not going."

Mia shook his head. "Phillip, go. It's the derby for God's sake. It's not like I'm on house arrest. I'm fine, seriously."

"I'll watch it here."

At least one city in every soccer-crazed country has one. Like those other major cities, Vienna's happens twice a year. Phillip followed Rapid Vienna, currently in third place, two points behind Austria Vienna. None of the players would be in the 2010 World Cup in South Africa this summer, so this game was their biggest. The winner could also climb within two points of leading FC Salzburg. It may not be AC Milan v Inter Milan, Real Madrid v Atlético Madrid, but the city of Vienna basically shuts down on game day.

For the last seven years, Phillip was either at Gerhard Hanappi Stadium or at a bar with friends to watch it. After moving to Vienna with Mia, he called Rapid his hometown team, unless they played Wolfsberger, where his father had taken him to his first game when he was six.

Mia went back to playing with his hair. On the outside she was glad he was going to watch it. On the inside, she was a sixteen year old with her first crush. Phillip kissed his way to her neck, snaking his way up.

Her eyes closed, her hands continued. "Phillip keep doing this and we're going to find out if you're empty right now."

By Monday, Mia needed to get out of the apartment. It wasn't being alone, as Phillip reluctantly went in to the office, it was trying to move on with the confidence like being at 31,000 feet. But every time she picked up the phone to call Anna, she couldn't press send. She just stared out onto the street.

An hour later, she left a thumbprint.

"Mia, come on. I'm coming to get you like it or not."

"Okay okay, I'm not 12. I'll meet you."

"How about Hawelka, like we use to. There shouldn't be any tourists now either."

Mia leaned into the frame of the floor to ceiling window on the second floor. Floors of parquet stretched out below, elaborately decorated crown molding edging the ceiling. She started tapping a toe, then a finger on her forearms. She gazed down at the street as if through a store window at shoes or jewelry she longed to have, but couldn't quite afford yet.

"Okay, 20 minutes. See you then." She pressed the button and her arm fell to her side. She stood still and window shopped for another four minutes.

Café Hawelka was close. She slipped into her favorite jeans and boots, and grabbed her purse, which was still by the front door since Friday. Going out the door was easy. Once her boots tapped on the sidewalk, her steps took thought. They were calculated going down Annagasse. Walking on Spiegelgasse she noticed shops and cars. By the time she got to Dorotheergasse, she saw faces and birds. The city was giving her energy, warmth in her flesh, and bringing her back to life. They city didn't know who Syler was.

Anna hugged Mia as if it would be the last time she would ever see her. It was crowded for a Monday afternoon and they found a booth along the front windows. Both ordered mélanges, Mia's with sugar. For a cafe that opened just after the war, one gets the feel it's as old as the clock towers peeking above the rooftops. That every second inside turns back the pages of its own autobiography. You'd swear there were ghosts from those pages floating around you. Maybe it's the pictures and posters on the wall that seem thrown up without care, before a level was invented. Perhaps it's the dark wood closing in on you. Maybe it's the coat rack at the end of every booth, with its reflection in the windows like bookends, squeezing between them a booth of burgundy and white stripes. Mia and Anna spent 45 minutes in comfort.

Eventually Anna's phone started vibrating on the table and she glanced down. She reached over touching Mia's arm. "Let me get this." She picked it up and sat back. Mia looked out the window, supporting her chin in her palm. A mother pushed a baby stroller by, which brought down Mia's teeth on her nails. She thought of Phillip and reached into her purse to check her phone for messages. She tilted her head to the left watching them continue down the street while her hand dug around in her purse. She found something similarly shaped, but miles apart. The only thing they had in common were the numbers on them.

Anna ended her call and hesitantly looked up. "Mia, I'm sorry I gotta go."

Mia was narrowing her eyes in her purse at the playing cards she was holding. *What…are these?* She pulled them completely out and held them down in her lap. Her look made Anna feel worse. *Where did…*

"Oh Mia, I'm so sorry, let's meet again tomorrow, I'll come get you for a movie or the museum." She reached over and grabbed her hand.

Mis looked up and laughed. "Oh no it's not you." She put the cards in her purse. "It was just a message from work," she lied. "Go Anna, no worries."

Anna was relieved and sat back hoisting her purse up on her shoulder. "I'll call you tomorrow. Promise." She slid out and came over to lean down and kiss cheeks. Then she hurried out of the cafe. Mia watched her go and then looked back in her purse.

She pulled out the cards and held them in front of her. *What is Eastern?* She turned them over and then opened them. Mia knew her purse never left her side on the train and Zürich. Once home, she even forgot that it sat by the door where she dropped it once stepping inside. *How did these get here?*

She pinched out the cards and flipped through them. They were just normal playing cards. She was about to slip them back in when something pulled her eyes to the bottom card. With a twist of her wrist, the four of diamonds appeared. She squinted her eyes as she read the numbers along the edge, then cocked her head the other way as she read the name on the other edge.

"*Barnstation*?"

Mia's curiosity was heard by no one, other than possibly those ghosts one felt may be lurking around the old cafe and Vienna block. Mia closed her eyes tightly, as she had to think back to her past. Unfortunately, it was the recent past.

She shut her eyes and rewound back to Thursday. Something she swore she wouldn't do for some time. These were not in her purse on the train. When the train crossed the border, they came around verifying tickets. She remembers sitting her purse in her lap and shifting things around to dig out the ticket. She thought of the ambulance and Markus. She thought of detective Brehmre, the officer standing behind her playing waiter.

She opened her eyes. Her thoughts then drifted to events between the train and ambulance. Those awful, middle five-minutes. The air in the cafe grew thick. The cards were stacked on the table now as she stared at *Barnstation* and the mystery numbers.

Fire ants then colonized her shoulders, neck, and insides. The feeling spread as she realized they had to be from him. He must have slipped them in her purse. After all, in her state at that moment, he could have tried shoving an espresso machine in her purse and she wouldn't have known. *Wasn't he kind of pointing at my side, my purse?*

It was as if Syler was there in her booth. He was in their apartment. He was next to her on the plane. He was sitting across from her in the ambulance. Syler was still all over her. 600 kilometers away.

Mia brought up both hands and covered her face. Her head became wobbly, light and full of air. She swiped her hair back and looked around. It felt like everyone's eyes were on her. All the ghosts in the cafe. All the faces on the posters and pictures on the wall, not level, but slanting because they are leaning over to glare down at her.

Then as if a guardian angel was among those ghosts, a waiter came from out of nowhere to the left of the coat rack. He seemed to ease her, blow cool air on her like a welcoming fan in summer. Life was continuing and he wasn't from Zürich, but here in Vienna. And he was a real waiter.

"Ma'am, may I get you another mélange with sugar?"

Damn he even remembers the sugar. She collected herself and looked up at him, her face pale despite the warmth flooding her. He unclasped his hands in front of him and one grabbed the coat rack. He tilted his head down a little.

"Ma'am, are you okay?"

She nodded. "Yes thank you. I could use a glass of water?"

"Certainly." He was off.

She licked her lips and picked up the cards, all but one that is, and slid them back into the blue box. The four of diamonds stayed on the table.

The glass of water was placed right next to it as the waiter smiled. "If there is anything else, please don't hesitate."

"Thank you." She gulped half the glass as he moved off to another table. She stared at the numbers while placing the glass down. Then the brave Mia, the one that announced to Syler where her watch came from, took on the person responsible for her new nightmare. In a cafe of ghosts, she tried to speak to one.

She picked up the card and leaned on the table studying it, and the hand that passed it on to her.

Why did you give this to me? You were ad-libbing, adapting. You were running, we were running. You didn't write this with me, you did it early when things first went bad didn't you? For someone unknown at the time, some unknown soul that would be me. It's too big for a locker combination. Bank account? You gave me a phone number? You gave me your phone number. No why would you give me yours? Mia dropped the card and sat back in the booth. *You gave me their phone number......oh my god.*

If Syler was evil, then 'they' were worse. Those that did this to him, and in doing so, to her. She scrambled to find Brehmre's card in her purse and picked up her phone. It was a phone number, maybe a bank account, it had to be. She began dialing. She was about to press the last digit, a five, when her thumb froze, the red nail pulling it back. It hovered. Her thumb never moved, but her top finger did. It extended up and pressed the iPhone off. Her hand fell to her lap still holding the phone, still staring at the playing card. *Barnstation.* She couldn't do it. That part of her past, all five minutes of it, was closed. It needed to stay closed.

What if they found out Syler gave it to her? What if they figure out she, the main witness, tipped the authorities off? There's only one way she, and then the police, could get that number. Mia's icebergs were approaching. They were on the horizon as her ship sailed by them. Phillip and her children pointed in awe, but she knew what was underneath. She knew the extent it could reach out for them.

She slid the card to her and snapped it off the edge of the table. She pushed it inside the deck, somewhere near the middle, and it disappeared. They disappeared.

Then Phillip appeared, a baby appeared, followed by more babies. Her world appeared. Mia knew 'they' were not that important in her world. They weren't worth it. She wouldn't let those five minutes turn into more.

On her way out, Mia walked to the back of the cafe with the deck of cards in her hand. She placed them on the counter and stepped back slowly, still looking at them. *Goodbye you. Goodbye them. Goodbye Barnstation.* Mia Strobl breathed out and turned her back on them. Cards that were more than playing cards. She left Café Hawelka on a cool Monday afternoon, leaving a past to forget for a future to cherish.

Unfortunately one of those ghosts in the cafe would follow her. It would follow her forever, wherever she went, into whatever closet was in her home, for as long as she lived. Like some women, she would now hold a dark secret. Something she would tell no one. Ever.

Mia's wasn't an affair, a child out of wedlock, an accidental death, or some deadly backstab. Mia's was a deck of playing cards. A possible clue leading to one of the deadliest organizations in the world.

A little over three years later, the ghosts were still there. The posters still watched over the tables. The espresso machines hissed, always keeping up with requests. The coat racks were still there, standing at attention. Other than some chips of paint off them, some more scratches on the floor, and a millimeter of varnish worn off the tables and chairs after countless wipes of a rag, the cafe in Vienna was the same.

Who came in and what emotions they brought with them, changed as much as the shadows seeping through the windows. Their stories and conversations seem to stay suspended in the air, swirling around for all. Maybe some became new ghosts. Some worn, used books with so many creases, it took twice as long to read the title and author, came and went on a far table. A dominos box and the Eastern cards were still there as well, never resting in the same place each week.

Miriam Koell was wiping down an espresso machine in the back. It was 10:15, but felt more like midnight. Midnight after a cloudy, dim winter day. Or was it a week? The coffee orders, her outfits, and the receipts all merged into one spinning, revolving moon cycle. To keep up, Miriam almost needed her watch not to show the date, but the month.

"Kilian," she tossed the rag in the sink and grabbed two mugs with one hand. They clinked as she put them in another sink behind the counter. She glanced up as he walked around the corner. "Hey the three top in the corner just left. We're done."

"About time." Kilian grabbed a bin and walked over to the round table. He pulled out a chair, sat the bin down, and picked up a glass and two mugs on saucers. One was still half-full, a mélange with an orange peel he made 30 minutes ago. He then shook his head. He saw the playing cards.

He scooped up the cards that were all scattered in a pile, Eastern showing on some, red and black numbers on the others. The 30 year-old's hands meshed them into one pile and he slid them into the box. Then his pocket, forcefully.

"Where's Jacob?"

"Left a half hour ago."

His head snapped up. "Well well, look who's in charge." Kilian lifted the bin up, slid the chair in with his hip, and turned towards the back.

She rolled her eyes and threw a rag at him. He smiled while heaving the bin up on the counter and reached into his pocket. He tossed the deck of cards on the counter. They slid into a dimming lamp begging for a battery. She noticed and grinned.

"Ah, your favorites."

"Why can't anyone put things away? The domino's get put away, the books are stacked, but not these. How hard is it to get them back into a damn box?" He wiped his hands on his pants. "Picking up playing cards nightly after people was not in the job interview. Where did those come from anyways?"

Miriam was sorting receipts. "Not sure, one day they just appeared." She reached for a stapler. "Jan Tríska played with them the other day when he was here."

"Why do I know that name?"

"Actor that lives in Prague. He's here a lot actually." With a squeeze, the stapler began pinching receipts with a deep clicking sound.

"So is he a method actor, or would you call him classical? How about Meisner philosophy?" Kilian continued stacking mugs, now with a grin.

The stapler stopped. "You mean Meisner technique?" She eyed him as the stapler resumed.

"Whatever. Acting's acting for god's sake." He enjoyed teasing her and getting her on her acting and theater soapbox. She took it seriously.

"Sometimes you just have to let art flow through you."

"Right. Well, I bet he put the cards away."

She laughed. "Linda Chuckman and three others played with them too last week."

"Who the hell is that?"

"Not sure, someone said she's known in America. She never stopped smiling when she was here." Miriam watched him walk away biting her lip, then closed her eyes and tried picturing the blueness of the Indian Ocean. All she saw was the blueness of the pool and him in a speedo diving in.

Kilian was an ex-swimming champion, turned coach. He's of African descent, grandparents from the Ivory Coast, parents from outskirts of Vienna. He basically lives at the natatorium or the cafe. Miriam's uncle was an original owner of the cafe, and she asked to have Kilian hired part-time. His shifts turned into teases. Miriam was in love with Stefan, but she'd be lying if Kilian's arms and shoulders didn't creep into her closed eyelids like a brochure at times.

"When do you leave tomorrow?"

"3:00."

"Nice. Should be there for the sunset."

Miriam shook her head. "Not going down to the Adriatic this time. Maldives, Indian Ocean."

"Wow. Always wanted to go there." Kilian slid a stool over, sat, and started filling sugar jars.

"We were there two years ago. It was a different place, but similar. We have a villa, Stefan wanted to splurge."

"Good for you guys."

She reached up and pulled out a tin coffee can from a cupboard. Kilian had never seen it before and noticed she had to do some rearranging to get it out. He narrowed his eyes at it and then her. She smiled.

"Little treat for the trip." She opened the lid that didn't have coffee in it, but like coffee, had its own unique smell.

"Ahh, now we're talking. Although you do know what they do to people caught with cannabis in Indonesia?"

She pulled out a bag continuing to smile, now up at him.

"Yes and the Maldives aren't part of Indonesia."

"Oh," he picked up another jar. "What are they?"

She shrugged. "Beautiful?"

He laughed, "I'll take it. How are you going to get it there?"

"Not sure, I've used books before and old CD jackets."

Kilian put the dried mug in a stack he was making and tilted his head to look around it. He decided to kill two birds with one stone. "Give me those damn cards."

"Kilian, what if they open the box?"

"They'll see a deck of cards Miriam." He pulled out a knife from his pocket and slid out the cards. He took four or five from the top and bottom and put them to the side. "They won't see the middle." He would cut out the middle of the thicker stack, making a hidden hole for the small bag. Kilian thumbed out the smooth, silver blade, clicking it into place. The point just touched the top card where he wanted to puncture.

"Wait!" She put the bag on top of the cards. "The box is too small."

"Oh, it is." He pinched his eyebrows. His head swept left and right looking for something.

"It's okay, I'll get it there another way." She put the bag in her purse. "Why don't you put those cards away for once." She smirked at him.

"Funny."

She stepped away towards the back and turned out some lights. Kilian put the cards in the box and then slipped them in her purse.

"Good riddance." Only the ghosts heard him.

She grabbed the purse and they headed out the door. They kissed on the cheeks as they said goodbye and he wished her a safe trip. Miriam Koell left Café Hawelka and weaved her way through the Vienna buildings towards home. The girl that was a reflection in every street window, bounded home with excitement, an illegal drug, a deck of cards, and mace in her purse. The mace would not make the trip to the Maldives.

From March 2010 to October 2014……

3 games of Accordion Solitaire
14 games of Bieten
1 game of Dobbm
10 games of Giltspiel
7 games of Hasenpfeffer Euchre
5 games of Klondike Solitaire
21 games of Preference
9 games of Schafkopf
32 games of Watten

PART III

6.8 Magnitude Earthquake, Niigata, Japan
Mine Explosion, Ulynovskaya, Russia
Virginia Tech Massacre, Blacksburg, Virginia
TAM Airlines, Flight 3054 Crashes, Sao Paulo, Brazil
Flash Flooding, Central Sudan, Africa

CHAPTER SIX

"Say, Charleston."

"Charleston."

"Say, spaghetti."

"Spaghetti."

Her eyes scanned the brick wall for ideas. "Say, watermelon banana rainbow smoothie." Her eyes found him again.

Danby licked his lips. He obeyed. She giggled. He then inhaled and blew out 12 hours of frustration. He held up his glass of melting ice with a fake smile.

"Another double sir?"

"Say, hurry please." He said it with a straight face.

She laughed and turned to the table behind her, grabbing the check and credit card.

Danby Lewis got in from Philadelphia 35 minutes ago. He arrived at Heathrow 12 hours ago. He spent most of the flight over the Atlantic looking over charts, studying graphs, and clicking between Excel pages. On the way down the east coast to Charleston, he summarized it all. After staring at data and using that to type reports, and traveling for almost a whole day, the last thing he wanted was to play circus performer for a 20 year-old waitress, who loves British accents.

With his work done and off his shoulders, he could completely relax for the next week. He hoped it would finally begin with his second Johnny Walker. He twisted his wrist and checked his watch. He figured he had a little less than two hours before his friend from Spain would arrive. He was coming through Dulles and last he heard, left Madrid on time. He checked his phone to find out.

His was one of the first in the office to get the new iPhone by Apple. For someone always trying to improve and get things down faster, this new device was perfect. In six minutes, he read 14 work emails, checked flight information, read the weather in two cities for the next week, read soccer and cricket news from England, and called the hotel in Charleston. He felt bad for the five secretaries in the office. He then started thinking what the office could do with the space once most were gone.

Two minutes later, a nod greeted her carrying Mr. Walker, as Danby was afraid to open his mouth anymore. The 41 year-old brought up the glass and inhaled, this time not to help push out annoyance, but suck in satisfaction. He sipped and swallowed, then looked out a nearby window. The Charleston air even looked thick and heavy. The heat was simmering at the end of the runway and tarmac. A stream of swimming blurriness just above the blue and red lights. He wondered if the pilots tried to catch it, fly through it, only to lean back and lift above it. The northern runway angled off behind a hanger, with row after row of sable palms beyond. He couldn't remember the last time he'd seen a palm tree and knew he'd see plenty of them over the next two days. He could tell they weren't fake or planted for scenery. They were the land. He was pretty sure they laid the runways to avoid them.

Two more drinks later, he checked his watch again. It was the middle of the night back home, so no need to call. His wife and son would be asleep. His wife probably fell asleep with her book next to her, maybe sliding down from her chest as she rolled over starting a dream. He had no doubt their 12 year-old son fell asleep in his white Fulham FC jersey, which he wore to bed the night before every game. With only two points separating them from Sheffield United and relegation, every match was huge. As for his 17 year-old daughter, well he just hoped she was home. Danby closed his eyes and shook his head, as if trying to whip that thought out of his brain. He then took another long sip fathers tend to take to wash away thoughts of a teenage daughter.

He hadn't seen Nestor in three years. Business brought them together at first, now it was golf and memories. The Ryder Cup at Oakland Hills on TV and four days of golf at Club de Campo Villa in Madrid, Nestor's hometown club, was their escape from life's stresses then. This time it would be iconic golf on two opposite coasts and Ryder Cup lore. Their first stop would be Kiawah Island and the Ocean Course, the site of the famous 1991 Ryder Cup. There were no matches to watch this time, only old ones to relive. They weren't sure what they were more excited about, the actually golf on one of the most demanding courses in the world, or the stories and footsteps of those made that Fall?

On Monday they would fly to San Francisco and play three courses at Pebble Beach.

"How are we doing sir, another?" The bar's sociolinguistics expert pulled his attention back in from the sable palms, and to his drink.

Blimey. He shook his head, still afraid to speak, and reached down to unclasp his briefcase latches. He pulled out the Kiawah Island Ocean Course yardage guide and started flipping through the holes. Each page has a detailed picture of the hole, with yardages and distances to help. He knew the second time they played it, there would be money involved. Nestor played more than him, and he'd take every little advantage there is.

By the time he was figuring out if a 3 or 4 iron would be the club on the 17th, a slap on the shoulder startled him. Then a thick Castilian Spanish voice fell upon him and his cheat sheet.

"That shit ain't going to help you." Nestor Barros dropped his duffle bag by the table and smiled down at Danby. Danby was up and they hugged, slapping each other on the backs. Danby sat down and leaned over, slipping the course guide into his briefcase and pulling over the large flap. They discussed their flights for the next five minutes, until the waitress walked over. Danby bit his lip and couldn't look. He brought up his hand to his forehead.

"Good evening sir, may I get you something to drink?"

"A double of what he's having." He nodded across the table.

"Sure thing. Where are you from?" The last question oozed excitement.

"Madrid." He started shrugging off his jacket.

"I love your voice. Say something in Spanish."

"Eres caliente, ven siéntate en mi regazo." He winked at her.

She smiled and walked off.

Danby brought down his hand. He was almost afraid to ask. "What did you say?"

Nestor leaned on the table. "That she has a wholesome, wonderful smile that makes rain clouds disappear."

"Bull shit." They both laughed.

"What's the age limit over here?"

Danby shook his head.

"16?"

"We're good." Nestor leaned back and stretched. He worked hard and played hard. He was a womanizer, and liked his woman with his drink and fast cars. He was only divorced once, but that was only because he liked his women smart as well. They would eventually figure him out before it was too late. He lived life as if no mulligans.

He and his ex-wife had a son, Alex. He was 16 now and an excellent tennis and golfer himself. He played daily at the same club his father played his golf at.

"We're not eating here are we?" Nestor finally got his drink and was happy he did't have to say super cali fragilistic expialidocious.

"No, let's check in first. Plenty to choose from in town."

"Sounds good." Nestor tipped back his drink and eyed the waitress. He loved skirts.

They picked up their rental car, a two year-old Ford Escape, and headed for the Francis Marion Hotel. They showered, changed, and were down in the lobby 45 minutes later for drinks. The lobby was nearly enough. After just 10 minutes in the lobby, they were deliriously drunk on southern charm. Wall papered posts seemed to be supported by green, rich ferns. Floral print sofas and chairs beckoned those whose conversation required sitting, while soft tan and burgundy print Persian rugs seem to carry minglers to groups. Danby figured the hotel looked the same 50 years ago.

One of the guests decided to play the piano, and as his versions of *Für Elise* and *Claire de Lune* filled the vintage hotel's gathering space to zero complaints. Two rounds later, they walked to Oak Steakhouse on Broad Street. Without a reservation, they were seated downstairs, across from the bar. The two friends of 22 years didn't care where the table was, it's what was on the table and the conversation that swirled over it that mattered. It was mouthwatering.

"That was the best 4-iron I've ever seen you hit." Nestor raised his Macallan above the table. Danby smiled and tapped glasses. It was a clinking sound they couldn't wait to hear for the last five-hours. Or was it three years?

"Hey," he took a sip, "what can I say, I'm a closer. Besides I had to do something to answer your birdie at seventeen." They both sat back and took long, savory sips. "Wasn't that around the same place Seve made his that morning?"

Nestor didn't need to respond, just smile and nod slowly. He then picked up his cards and discarded. They had asked the bartender if by chance he had a deck of cards. A caddie in the bar with his group enjoying a drink knew where some were.

"Look over by the phone, Tom. That old Eastern deck was there last week," he had said.

The bar at the Ocean Course is smaller than you'd think. For a course at the scale it resides at, you might think it would be huge and fancy. Instead, its simple and plain. The classic places don't need to show off. It's a given.

The wrap around porch with tables and chairs is just outside the windows. The eighteenth green is off to the right. The putting green sits around to the left. And of course, the shimmering waves of the Atlantic is the wallpaper behind it all.

Four other players were in the bar area, two tables away against the wall. A green pin flag from the Ryder Cup framed on the wall above them. Nestor and Danby's table was against the windows next to the bar stools.

Their first drink brought out a front nine discussion, an Englishman's 38 and Spaniard's 37. The second drink wrapped up the round, two 40's. The next three drinks covered nothing to do with a shot made earlier. It was about the footsteps they took that morning, refreshing stories hidden in the sand from 16 years ago.

The first drink took them to the second hole. It was the place of Friday morning's Foursomes from '91. Where it all started. Especially as far as Nestor was concerned.

"So this is where Seve pull-hooked his drive right?" Nestor asked while being handed his driver.

"Yep, lost ball in that marsh over there, where you do not want to aim." The caddie leaned up against Nestor's shoulder and pointed to a tree far away. "That's your aiming point."

"Gotcha."

"Didn't he then try to drop farther up?" Danby asked and then everyone waited for Nestor to swing. He did and his ProV1 sailed off in a slight draw towards the distant tree.

"Yeah, Azinger nipped that in the bud right away, then never left his side, literally." Nestor's caddie took the driver with a nod, and started slipping on the head cover.

Danby's caddie added, "Azinger was never farther than 10 feet away from him hitting a shot from then on. Closest awkward proximity I've ever seen."

Danby and Nestor exchanged glances and smiles. They were loving this.

The caddies nodded and gave each other the customary smirk of approval on the third hole. It wasn't that their golfers weren't hacks, but they would be easy and take advice without questioning. They seemed more concerned with what happened 16 years ago than the present. They would enjoy the walk as much as the Englishman and Spaniard. They cringed at the asshole who wouldn't trust their lines and questioned their club selections.

On the fourth hole, Nestor's biggest concern wasn't how much his five footer would break, but where Seve made his 15 footer that halved the hole, so he could try to duplicate it. If anyone questions how hard the course was for that Ryder Cup, four of the best golfers in the world halved (tied) the hole with double bogey.

On the seventh, they discussed the American's mixing up the correct ball to hit. It was an odd number hole and the 'correct golf ball' sage spun to a start. The ninth saw another questionable ball drop from Seve. Azinger was furious. Seve was yelling. Nestor and Danny were almost giddy.

Back in the clubhouse, Danby was holding the nine of spades that he thought Nestor was waiting for. He needed two more tricks. That fourth drink arrived. It took them to the tenth tee. Sight of arguably the most famous and dubious incident in Ryder Cup lore.

They trudged up to the tenth tee, the highest point of the course, with a stunning view of the back nine stretching out in the distance. Swamp and plantation houses on the right. Furry sand dunes rising out of the ocean to the left. Nestor's green glory down the middle. Danby's caddie put the bag down and turned to them at the back of the tee.

"This is where they were all standing. This is where they argued."

"In all my years," Nestor's caddie reached the tee, walking up near Danby's caddie, "I've never seen so many people on a tee box before. Ever. It bordered on eerie." He plopped the bag down, clubs rattling around, and pointed behind them to various spots. "They argued so long, the foursome behind caught up. Couples and Floyd were over there, shocked. James and Longer were over there, all with their caddies mind you. Langer looked confused, not believing this was all happening. It lasted almost 15 minutes."

Danby, with honor after a par at nine, was wiggling his fingers into his glove like a surgeon.

"I really thought they were going to push and shove." Both caddies nodded in agreement. Danby was shaking his head. Nestor crossed his arms across his chest, like his idol 16 years earlier, and stood looking down at his feet.

"I remember Olazábal even getting into it and he never raises his voice." Nestor then looked around, as if looking at the ghosts of those that were huddled around the tee box from years ago, in jealously. "They hit the fairway didn't they?" Nestor reached into this pocket for his glove looking at the caddies.

Nestor's caddie gave an impressed nod.

"That's the incredible thing that most people don't know or think about" He gazed down the fairway, then back to the group. "After all that fuss and emotions boiling over, to almost getting physical, both Azinger and Seve controlled it all and split the fairway with irons." He shook his head, gazing back at the fairway, speaking to it.

"Can you imagine that? Most people hate to wait on slow players for even three or four minutes, then of course end up hitting awful shots." He found his small classroom again, between tee markers not whiteboards. "Those two were shaking and basically screaming for 15 minutes and still calmly nailed the fairway. In a Ryder Cup!"

The other caddie concluded the lecture.

"Unreal."

Danby found the left side of the fairway with his 3-metal. Nestor's caddie handed him his 3 metal. Nestor was staring down the fairway, and all nine holes for that matter, and shook his head. He then thought about Seve, on this very spot, telling José Maria to play as well as possible, that they were going to win somehow. Seve igniting José Maria with floods of galvanized inspiration. A feeling an entire continent would know.

"Give me my 2-iron please."

Six holes later, Nestor was on the par 5 fifteenth in three. Despite his ball being 15 feet above the pin, Nestor was headed for the sand on to the right of the green. With the Atlantic just over a wispy dune, Nestor dropped a ball in the huge bunker. Danby craned his neck to look what he was doing. Both caddies shrugged their shoulders.

From the green the first, and only thing they saw, was a tiny explosion of sand flying into the air, then a white ball arch up and down onto the front of the green. Then Nestor climbed up and slapped the underside of his shoes with his wedge. The ball wasn't near the hole.

"What hole were you aiming at?" Danby asked with a hand on his hip, leaning on his Scotty Cameron.

"The one Chema put it to within three feet of that morning." Nestor walked over, picked up the bunker shot, and looked at the ball. He wondered if he could have pulled that off under the pressure of that morning. 'Not a chance,' he thought.

Danby pinched the jack of clubs and slid it up half way, eyeing Nestor across from him. He was no mind reader though. He slid it back down and pulled the five of hearts to discard. Half out of excitement, half out of nervousness to see what Nestor would do. Nestor grimaced at the red five and drew. Danby blew out easily. Their conversations continued to cover the morning's walk, now the seventeenth hole, while their minds were on the cards in their hands.

They reached the par 3 seventeenth, which needed no introduction. A carry over an alligator infested pond that could feel like an ocean depending on the winds, to a thin green with bunkers behind. Piece of cake.

They both found the green with nice shots, but there was only a modest breeze of 10 knots. Then the caddies took them to the seventeenth and a half hole. The tees used for the Ryder Cup. The caddies plopped the bags down at the tees.

"Okay gentlemen. Play time is over."

Most legendary courses have that hole or shot from a tournament that everyone playing must try. As bland as it is to the caddies, they know to the men they're carry bags for, it is a once in a lifetime event. The caddies at Merion know this, thanks to Ben Hogan. The ones at Baltusrol can thank Jack

Nicklaus. Both 1-iron shots seem impossible to duplicate. The Kiawah caddies, like those at all those iconic courses, are good sports too.

The "Calcavecchia Tees" are no different. Unfortunately, it is not famous for a flush, pure strike from a blade iron. It is known for a topped tee shot, sending the ball skipping across the water like a shell or rock thrown by a child. All triggered from the vomiting, seizure-like induced pressure.

Just as Nestor bent down to tee up his ball, his caddie tried to put it in context.

"Oh, and imagine gusts of 30 mph."

"And you've just lost the last two holes and you're trying not to do the biggest choke in Ryder Cup history," the other added.

"Oh not to mention the hundreds of people around the pond watching."

"Or the millions watching you on television."

"Good luck."

This was the caddies' favorite part. Unlike the shot for their golfers, this never got old. Nestor stood up and waggled his club while grinning.

Nestor's splashed into the water like a depth charge. Danby's made it over, but was nearly sculled and came in sharp, skidding of the green into the back bunker. Plugged. A sand mine.

Danby pulled out his tee, "How the hell did they hit that green? Seriously."

"Did anyone birdie it Sunday?" Nestor was pulling on each finger of his glove.

Both caddies looked at each other. Danby's spoke up, "I'm not sure, I don't think so."

They walked around the pond. With each step closer, Nestor's pulse grew. He tried peering onto the green for his ball. As he got closer, his perspective improved. His putt was getting shorter and shorter. They got up to the green and Nestor walked over to his ball. He was 20 feet away. 20 feet from a birdie. Just like someone else 16 years ago.

He marked his ball and tossed it to his caddie walking by. They moved and stood on the edge of the green with the bunkers behind them. While Danby and his caddie talked about his long putt from the left side, Nestor's caddie cleaned his ball. Nestor grabbed his putter, pulling off the head cover.

"You need a read?" He asked.

"No." Nestor's eyes was undressing each blade of grass from the hole to his coin.

His caddie nodded and shot a glance over at him. He knew better to bring up that Seve had a similar putt.

"Just release that putter like you have all day. Get it to the hole, you got this." He handed Nestor the ball and walked away. He was good.

It's what made a caddie great. Nestor hadn't released the putter all day. His first two putts on the other side of the course and last two putts at fifteen and sixteen were his worst. But as far as the caddie was concerned, it never happened. Happy thoughts. Confident thoughts. The only thoughts.

Danby putted to within four feet. Nestor then positioned himself behind the hole and squatted down, seeing how his putt should fall in. Then he moved behind his coin, a gold 100 Spanish Peseta coin dated 1979, and exchanged it for the ball. He saw it left at first, then straight the last half.

He took a deep breath and stood over the ball. His putter wasn't a bronze Anser. He wasn't wearing all navy blue. His name wasn't on the Claret Jug three times. He didn't have 50 European wins. He wasn't a legend. But he had Castilian coursing through his veins. He lived passionately. And his putter's toe was pointing up.

He pulled the putter back with his light grip and swung it forward, tapping the ball. It felt solid, sounded deep, but came off fast. With each foot, his grip tightened. The ball curled for the first 15 feet, longer than he thought. 'No no, come on…' he thought. He misread it.

He stood up and leaned back slightly, trying to will the ball back up higher, like a healing sailboat. It was still curling unfortunately, but something or someone was helping.

His adrenaline and confident stroke rolled it a bit too hard. He would later call it his passion, channeled from his idol. The speed countered the break, and the ball rolled through it, staying high. With five feet left, it was either going to bang into the middle of the hole, or power lip-out into the pond, or ocean for that matter. With a foot left, his teeth dug into his lower lip holding his breath. He wanted this putt like it was his last meal.

He exhaled as the ball disappeared into the hole, slamming into the back of the lip... Then a grin spread on his face as he looked over at Danby, then at his caddie who held a fist in the air.

While walking back around the pond to the eighteenth tee, his caddie turned to Nestor with a curious grin. "So, mis-read or mis-hit?"

Nestor looked over.

"Si."

Their glasses were empty, the ice in pools at the bottom. Nestor beat Danby by a shot on the course, but got shellacked in the bar's game of gin. With the weekend's matches to relive, and Nestor changing up the card game, the two old friends ordered that fifth drink. They would enjoy it outside on the wrap around porch in wicker chairs.

Danby grabbed the drinks, two-fisted, and headed out of the bar and through the lobby. Nestor paid while gritting his teeth, and weaved his way over to the table to thank the caddie for finding the cards. They all looked up as he stood above them. He reached out his hand to the caddie.

"Thanks for finding those cards for us. What's your name?"

"Henry."

"Nestor," they shook hands. "I'll remember you Henry if we make it back here."

"Please do. Where are you from Nestor?"

"Madrid."

"So what'd you think?" Henry nodded out to the windows, out towards the 18th green that's bookended by sandy dunes and wooden lawn chairs.

"Wonderful."

One of the players Henry caddied for reached up an offering hand.

"Nestor, Jay Willets."

"Jay, nice to meet you."

Jay sat back and reached for his drink. "So what did your partner hit on 18? That was incredible from there."

"4-iron," Nestor smiled. "Was that you guys walking off the green."

"Yeah. Great shot."

"I'll make sure to tell him. I better get going. You all have a great day." They all nodded and waved each other off. He found Danby outside shuffling the cards. Despite the Atlantic being a sand wedge away, it was relatively quiet. Wooden lawn chairs were arched in a crescent moon shape facing the eighteenth green. A threesome was approaching the green as one of the caddies pulled the flag. Nestor pulled out his chair and turned to face the view.

"What do you want to lose in? Gin? Canasta? Noddy?"

Nestor sipped his drink and eyed the Englishman.

"You pick. I wish we could play Mus." He crossed his leg over his knee and watched the American flag hang limp off to their left.

"I wonder if we're going to be lucky with the wind tomorrow?"

Danby knew Nestor was a better wind player.

"Yeah, would be fun though if it was up there. It would make the stories even richer."

Nestor raised his glass in approval. Each card then evoked another memory from 1991. Not so much through the television, but also blended with their walk today.

On Monday, they flew to San Francisco. Bunched up clouds hung over the coast, appearing to be stuck on Point Reyes and not able to slide east. The city and bay was bright with sunshine. An hour drive down California HWY 1, banked by those clouds, they were in Monterey. Their Toyota Camry entered Pebble Beach through the north gate. They weaved their way through real life gingerbread houses tucked away under thick sheltering trees, to the Lodge. Their home for the next four nights.

They finished the late afternoon, with a cruise around the famous 17 Mile Drive. Even Nestor would agree, going less than 10 mph in a car is never more thrilling. The seals, pounding surf, and rocks buffering the Pacific lulled them into submission. They finished the evening in the Tap Room, which they would admit topped the bar at Kiawah. They started brainstorming all the names of those that possibly sat at the table they were at. They gave up at 15. And those were just actors, not even golfers or other celebrities. Nestor also got some revenge in gin, showing Danby a notepad of lopsided scores.

They played Pebble Beach the next morning, then Spanish Bay on Wednesday. They were surprised that Spanish Bay, not Pebble, was their favorite course. The bagpiper standing out from the clubhouse at sunset, Scottish kilt and all, was the cherry on top. They found a fire pit in need of some attention. Others would join, adding to the conversations. The wine flowed. The fire flickered and glowed. The drones of the bagpipe hummed the setting sun into submission. They decided if they had time, they would play it again. They were busy tomorrow, however.

Thanks to a business friend of Danby's, they had a 9:45 a.m. tee time at Cypress Point. If anything on the American trip could match last weekend's stroll around Kiawah with stories floating around like their cigar smoke, it was playing Cypress Point. Getting a chance to play on the most private of all private golf courses in the world is usually the hard part. It turns out, the tricky part was finding it.

"Where is it?" Nestor's head was twisting around while trying to stay on the road.

"Hell if I know," Danby was in the passenger seat holding the official 17 Mile Drive map. "It should be right back there." He shook he head, "How is this hard? There is one road and we're on it."

"I'm turning back." Nestor pulled into a private driveway and backed out. They headed back where they had come from. He leaned down looking out and up the windshield.

"Okay, it's got to be up here before that bend in the road." Danby held the map up closer like that would help. The car slowed and Nestor rolled down his window. With his elbow on the doorframe, he looked out at a road in a tunnel of trees. Danby leaned forward looking around him.

"That has to be it, but there's nothing there?"

The car stopped as Nestor saw a sign, hidden in the shadows. The sign was green making it harder to read. They looked at each other with a 'you gotta be kidding me' expression. With a spin of the wheel, Nestor pulled the rental to the left and up the driveway. 15 seconds later, they were at the most exclusive golf club in the universe. They had passed it twice.

There was no gate. No security guards. No video cameras. No fancy sign or guardhouse. Just a simple sign that read, *Cypress Point Club, Members Only,* the size of a No U-Turn sign. In the perfect world, all golf course entrances are like this.

They were still shaking their heads and smiling in the parking lot. Nestor was pulling out the golf bags from the trunk, while Danby sat on the bumper. He was tying his shoes and looked up. "You know, you can't even stand to look through the gates at Augusta without someone yelling at you to go away."

They met up with Mitch, the member which roughly translates into, 'one of the luckiest .1% of the people in the world', out in front of the two-story clubhouse. They shook hands and Danby introduced Mitch to Nestor.

"Mitch, do we have time to hit some balls?" Danby shrugged off his bag from over his shoulder.

"Well, you'll have to go to Pebble or Spyglass," he said with a smirk. "No driving range here."

Nestor and Danby looked at each other and nodded. It seemed fitting.

"You do get a breakfast ball though." Mitch mentioned while the caddies came over. After more introductions, they headed to the first tee. Nestor and Danby were shaking they were so excited. Another caddie brought out a tray with mimosas.

On the eleventh hole, Danby was looking around. Fairways were on either side and holes up ahead. *Where is everybody?*

"Are we the only people out here?" He said it as a joke.

"Yes." His caddie wasn't.

Nestor joined Danby in a confused look at the caddie.

"Rick, is Michael and his gang going out later?" They reached Danby's ball and his caddie propped up Danby's bag on its kickstands. He felt around for the 9-iron.

"Yeah, I think pretty soon actually." Rick stopped with Nestor to watch Danby's shot. 115 yards into a 15 mph ocean breeze.

Danby's caddie handed him the 9-iron. "Just two groups today. A busy day here is nine golfers."

Danby shook his head. The most famous golf course in the world and maybe 20 golfers play it on a weekend. It made sense now. Both he and Nestor noticed the lack of annoying divots in the fairways. Danby thought maybe the course was closed for the last week.

The first 14 holes were marvelous. Green rolling fairways in a strategic layout, blended with sand. And those trees. Those beautiful majestic cypress trees all leaning away from the ocean, as if frozen in the middle of a gale. Their trunks so wrinkly and tan, they look fake.

Holes 15-17 were another story.

One could argue they are not even golf holes or fairways, but bold cliffs of jagged rock, with whitewash constantly swirling around and between them like simmering stew. All there with the constant hum of the ocean and splashing spray. It was like playing golf on the edge of a rocky, forest world in a children's fantasy book. It was the type of view and setting that muted voices. There was nothing to say on those tee boxes, no description needed, no comment to try to spurt out. You just listened. You just stared shaking your head at the whole scene. Then realize, *oh wait I have to hit a golf ball.*

While they were walking to the eighteenth tee, Danby stopped and looked back at the 17th. He then looked up quickly at the puffy white brushstrokes on the light blue background, then the trees on the right, the ocean on the left, and finally Nestor walked up behind him.

"Not a bad view huh?" Nestor was just about to him.

Danby nodded, his eyes and ears still memorizing his surroundings. Nestor's own eyes squinted at his friend.

"You okay?"

Danby nodded, "yeah, I'll tell you later."

They finished and were in the bar enjoying their first scotch. Danby pulled out the Eastern cards and started shuffling. Mitch joined them and brought over some pretzels. "You know Jack Welch sat at this table two weeks ago?"

Nestor swallowed his sip and put his glass down. "Impressive."

Mitch nodded while taking his first sip. "Eastern? Wow, how long have you had those things?" He nodded to the cards meshing in Danby's enclosed hands.

"Well I hate to admit this, but we took them from the bar at Kiawah Island."

"That's funny. I flew them a few times back in the day." He leaned on the table looking at Nestor. "So Nestor, what club do you play at in Madrid?"

They drank their scotch and played cards while discussing business and golf for the next 45 minutes. Eventually Mitch needed to leave and tipped back his glass, finishing his third.

"Okay ladies, I've got to run unfortunately. You stay as long as you want, trust me." Mitch swiped up his glasses and phone from the table.

Danby looked over at him. "We still on for tomorrow?"

"Dinner, you bet." He stood and slapped Danby on the shoulder. "6:15 at L'Auberge Carmel. Nestor it was great meeting you. Nice score out there."

Nestor stood up and they shook hands. "Likewise, thanks so much for today. This was mind blowing."

"Yes it is. Yes it is." Mitch only got three steps away when someone came up to him and they shook hands. One hand came up, gripping Eric's shoulder.

"Where are you off to?"

"Ugh, gotta run. Did you play today?" Mitch wondered.

"Yeah, quite awful actually. Paul and David kicked my ass out there."

"Well tell you what," he turned and pointed at Nestor, "there's the man you need to talk to about that. And you can take my place."

"Gotcha." He pointed to the bartender and nodded, who immediately started filling a glass with ice. Michael Dell then sat down and they all introduced each other. Nestor and Danby gave each other a look like you would when hanging out with someone you saw on Bloomberg last week.

The bartender came over and placed the glass of ice in front of him, then poured a 25-year-old scotch into the glass half way. He left the bottle.

"Thanks Tom. So Danby, how do you know Mitch You at JMS Capital?"

"Yep. Nestor was too, up until last year."

Nestor raised his glass. "Who knew we'd make so much bread. Two revolutionaries."

He nodded and sat back, taking a deep breath. "What are we playing?"

"Five-card," said Danby.

"Excellent." He took a slow sip, swallowing seconds later.

"So Nestor, I'm blocking my irons."

Michael Dell lost money on the course, but was winning some in the bar. All three were good at reading the cards and reading faces. Michael won the last hand with four 10's. Danby and Nestor shook their heads.

"What movie did that happen in?" Danby looked around at them.

"*The Sting*." Michael answered.

Danby nodded, then quickly swallowed. "But wasn't it nines?"

Michael was about to take a drink, but paused thinking.

"Yes it was, you're right. Good call."

"Never saw that." Nestor admitted. Both Michael and Danby turned to him surprised.

"Really?" Danby narrowed his eyes.

Nestor shrugged his shoulders and took a sip. He continued shuffling. Just then, Michael's phone buzzed. He leaned over sliding it out of his pocket and looked at the screen. "Excuse me guys. I need to take this."

He brought up the phone to his ear.

"Hey Jerry." Nestor began dealing the cards and Michael nodded at him to continue. He brought up his shoulder to hold the phone in place and scooped up the five cards and fanned them out.

"What's her name……Erin Tanvary?" His eyes peeked up at Danby and Nestor, as if they may recognize the name and give him a sign, but they both stuck to their cards.

"Erin Tanvary. No, never heard of her…okay I'll take your word for it. I trust you…yeah sounds good." He clicked his phone dead and put it on the table.

"You guys ever heard of Erin Tanvary?"

Nestor and Danby shook their heads. "Nope, sorry." Danby said after swallowing another sip of scotch.

"Me either. I need a photographer and apparently, she is the next big thing. We'll see." He moved some cards around and tossed in his ante.

After the hand, Michael had to leave. They shook hands and said their good-byes before he headed out of the bar. While walking away, he pointed to the bottle on the table. "Enjoy boys. It's on me."

It was Nestor's turn to shuffle. "Nicest billionaire I've ever met." They both grinned and Danby's eyes scanned the bar. It was like Kiawah's in that it was simple yet classy, even bordering on plain. It matched the entrance.

They continued playing poker. Nestor was dealing Danby his cards across the table.

"So, what was going on back at seventeen? It's *later*."

Danby scooped up his cards nodding.

"I'm quitting golf." He organized his cards in suits. A five and eight of hearts, ace and queen of clubs, and six of spades. He shot a glance up at Nestor.

Nestor just stared at him, then moved some of his cards around.

"And what brought this on? Two." He put down two cards and Danby slid him two new ones.

Danby thumbed the ace and queen, then pulled them out and put them on top of Nestor's two discards.

"I'll take two as well." He slid off two new cards from the pile. "That was my last round of golf out there. Those holes, the views, that ocean. Us. That's it."

"Just like that?" Nestor pushed his cards together in his hands and laid them on the table in one tiny stack. He reached for his scotch. Poker would have to wait.

Danby sat back in his chair.

"It hit me out there, walking away from the 17th. That's how I want to remember it. My last round." He looked down at his cards, fanning them out again in his fingers, afraid to look up at Nestor. His two new cards were two aces, the ace of hearts and diamonds. *Of course I get two aces!* He pushed his cards together and put them in his lap. He reached for his drink and finally stole a glance at Nestor.

"So if we didn't play this course today, you're still playing golf?"

"I guess so. It was a moment of clarity out there." He shrugged, "I just want that to be it."

"You didn't know this morning?"

Danby shook his head.

"You're not going to sleep on it?"

Another head shake.

"Well it would have been nice to know before playing, knowing your putt on 18 was it."

Nestor held his drink and rested it on his knee. He was studying Danby and could tell in his eyes, he was serious. They were also close enough that he wasn't going to challenge him.

"So you're the star athlete who decides to retire after winning the European Cup and not drag out a career with teams he shouldn't play with?"

Danby bit his lip and nodded, approving of the association. "I am George Best. Kevin Keegan."

"Well shit," Nestor sighed and looked off towards the bar for a second, "so much for Spanish Bay tomorrow?" He then raised his eyebrows at

Danby. Nestor tipped back his drink gulping down more than usual. *So much for, well, a lot of things.*

"I need a drink, how 'bout you." He leaned forward and grabbed the scotch bottle. Danby pushed his glass out to the middle of the round table. Nestor angled the bottle down over Danby's glass, but then stopped. It was now pointing up to the ceiling.

"No." He sat back, holding the bottle.

Danby smiled. "What do you mean no?"

"I mean no. No, you have to play tomorrow."

"Nestor, don't-"

"Tomorrow can be it, then quit." He cocked his head to the left. "Look I get it, well sort of I mean, it was stunning today, and I could see where you want that to be the grand finale. But you have to play with me one more time. We, I, have to play knowing this is it for you. You owe me that walk up 18."

Danby took a breath and licked his lips. He didn't want to, but felt like he owed his longtime friend that. If the roles were reversed, he'd ask the same. Nestor could see the struggle and indecision in Danby's face.

"If it helps, I won't tell anyone we played again. It will be our secret. Only your clubs will know." He leaned forward, the 35-year-old scotch poised over the thirsty glass.

"Fine." Danby picked up his cards, fanning them out.

Nestor poured. "We're getting drunk."

Danby took his glass and tapped Nestor's.

"This is bloody good stuff."

"Don't tell me," Nestor took a sip. "This is your last scotch ever."

Danby laughed. "Hell no."

"Good." Nestor put his drink down and laid his cards out. "Three kings."

"Two aces," came in a dejected voice.

Nestor smiled. "That's what you get for quitting." He started scooping the cards into a pile to shuffle. "Quitting after tomorrow, that is."

CHAPTER SEVEN

Although the Boeing 777 can fly up to 43,000 feet, it tends to cruise between 31,000 and 40,000 feet. Most of the 414 passengers on United Airlines flight 3285 from Chicago to Madrid, wished it could have been 80,000 feet.

Tropical Storm Noel, the 14th named storm of 2007, spun over Haiti and the Dominican Republic. Then curled its way north out of the Caribbean. A storm known for its rain rather than wind, it left the two nations as giant mudslides. A day later, it was a hurricane as it raced up the Atlantic, mirroring the US coast. By the time it reached the coast of Labrador, it wasn't a hurricane, but an extratropical cyclone. That is a fancy meteorological term for a giant mess.

As customary with ex-hurricanes headed up to Greenland and possibly the UK, it picked up speed with the Gulf Stream tugging it. On its way past Newfoundland, a weak northeaster merged into it like a tail, hooking on. There wasn't blue sky from Cape Cod to Reykjavik.

If only the flight path was on a flat map, rather than a sphere, they would have stayed south of it. The pilot tried going above it, but this wasn't just a common storm ceiling out at 21,000. This seemed to skim the heavens.

The cruel part was after dealing with the lines like cattle, winding its way to be slaughtered, stripping off clothes, unpacking half their carry-ons, that now cost $50, and then redoing it all over again like it was 30 minutes ago, the passengers were rewarded with a stressful flight.

Nestor slept for the entire flight from San Francisco to Chicago. There would be no sleeping on this flight. At 6:15, an hour after takeoff, it was bumpy and full of rolls. At least he would be comfortable in first class. Nestor shook his head at the irony. He was supposed to be home yesterday. But since he wasn't in a hurry to get home with any pressing engagements, he gave up his seat after overbooking, to be bumped to a later flight with an upgrade. The next day was treated with a first class seat, 9F.

A fourth of the first class was empty. Each seat was in a shell about waist high. When reclined back into a flat bed, your seat was down in it like your own private cocoon. Nestor was in the middle of the plane, with a bed seat next to him and one across the aisle against the windows. He was nursing champagne and replaying this last week in his head.

The Boeing bounced, so did his thoughts. Danby, Seve, José Maria, Cypress Point, Oak Steakhouse, Kiawah, Michael Dell, a son……and the rattling. The rattling and noise was the worst part about turbulence. Even up front in this comfort, stuff shifts, slides, bangs around, and rattles like the plane is breaking apart. The little sounds were unnerving. No matter what he was thinking of, it was there. Especially to the passenger over in 9A.

Nestor, of course, noticed her the second she came on board. She was wearing a tan women's suit over a white blouse. Her hair came down in waves, cresting on her shoulders. She was tapping her laptop for the first 30 minutes, but typed in bunches. The bouncing and shuttering paused her in mid sentences. After one rather obnoxious bounce, she slammed the laptop closed as if trying to shut it away, like slamming the basement doors as a tornado rips through a cornfield outside.

Her left hand gripped the arm of the seat as she closed her eyes, as the blankness of her eyelids became a movie screen. She was looking at that shirtless Ralph Lauren model on the bow of the sailboat, the dark hard guy for D&G in underwear on the black sand beach, that ocean cabana in the Bora Bora ad, her bathtub at home, her mom and dad, and other random images and magazine ads she flipped through while waiting at the gate to board. Anything other than a plane, clouds, or kite flying.

She opened her eyes and licked her lips, then suddenly glanced over at Nestor across from her. She let go of the armrest and started rubbing her hands together while tossing some hair away. Then she crossed her legs as if sitting in a cafe back in Lisbon, or any level, still table in a calm quiet street in Europe. Another stomach twisting bounce brought her back to 41,000 feet and kite flying.

"Isn't flying great." Nestor tried some sarcasm.

"I'm fine," the woman lied as she shifted in her seat, crossing her other leg.

Nestor smiled at it. "Get away from the window, it just makes it worse. Come over here." Nestor unbuckled and moved to the vacant seat next to him. He was buckling up when he looked over and patted his old seat, still warm. "Come on, we'll keep each other company."

She didn't move, just gripped the left arm rest again, so this stranger couldn't see it. She put her head back into the seat and turned to him.

"We got six and a half more hours to go." Nestor buzzed for the flight attendant.

Her travel defenses gave in, allowing a smile to surface. She unclasped her buckle letting it fall to her side, like those defenses, and smiled as she moved over next to Nestor, using hands to brace herself. She could use a gentleman right now.

"Nestor Barros." He held out his hand.

"Daniela Brandao." She twisted to reach over her left hand. He took it and brought it up for a kiss.

"My my, so old fashioned." She smiled. "Men and women kiss on the cheeks now." She eyed him in victory.

"Yes, well I figured that hand was sore from gripping the arm rest so I thought I'd kiss it and make it better." He returned the smile and took back the lead again. They both laughed as their gamesmanship was put to rest and relaxed.

"Daniela, where are you from?"

"Lisbon, originally from Coimbra. Was in Chicago on business and now I'm needed in Madrid. And you?"

The flight attendant arrived and Nestor asked for another glass. "Home to Madrid." She came back with a flute glass and Nestor picked up the champagne bottle and started to pour. He then paused, waited for some bumps to pass, and quickly poured Daniela a drink while he could. The plane was never still and Nestor was surprised the flight attendants were still walking around.

"Thank you Nestor." She sipped hers.

"Where are you staying?"

"The Principal Madrid."

Nestor nodded in approval. “Excellent place. What took you to Chicago and onto my hometown?”

Nestor sipped his own, which was almost empty. They chatted and talked about their lives for the next ten minutes, while swaying, and at times, vibrating. Daniela found Nestor beyond charming and noticed her foot was not tapping furiously in the air and her hands were a little more relaxed. The haunted house was still there around the corner, but for now she didn’t have to walk past it yet.

The captain’s voice filled the cabin and skeptical minds soon after, telling everyone to make sure they were buckled up and for the flight crew to take their seats. Nestor bit his lip. That’s never a good sign. He could tell she picked up on it. Her eyes were as turbulent as the fuselage. At one bounce and drop, her arm shot over and grabbed his forearm, squeezing until the jolting subsided. She wasn’t even embarrassed anymore.

Nestor reached down into his bag and pulled out the Eastern cards. “Come on, let’s play cards. What do you like to play?”

She looked at him like he was causing the turbulence. “You want to play cards right now?”

Nestor nodded. “Let’s get your mind off this flight.” He eyed her. “Mine too. Trust me.”

Daniela smiled hesitantly and nodded. Right now, he could have told her there were propellers on the wings and she would have believed in him. He started shuffling.

“I had an uncle that played Briscola, I kind of remember.” She looked down at the cards arching into each other in a blur.

Nestor cut the deck. “Love your uncle.” He then passed out the cards and put the pile down on the table between them.

“Let’s play an open hand and see how it works.”

Within 10 minutes, she was staying right with him and no push over. The game was helping with the nerves as well. Imagining shirtless models or picturing the coastline of Madeira is one thing, but actively thinking and using strategy with numbers and chance is another. She still looked around during rough bounces and sways, as if listening for cracks, but was doing much better.

The talking helped too, which the cards brought out. Nestor noticed the body at first, but was now picking out a bright mind and spirit from her stories and thoughts. There was only an eight year age gap. It was a blending of the generation, not crossing them.

Daniela curled up her legs on the seat and leaned into the leather. Nestor was rearranging his cards, and she was studying his face. His eyes were dark and his jaw was rigid. She got the sense he was the type of guy that was cute when younger, but got better with age. Nestor looked up catching her eyes floating over his face and smiled. She looked down at her cards and then the pile. She picked up the four of diamonds and licked her lips, thinking she can use it.

Just then, the plane rose up quickly, shoving everyone down in their seats like a rocket had taken off vertically. Everyone gripped their seats or something close. Gasps squeaked out everywhere. Curiosity mixed with the wide scared eyes. Daniela shut hers, as if bracing to be punched. After five-seconds the plane became a yo-yo, and as high as it rose unexpectedly, it plummeted even farther.

Beverages became colorful fountains. Reclined seats vibrated as if a quarter had been deposited. Eyelids shut, jaws tensed. The cards joined snacks, magazines, pens, iPods, and books, and became popcorn. Daniela was yanked back down into the seat by the seatbelt. Her yelp was muffled by clenched teeth. Everything shook uncontrollably. Nestor reached for the seat in front of him to brace himself, thinking he was in coach like normal, but it wasn't there. It was a curse of first class, leg room.

Daniela was seasick, her head pushed back into her seat, gripping the arm rest and Nestor's arm like the deck chairs of an ocean liner in 50 foot swells going 450 knots. Nestor saw his son behind his closed eyes. One shake was him holding his Real Madrid soccer ball signed by Raul when he was little. Another drop of the plane produced another of him holding his tennis racket on the red clay of Roland Garros with his mother.

The good news was the noise of the plane wasn't as horrible, as the screams and noise of the terrified filled the cabin. Those not screaming out loud were screaming prayers in their heads. It wasn't bumpy anymore, just violently down in a dive. Nestor reached over and grabbed Daniela, their fingers like claws on each other's sleeves. After 15 seconds, the plane began pulling up. Daniela slowly peeked out her eyelids as if not wanting to. Nestor was stroking her hair away from her face.

"Daniela. Daniela, you okay? It's over."

She put her hand to her chest trying to keep it still, or at least down a little, and looked over at him. She nodded, still in shock. Everyone began gathering their items and trying to find everything else. The plane still shook and vibrated, but after the sudden Disney ride, no one seemed to mind. First aid was administered to two people with bumps and bruises, even a trickle of blood down one temple.

Voices and conversations were bounced around the cabin. So many from so many seats, even an operator from the 60's couldn't keep up, connect them all and push in those plugs in all those holes.

Within five minutes, the cabin returned to normal as if nothing happened. All that remained was answered prayers and new goals to follow through on. Nestor gathered the cards, shoved them in the box and slid them into the seat pocket. Food arrived, but few were hungry. Daniela and Nestor ordered more champagne. They, like all the other 412 passengers on the plane, talked to each other and acted differently. They all had something in common now, a badge on their sleeve. They had flight 3285. Their own haunted house in the sky.

Within two hours Noel was back to being just a Christmas term and the flight was as smooth as wrapping paper. With nothing but cirrus clouds between the plane and Gibraltar, it was how a flight should be.

Within two years, Nestor and Daniela were married. Danby was forced out of retirement to play one more round of golf with Nestor and his 19-year-old son. The day before Nestor walked down the aisle, they walked the fairways of Valderrama, the site of the 1997 Ryder Cup. The European team captain was Severiano Ballesteros.

Radley Smith was afraid to unbuckle and he had the most secure seatbelt on the plane. It came over his shoulders and clicked into the seat between his legs. After 21 years in the cockpit and the last 10 in the pilot's seat, he had never experienced that much turbulence. No simulator could prepare him. No stories of wisdom passed down from veterans was enough. The wings on his shirt didn't make him an angel. He was flesh and blood, getting scared like anyone. No not scared, petrified.

He also had the best view on the plane. There were a couple flights he will always remember. His first flight, in a 737 as a rookie co-pilot.

His first ocean view in a 767 crossing the Atlantic. And that first sunset, followed by full moon, from the pilot's seat of the 757 from Seattle to LA. This current view would join those.

Looking out now, over the nose of the triple seven, that view was the giant windows of terminal 4 in Madrid's airport. Not the view most people think of, but six hours ago, he questioned if they would ever see the gate, let alone something on the ground.

He finally reached down and pushed the release button with a 'click'. Then slid each harness up and over his shoulders. Radley took a deep breath, blowing out his chest without any restraints, then looked out his side window to the tarmac.

"Post flight checklist complete Captain."

The pilot brought his head back inside the cockpit to the instrument panel between them. Under the flaps levers, he flipped down three switches and then looked up to the ceiling. He located two more and pushed them. Radley then glanced down at the co-pilot's hand, scribbling down log information in his lap. It was still shaking.

Chris Pariso was young. Younger than Radley when he was a co-pilot on a plane this size, and sometimes needed to be reminded of that. He was good and trustworthy though, that's what Radley cared about. They had only flown together for a month.

Radley glanced at his watch; they had two hours before leaving for Genéva. He liked Genéva, and looked forward to two days of relaxing before heading back to the States. After this last flight, he deserved a treat too. It would be a special one he only splurged on once a year or two.

"Weather looks better sir, a lot better. We may have a satellite lens even." That's what they called clear skies where even from more than 30,000 feet, it looked like zoomed-in satellite images.

"Good." Radley picked up his phone and a small notebook from the floor to his left. It was his bible; 21 years' worth of notes and information from his travels. Which hotels he liked, and rooms and floors to steer clear of. Notes on bars and resturants in every city. Airport info. Terminals with the best shops for clothing when pressed for time. Who to call for tickets when in certain American cities. There were even drawings and sketches.

Some of it was in pencil, some in blue ink, and some in black, whatever pen was handy. He tended to write in cursive when driving in a taxi or even flying on autopilot. The flowing writing was easier when moving. The print told him he was at a restaurant, hotel lobby, or airport lounge. What he would refer to soon was in print, written in the American Airlines Admiral Club at Paris' Charles de Gaulle some years before.

Thirty minutes later, he was sitting in La Mary's with his co-pilot. Although it's written in his notebook, about 2/3 of the way into it as he finally earned European routes, he didn't need to look it up. He knew where the restaurant was. Radley always ate here.

For the first time in his life, he was having a drink between flights. He sipped his red wine without a care. After getting flight 3285 on the ground, he would have ordered the bottle if not for the Genéva trip.

They sat at round cafe tables, spaced out along a railing. Busy travelers and families funneling by on one side, windows to the restaurant on the other.

"My turn Radley," Chris leaned over to pull out his wallet. He placed his card on the tray and finished his San Pellegrino.

"Thanks Chris. I'll see you back on board in ten minutes. Need to take care of something." He got up, slapped Chris on the shoulder, and weaved through the tables to the exit. He found a chair in the nearest gate, an Iberia flight to Berlin, and pulled out the notebook.

What Radley did look up, was 11 pages after La Mary's entry. It was just a bunch of confusing, random numbers and letters to anybody else. The 8 in front was just his lucky number growing up. The phone number started after it, beginning with two 3's. The calling code for France. Then the nine-digit phone number. Right after the phone number was a code of five numbers and two letters. There were no spaces, no dashes, no nothing. Just 17 numbers and two letters on a blank page.

He dialed the number with the open notebook resting in his lap. It was April, an even number month. That meant he let it beep twice before ending the call and hanging up. In a week, he would let it beep three times before hanging up. His eyes scanned around the gate out of habit, as if everyone could read his mind, and waited a few seconds. Then he dialed it again, this time not ending the call. A female voice came on the line. He always wished to see the face that matched the voice. He knew he never would.

"Good afternoon. May I have your code please?"

Radley bent his head down and whispered, half to read the code and half to be discreet.

"Thank you sir, please hold."

Radley closed his notebook and crossed his leg. He looked up and found his voice shaky for some childish reason. His nerves pumped his heart faster. 15 seconds later, she was back.

"Yes, welcome back sir. It has been almost a year I see. What city will you be in and when is your desired arrival time?"

"Genéva, this evening. I know it's short notice."

"Not a problem sir, although it may limit some personal preferences."

Radley noticed Chris walking past, presumably back to the plane. "Yes, of course. I understand." He brought up his arm and twisted his wrist, checking the time.

"Will we be using your usual profile this evening?"

"Yes."

"Excellent. And do you have a preference?"

He bit his lip and looked around the gate quickly, as if seeing a hair color would trigger a name.

"Maybe a usual, if possible. And for tomorrow as well."

"Of course sir, we'll see what we can do. Where will you be staying?"

"Hôtel de la Paix."

There was a pause. "Okay sir, someone will contact you before seven o'clock this evening."

"Thank you." He ended the call and let his head fall back, then rolled it around half way. His heart was still swelling as he left the gate for his plane. There was a lightness in his steps despite the pounding heart. He was already thinking about what champagne to have brought up.

Radley stepped on board and smiled at Lisa pouring coffee in the galley. Her brown eyes flashed up quickly.

"Can't get enough of us can you?"

"Nope." He took off his hat and put it under his arm at his side. "Lisa may I-"

"Have a cup of coffee? Why of course captain." She grinned at him and looked back down at the cup, now almost full.

Radley just smiled to himself. "Best mind reader I've ever known." He walked up to the front of the plane towards the cockpit. Lisa leaned to her left watching him go. Another flight attendant walked by shaking her head.

"Now now Lisa. No dating pilots." She waved her finger at Lisa like a teacher at a cheating child. She grinned and raised an eyebrow at Lisa as she started putting ice in a bucket.

Lisa, 26 with short black hair just below her ears, gave her own smile and tilted her head back and forth like a clock pendulum. "Yeah yeah." She put the coffee pot down and headed to the cockpit. The other woman laughed and finished with the ice.

Lisa came in with a knock. Radley was storing some things and glancing through a three ring binder by the door.

"Here you go Radley." Lisa smiled at him wondering if he knew she wanted to be that flight attendant in every boy's fantasy.

"Thanks Lisa. This flight should be much better than the last."

Lisa left Radley alone in the cockpit. He bit his lip and looked back at the closed door, knowing what was walking away. A child. Radley knew it wouldn't be a child walking in and out of tonight's door.

He moved around into his seat and looked at the terminal windows just to his left, reflecting the late afternoon sun like a mirror. The glare was like standing on the top of a lighthouse. He blinked and looked away, still seeing it in his eyes. He was looking down at the instrument panel between his seat and the co-pilot's. Rings of dazzling light began to fade. He continued blinking, focusing better on details. He squinted at the panel as he saw a small blue box with Eastern written across it. It appeared like a mirage through his eyes. A memory. Radley shook his head as the lighthouse's beam finally swept around. The glare was gone. The box wasn't. He reached for the box and picked it up. He was surprised it was a deck of cards. "What the hell?"

He sat back in his seat and looked down at the box in his hand. He turned it over, the back was the same as the front. He immediately got goosebumps, like seeing an ad for a favorite childhood movie he hasn't seen in too long.

"Didn't you use to fly them?"

Radley nearly jumped out of his seat, as Chris had slipped in behind him unknowing. Chris bent down getting into his seat and looked over at Radley. He then realized he hadn't heard him come in.

"Oh man I'm sorry, I thought you heard me." He was laughing and looking over at Radley. He softly slapped his shoulder.

"It's okay." Radley looked back down at the cards. "Where did this come from?"

"Cleaning crew. They found them in a seat pocket back in first class. They thought you'd like them." Chris looked down at the box, then up to his captain. "I guess they think you're old."

Radley narrowed his eyes at him, the look saying enough.

Chris chuckled, then looked back at the box. "So? Did you?"

Radley shook his head.

"No." He then opened the box and pulled out half the deck, flipping through what was sticking out. "I once co-piloted for a guy who did though, when I first started with United. Damn legend. Wyatt…" he pushed the cards back into the box.

"God what was his last name…" he closed the box, "Cavanaugh. Wyatt Cavanaugh." He matched eyes with Chris. "If he was on that last flight, he would have turned the plane around and flown back through that turbulence just to do it better."

He looked down at the closed box and ran his thumb over *Eastern*. "He started out with Eastern and then in the early 80's moved to United. I was only in the cockpit with him a few times though." He ended the story before getting to the bad part. He licked his lips and let it rest. Like Wyatt.

"I think I will take these actually." He put them in his jacket pocket.

Chris nodded and made a note to remember that name. He then shot a quick glance at Radley before his checklist. He looked forward to giving a similar speech to his co-pilot someday. He then peered over his left shoulder to the closed door and back to Radley.

"So, the one with short hair and solid rack that brought your coffee, what's her name?"

"Hello."

"Is this Mr. Lindbergh?"

Radley picked up his head from the ice bucket.

"Yes."

"Good evening. This is Elena."

He closed his eyes trying to picture the name. He envisioned a blond from two years ago.

"Ah Elena, wonderful to hear your voice again. It's been a while." He reopened his eyes and continued spinning the champagne bottle in the ice bucket.

"Yes, it's been too long," came her response. It was only half a lie. It wasn't a complete lie because Elena was half excited. Radley wasn't a freak or into crazy stuff. She made $7,000 an evening, and has done everything there is. Tonight, there would be no role playing, nothing gross, nothing dangerous. Another woman would not be involved.

"Are we meeting upstairs?"

"Well I thought we'd have a drink first, in the bar." The hotel dining room downstairs was one of his favorites in all of Europe. One felt like royalty in it.

"I have some champagne chilling right now. Let's have a cocktail downstairs."

"That sounds lovely. I can be there in 45 minutes."

"Wonderful. I'll see you then Elena."

Radley ended the call and put the phone down on the table. He slid the bucket to the middle of the table and moved the flutes in front of it. He showered and put on jeans, a white button down, and his navy wool blazer. He turned off all the lights in the room except for the bathroom light. With the bathroom door opened, it spilled out into the room's carpet, a long gold rhombus dimming the room perfectly.

He sat by his window looking out on Genéva. A bright, vivid city that even sprays its richness 400 feet into the air. Its special mist kissing all those strolling along the lake's railing on the south bank.

His life was in the sky. His family every co-pilot, flight crew, ground crew, and tower controller on every flight. And his loves were women in various cities. He didn't want to get married, because he had three wives. Amy was in Denver, Sophie in Washington DC, and the Madame on the other end of that phone call that finds him one in Europe and Dubai.

That passion that was flying a jet, shocked him earlier in the day. He was never that scared before behind the yoke. He wondered how Wyatt would have felt. He was a legend, and there weren't many pilots like him, but of course he had exaggerated to Chris earlier. He hadn't thought of him in years, and did of all days, today.

He was staring out at Lake Genéva through the window, with the lake and his room's reflection blending together. Radley narrowed his eyes and focused on the table by the door. He turned to look at it, and the playing cards on it. It was as if Wyatt was reaching out to him, reminding him what it takes to be a pilot. With every flip of a card earlier, it was another lesson, point, or counseling coming from the captain of all airline captains.

Radley pulled back his sleeve and checked his watch, another piece of advice from Wyatt to purchase. It was 7:10. Elena would be downstairs in 20 minutes. They were never late. He would enjoy her more than usual tonight, even if she never exactly knew why.

The dining room was busy. There was a murmur, more than a whisper but less than normal conversations. The walls and ceiling were crimson red, with red velvet chairs. In places where red didn't reach your eye, wood was between. Radley nodded and smiled at the table he was shown to, along the left side wall. He faced the entrance, redness looming over him on the right, and ordered two dry martinis. At 7:29, a 5'10" brown haired vision stood at the entrance in a black Versace sleeveless dress. It was like seeing northern lights for the first time.

Radley didn't blink for a few seconds. He barely breathed. He remembered her from three years ago, on a trip in Marseille. Radley's eyes slid up and down her body as she strolled across the hard wood floor towards him. The tapping of her heels grew with each step. He stood as she approached.

"Elena."

"Hello Charles." No one said he didn't have a sense of humor. Even Elena smiled inside. After all, she went by Elena for an ironic reason as well. They kissed on each cheek, his hand touching her side.

"You look wonderful."

He pushed in her chair as she placed her small black purse on the table. He came around to his seat and scooted up. Their glasses pinged over the candle and both sipped the icy cold gin and vermouth. She was elegant and breathtaking, but not in a flashy exotic way. She wasn't fake thanks to surgery, just naturally stunning. That was given to her. Her talents were learned.

They talked for 20 minutes nursing their martinis. Both leaned on the table with their elbows, breaking all etiquette rules, and talked. Even knowing he was going to be within 5 feet of her for the next 36 hours, he still desired to be as close to her as possible. She smelled like flowers. There was no rush, no deadline. Just a timeless bliss of endless possibilities.

He charged the bill to his room as she plucked out the olive from her empty martini glass. They walked out and through the marble lobby to the elevators, arms interlocked at the elbows. They strolled into room 812. She placed her purse down on a table next to the door. She had never been in a room at the hotel before, just met clients in the lobby once and bar twice. She gazed around and noticed the champagne bottle by the window and a table with playing cards scattered about by the far wall.

She kicked up a leg to remove a heel when Radley turned and looked at her over his shoulder.

"Leave those on."

He foot stopped in midair and slowly lowered. She smiled and walked to the table with the cards.

"Aye aye captain." She put the olive down on the table as the bottle popped to life across the room. He did a double take at the olive.

"Hungry?"

"No," she looked at him sliding some hair off her cheek. "But you may want it later. I'm sure I can think of someplace to put it."

"Well how about we cleanse our palates with this." He handed her a champagne flute and they sipped. He then turned on a lamp in the corner. She eyed him over the rim thinking of a way to get started. She placed the glass down next to the cards and picked up a couple.

"Card player?"

He leaned against the bedpost sipping his Dom Pérignon, staring at her in the dim light. He was thinking the only thing better than drinking this is licking it off her. He may have plenty of time with her, but with her body in that dress and knowing the things she could do with it, she began tugging at his nerves. Her soft face downstairs by the candle had put him into a trance. The body in the dim room was a steroid pumping him.

She made a quick pile and spread them out like a fan. She walked over to him holding them out.

"Pick a card."

"Hmm, what are we playing?"

"Chance."

Radley never looked down at the cards, just stared at her face. He reached out feeling a couple and eventually pulled out a card. He held it with *Eastern* facing the chandelier above them.

"Can I look?"

"Sure."

Radley took a swallow still staring at her. He then twisted his wrist and looked down at the six of spades. He peered up to Elena, who was taking her final sip for now. She walked over to the table and placed the remaining cards and drink down. She unclasped her Rolex and diamond bracelet, then put them in her purse. She turned to him, leaning back on the table.

"So what is it?"

"You're not a mind reader?" Radley held up the card shaking it, *Eastern* now a blur.

She shook her head. "That's one thing I can't do." She stood up straight and headed for the bed, grabbing a pillow.

"One thing I can do, is make you very noisy." She came around the bed running her fingers down the opposite bed post and locked eyes with him. She strutted to the window and dropped the pillow on the floor, then turned around.

"I'm going to get you off that many times," she nodded at the card, "before taking off these heels you like so much."

Radley tilted back and finished his champagne in three-seconds. His pounding heart almost didn't let it flow past into his stomach. He turned the card around. The 6 showing.

Elena raised an eyebrow. "Well I better get busy." She walked over and grabbed both his hands and brought him to the window.

"Which view are you going to look at?" She kneeled in front of him, the pillow her cushion, with the window inches behind her.

Radley peeked out the window at the view he looked at earlier. That only last about five-seconds though.

The dress finally slinked off her body half way to the goal. Instead of a wrinkled pile next to the bed or wing-back chair, it was hanging in the closet neatly. She would have to wear it tomorrow as they shopped for tomorrow night's dress. Something Radley enjoyed doing with his Europe wife.

By three in the morning, the heels were placed in front of the closet and both fell asleep in the king size bed. The curtains were half open, allowing some light of the city to cast into the room, adding a light glow to the ceiling. Radley always loved watching a beautiful woman sleep next to him, or on him, in moonlight-like conditions.

They enjoyed the city the next day, shopped, and had pizza for lunch. In the afternoon, they went to the airport and he gave her a tour of the behind the scenes at United. They were able to get into a hanger and he showed her the cockpit of one plane, a Boeing 747-400. Elena mentioned to him that other than a private jet, she had never had sex on a plane before. Radley was more than happy to help out with that checklist item, even if it wasn't at 30,000 feet. That night they dined at Domaine de Châteauvieux, before returning to the hotel for drinks and more play.

He woke up to Elena curled up next to him, her skin paired with the Egyptian 1800 thread count sheets was numbing. They showered and left the hotel together as husband and wife, from his stand point. She left for home, some place within a couple hours by train, and he taxied to the airport.

Radley flew out of Genéva for Washington DC. He was over the Bay of Biscay going 475 mph when he shut his eyes in a grimace, and realized he forgot the Eastern cards in the hotel room. The two days with his Elena were so marvelous, even memories of Wyatt and his past got lost in her flowing hair, curves, and lips.

Radley opened his eyes shaking his head. He at least had the comfort of knowing he had a great reason to forget them. They also helped make the first evening something he will never forget for the rest of his life. The Italian couple next door won't forget it either, hearing him like Elena promised.

He would have remembered to take the cards if he had seen them. The problem was Elena's eyes fell on them first. While slipping on her bracelets, she grabbed the cards and held them. She grinned. For some odd reason, she wanted them. The box of cards was her new passport. It wasn't so much how she used them unexpectedly, but the name that made her narrow her eyes.

Eastern.

All the clients, all her tricks, all the sins, all the things she had to do, was to travel that way someday. The place was Waiheke Island in New Zealand. A quiet, innocent place untouched by her clients and trips. It wouldn't know what she'd done, where she'd been, or who she served. The only bed she would know is the bed of sand at low tide. The most important bank would be the walkable edges of the Pelorus River near Marlborough. The peaks of Milford Sound would be her towering hotels and skyscrapers. There were no more threesomes, just the foursomes of the Four Sisters Waterfall.

It would be a new destination for a new life. It was where her life was aiming. It was the course she entered on her plane. The pilot was a gentlemen, and treated her like a princess. She was and gift, wrapped in lingerie not wrapping paper. It was a lovely day in a lovely city, buying nice clothing and eating scrumptious food. And full of fantasies in bed, the shower, a chair, and a 747 jumbo jet. And every time she had to do something, she heard a cash register ding, as her account and the Madame's grew and grew. She put up with some of the crazy stuff, things some only hear about in movies or stories. She was in her own movie with her own script on each evening with someone.

As Charles Lindbergh lightly touched her lower back, ready to leave the room, she slipped them in her purse.

"Come on, I'll walk you downstairs."

"Thank you. Where are you flying today?"

"U.S. Washington DC."

They hailed separate taxis that even turned in opposite directions form the hotel. One to the train station, one to the airport. Elena looked up at the hotel through the windshield one last time, and saw an enchanted castle she was leaving. She pictured the drawbridge raising up. She was headed to her apartment, and then off to the shops of the Riviera before this weekend's regular client in Nice. His villa on the mountainside overlooking the ocean was her next castle. The yachts entering and leaving the harbor like carriages.

CHAPTER EIGHT

Another camera in the corner, followed by another disapproving exhale. He hated cameras. He tried spinning this annoyance into a positive. This new trend of cameras everywhere around the world was separating the men from the boys. Fortunately, he wasn't a boy. It just made him think and plan harder, and execute despite the hinder. It's what put him with the men near the very, very top.

Hôtel de la Paix was busy. The hotel drew return customers. The lake pulled couples. The street life's aromas and charms appealed to tourists. The weather lured skiers on their way south. The restaurant and bar brought in the tired needing a break. And the Austrian security detail interested the backpacker staring at his *Eyewitness* guide book.

They would be here next week. It wasn't the President's or the Chancellor's, but even the smaller detail that would follow the Internal Affairs and Finance Ministers would require attention. Then again, Syler tends to give even pigeons and park benches attention.

Two weeks ago, he was in Vienna following around the Internal Affairs Minister. Vienna focused on personality and mannerisms. He watched what he ate, how he ate, and where he tended to eat. Syler noticed he always ended his meals with tea, and did not drink coffee. He rarely sat down for lunch, as breakfast and dinner took precedence. He didn't carry around a phone, his assistants did. He was a reader. He was punctual. He enjoyed art, and had an eye for architecture around streets and buildings. Syler also noticed something else his eyes tended to fall upon and appreciate. Women.

That little piece of knowledge stuck with Syler the most. It took him four days, but he felt he had gathered enough information.

Now in Genéva, it was time for geography. The maze and trap that his mark and security would enter. He spent a day at the airport and every day at the train station. The blocks around the hotel garnered two days. Finally the hotel itself, which was the most important.

He tugged his FC Basel hat brim down to his eyebrows and turned the page. He was scribbling down notes and diagrams, but not about Victoria Hall or the Barbier-Mueller Museum from the pages, but the lobby, elevators, and employees from his senses. Syler figured out the shifts at the front desk and would not be able to count on any slack. This wasn't a five-star hotel for nothing.

The minister would be walking into the lobby in two days. Two days. Two, long days. If all goes according to plan, and there was no sign it shouldn't, the minister's stopped breath would signal the end of two careers. Syler was done. He was in the rare position to walk away and go live some place quietly. And like Karl, he was damn well going to do it.

He was summoned out of military barracks in his native Denmark at 19. Pulled out not because of his family name or for a special assignment, but to disappear thanks to natural, innate talents.

Syler knew something was different when his meeting was in the mess hall of all places. Karl lead him past offices, ranges, and even awaiting jeeps full of fuel. There were even people eating around them. Karl had no office. Karl never had a desk. Karl had no official job. Karl didn't exist.

"How's the food these days?" Karl never looked at him, but glanced around at others eating.

"Not bad." Syler tilted his head eyeing the stranger. No one looked at him while walking. No one saluted him. No one seemed to know who he was, yet he walked around like he owned the place. Syler couldn't tell if that was good or bad.

Karl brought up his coffee in a plain Styrofoam cup and blew in it. Then shot a glance up at the 19 year old.

"I guess it beats stale bread and cans of soup every day." He took a sip, a proud sip like he had something on the youngster. Which he did of course. Karl did his homework.

Syler sat back in his chair, failing to show he was surprised. Syler was half proud of raising himself the last half of his life. After his grandfather died when he was 14, several things seem to end. The wonderful trips to Austria. His mother's steady job. The guidance of a former Norwegian champion, and the dreams of Olympic biathlons. Related or not, it didn't matter to Syler. There was the other half that was furious someone teased him about it. He leaned forward about to say something when Karl beat him to it, shaking his head as if to say, 'don't bother'.

"Look kid. There's a talent, isolation, and bitterness in you that needs to be unleashed in other ways than the Danish Defense. I didn't like team sports growing up either."

Syler now didn't bother trying to hide anything. *Where the hell is he getting all-?*

Karl stood up. "Come on, let's go for a walk."

Syler didn't get up at first, but after a few seconds, gave in like Karl knew he would.

Twenty minutes later they were outside the fences, trudging along with hands pushed deep into warm jackets. The North Sea, with its thick wind lashing at them, was marking its authority 50 meters away. It almost leaned them to the right as they followed a tiny path though reeds and dunes. The sea and sky so gray, the only way to find the horizon was the last row of bumpy white caps. It was hard to tell if the wind was stirring up the waves, or were those waves pushing the wind.

"Sir, may I ask your rank?" Syler spoke to his footsteps. The gale coming off the gray sea to his left, pushed his question to Karl.

Karl shook his head. "I'm no longer with the Royal Danish Army or Danish Defense." He turned looking off at the North Sea to his left.

"Officially left last year. Unofficially left eight years ago. I moved on past these borders, to where there are no borders. No flags. No bureaucracy. No restraints."

They walked on for another 30 minutes, and continued walking and talking for five more years. Karl finally told him his name after two. A bond grew between the two, tougher than blood family that Syler never had. It lasted until Karl stacked several coins neatly on the table next to their empty coffee cups, and walked out of Bevar's and left Syler alone, educated, and ready. Syler watched the only father figure he knew disappear around a corner.

Now in a five star hotel lobby, the much older and wiser Syler screwed the cap on his pen and tucked it in his backpack. Then his notebook and guidebook found another zipper compartment. He sat back and scanned the lobby, then sipped his espresso. He wondered where Karl was now, hoping he was still alive. Then he realized he didn't want to know, that was part of it all. Vanishing without a trace. He knew his cabin in Austria would help him do the same soon.

He decided to check out a restaurant and cafe around the corner, both having back exits through the kitchens leading to an alley. An alley dark, quiet, and lost among busy streets he could use if needed. Ten minutes later, he was in his hotel, asleep. He tried dreaming of the cabin and its porch covered in new snow, but like so many times, never got past the dream of the river. A river with all the people he killed, floating and bobbing up and down like empty bottles, as he wades through trying to get to shore.

Three years after Elena walked out Hôtel de la Paix with Charles Lindbergh, she strutted back in for an Austrian elected official. She was wearing a navy coat down to her heels. It had been a while, but she remembered it vaguely. Like flipping through a slide show of men and locations, she stopped the projector at the one of the lobby. She remembers the unique floor and meeting him in the bar. It was only three years, but seemed like three decades. She didn't even know that person. A 27 year old full of ideas and plans, and a body to pave the road to them.

She remembered leaving the hotel as if it was a castle. As she entered it now, it still was a castle, but in Transylvania with an eerie full moon illuminating a dull, hard hill with leafless branches and howling animals. She pictured the rooms upstairs like damp, candle-lit dungeons full of creepy flickering shadows. The only book found in the bedside drawer was by Edgar Allan Poe.

She ate and shopped like a princess, and traveled around like one too. She had flown enough private jets to know where the extra silverware was stored. She was on board enough mega yachts to know which rooms were the smoothest and quietest. And enough suites and penthouses to not even be impressed anymore. It was all getting old.

Her nest egg was growing, that's what kept her going. Every time she thought about declining or cringing at what she was asked to do, the money flashed in front of her, running through a mental counting machine drug dealers own. She made $9,000 three weeks ago for three days on a millionaire's yacht. $2,000 was already wired into the account for tonight's services. She never saw all of her pay, but enough that her plan would work to retire younger than most at this rate. Breathing was important though.

It was the first time she was scared with a client or clients. 10 more seconds and the erotic asphyxiation the man was into would have killed her. Luckily her skills with her body finished him off early, releasing the grip around her neck a little. She laid in bed shaking slightly, and said it was her aftershocks. A minute later, she was in the bathroom with the door closed. She turned the 22-karat gold faucet handle all the way over. The Murano bathroom fixture became Niagara Falls. The noise covered her crying. She didn't think she could walk back out.

The same guy that spent $3,000 on faucets and $5,000 a night for her body nearly killed her. He wasn't trying to kill her, but he wouldn't be devastated if he did. She was a name, an account number from a phone number and code, and there were others. The erotic pleasure was the most important. She realized this while controlling her breathing and wiping her face in the mirror. She eyed the faucet as she reached for it to turn the water off. She was basically a bathroom fixture. That replaceable.

Her brain knew this, that first time in Paris, with the banker from America when she was 23. Her first call. She was able to look past it all. It didn't hurt that he reminded her of her father. A man who never physically did anything to her and her mother, but mentally did plenty. She had no idea where he was, who he was with, what he was doing. But that first American client was a way of getting back at him, his kind.

Seven years later, now her heart realized it. She could trick her brain, but her heart knew a hoax. Her father, like that first man in Paris was long gone, with all the others. A lifetime ago from the yacht in Dubai.

The only thing that got her out of that bathroom was she could do things to control his hands, make them immobile. She left the comfort of the bright bathroom and headed into the dim bedroom, like going into a dark cave knowing the beasts that were lurking. Her defense was his dress shirt. A tailored shirt from Savile Row in London that cost what the faucet did, or close to her for that matter. Elena tied up his hands to the bedpost for the next two hours.

The worst part was she had to lay with him, even caress and touch him as they slept until morning when she could leave. Just before falling asleep, she thought of the Madame in Paris that was seeing some of this money. She saw it from the comfort of her apartment in the Eighth Arrondissement. A couple thousand miles in geography from Dubai. A couple thousand lightyears from the bed.

Elena boarded the Dassault Falcon 900 clutching her Louis Vuitton duffle bag with both arms, tight against her body. It became her teddy bear. She was headed to Paris to shop, then head home by the TGV. Another private jet, leaving another exotic city, after another nameless man, to stroll another fancy store. As the jet reached 47,000 feet somewhere over the Mediterranean, she couldn't take it anymore.

She crossed her leg and rested her head back into the plush seat. She turned glancing out the window at the blinking, pulsing wingtip. It was like a lighthouse warning sailors, warning her of a rocky shoreline she was now skirting. She felt a single tear meander down her check, matching the drop down her champagne flute. And as usual she was alone, no one there to see the symbolism or even the coincidence. No one there to sit next to her and rub her shoulder and back telling her it will be okay. There was just her expensive bag, her fashionable clothing, more expensive things in her fashionable purse, that all surrounding flesh and blood could care less.

There was also the constant hum of engines filling her thoughts. The three Honeywell geared turbofan engines triggered another thought. Formula One engines. Monte Carlo would be it.

Like every year, she knew she would be called upon to be in Monaco for the Grand Prix later that month. She decided it would be over then. The checkered flag would wave and flutter the conclusion of two things.

Now in Genéva, it was the white flag above her track. Her race was almost over. With her tiny purse swaying back and forth at her side, her other hand came up and checked the top button of her coat. Her heels beat across the checkered lobby. Eyes followed the sound, then stared at the source. The fake ring on her finger made those that notice think she was a wife. A trophy wife to sneering women. A prize to jealous men. Like the last time she was here, she looked forward to no thrills and nothing taboo. Just another notch on the bedpost that was her globe bedroom.

Elena looked up as the lobby reached to the ceiling seven floors up, taking up the middle portion of the hotel. Checkerboard floors framing the square hole down the middle like a picture frame. She remembered where the elevators were and headed in that direction, pushed by new goals. Monaco was just around the corner. She could almost smell the exhaust, hear the roar of the engines, feel the rocking of the mega yachts docked at the exit of the famous tunnel at turn nine.

She would meet the Minister in his room. She was dressed as he requested, carrying an item in her purse he asked for as well. There was another item in her purse that was a little odd, and most likely wouldn't be used. They were there so she could leave them here tonight, in the same place she got them. She wanted them gone.

They had sat in a drawer in her living room for three years. As if they shuffled themselves, they morphed into a different symbol. For some time now, they no longer reminded her of a princess soaring off to the east, to New Zealand and the blue waters of the Hauraki Gulf. She now saw a gold faucet. She felt her throat closing. She tasted caviar she had never really liked. She heard her fake screams and moans for rich men.

Like the hotel that was once a castle from a fairy tale, but now a horror story, she saw the cards differently too. She wasn't sure if she could make it to the South Pacific anymore. Elena didn't care. She realized she didn't need to go half way around the world to escape a life, feel fresh, and purge herself. She just needed to venture around the block to something common to fill with pristine ideas. Looking at the Eastern cards only reminded her of a life she was going to try to forget.

Daniel Bohm's two personal assistants use their phones a lot.

Not only do they have lives and responsibilities, but the Minister of Internal Affairs has even more. Either Thomas or Nina is always within an arm's reach of him. Despite seeing Nina more often and her being a little more careless with hers, the part-time waiter choose Thomas' phone instead. He also arrived in Genéva the day before his boss. There were just some things a guy would ask another guy to do.

Thomas and two others sat in the bar downstairs, at a table out in the middle of the room. The waiter shook his head, *they never learn.* He was standing just out in the lobby from the entrance, looking in and waiting. Just as they sat down and got comfortable, he stepped through the open French doors and grabbed a rag and candle jar. Despite never mixing a drink or taking an order, the waiter smiled, nodded, and walked with a pace as if he belonged. Confident and with purpose. Like always.

Thirty-seconds before the real waiter of 17 years would take their orders, Syler moved in. Between greeting them, taking the candle, and wiping the edge of the table of crumbs, no one saw the phone get snatched up in the rag. Syler smiled and headed off.

In the corner with his back to them, he spent 30 seconds with the phone. He pulled out the memory chip, put in something similar, and headed back to the table. He replaced the candle with a smile and then looked down at the floor, bending down. There was nothing there but expensive shoes.

"Did someone drop a phone?" He stood back up holding the phone over the table, now in his other hand.

"Oh," Thomas searched the table and looked back up. "Yes, thank you." Thomas took it with a smile, shook his head, and placed it next to his sunglasses. Syler then stepped out into the lobby and turned his back on a two-minute career as a busboy.

For the next 17 hours, Syler monitored all calls going in and out on the phone. Nothing was alarming and everything seemed fine. There were calls home. Calls from Nina. Calls from Vienna. Syler almost thought things were going too well, too quiet. The evening finally arrived. Syler was in Bohm's hotel room by 7:00. Standing in the large walk-in closet that's found in most bedrooms, it was easy to be a shadow. The door's latch bolt had been taped over. He now wouldn't have to turn the doorknob to open the door making noise. Syler leaned against the wall with a silenced Sig Sauer P239 in his jacket pocket and a capped syringe with 10ML of Succinylcholine ready to flow out. Plan A was the needle. Plan B was the Sig.

He then waited. And waited.

He wondered how many hours he had spent standing in one spot, just waiting to reward his patience. Or sitting in a car seat watching his breath float away to the rearview mirror. And lying in a made bed, thinking and relaxing while waiting for a phone call that hopefully would come in the next day, or the next rainy night.

This would be the easiest few hours ever, knowing it was the last time. The next time he would stand in one spot like this, showing the scary patience he possessed, would be behind a tree near the cabin hunting for deer. His cabin was so close.

The Austrian Minister of Internal Affairs finished dinner at Chez Costa around 8:00. He declined on dessert. He would wait to get to his hotel room to enjoy his bad habit.

He has had a revolving door, no more like a whirlpool, of women. They came and went before and after going into politics and government. Amongst the women, were the girlfriends. The latest was Camille who had lasted the longest. The last time he plunged into the "whirlpool", with her supposedly at his side, was three months ago in Salzburg. He had said to himself that was the last time, that Camille was special and changed him. It was his plastic surgery. He just couldn't stop no matter what.

This trip was no different. It may have been the secretary in the short skirt and heels that morning, but while back at the hotel before lunch, he asked Thomas to take care of something. Thomas just didn't use the phone, like Syler thought.

Thomas walked away from a certain concierge, who then picked up his phone. He called a friend, who called a friend.

"May I help you?"

"Yes, I have a possible client seeking a lady tonight."

"Who is our mutual friend?"

"The Johann Strauss fan."

Not bad, how about this. "What's his favorite piece?"

"*Vienna Blood*."

Good enough. "Okay. Is he still in Genéva?"

"Yes."

"What class are we talking about?"

"Caviar and DP."

"That will take me some time. Who is it for? Title?"

"Similar to that Ambassador last summer. Official from Austria, ironically."

"Okay, give me the afternoon. I will redial this number before dinner."

By the time Mr. Bohm was shown his seat for dinner, his secret dessert was taken care of. At 8:15 he was in his room splashing water on his face and slipping into a satin robe. He moved some items on the table to make room for the champagne. He walked to the curtains and eased them to the side with the back of his hand. A light drizzle was coating the city in beads. He cocked his head to the left in search of the fountain, when a gentle knock at the door turned him around. The curtain swayed closed as he moved to the door and pulled it inward.

"Mr. Von Trapp?"

Daniel pulled the door completely in and stepped back. "Yes, come in."

Elena smiled and extended her hand, angled down slightly. He took it gently and brought it up to his lips. "Welcome. You are simply stunning."

She smiled again. "Thank you. I'm glad I could be here tonight for you." She walked in and placed her purse on a table by the door. She quickly scanned the room and found him again, staring at her. He was good looking and fit, and judging by the Austrian security man outside, wearing a tux, that searched her purse, he was important.

"Would you care for some champagne? I apologize; it should be here any minute." He moved to the small velvet ottoman bench at the foot of the bed and sat, crossing his leg eyeing her up and down.

"That would be lovely, yes." Elena then began unbuttoning her coat and shrugged her shoulders out of it, folding it in half and placing it over the chair by her purse. As per request, she was now left in only a negligée. Shimmering silk and teasing. She pulled out two clips releasing her flowing hair.

She took three long, tantalizing steps to him and straddled him, the beige silk hiking up to her waist leaving nothing but smooth, tan legs enclosing around his robe. She ran her hands through his hair, fingers and thumbs pressing. He sighed and closed his eyes, tilting back slightly.

"Long day?"

A combination of a moan and sigh was released.

"Too long."

"Well the night can be long too, if you'd like."

He opened his eyes and found her mouth and moist lips. "Only not as stressful I hope." His eyes then slid down to her breasts pushing out her negligée and thin straps over each shoulder.

She shook her head. "Not stressful at all."

She continued slithering her fingers through his hair, messaging his head, coaxing out another relaxing sigh.

A heavier knock came from the door and she got off of him. He adjusted his robe and walked to the door, opening it a little for his head. Elena sat on the ottoman crossing each leg in turn to take off her heels. The door opened just enough for the cart to wheel in. The security man's hands let go of the cart to pull the door closed. Daniel pushed the cart to the window.

"Come."

He poured two glasses and while stealing another glimpse down at her; they toasted each other. "Where are you from? I hear several places in your voice."

"Close by."

He nodded and took an understanding sip.

"And you?" She tilted her head to the left exposing a hoop earring.

"Vienna."

They both moved to the intimate couch this time, on the opposite wall from the bed, holding their golden flutes. She looked at him.

"I love Vienna. Only been there twice though." "The most beautiful city in the world. Art. Culture. Music. It has everything. Except you I guess?"

She laughed and looked away at the rest of the room. The window in a veil of curtains. The trellis of the double doors to the closet. The rectangular lamps of the oak desk. Then there was the ceiling that wasn't painted, but rather took the impression of pinned fabric in waves, like a knife smoothing over layers of a delicate cake made of rich fabric.

She returned her eyes to him and sipped her drink, leaving pinkish smudges on her Waterford flute. He was eyeing her body again before finding her eyes. She sensed he was ready and the talking was getting in the way of what he had longed for since 9am. She looked at her glass and held it up in front of him.

"Just look what I've done to the glass." She licked her lips and locked onto his eyes speaking slowly, deeply. "Looks like I got lipstick all over this." She held the erotic stare as she reached over and put the glass down on the table, her eyes never leaving his. His chest was now on fire and his eyes danced everywhere in eagerness. An eagerness to explode.

With her eyes still sucking his into her, she stood up and moved in front of him. She pushed his knees apart and then pulled each robe string out and loose. The robe opened. He was mush. Throbbing mush.

For the next six minutes, she did things to him no one has even come close to. For the first two minutes, he continued to sip his champagne and enjoy. Eventually he couldn't hold the glass still or control his breathing to drink anything other than saliva. By the time his breathing returned to normal, she raised up, bending over at the waist, and kissed him on the cheek.

"So Mr. Van Trapp, still feeling the stress of the day?"

"Jesus Christ no." He looked at her shaking his head and played with her hair. He would have said he was speechless, but he wasn't. His grunting scream was only muffled by gritting teeth.

"May I use your bathroom. I will be right back." She only knew one guy who would kiss after doing that. She stood up.

"Please, go right ahead. I'll get you more champagne and see you in bed."

She slid some hair over her left ear and strutted into the bathroom, closing the door behind her. Daniel Bohm would have some help getting to the bed.

She turned the faucet handle on, eyeing it as if the one on the yacht in Dubai. A slight hesitation was present before gripping the handle. She leaned down, cupping cold water in her hands. She splashed her face lightly. Then rinsed, and spit. She stood up and pulled off the hand towel, dabbing her face and chin. She looked at the 30 year old in the mirror and wondered if she would ever see Vienna again through the eyes of a woman in love, not a woman giving love. Monaco was getting closer. She was so close.

She flipped off the light switch and opened the door. The room was glowing light blue thanks to the thin curtains playing a camera filter. He was lying in bed on his back. The champagne still on the table and flutes on the floor where they had been left.

"No more bubbly honey?"

A gloved hand suddenly wrapped around her mouth pressing in. It pulled her head back into a chest and shoulder. Then a circle of hard metal pressed into the side of her head above the ear. Her eyes exploded open, but unlike her client two minutes ago, it wasn't because of erotic euphoria, but sheer panic. She was now in the midst of plan B.

As her coat was coming off exposing a body that made grown men whimper, Syler was in the closet watching, biting his own teeth in thought. And Irony. Karl said, *'there's always a catch.'* He knew things were going too smoothly for the last time.

Thanks to her, he needed an alternative plan. By the time his target's eyes rolled into the back of his head on the couch, Syler rolled his own knowing he would have to kill her too.

Syler assumed the security man outside wasn't at the door, he wasn't the chancellor after all, but most likely down the hall a little. He was probably by the elevators to the left. That's what it was like at the hotel in Graz when following Mr. Bohm out of Vienna for a day. A silencer would not be heard. But the little voice in his head, that Karl planted there, knew better. He hadn't come this far to take a childish chance like that now. If he was just outside the door, just happened to be walking by, could a spitting gun be heard? Possibly. The word possibly didn't register with Syler at all. The gun would only be used to get his point across. He would have to kill her with his bare hands. It wouldn't be the first time. More importantly, it would look like a crime of passion, and fit the atmosphere of the moment. Syler was still relaxed. It's what separated him from the boys.

The Austrian never knew what happened. It took Syler four-seconds to come out from the closet, take three stealthy steps to him, and plunge in the needle. He covered his mouth and cradled his head as the chemical began working quickly, like always. Within 12 seconds, most of his body's muscles gave way, and Syler was holding a 6'1" rag doll. He dragged him to the bed, his heels leaving parallel marks in the plush carpet.

Succinylcholine paralyzes all the muscles in the body. Including the ones that allow a person to breath. It doesn't kill you directly, it kills the muscles. Without them, you will die. The evil part is the brain continues to work and figures out what is going on. Pretty soon even his eye muscles gave in, and the slow agonizing death took place. By the time she had entered the room, questioning where the Dom Pérignon was, he was a statue looking up at the ceiling, comprehending what was happening to him, unable to do anything about it. Even her body, skills, and mouth couldn't awaken anything in him.

She was able to breath out of her nose, just above his thumb. Her eyes were not as wide open anymore, but rather filling with water. Syler pulled the gun away and slid it inside the back of his waistband. Then his right hand reached up, barely touching the back of her head. All he had to do was forcefully spin his hands, snapping her neck.

"Please, I'm all alone." She began pleading, shaking. "I have no one. Please don't kill me." The 'e' sound elongated as she began crying uncontrollably under his gloved hand. She shut her eyes, tears leaking out the corners.

Syler paused at this, as it all registered in his head. It's what they all want to hear. Someone by themselves, not attached to anyone. No ties anywhere. No one expecting them the next day. And most likely depressed. She was a number, a statistic, data that would not be missed.

It was like he was looking in a mirror and hearing himself.

His right hand came off her head. He blinked a couple of times as the robot-mode he was in short circuited, overheated. Syler swallowed and his hand slid down to her upper arm and gripped it.

"Do not scream." His hand pulled away from covering her mouth a fraction. "What's your name?"

She sucked in a breath, tears still streaming down her checks, running into his glove.

"Elena."

"Your real name."

A pause. "Lucie." She had to actually think about it. She had forgotten her.

"How old are you?"

She needed three gulping breaths before she could answer.

"30." Her eyes were now open, vision blurred like a kaleidoscope.

He licked his lips and shut his eyes knowing he should kill her instantly, quietly. *Do it, do it, do it. Now! Come on, just…*

His hands couldn't, as if the syringe had found his arms. They didn't move. He couldn't kill her, kill himself. He opened his eyes staring at the back of her head, shaking his in disbelief.

"Please mister, let me be some…" Her lungs needed another gulp of air. She no longer saw a checkered flag in Monaco, but the checkered floor of the lobby as she walked out, sprinting far away leaving everything behind. Hopefully. The homes of Monte Carlo and cabins of Austria couldn't be further apart, but from room 406's perspective, there is so much more to the story than meets the eye.

Syler tilted his head, as if trying to look around to her face. "Where are you from?" His hand pulled away from her mouth and gripped the back of her neck, keeping her still and facing forward.

"Brussels."

"Where do you live now?" His eyes shot over to the door before returning to her head.

"Marseille." She could hear frustration in his voice. She could feel indecision in the air. Her breaths were just tiny gasps now.

"Where is your family?"

Her eyes searched the room for that indecision she felt in him. Her chest was still heaving, but less.

"I don't know. My father…" she began crying again.

Five-seconds later, Syler moved her to the chair with her coat. He let go of her upper arm and pulled out the Sig from his waist and held it up against her head. The round, smooth end of the silencer pushed her head forward a bit, again to make a point.

"You are going to put on your coat and shoes. I'm right behind you." He didn't bother saying, *move slowly*. She was a wounded orphan doe right now.

She sniffed and nodded as she lifted the coat from the chair and stretched her arms into it. She brought up her hands to button the coat, but couldn't keep her hands from shaking. The button was missing the hole each time. He helped her from behind and then moved her to the ottoman for her heels. She kicked up both legs and eventually had them on somewhat strapped.

The tip of the silencer moved her to the door. "If this is going to work and you want to live, you need to calm down. Otherwise, that guard out there will suspect something. You will count to 20 and open this door. Then leave to the right as normal as possible. Face forward, do not turn around or look back in the hallway. Go down the stairs, stay along the walls, leave out the restaurant exit, not the lobby. Do you understand?"

She eventually nodded and took a deep breath, less nasally.

"Yes."

He reached for her purse, unclasped it open.

"Take out your money and give me your wallet." She did, about 340

Euros now in her damp hand. He slipped the wallet back into her purse, closing it against his leg.

"I'm taking your purse. The gun is going to be pointing at your head for the next 20 seconds. Do not turn around. Start counting." *And for God's sake go find someone.*

Despite what he claimed, the gun immediately went into his pants. By the time she got to seven, he was on the balcony quietly closing the French doors that locked from the inside. By the time she counted to 12, he was climbing the knotted rope that dangled from the balcony directly above. As she opened the door to room 406, he opened the balcony doors to room 506. He then put her purse in a duffle bag, slung a backpack over his left shoulder, and left his room of two days.

The two loners left the hotel in opposite directions, both finally ready to move on in their lives.

The train ride to Lausanne, hugging the north shore of the Lake Genéva, was 50 minutes. His new room at the Novotel Lausanne Bussigny, was under the name and credit card of Morton Laudrup. Of the list of aliases he had come up with decades ago, this one was his favorite. He had saved it for his last job. When the man behind the counter in Lusanne asked for his passport, Syler handed it over with a quivering hand. A hand that had touched a great many things in those decades, but only wanted to touch Mr. Laudrup's passport.

He was up past midnight. With no lights, Syler sat in a chair by his room's window with his gun. He was paying attention to all the activity on Thomas' phone through his. He watched the street from his perch, peeking under the door for any movement. Then there was his pulse. Slow and calm, as if his heart was beating to the whisper of falling snow. He was so close, he could hear the crackle of the fire inside. He could smell the wood stacked on the back porch in its own short wall.

Before going to bed, he pulled out Lucie's purse. Syler spread a hotel towel on the bed, and dumped the contents out. He raised his eyebrows at the handcuffs. He knew handcuffs of course, but not for how she had used them. He then pulled out her ID and credit cards, burning them in an ashtray. His fingers brushed aside lipstick and a perfume bottle. Some hotel matches were tossed on the end table. Syler flipped a blindfold, resembling a mask, to the side that uncovered something. He leaned down slightly as his eyes found a deck of playing cards.

Are those…?

He picked them up. He then sat up straighter smiling at the thought of Lucie, knowing very well what she could do after seeing it in person, using these cards in some kinky, creative way. He wondered where she got them and how long she'd had them. It also dawned on him, that the closest person he had to a father once flew that airline in America.

The cards, like a torch, had been passed from one father-less child to another.

From April 2007 to March 2010……

1 game of Briscola
1 game of Chance
1 games of Chinchón
4 games of Gin
1 game of Napoleon Triumph
2 game of Noddy

PART IV

The Summons
The Nanny Diaries
Red Rabbit
Prey
The Lovely Bones

CHAPTER NINE

The early November sun was just beginning to wink above the Atlantic. The palm fronds were slowly beginning to bend and flutter to life, carelessly waving at the chirping birds that were around. The song of the birds was constant, coming from everywhere. Squirrels leapt from branches and porch railings. The blue water began to lighten with every degree the sun rose. Surrounded by marshes, ponds, and the ocean a half mile away, the sounds of nature held the mic.

A quarter mile past the guard gate, Governors Drive turns and sways its way through these marshes and ponds. It gives way to golf courses and select homes scattered between large, sheltering oak trees. One moment you are driving in a tunnel of oaks, with moss dangling down like forgotten party streamers. And the next you're out into an opening with a body water on one side and inviting homes on the other.

Two miles from that guard gate, it swings south in the direction of the ocean. Jutting off to the left and tucked behind a row of full oaks, is a quiet lane named after a local fern. The street sticks out into a marsh like a finger with seven houses.

The third house on the left is a light blue, two-story Victorian with a wraparound porch. As with most houses in the low country, wide stairs lead up to the 'first' floor at the porch. Oaks surround the sides and back of the house, with five huge sable palms standing guard in the front. A white gravel driveway curves in front of the house. On the right, the east side, the wooden balcony from a small guest room covered in shade from the trees overhead. The sunrise just seeping through in splotches.

It was in this room that Hunter awoke on his side facing the sliding glass door. His eyes opened slowly, then blinked rapidly for a second until focusing on the closed curtains. Thanks to being on the east side, the glow from the early morning sun was the only, and perfect, alarm needed.

Under a glass lamp full of seashells, was an alarm clock an arm's length away just in case. Hunter peered at it and enjoyed reading the time without the instinctive urge to get up. Also, he was alone.

He had gotten used to waking up next to his fiancé, since the engagement. His hand stroking her hair or shoulder, or her fingertips caressing his chest was the tantalizing alarm occasionally. As of two weeks ago, it was every morning. She sold her place and moved in with him until they would close on their new house they had purchased. He didn't mind his place being turned into a storage facility, with boxes, bins, her shoes, and her bags everywhere. Her shoes alone took up a closet. As long as she was there, strolling through and around it all like a minefield, he was happy.

He still remembers their first cup of coffee together in his place, called home by both of them for the first time. He was on the hardwood floor, leaning back against a moving box, coffee at his side. She was sitting up on a dresser from her bedroom that was now in the middle of his living room. She was cupping her coffee in front of her, swinging her legs slowly. He just stared up at her. Her hair was messy, her tiny tank top she sleeps in was wrinkly, and she probably had morning breath. He couldn't wait to do this again tomorrow morning. And the next.

Yesterday in bed, she clung to him, not letting him get up. After a month being each other's alarm, she would wake up without him for three days. She almost cried. Hunter called in sick until lunch, so he could stay in her arms. They were each other's drug dealer, supplying their addicting fix of closeness, flesh, and thoughts.

For his weekend in Kiawah, she had to pull out her 8x10 picture of him she had kept at her place. Finding it was no simple task, with moving boxes the ocean, the frame a shell. It was the last thing she packed from her place. She loved the fact that she would never need it again, since she now had the real thing every day. It was called to duty one more time.

Through the curtains the shadow of a small squirrel, out on the balcony railing, dragged his attention back outside. He sucked in a long breath and rolled onto his back, bringing both hands up to his face. He rubbed his eyes and ran his fingers throughout his messy hair. He let his arms fall to his sides and stared up at the ceiling fan slowly spinning.

Hunter hadn't slept in flannel sheets in years, maybe since college.

They felt so soft. He thought about putting them on their registry. They smelled refreshing too, noticing from the pillowcase his head sunk into. Some spring flowery detergent hinting they were just washed. Heather had something to do with this, no doubt. He probably could have fallen back to sleep if he wanted, but decided to get up.

He reached over and lifted the feather comforter up to swing his legs out. He sat on the edge of the bed and rubbed the back of his neck. There was still a hint of the beer he helped drink last night behind his forehead, but nothing coffee couldn't fix.

Hunter stepped out on the balcony. The squirrel gave him a look, and moved away. Some birds flew off too, eventually. He walked to the railing and leaned into it. Half the orangish-yellow sun was hiding behind the neighbor's roof through swaying moss. He looked to his left. The backyard stretched back about 75 feet to a white, chipped pier. It extended out into the marsh with clumps of reeds and sand scattered throughout. Across the marsh, another line of homes was visible, with the mainland way off in the distance. He looked to his right towards the front of the house and the street. A woman was walking a golden retriever, passing by the mailbox. On the other side of the street was another house, three stories and yellow.

It felt funny to Hunter that it was 9:15 on a Friday morning. It felt more like a Sunday morning. Nothing was rushed. No one hurried out to the mailbox. Bush and plant trimmings were left littering the flowerbeds and mulch, waiting to be picked up later. The squirrels and birds were more annoyed than scared of people. The pulse of the island seemed to keep up with the pace of the tides.

He looked forward to two full days of relaxing, golf, and hanging out with Will and Heather. Today was Cougar Point and Turtle Point. Saturday was the Ocean Course. They were also having a bunch of people over tomorrow night for a party.

He turned his head to the house next door. The sun was much brighter now and above the peaked roof. Hunter squinted at it through the branches and hairy moss, as the sun turned the tree into a lifeless silhouette. He stretched and headed back inside, retying his pajama pants strings. He pulled out a plain navy t-shirt from his duffle and slid it on while walking out of the guest room.

To the left, the hallway opened up with a railing looking down into the first floor living room. Hunter turned right and across from a sewing room, was a second set of stairs, much smaller than the main stairs. These made an *L* shape, and at the bottom, Hunter turned left to hop down the last three steps. He came out into the wide-open kitchen.

"Morning honey," Will said without looking back.

Hunter scanned the kitchen while walking past the fridge and heading around the island. He pulled open both cabinets above the coffee maker. He then tried two more before giving up.

"Where the hell are the mugs?"

Will put the paper down and twisted around in his chair to look back.

"Oh, actually they are over there by the sink." Will nodded his head to the other side of the kitchen by the windows.

"Well, that makes sense." Hunter looked at him while walking back around the island.

"Yeah," Will laughed a little. "We had to move the coffee maker for the outlet. Long story." He turned back around, crossed his leg at the knee, and brought up the paper.

Hunter reached the far side and peered out the window. The long backyard stretching to the marsh, filling the window like a mural. It was the kind of view that made any cup of coffee, no matter how early, quite extraordinary. He reached up, pulled open the cabinet, and surveyed the mugs.

There was a hunter green Pebble Beach mug, with the famous cypress tree on it, and a Master's one, but he'd never been to either and felt like he couldn't take them. Hunter felt it was like someone from his generation wearing a Led Zeppelin or Pink Floyd t-shirt. A yellow one was boring. His Tar Heel mug at home wouldn't allow him to grab the Wake Forest mug, Hunter's would break out of jealousy the next time he reached for it. He was about grab the brown 'Wake Up' mug, named after a coffee shop in St. Simon's Island, when one behind it made him smile. *Wow, he still has it.*

It was red at one point, but now over time and years of dishwashing, was a hideous orangish. The white lettering, if found down a hardware store paint aisle, would be called egg shell or bone, something other than a bright white. The picture on it wasn't even clear anymore and a fourth of it was missing. Hunter didn't need to see it anymore, neither did Will. They both knew it well. He pulled it off the shelf and closed the cabinet.

He held it by the curved handle and ran his thumb over the letters at the top: De Meer Stadium

He turned and was walking clockwise around the island when Heather came into the kitchen. She was wearing gray sweats and a pink tank top. Her strawberry blond hair was twisted in a pin behind her head. He put down the mug, smiled, and walked over towards her. They met in front of the stovetop.

"Hunter!" She walked into him with open arms and hugged him. "I'm sorry I missed you last night. I was exhausted." They let go and she brought up her hands to his face.

"Let me look at you." Then they slid down to his shoulders. "Your hair is short, I like it." Her right hand patted his chest twice and then grabbed a banana out of a bowl. She started walking around to the sink.

"Sweetie, would you mind if I run away with Hunter this weekend?"

"Sure. As long as it's okay with him."

Hunter replaced the carafe and turned, placing his coffee down on the island.

"Absolutely," Hunter said with a smile while he scooped a spoon of sugar into his coffee. Heather was peeling her banana and facing him, leaning back on the sink.

"You two certainly did some catching up last night, judging by the recycling bin." She tiled her head towards the stairs that led to the garage. "How was the drive?" She bit into the banana.

"Not bad." While stirring his coffee he raised his other hand and gave it a shake.

"Little iffy driving out here at night I might say." He placed the spoon down and brought up his mug for a sip. He looked at her over the rim.

"Was the bed okay?"

He nodded until done swallowing. "Yeah it was fine. I forgot how nice flannel sheets are."

Will continued reading and talked into the newspaper. "So is that why you slept so hard? I tried waking you for a little action around three and you just rolled over."

Hunter took another sip, "You wore me out."

Will smiled and Heather rolled her eyes as she turned towards the sink behind her to wash her hands.

"You guys never change." She then threw the banana peel into the trash and retied her hair. She looked at Will. "Where are you guys playing today?"

"Cougar and Turtle."

She looked across the island to Hunter sipping his coffee. "Have you played out here?"

He shook his head.

After finishing her hair, she walked over to Will, put her hands on his shoulders, and leaned down.

"Did you call Jaimie?" She started massaging his shoulders.

"Ohhhh don't stop." Will stopped reading and put the paper down.

"He's like a dog. Pretty soon his leg will start shaking." She stopped and leaned over right in front of him, still waiting for an answer.

"I had to leave a message, I'll try again today."

"Don't forget." She turned and walked past Hunter, grabbing her coffee.

"So the kids are at your parents?" Hunter asked.

She put her coffee in the microwave and pushed some buttons, then with her hand still on the door handle, turned to Hunter.

"Yeah. They came and got them yesterday. This is their first long weekend with them so it should be interesting." She started smiling. It beeped and she pulled open the door.

"Colleen is just about potty trained so hopefully she doesn't regress."

Hunter nodded.

"So when are you and Riley going to start having kids?"

Hunter finished his first cup. "Well, I'd like to get married first. Call me old-fashioned."

Will finally entered the conversation.

"But that's the new celebrity thing, be like six months pregnant walking down the aisle." He closed the paper, folded it, and picked up another section. "Then call your kid a screwed up name like Moon or Natural."

Hunter opened the sugar. "I like Tangerine." Everyone laughed.

Heather picked up some papers from the desk and walked past Hunter, patting him on the back.

"April 5th, right?"

"Yep."

"Will she keep the name Cobb?" Heather glanced back.

Hunter shook his head.

Heather nodded. "Hunter and Riley Grace. I like that." She smiled.

Will turned. "April 5th, that isn't Masters week is it?" He turned back around and crossed his other leg. "Cause if so, Heather may be coming alone."

"It's that Tuesday night," Hunter took a sip, "we're having the ceremony out on the lawn under the famous oak and the reception upstairs at the Champions' Dinner."

"Excellent. What are you putting on the menu?" Will turned back around.

"Tiger and I are discussing that now."

Heather had had enough. "You all are so retarded." She looked at Will. "You grilling tonight?"

"Yeah, it's all marinating in the downstairs fridge."

"How about the ice for tomorrow night?"

"Get it on the way home."

"Okay. Well, you two have fun." Heather kissed him on the cheek. "Oh Hunter, I need your new address, help me remember okay?"

Hunter nodded, "Yeah, I've got it upstairs, I haven't memorized it yet."

"Is it Raleigh or Chapel Hill?"

"Well we're going to be almost in between, but I think it's technically Raleigh."

"Okay. Are you building?"

He swallowed and brought his mug down. "No, found an older house, built in the 50's. It's really cool. Can't believe we found it. Great shape."

"Nice." She turned towards the family room and out of sight. Hunter closed the sugar lid and walked over to the table, and picked out a chair across from Will. He put his mug down and grabbed the top section of the paper. Will bent his paper down and peered over it at Hunter's mug.

"Still take it black, huh."

Hunter was unfolding a section and with a straight face replied, "Like my men." Will laughed.

They could have entire conversations in movie lines and inside jokes. Hunter had given up on the top section of the paper and plopped it down to his right. Will was still nursing the sports section, so Hunter slid some out of the way until finding the local. He looked up at Will then back down to the page.

"When's the last time you were without kids around here?"

As if searching for an answer, Will looked up to the light hanging over the table. Then down to Hunter.

"I guess a year." He nodded, "My parents came here to house sit while we went down to Savannah for a weekend." He looked down at the page.

"I can imagine it's nice, but funny at the same time."

"Yeah," Will replied.

They read the paper for the next 15 minutes, occasionally commenting on business and finance stuff, comparing Charlotte and Charleston, and events in Europe.

Will's eyes moved to the top of the next page.

"Are you hungry? There are muffins, some fruit, and stuff over by the bread basket and on the island."

"You're not making me an omelet?"

"No."

"Do you even know how?"

Will smiled. "Probably not very well."

Hunter brought up his mug for a sip. "I'll grab something in a minute. When's our tee time?" He finished his second cup.

"10:45." The paper tilted down as Will looked at the sport watch on his turned wrist. "We don't need to leave for another hour."

"Cool." Hunter turned and looked through the French doors to the backyard. He wanted to go out there. He looked back at Will wondering why he sat in here when he had that out there. He guessed it was one of those things that when you have it in your daily life, it just becomes ordinary.

"Could you hurry up with that? I want to check the MLS standings."

Will shut his eyes and started laughing. He then looked up at Hunter.

"How's your fantasy team doing?"

Hunter smiled and couldn't think of a quick response. He just kept grinning.

"Are they even playing right now?"

Will tossed the paper in front of him and got up, holding his mug.

"Does anyone care?" He walked over to the coffee pot. "You're going to like Ocean tomorrow. Rumor is it's going to get a PGA soon. Pete Dye was just out here a month ago, saying it's so hard he won't have to change much if they do."

"Too bad it's not an Open, then it would be a real major."

Will laughed. "Very true." He grabbed the carafe and pulled it out.

"It's not supposed to be too windy tomorrow, so that will help." Will poured and headed to the fridge for the creamer. "I played in the summer and the winds were 30 mph. It's almost unplayable. I shot an 81."

Hunter raised his eyebrows. He never knew Will to shoot anything more than a 75, even on a bad day.

"Are we walking today?" asked Hunter.

"Let's walk Turtle this morning, then ride at Cougar."

Hunter was looking forward to that almost as much as playing the course. To him, walking and golf were a tandem. It was the only way to experience the game. The other thing paired with golf would take place afterwards. He hoped Will had some.

"You got any cards?"

Will was shaking the creamer jug when he stopped to think.

"Yeah, somewhere. I think they'll be over there in a drawer," he pointed the creamer jug to the desk in the corner, then poured some in his mug.

Hunter refolded the finished sports section and tossed it on top of the front page. He walked around to the sink and placed the mug in the sink. He grabbed a banana from a mesh basket on the island and started peeling.

"I need to hit some balls first."

"We'll have time."

Hunter continued talking through chewing.

"I'm going to shower." He swallowed and tossed the large strings of peel in the trash. "Will you come up and get my back?"

"I thought you'd never ask."

Hunter smiled and headed over to the desk. Papers were scattered everywhere, the computer cove taking the form of the temporary place for everything until going upstairs into the den where the real desk was. He pulled open one drawer and found an iPod, sunglasses, and bags of M&M's Heather used for treats. He tried the second and found pens, notebooks, and playing cards.

"Bingo."

One was a Master's deck, green with the famous yellow logo, that like the mug earlier, he didn't feel right using. He pushed them towards the back. He chuckled to himself as he pulled out a blue box.

"Eastern? Wow." He turned holding them up to Will. "Where the hell did you get these?"

Will was finding his seat again and putting his coffee down.

"Uh, not sure. Oh wait, we brought those back from Colorado a couple of years ago. We rented a house out there one Christmas with some other couples. Drove the entire way. Heather brought them back. Kind of a funny, long story."

"You drove out there?"

Will gave him a look. "Yeah, didn't want to fly with a little one."

Hunter nodded, kind of understanding. He looked back down at the cards.

"My dad use to fly Eastern. Charlotte was a hub."

"You can play *Go Fish* with them, right?" Will brought up his mug for a sip.

Hunter rolled his eyes. "Jesus, you still haven't learned any other games."

Will laughed. "Not really."

"You have Masters cards for God's sake, sitting in here wasting away."

Will looked over and raised his coffee mug in a sarcastic toast.

"Cheers!"

"You're pathetic." Hunter smiled and eyed the backyard one more time before heading to the left of the fridge and disappearing up the stairs.

Will called out. "You know I love you!"

Due to fantastic water pressure, he took a soothing 20-minute hot shower. Hunter adored long showers, something that most mornings didn't allow. He pulled on a white Lacoste shirt and tucked it inside light khaki shorts. He sat down on the edge of the bed and reached for his watch on the bureau. While strapping it on, he noticed a wedding picture next to the mirror. It froze him for an instant. He couldn't believe it was taken six years ago. *How has it been that long?*

He was their best man and it seemed like yesterday. He thought about how much things had changed. He also thought how little had changed. He and Will have known each other since they were eight, playing soccer together and going to the same elementary school. Hunter's mom and

Will's dad would sit on the bleachers at soccer practice and talk. They would invite Hunter and his mom over for holiday dinners. Both family photo albums had the other in them. Every now and then, Hunter would pop in for a visit unannounced while Will was off getting his MBA. He and Will's parents would sit and catch up over coffee. It was these little memories that Hunter remembered most.

Because of this, being the best man at Will's wedding was one of the top five memories of his life. That, and nailing the best man toast, which was made all the better by coming in front of 200 people. He never felt the need to be in the spotlight, but he had it then. And the quiet, even shy guy, who played wingman to Will his whole life when it came to girls, soccer, golf, school, and just about everything else, took it and ran with it.

"Good evening. If I could have everyone's attention." He held up his flute glass, then looked at Vanessa, the wedding organizer who had just announced him and asked everyone to refill their glasses.

"Thank you Vanessa. I need to thank and recognize a few people here tonight. First off the bridesmaids. I'd like to toast the lovely ladies for looking radiant today and making Heather look even more so. Cheers." Everyone raised their glasses and yelled.

"Next the Davenports, for this wonderful evening and setting. Something that none of us will soon forget." More cheers.

"I would also like to thank them for being so nice and welcoming to me over this past week. It's been very nice getting to know you all, all 500 of you." He smiled and the room laughed. "And I think it's good we do this now, meeting everyone here tonight, seeing that the next time I see you, I probably will have no clue who you are." More laughter and howls. Hunter smiled and the room's loud affection pumped his heart.

The crowd softened. "Anyway, all kidding aside," he cocked his head to the left to find their table, "a toast to the Davenport's. Thank you for this evening." Hunter tried to slow down and not get ahead of himself; he didn't want to rush things. He realized simply scanning the room from side to side without really locking into someone made it easier. Eye contact was where he felt rushed.

The room quieted. A glass clinked off in the corner. Up to now, he had followed the blueprint from etiquette guides on classy toasts. *Okay, time to get personal.*

"I'd also like to recognize the Ramsey's and give a toast to them for last night's rehearsal dinner. The food, spirits, and company was the perfect start to a memorable weekend. Cheers!" He found them, and locked eyes with both Will's mom and dad. He raised his glass, now half-empty. Then had to wait 10 seconds.

"I would also like to take a second and thank them personally, for everything they've done for me over the last 19 some years that I can't possibly sum up in 10 seconds." He smiled and paused. "But of which includes all those carpools to soccer games, many chats over coffee, and simply being like a family to me when you didn't have to." Some awes filled the room and that felt about right. Will's mom touched her chest.

"Vanessa can I get more champagne?" He looked over at her. People laughed, but he was serious. He needed a drink. He took half the glass in one smooth sip and looked out at the vast, candlelit room. *Deep breath... and...go...*

"So Will and I have known each other since we were eight years old. And in that time, we did a lot of stupid, childish things." Typical little smirks filled the air. "But one evening comes to mind more than others tonight." Hunter smiled, knowing everyone's immediate thought of, *oh and now comes the cliché' speech*, was just about to get crushed.

"We were at the beach sitting in my convertible one night with some beverages, of course, when out of nowhere, Will said, 'I wonder what my wife is doing right now?'"

Silence. The indoor water fountain gurgled. That was it. The room was frozen and everyone stared at him. Hunter paused and looked around. They were hooked.

"He looked at me and said, 'Where is she, what is she doing, what is she wearing at this exact moment?' and I had never seen that side of Will. So we sat there and started talking about it. What were our future wives doing that night, wherever they were? How would we meet? Would it be around the corner in five minutes? In college? Work? And as we talked, I remember feeling a little envious because if you knew Will growing up, everything came easy to him, everything was natural for him. It always, always worked out." Hunter found Chris, a mutual friend from childhood, and pointed at him. "Am I right?" Chris raised his eyebrows and nodded. Hunter then addressed the room again, which was on the edge of their plush seats.

"I remember being even a little annoyed thinking, man what are you worried about? Of course you will find your true love, your fairytale; this is you we're talking about." Hunter took a sip and finished his champagne. He could have started singing the Bulgarian national anthem and everyone would have rose up to sing it with him, not even knowing the verses.

"So tonight, I think it's pretty cool, we can look back and answer all those questions from that night years and years ago. We know who..." Hunter's eyes found Heather, followed by the rest of the room.

"We know where she was that night we were at the beach; Thomasville, just outside Phoenix. We can also answer how they would meet. I," Hunter swept his hand across the room, his glass pointing to four or five guys in the audience. "Along with several guys in here, were all at Molly's Tunnel on St. Patrick's Day night a couple years ago, and watched Will go over to get introduced to this 'Heather' girl that no one knew." Heather reached under the table and grabbed Will's knee, and started crying. Half the eyes in the room blurred vision. Then the grand finale, that had come to him this morning in the shower, wrapping up an old story to the present day like only a Pulitzer winner could have done.

"And as far as what she was doing at the *exact* moment we were sitting in that old convertible all those years ago, as hard as it seems, I think I actually have an answer. And it came to me last night during-," Hunter looked over to a far table and extended his index finger, unwrapping it from his champagne flute, pointing to one of Heather's childhood friends who spoke at the rehearsal dinner.

"Daphne's speech." He grinned at her and those 80 or so that were there last night started roaring. They all knew what was brilliantly, coming next. Hunter's gaze looked away and found Will.

"Will. They were shopping. And trying on everything in the aisle." The roof lifted off the banquet hall. Candle flames flickered at the rush of laughter like they were being blown out. Hunter smiled and licked his lips to the reaction and couldn't believe it. He then took a deep breath and reminded himself to stay calm and don't forget the actually toast. After about 30 seconds of laughter and applause, Hunter was able to continue and wrap it up.

"So Will, I'm glad I was right way back then, you did fine your fairytale true love like I knew you would. So, would everyone raise your glasses in a toast. To Will and Heather. May you find years of joy and happiness."

Hunter put the mic down and turned to Vanessa. She was even crying. If not for the huge rock on her finger, he would have grabbed her, tilted her over in a bow and kissed her like a returning World War II sailor. Hunter made his way through the crowd to hugs, handshakes, and comments. As he walked by Will's parents, they both hugged him.

Then in typical Mr. Ramsey fashion asked, "And just how many beers did you all have before driving home that night?"

At the same time two tables away, Vanessa moved over to Lainie, Heather's sister and maid of honor, to tell her it was her turn to speak.

Lainie refused. She looked up at Vanessa.

"I can't follow that."

Hunter now sat on the bed and finished with the watch strap. He then turned his hand back over. He looked at the second finger from the left. There would be a ring there in less than six months. It took three or four years longer than he had dreamt, but oh well, it was certainly worth it.

Like Will, he was introduced to her in a way. Hunter accompanied a friend, Nicholas, to a street festival and met up with Riley and two of her friends. Riley had just moved to the area after taking a ballet instructor's job, and moving in with Nick's sister, Mariah. After 30 minutes, it was obvious that Riley had eyes for Hunter. He'd fallen hard for Riley, but couldn't get a read on her. No other girl had that effect on him and he assumed she just thought he was nice.

Almost a month went by and Hunter was going to be passing through. He decided to give it a shot. He asked Nick for her number and called her out of nowhere.

"Hello."

"Is Riley there?"

Her head shot upward as she recognized the voice. "This is she." Her back straightened, she drug her teeth over her bottom lip.

"Hi, this is Hunter. I came down with Nick a couple of weeks ago."

Riley pulled the phone away and covered her mouth. Then brought it back, "Yes I remember you. How are you?"

"I'm good, I'm good. Listen if it's okay, I um, was going to be passing through town in a couple hours and was wondering if I could stop by?" He paused. "Maybe grab something to eat, a cup of coffee?"

Riley ran her free hand through her hair. She looked up at the clock above the back door. *I have to wait a couple hours?*

"Sure that would be fine." 'Fine' almost come out in a high-pitched voice she was trying to hide.

"Great. I guess I'll be there around 4ish?"

"Okay sounds good. I'll be here."

Hunter was happy, but couldn't get a feel from her voice or answers. He then assumed it would just be a friendly occasion.

Upon hanging up, Riley ran both hands through her hair and stood up while a quick little scream left her mouth in a burst. Behind her on the couch, Kevin had just started on his beer. He leaned back and rested his beer on his leg, a small wet ring on his jeans. He stopped by to hang out, continuing to hope that after three months that they would become more than friends.

"So I guess this means I need to leave?" He said with a smile, half-funny, half-serious. He was expecting a funny reply back from Riley. He didn't get it.

"Uh, yes."

That was all she said. Just then, Mariah bounced down the stairs and once she reached the bottom banister, swung around it and found Riley.

"Are you okay?" She asked worried, but then relaxed and smiled after seeing the look on Riley's face.

The girls began talking and Kevin was shell-shocked. *Wait, that's it?*

He put his beer down on the coffee table and walked over to grab his keys. He then looked back to Riley hoping for a life vest. He wanted a wave, a smile, a comment, something. All he got was, 'Oh, I'll talk to you later'. She didn't even move his way. She just stood there talking to Mariah. *Who the hell is this guy?* Kevin left and cursed the person on the other end of the line.

Upon getting a tour of the two-story apartment, Hunter knew this was more than just a friendly meeting, and would lead to storybook feelings. As they were leaving, Mariah smiled and said have fun from the chair by the door. That's when Hunter knew for sure. He could see it in Mariah's face. He had been the center of their conversation from the time he had hung up, to knocking on the door seven minutes ago. He was the reason her room was a mess, with clothes all over the place, as she tried on six different outfits like a schoolgirl. After all, she had to find just the right one.

On a cool October Thursday, under a cloudless blue sky so rich that planes were diverted, they walked seven blocks to a street lined with trees and brick sidewalks. Store and restaurant windows spilled their light down on the brick, as Hunter and Riley floated on the bricks. The leaves had all fallen, now brown, yellow, orange and dead. All they had left was one last crunch as they got in the way of everyone strolling by.

They walked into *Sparky's* and their table was in the front, up against one of those windows. As they slid into the booth on opposite sides, they instinctively placed their keys at the end of the table, up against the window. Their key chains were similar. They were nothing special, even considered cheap. You could find them in one of those stands in the middle of the mall, with flags, stickers, t-shirts, and other tacky trinkets of countries from around the world. Both keychains had flags on them. Hers was Austrian, his was Irish. Hunter noticed it and smiled.

"Nice key chain."

Riley saw his and returned the smile. "Oh my god that's crazy." She looked at him. "Why Ireland?" She leaned on the table towards him.

"Was there two years ago. Wandered around for a week aimlessly. Played golf too. It was wonderful." He shrugged, "And I'm-"

"Irish," she finished for him.

He smiled, then matched her lean. "Why Austria?"

"I was there a couple years ago with a ballet company. Spent a week in Vienna, Linz, and Salzburg. It was breathtaking."

Two minutes later, between a roommate's facial expression and two cheap $4.95 key chains, Hunter realized he was ordering beers for himself and his future wife. It turned out to be just that simple. That this would be their first drink together, their first street stroll, their first talk together. The restaurant, day, and beer would be the answers to their very own private trivia questions years later.

Hunter slid into his flip flops and stood up to loop his belt on. He snatched his money clip and keys from in front of him and exited the room.

He bounded down the steps and emerged into the bright living room. There were no lights on and the sun wasn't directly streaming through any of the windows, yet it had a bright cheery feel. The light wood floor, white furniture, and light blue walls gave off a Key West feel, and was right at home with the palm trees outside through the double panes.

Hunter pushed open the front door and swung it closed behind him as he walked down the six steps to the driveway. He reached into his pocket and his thumb found the small button. His six-year-old Volvo beeped twice and locks thumped open. He then stopped and looked around, almost in embarrassment as the alarm sound interrupted nature. He was fairly certain if someone was walking by the house just then, they would stop and stare in disbelief.

He worked his way around to the trunk and popped it open. He pulled out his golf bag and a small black bag holding his shoes. He closed the trunk and walked his clubs over near the garage.

He reached into his pocket and pulled out his Nokia phone. With one hand outstretched against the house, his other flipped open the phone and he swiped through any missed calls. Will emerged out of the shadows of the garage, walked around his black BMW, and opened the trunk.

"Put your sticks in." Will pushed his bag farther back to make room for Hunter's.

"You get a new bag?" Hunter asked Will as he leaned down to place his in front of Will's.

"Yeah, finally had to break down and get one. I'd had that old one since college."

"It looks brand new."

"Just got it a month ago. Took it on a business trip to Philly last week. First time I used it"

Will handed Hunter a plastic cup with something yellowish in it.

"Here, see if that is strong enough."

The trunk slammed closed as Hunter took a sip and looked around in the garage.

He nodded. "Yep."

Will tilted his own into his mouth and swallowed. He was gazing out onto the street now.

"I love yoga pants."

Hunter took another sip while looking at Will, then leaned to the left to peer around Will. Two women in yoga pants were walking past, chatting about something with little weights swinging in their hands.

Hunter brought his drink up. "If you're into that," he said between sips.

"Right. I have to look away." Will put his hand on his hip and looked at Hunter. "Good drink huh?"

Hunter smiled. Will always took pleasure in making drinks despite the fact he couldn't make good ones. They were just really strong. Hunter usually didn't mind that. He held it in front of him looking at the cup.

"Always." He twisted it around reading it. "I like the cup better."

"I knew you would."

The late morning screwdrivers were in green plastic Master's cups. Will had some stacked above the fridge. In one of the many Augusta traditions, as you buy beers you save the cups, stacking them in one another throughout the day. Will had been to The Masters six times. Each time getting badges from clients or friends who couldn't use theirs.

In his inaugural trip, Will the rookie, finished his first beer behind the grandstands on the twelfth tee. The botanical garden off the thirteenth was off to their right. The Bermuda Triangle of a pond at 11 was to their left. He looked at a trashcan and then shook his head.

"I just can't throw it away, but I guess I have to huh?" He looked at the two guys he was with, assuming he'd just eventually save the last one.

Robert, who along with the other guy went every year like a rite of passage, grinned and with the back of his hand, slapped Will's chest.

"Of course you don't." He then pointed over Will's shoulder behind him. "That's what you do."

Will twisted around. Three guys behind him were walking past, each drinking their third beer. You could tell it was their third because the fresh one was stacked inside the first two. Will smiled and gladly held onto it.

"You aren't keeping yours?" Will looked up at his client.

"Nah, we have enough."

Will couldn't believe someone would say that, not treasuring every little thing about this place, every time you set foot on it. Of course, seven years later and on his fourth visit to the green hills and ski slopes of Augusta National, he found himself saying the same thing. He knew between work and golfers he knew, he would come back again. That was one of the differences between Will and Hunter. Hunter could come to Augusta every year and still walk out with five or six plastic cups. It wasn't in his DNA to throw one out, no matter how many times he would return.

Standing on the gravel of Will's driveway, Hunter rubbed his thumb over the famous circled flag of the Masters logo, swiping away tiny droplets of moisture that had collected on the side. *Someday,* he promised to himself.

The driver and passenger doors closed almost simultaneously as they sunk into the tan leather seats. Will set his drink in the cup holder behind the gearshift and plugged his phone into the cord. He then twisted around in his seat to back out. Hunter took a sip and held out his cup in front of him towards the garage, now disappearing behind the door lowering as they backed out.

"Where are your tools?"

Will faced forward as his right hand grabbed the gear knob, pulling it down two slots. The BMW moved forward and swung around a Sable Palm crunching gravel. Hunter slipped on his sunglasses.

"I don't do home improvement." Will looked off to his left down the street and turned right. His right hand left the wheel and found his drink.

"This is the only screwdriver I need." He swallowed a gulp and began chewing on an ice cube. "I have a few I guess."

Hunter shook his head. "That garage is begging for tools on the walls."

"You should see the guy's down the street. Greg. He has every tool ever made. I've never been in his garage and there isn't sawdust or wires all over the floor." The car braked at a stop sign and then swung around to the right as Will pressed the pedal down. The German machine accelerated under the canopy of oaks.

"He built a boat in there for Christ's sake. And he lets me borrow anything I need." Hunter looked over at Will, then back out front. He desperately wanted to meet that guy. Just then, Will braked as they approached a man jogging on their side of the road. Will pulled up slowly and lowered Hunter's window. He leaned down to look out past Hunter.

"Uh, excuse me. Are those Bugle Boy jeans you're wearing?"

The man stopped, chest heaving, and put his hands on his hips.

"Why yes, yes they are Bugle Boy jeans."

Hunter grinned, remembering that old ad. The jogger leaned down, resting two sweaty hands on the door frame, smiling. "Do you ever work?"

"Yeah, working on my baby fade today."

He looked down at Hunter. "I've seen this guy passing three or four times in the last two weeks, all he does is play."

"Jud, this is Hunter, childhood friend. We're heading to Cougar and Turtle today."

Jud shook his head. "It's your world and we're all just jogging through it." He looked down at Hunter.

"Jud Strickland. Good to meet you."

"Yeah, same here. Hunter."

"You guys coming tomorrow night, right?" Will took a sip of his drink.

"Absolutely. Can I crash there?" He reached in for Will's cup. "Let's have a taste."

"If you're too drunk to stagger home next door, I guess so. I'd pay to see that."

"So would Lisa."

Both guys laughed. "I bet." Will looked out front, as a SUV passed him, going around.

"That's good." Jud handed the drink back to Will. "So how was Philadelphia?" Hunter was going to turn to Will, but stayed on Jud. The jokes and sarcasm were pulled away by the passing Escalade. There was a curiosity and envy in the question, mixed with a tease. Then there was Jud's face. The corner of his mouth, an eyebrow, his longing stare across the interior of the car. Hunter felt awkward all of a sudden.

"Oh not bad, cold."

Jud gave him a look. "I'm sure you stayed warm."

Will nodded and sipped his drink.

"Hey, we gotta run. Talk to you later."

"You bet. Hunter see you tomorrow night." He took off continuing down the road. Hunter glanced at Jud in the mirror on his door, who was shaking his head, then at Will next to him. There was something going on. He didn't feel awkward anymore. He felt confused and left out. *Stayed warm? Who says that?*

Will accelerated on, sipping more drink.

"He's a good guy, neighbor of ours. They'll be over tomorrow night. Lisa's his wife."

Hunter nodded, sipping his cup. "The more the merrier. Did you grab the cards?"

Will nodded. "Put them in my bag, along with Old Maid."

Hunter smiled and shook his head as he gazed out his window. Will steered the car through the twists and turns with his left hand as his right rested on the gear knob, two fingers rhythmically tapping it. The new Interpol CD, "Turn on Your Bright Lights" filled the car's interior and seeped out into the Kiawah Island air, tickling the hanging moss.

CHAPTER TEN

The weathered, shingled roof of the Ocean Course Clubhouse and salty windows banked the putting green to their left. Row after row of pushed white caps were to the right, rolling at them from as far as they could see. The Atlantic was raging from 25-30 mph winds. If there were clouds at sunrise, they were probably in Tennessee by now.

The winds were nonexistent Friday, and even on the exposed holes at Turtle Point, it was barely a breath. The Atlantic was a table. Today the wind was obnoxious. Blustery and bold out of the east-southeast. Will would have given up on wearing a hat, but the bright sun in an endless sky of blue would scorch a face today.

Hunter stood over his three Titleist Professional 90's, his putter shaft glistening the sunshine every few seconds, figuring out how much the wind would affect his putts. Will only practiced with one ball, like one of his idols, and his lone ball curved down a slope and into Hunter's three, scattering them like shuffleboard.

"Nice." Hunter's putter corralled one loose ball and brought it back in front of him. He leaned back over it.

"You still use those old things?" Will stood in front of him, crossing his feet and leaning on his putter. He was looking down at Hunter's ball and putter face. Then his eyes slid up to his hands and shoulders, watching Hunter putt. There were no moving parts in his stroke, it was one motion from shoulders to hands, to putter blade. Hunter was a good putter, maybe better than Will. Will could admit this, because as far as the other 13 clubs, Hunter trailed. If Will had Hunter's talent for putting, he'd have endorsements.

"What do you use now?"

"The Pro V1. They're new." Will followed Hunter's ball roll towards the white hole.

"Did those replace the Balata?"

"Yeah." Will then stood over his ball, hovering Scotty Cameron just behind his ball. "I'm going low today." Will oozed cockiness.

"You better. I didn't come all the way down here to see you shoot 73. By the way your ass looks awesome in those shorts."

"Thanks, I squeeze my ass cheeks together on my drive for more power."

Hunter grinned and strolled to his bag shaking his head.

Will joined him and they zipped away their golf balls. Will took off his watch. Hunter started spraying sunscreen on, when a cart motored over to them.

"Mr. Ramsey? Mr. Grace" An Ocean Course official was on a dark green gold cart with no top. It was longer than most, with a flatbed for golf bags in the rear. The Ocean Course's famous orange Palmetto tree logo on the side.

"Good morning gentleman. Your 10:05 tee time is ready. Have you played here before?"

Right before Will could answer; the man cocked his head to the left and pointed his clipboard up towards Will.

"Mr. Ramsey, you look familiar."

"Yes, I've played here several times."

"Outstanding, welcome back." They shook hands. He turned to Hunter, who was wiping his sunglasses.

"My first time."

"Well welcome Mr. Grace, you won't forget it. Henry here will see that you two make your way around."

The caddie moved around the cart and shook hands. He then grabbed both bags and laid them on the back. The first tee is far from the clubhouse, and the 50-second ride through seagrass and dunes, and even what appears like a swamp to the left, allows for more introductions.

"Will, where are you from? Close by I presume." Henry turned, resting his elbow on the seat's back cushion. Some of his black hair now pushed in front of his glasses.

"Just up the road actually, maybe a mile or so."

"Very nice. Hunter, what about you?"

"Charlotte. Moving to Raleigh soon."

"Ahh, been to both many times. Hunter you are in for a treat today. Especially with the winds." That last comment came with a grin.

Hunter glanced over at Will. "Yeah, fancy that."

Will rolled his eyes. "Yeah, yeah."

They reached the first tee, perched up from the sandy path like a dome. It would be a recurring theme.

Henry checked their bags, clubs, and balls they were playing.

"Will, what do you play to?"

"Three or four."

"Hunter?"

"Better say 8. I've haven't played in three months."

Henry stood around the bronze tees. "How about here then, it's really a blend tee. This course plays a lot longer than the yardage shows. It will read sixty-four hundred for us, but will feel like sixty-eight or sixty-nine hundred. Especially in this wind."

Will nodded, knowing this to be true. He and Hunter stood on the tee, extending their fingers into their white gloves. They looked off down the first hole, which was blind somewhat. Will looked over at his childhood friend. "You ready?"

Hunter nodded.

Henry and Hunter watched Will waggle his 3-metal and then send his drive out toward his usual tree. The wind pushing on his speck of a ball, easing it down quicker than normal.

Will was awesome off the tee and Hunter forgot how much he hated following his drives all the time.

"Nice." He teed up his ball and took a couple steps back behind it. Henry was over his shoulder after taking Will's club, and used it to point with.

"Okay, see that tree?" Hunter followed the club and grip to it. It was farther right than he would have thought to aim.

"Uh, yes."

"That's your mark; you want to go where Will went."

But I never do. "Gotcha."

"You sure you want 3-metal in this wind?"

"Yeah, I can keep this down better than my driver."

Henry joined Will back by the bags, slipping the Demon Deacons head cover over his driver. Will's eyes were down on Hunter's ball, waiting for him to hit. Henry's usually is too, but only for 17 of the 18 holes. Not the first.

Caddies won't say they hate hacks, but they won't say they love them either. Most caddies can watch someone swing, even just address the ball, and know immediately what they're dealing with. There was no question about Will, he looked like Ernie Els. Henry now wondered about his partner, *Mister I haven't played in a while.* The common quote that can sum up any player, from scratch to a 23 handicap.

Hunter did keep the ball low out of the wind, 10 feet above the ground. It sliced off to the right, swerving out of bounds into either sand or a pond. Hunter chuckled out loud.

"Jesus Christ Hunter, are we going to put up with this all day?" Will made everyone laugh more. Henry, being the caddie he was, already had a ball ready in his palm out of sight. He'd been here before.

"Here you go, Ocean Course brunch ball!" Henry tossed him another Titleist 90. Henry took a deep, satisfying breath. Hunter's stance, take-away, and swing were good. It was just caked in rust.

"Hey Henry, where are the ladies' tees?" Will asked louder than normal. He enjoyed teasing Hunter on the golf course. Henry smiled and nodded. *Come on Hunter, relax and just swing.*

Hunter took a deep breath, his chest puffing out, then shrinking between his outstretched arms, swung. The ball curled out towards the tree in little low draw. Hunter's follow-through wrapping the club around his neck, with the club head pointing to the tree.

"There you go." Henry nodded and grabbed his argyle head cover. "Hey, relax buddy, your mother and girlfriend still love you no matter what your shoot out here."

Henry knew exactly what to say, how to say it, and when to say it. He also had everything needed for his players. The pockets of his caddie jump suit were an endless pit of necessary items. Hunter would joke it was like Mary Poppins' tote bag. Hunter thought about coughing and wanted to see if Henry would pull out a lozenge and toss it to him.

Hunter smiled and nodded.

Hunter walked back to put the club away, but Henry didn't let him.

"Here, I got it." Henry picked up both bags and slung them over his shoulder. Hunter shook his head.

"Henry, let me carry one."

"Hunter I do it all the time buddy," came with a smile.

"No, no really, I want to. I don't play that much anymore and when I do, I am herded onto a golf cart. I love walking and hearing them rattle and clink around." Hunter reached for the strap. "It's half the reason to play Henry."

Henry bit his lip, loving the response, but the proud caddie in him not wanting his players to carry a bag on one of the longest walks in golf. Will stepped in.

"Hey, how about nine holes, then I'll carry mine on the back."

Henry gave in. "Okay."

Hunter double-strapped his old black Ping bag behind him, and headed off with Will and Henry.

Hunter was amazed, like any first time golfer here, how the course was half beach half marsh. Sand was everywhere. Hunter thought the palm trees had to be fake, sticking out of the sand like cake decorations.

They stepped off the perched up tee and walked 50 yards through sand to the fairway, also perched up. Three wooden steps lead them up to the fairway, a long, narrow green island surround by a sea of white sand.

"Wow, I knew the greens were domed, but had no idea the fairways were too."

Will got up and down for par, Hunter carded a bogey. They both parred the second, a 500-yard par five with dissecting fairways that played twice as long into the stiff wind. Hunter was calmer though and the nerves were gone, blown away by the offshore wind and Henry's psychology lessons.

All three continued to talk golf, work, and their lives throughout the outward four holes leading away from the clubhouse, finally reaching the par 4 ninth. That's when the round would change, and it wasn't just their direction. It had nothing to do with golf or Pete Dye's course architecture.

Hunter understood his role with Will since the fourth grade. He was always handed his medal before Will. His trophy was smaller if he got one.

His AP tests were harder. And his girlfriends were pretty, just not mouth watering.

Even best friends can have this disparity. They are best friends because it doesn't get between them. Hunter had to learn this first, being the trailing one and the one with a hint of jealousy that came natural. It hit him in sophomore year of high school where Will placed Hunter in his life. It wasn't the number of times he got a phone call from Will; it was when he got the call.

Will didn't always call him first when going out, getting Master's badges, or scoring tickets to some events at the Atlanta Olympics. Hunter wasn't always the first to hear about the new girl while getting ice cream outside the theater, or to get a note passed to him in class about a party. Hunter did get the first call when Will got into Wake, when he got engaged to Heather, and when his father was dying in front of him at hospice. Will only reached out to him in times of integrity.

Hunter knew his place in their relationship, and his best man speech was not made up, but legit. Everything did come easy to Will, it always worked out for Will. Will had the cream of the crop in most things, and Hunter often wondered what it would be like to be in his shoes. He wasn't always the most popular choice of audience for Will, but the most worthy one. That's why on the ninth tee box, it all made sense and didn't at the same time.

"Okay girls," Henry propped up Will's bag on the tee box. He flung the towel off his shoulder and started wiping Will's Pro V1 to a shinny white.

"Long par 4 with help from the wind though. It doglegs left. Aim at the bunker." Henry's extended arm lead their eyes to a large white bunker that looked to be in the middle of the fairway. It really was at the bend of the dogleg. It looked closer than it was. Henry handed Will the driver and its cleaned mate. Will, of course, had honor.

"Will we reach it?" Will wondered and turned to both of them. Henry had heard that question for years, day in, day out. He then replied with the same answer for all those mornings and afternoons.

"If you put it in that bunker, drinks and lunch are on me."

Hunter nodded. "Let me guess, you've never had to."

Henry shook his head. Then glanced at Will knowing with the wind and his length, he had a slight chance.

"One guy would have, but it drew slightly and curled at the dogleg. He's playing over on the European Tour right now."

Hunter pulled out his glove from his left pocket, then reached into his right for a tee. *Come on Will, reach it.*

There was no tee. He checked his bag. Not there either

"Shit. Will, I need a tee."

"Yeah, side zipper buddy. Henry is there more room up to the left?"

Henry pointed. "Yes. Aim at the bunker, but left of it is perfect."

Hunter squatted down and unzipped the pocket on Will's new Titleist bag. The wrong pocket.

The first thing he felt was the Eastern cards. He pulled out the small box and flipped it around looking at it. He knew his father flew out of Charlotte sometimes with them, possibly flew right over Kiawah on his way down the coast to Miami. He flew to Atlanta more often and knew two stewardesses by first name, one more than other. She knew about Hunter as much as some aunts. *God, what was her name?*

He pushed the cards in with that questioning memory, then he found a scorecard, which is nothing odd. He pulled it out with curiosity and it was from Merion, the famous private club outside Philadelphia. The front had the iconic wicker basket flagstick logo, and Merion written above it. He flipped it over. Penciled in numbers stretched across the boxes. Hunter figured Will had a client or knew someone who was a member. *Lucky Bastard.*

Just before flipping it back over, he noticed some other numbers on the bottom. Two phone numbers. Hunter stared at them and just felt weird. The handwriting was slanting and uneven in color, with some strokes dark gray and thick, others thin, and light gray, almost wispy. The lead had been quickly scribbled across the card. *And what the hell is this doing in a golf bag?*

Hunter may not play much anymore, had lost some of the passion for the game, but he still knew the game. And he knew where Merion ranked on the "bucket list" of golf courses. Hunter probably had an old scorecard in his bag, but from Ballantyne, the Tradition, or Rocky River. Not Merion. Like Cypress Point, Shinnecock, Oakmont, and Augusta, a Merion scorecard isn't left wrinkling and creased in a golf bag. It's in a frame behind your desk, on the fridge, or in the liquor cabinet at home, that brings out a story while the ice is coated with the liquor of choice.

Hunter made a face and slid it back in, then pushed his fingers in deeper in the hope of being stabbed by pointy golf tees. He was stabbed all right, but he wasn't stabbed by wood in the fingers. It was steel in his heart. His eyebrows seem to push down his jaw as he pulled out a package of condoms.

"You get some?"

Hunter jumped slightly, teetering on his heels. Will was bending down and picking up his tee that somersaulted forward out of the ground. His drive floated down 15 feet in front of the bunker.

"Uh no, wrong pocket."

He shoved the condoms in quickly, mashed up against the Eastern deck. He leaned over, tried the other compartment, and pulled out four or five tees. He stood up and came from behind the bag. Henry held Will's driver, walking to Hunter's bag to grab his.

The scorecard, phone numbers, and condoms were like finding dead puppies. Hunter knew why they were there. Wives, Heather in this real life scenario, would never look in a golf bag.

Hunter staggered to his bag, almost drunk, hoping the gusty ocean wind would capture his thoughts and take them away like a lost kite. Henry handed him his driver and said something, but Hunter only heard wind. Laughing wind. Chills immersed him, like plunging through a hole in the ice. He pull-hooked his tee shot, his worst swing of the day. Henry shook his head wondering where that swing had come from. It came from a funeral. A death from ambush. The ninth hole just became his Trojan horse, and he brought it in the gates and opened it up all by himself.

Will of course birdied the hole, Hunter double-bogeyed. The hole was even following Hunter's new script. The same riding cart greeted them behind the green on the sandy path. All three hopped on, bouncing and swaying their way back to the clubhouse. Dust and sand kicked up in a cloudy trail. Just before crossing the tiny road leading to the 10th, they stopped at a small tent serving as the half-way-house. Drinks and food were available. Most was wrapped in plastic wrap, while hot dogs were wrapped up in aluminum foil.

Will whined like a 12 year-old. "I want a hamburg…no I want a cheeseburger, I want a hot dog, I want a milkshake."

"You'll get nothing and like it!" Henry snapped back at Will, playing along. The customary classic scene from *Caddyshack* was as common as the kegs being pumped.

"Henry what would you like?" Hunter bent over unzipping a side pocket and pulled out his money clip.

"Oh I'm fine."

"No you're not, come on, what do you want?"

Henry took a breath, "Well the hot dogs are really good."

"Done. Will?" Hunter didn't look at him, but at the cute girl working the tent, smiling at them. *Has he slept with you?*

Three hot dogs, two Heinekens, and a water were charged to Hunter's credit card. Hunter asked for scotch, but only beer was served out there. Will thanked Hunter and Hunter nodded, still refusing to look at him.

Henry can't drink alcohol on the course. Will slapped him on the back and told him they'd take care of that at the 19th hole. Henry turned to the girl serving.

"Trish, has Billy come through? Leave me something?" Henry screwed back on the cap to his water. Trisha was punching a cash machine.

"No Henry, but Alec and Greg are ahead of you and left this." Trisha handed him a ball marker that was as inside joke. Henry shook his head and gave it back.

"Throw that away immediately." Trish smiled and grabbed it, then thanked Hunter. The bubbly 20-year-old could sell beer to a Mormon.

They found the 10th tee. Henry took Hunter's bag, which was comforting with everything else on his shoulders. Henry did his customary Ryder Cup comment. Hunter looked down the fairway, laid out from the perched tee box like a rumply green carpet bordered by blue water. Million dollar palmetto homes lined the far side of the narrow pond. It may as well have been a lighted par 3 municipal course from back home. He had no desire to play golf anymore.

The inward nine was a daze. A daze of fuzzy images from a photo album, that the winds off the Atlantic flipped and turned so fast, it turned into a scary movie.

On the par 4 10th hole, he remembered the under-10 traveling soccer team's county semifinal. Dressed in orange and white like the teams from De Meer stadium, Hunter got by his marking midfielder and saw Will hovering in front of the off-sides trap. Will pointed, and then took off just as Hunter's instep curled the ball towards the top of the penalty area, where no one was. Yet.

The ball curled around one defender's outstretched leg in front of Hunter and slipped between two others as the sprinting center forward reached it in perfect timing. Will, alone on goal now, collected the pass, settled, and scored. As the bulging net came to rest and the ball was still spinning in the corner, Will raised his fist and turned towards the sideline. The ref's whistle blew 11 minute later. They won 2-1.

The coach hugged Hunter, praising his selflessness and touch. He passed on the chance to take on a defender and head to goal himself. Hunter may have passed on the opportunity, but he did pass the ball, which he feathered in perfectly from 20 yards to Will not breaking stride. The rest of the team, the girls U10 team that was there to watch, and an assistant converged on Will like he was Charlie Bucket holding the last Wonka Golden ticket.

The par 5 eleventh brought out Junior High. He was sitting in third period geometry passing yearbooks around. He was sitting on his desk with his feet in the chair, Melissa's yearbook in his lap. She was signing his and gave it back with a hug. They had known each other since fifth grade. She then huddled around Will two rows over, along with four others. Later in seventh period, world history, the other class they had together, they sat back to back. Will tossed his yearbook to Hunter over his shoulder.

"Hey scrotum, sign this."

Hunter was surprised. "Are you gay?" Boys didn't sign boy's yearbooks.

"Whatever, just do it dude." Hunter flipped through it, and flipped through it, and flipped through it. He couldn't find room. He finally found a page, the Clubs page along the border or margin. He wrote, *You Suck! From Hunter,* with a smile. While flipping though he noticed he was the only guy who had signed it. He had as many girls sign his, but the notes or messages were shorter. Will had no cliché yearbook quotes.

The par 4 twelfth fairway turned into Jessling Avenue, snaking its way along the quiet creek leaving the neighborhood and school behind. Hunter was in the backseat of Will's Jeep Cherokee, sandwiched between Molly and Jenna. Michelle, a cheerleader, was up front. They were headed to the mall after school. The topic of colleges came up. Michelle was headed to Appalachian State in Boone. The avid skier would never think of going east.

"So Hunter, are we the only ones going to Chapel Hill?" Jenna looked over at him, swinging her knee over into his.

"I guess so. Apparently it's not good enough for Big Man on Campus here?" Hunter tilted his head to see Will in the rearview mirror.

Michelle leaned into Hunter to catch the mirror too. "Will, did you hear from Georgetown?"

"Yeah. I'm in, but the scholarships at Wake and Vanderbilt are better. Georgetown and D.C. will be way too expensive."

"Hey," Michelle reached over touching his hand on the stick shift. "Are we still going to the movies?"

Will checked the lane next to them and changed lanes. "Yeah, definitely." Movies was the code word for the river and bluff, the popular hangout about 20 miles away. The brunette cheerleader wasn't going there to pep up a crowd, only the driver.

The par 4 thirteenth was the last hole with the wind, now close to 25 mph. The tee boxes are off to the right across the pond from the fairway. They were right up against the three story houses with the stunning views, including two alligators, one in the backyard of a light blue house. The occupants were on the top porch, which wrapped around the floor, leaning on the railing with pointing fingers.

Henry was out in the fairway, facing them, 250 yards away. He was trying to be a lightning rod. With Henry showing the aiming line, Will and Hunter were alone on the tee. It was awkward and normal at the same time. Of course, Will had honor and tried hitting a cut with the helping wind, but it stayed straight. The wind helped, but not as much as he would like. Henry turned to his right watching it land a foot into the rough.

Hunter pushed in his tee and ball, and like the last four holes, didn't bother looking for a target and took maybe two-seconds to swing. If it was the hurrying, seeing the alligators making him maybe lean back a little on his heels, or just luck, Hunter ripped his drive with a slight curl to the right. Will would call it a fade; Hunter would call a 15-foot slice. Hunter's eyes widened and stayed open. Henry looked up, then turned 180 degrees, and watched if sail over him. It landed 20 yards past him and bounced three more times before stopping 75 yards from the green. His wind pushed drive went 302 yards.

They reached the fairway and Henry was shaking his head. "You hit the hell out of that!"

"Hey Will, you're away." Hunter said it to Will walking over to his ball. He then turned to Henry.

"I've been waiting 31 years to say that." Henry smiled and slapped him on the shoulder, then propped up his bag. He swiped off the towel from his shoulder and headed over to Will.

From the peninsula tee box to his bag, Hunter thought about something he had done better than Will or had ever beat him in. It wasn't until halfway up the 13th that Hunter realized he never did until now. Leaning on his bag looking at the flag, he crossed his ankles and shook his head. He finally did something better than Will, and this was it. A longer drive that isn't on a scorecard, in a sport he didn't really care about much anymore. It seemed fitting. *I finally do it and this is it?*

The par 3 fourteenth, like the fifth, aims out to the ocean at the turn, before heading back to the clubhouse. The plateau green rises up 12 feet, with the rolling ocean in the background. The 165-yard shot is hard on a calm day, but today it was brutal. The winds were relentless, coming at them off the ocean at an angle.

Hitting from an elevated tee the same height as the domed green, it was like hitting from one castle turret to another, with arrows soaring at you. The flagstick was bending 30 degrees. The branches of the thick oaks behind them were swaying ripples of green waves. The sturdy trunks seemed to be the only thing that could care less. Will and Hunter missed, even laughing as their shots veered all over the place, leading to double bogeys.

They both leaned forward at times walking the last four holes, especially Henry. With the weight of a golf bag behind, and the wind pushing at them, if he stood up straight he would go right over backwards. All three shook hands on the 18th as Henry replaced the flagstick. He let go, and it instantly bent towards the clubhouse like a palm tree in Hugo.

For the last four holes back along the beach, into the wind, Hunter's thoughts weren't of Will. They were of Heather and Riley. At one point

Hunter was walking behind Will, following. He glanced down at Will's shadow angling off to the left. It was just a shadow, a boring common shadow now.

How the hell is she not good enough for you? You have everything, including my proud envy.

Heather is the wife of his best friend. She was like a sister in a way that he never had. They could talk, hug, dance, even kiss on the cheek, but it was chiseled out of friendship and love, not desire. Even after his chance meeting with the ballet instructor that would become his fiancé, he wouldn't lie that he had never wondered what it would be like to be married to Heather. He thought it was a guy thing. It was just something guys do, when their friend's wife is drop dead gorgeous.

And that was Heather. Beautiful. Even women looked at her twice and wouldn't get mad at their husbands after they do. She could make any hideous outfit look like a magazine cover. The former captain of the Arizona State dance team could wear her old uniform after just four months of giving birth. Both times. And she was no airhead either.

Hunter's eyes may stray to Heather, but his heart was pumped by Riley. Despite this, even he wondered: would he ever cheat on Riley? If Will cheats on Heather, where is the line drawn? Is it inevitable, just a given and natural thing now?

Will and Hunter tipped Henry generously, which was much deserved. Then the three ventured into the bar for drinks. Henry to celebrate a job well done in extreme conditions. Will to celebrate a round at the ocean course with his best friend. Hunter to try to figure out what to do with these Greek warriors now ransacking his walled fortress he swore was impenetrable. Helen wasn't kidnapped, just deceived.

CHAPTER ELEVEN

Cassandra.

That was her name. The stewardess on his father's Atlanta flights. Hunter rolled his eyes to the ceiling of the pro shop when it hit him. Thoughts of Heather and Riley finally were extinguished like a match in the winds on the 17th green. For some crazy reason, if it was a distraction from the recent findings or the playing cards, the mystery stewardess finally walked down the aisle to him.

"Hey, you should get something from here." Will pulled a golf shirt from the rack, eyed it, and hung it back up.

Hunter looked over at him startled. "Yeah. I will," he lied. Hunter bit his lip with a distaste of this place. He was still trying to figure out how to start the conversation with Will.

"I'm going to piss. I'll meet you in the bar. Henry should be there soon."

Hunter nodded. Then watched Will walk out. He surveyed the room. He wanted nothing, absolutely nothing from here. What he needed was a drink.

He slithered through the racks of clothes and tables of items for the bar. He glanced to his left and stopped in his tracks. A shelf of teddy bears clawed at his senses and emotions. They looked soft and furry. One was wearing a tiny knit sweater with the Kiawah Island logo and crest on it. As if hunting it, he seemed to slowly tip toe over to it. There were pink, light blue, and brown ones. The wall of kids' stuff had turtles, birds, and dolphins, animals you think of out here, along with beanie hats, and children's nature books. But the bear stood out. It had gun's crosshairs on it. He backed up, as if not wanting to disturb it, and headed for the bar.

Two steps out of the pro shop, Henry patted him on the back.

"Hey, you okay? You've been quieter."

Jesus he can read minds and greens. "Yeah fine, let's get that drink." Hunter then slapped his back, wondering how this bar scene would go.

Beer alone would not do.

With his foundation crumbling and left deserted, that began at the age of eight, Hunter came back to the round table, finally with his scotch. The whole bottle.

"Nice buddy." Will pointed to it as he found his chair. "Hey, I've got an 18 year-old from Scotland we can open up tonight. A Balvenie."

Of course you do. "Sounds good. Henry?" He poured a 'neat' in his tumbler and then held the bottle, hovering it over the caddie's glass. Henry gave in again. He poured, then poured Will's. He wished he could pour one for Cassandra.

"Hey go get the playing cards." He looked up at Will, who pushed back in the chair and nodded. "Wait and that Merion score card I saw. You didn't tell me you had played there?"

"Gotcha." Will walked out. Henry was turned in his chair talking to someone behind him. Everyone knew Henry. Hunter brought up his tumbler to his lips, inhaled the aroma, and sipped. The spreading burn down his throat, and tingling on his lips, he closed his eyes, and took a deep breath. He wondered where Cassandra was. He looked at the bottle in front of him on the table, and tipped back his tumbler for five-seconds. The burn was like gasoline.

His father joked that he had an affair monthly. His mother would play along, commenting, 'Well at least he did it at 30,000 feet and not around me'. By the fifth trip to Atlanta, they were real friends. By the 26th trip, she was another sister to him.

The story is that his father called home from a pay phone in the main terminal at Atlanta. He was just checking in on her, seeing if she was okay, and that his flight was on time. She then told him why she wasn't on time last month. The sentence came through the metal cord and into the phone with warmth, conduction in a way, and echoed in his head the entire train ride out to terminal C. The phrase that you always think about hearing, always plan on hearing, know you're going to hear, but never know how you will react to hearing it.

We're going to have a baby.

He was thrilled, scared, and nervous all at the same time.

Cassandra was the first person he told. She actually made him unbuckle and stand up in the aisle to hug him. She gave him a toy Eastern plane on his last flight before the due date. His father hung it up in the nursery. She saw through photos and stories, a boy grow up.

Will was back with the cards and tossed them to Hunter. Henry scooted up, sitting between them, and Will asked about Henry growing up in Charleston.

Hunter opened the box and pulled out the stack of cards. He started shuffling and did it slowly, wondering how many cards she had handed out over her lifetime. Where are her children now and how old are they? Is she still up there flying with someone else now?

Hunter shook his head and sat up straighter, as if he had just woken up. No matter what he was thinking, or trying to think about, his Trojan Horse had just galloped right into his head. It was a cancer. Would it ever leave him? He felt like it would be his Shingles, always residing just under the surface waiting, waiting to seep out and take over his body at any given time. But unlike Shingles, it wouldn't just surface once, but whenever it felt like.

Even with Henry right next to them, he wanted to look at Will and ask, *so how long have you been screwing around behind Heather's back?*

"What's the game boys?" Henry asked.

"I'm not the card player, he is. What will it be buddy?" Will raised his glass to Hunter.

"No gin with three of us. Hearts or poker?"

Will showed the scorecard. Henry had never played there, but knew people that did. They then talked about Pine Valley, close by in New Jersey. Hunter was studying the scorecard eventually, concerned with different numbers than Henry. About five minutes later, he excused himself to the bathroom. He just had to know.

Both numbers were 215 area codes. He called the first one. It was the Franklin Hotel at Independence Park in Philadelphia. The second was to the voice mail of someone named Arianna. He knew Will went there four or five times a year for business. He was obviously doing more than that.

He returned to the game and drinks. Despite the cards being up against the condoms for the last five hours in Will's bag, the cards eased him somewhat. They made him think of Cassandra, his father and mother, and the friendship an airline flight could make back in the day. Hunter wasn't sure when, but at some point during the third game, right about when he pulled a 9 of spades he knew Will was probably looking for, it finally hit him what he would be better at than Will.

At the same place he had found his Trojan Horse, he would take away another animal. This one more pleasant and hopeful. It came with a catch though; he was altering the common delivery. He wouldn't give it to his own baby or child someday, but he would give it to Riley. To a wife he would be faithful to, which would translate into parenthood, so she could give it their baby. It would be their first teddy bear. One day, when much older and they had probably forgotten all about it, they would find it tucked away somewhere, maybe in an attic, closet, or a chest.

Henry won in cards, with Hunter not far behind. Will did well for not having the card sense in his decisions and thoughts, but brought up the rear. They thanked Henry with strong, sturdy handshakes saved for those bound by memories. Will paid the tab.

"Hey, bring the car around; I'll meet you out there?" Hunter walked under the chandelier in the lobby, turning right.

"Yeah sure, where you headed?" Will was pushing his money clip into his pocket.

"Pro shop, gotta get something."

They had been back for an hour, just enough time to shower, change, and start drinking and grilling. Another couple from the street came over and Heather, with two of her friends, was on the way. There were already eleven people over, most from the Charleston area. From the street, every window was glowing with silhouettes of people moving about. The quiet street found five cars parked out on it with the driveway full.

"Mason, this is Hunter. We grew up together." Will handed Mason a drink and turned to Hunter.

"Hunter, great to meet you."

Hunter smiled, and took a sip of the 18 year-old Balvenie while they laughed. "Where do you live Mason?"

"Just around the corner. My wife is here someplace, Bess, I'll introduce you later."

"Sounds good." *Careful, Will may try and screw her out on the pier.* He then looked at Will. "This is good stuff." Hunter was determined to get pure drunk, still reeling from the day and thinking the fluids from the Scotland Highlands would find the cancer in his body and kill it. He also didn't know if he could bring it up.

They walked over to a group in mid conversation. Jud, from yesterday's odd meeting while jogging, was there with his wife Lisa and three others Hunter didn't know yet. One guy impressed him quickly.

"…if that's what you want. I'm telling you, our only hope is Rice running."

"Who?"

"Condoleezza Rice in '08. Hell, maybe even in two years."

"A woman huh?" Jud took a drink.

His wife Lisa elbowed him. "What's wrong with that?"

"Nothing pumpkin. She has my vote!" He smiled at her and raised his glass in a toast.

"Jud, we played Ocean today." Will clinked glasses with him.

"Whoa in these winds? That's crazy." Eyes shifted to Will.

They talked about the round that Hunter had already forgotten about. He had no desire to discuss golf. He smiled and nodded his head, but was able to slip over across the circle of people to the fellow Condi Rice fan.

"I'm Hunter by the way." He held out his hand.

They shook hands. "Hey Hunter, Edward. Came down from Charleston. How about you?"

"Moving to Raleigh-Chapel Hill area soon."

"Excellent." He took a sip. "So you've known Will forever huh?"

Hunter gulped a sip, realizing it was a super way to avoid talking about him.

"We were at the wedding, we never met you though. That was a fantastic speech man."

Hunter smiled, then changed topics. "So who do you think should be her VP?"

They chatted until Hunter finished his glass and headed off to refill it. Just as he pulled out the cork, the kitchen door next to him that led to the garage swung open. Heather strolled in, followed by two others toting leather overnight bags. Heather was in jeans and a sweater, with high heels tapping the hard wood floors.

"Hey Hunter, how was it?" She put some grocery bags on the counter and looked at him.

Well now that you mention it…

"Stunning." Hunter smiled at her. Half of him wanting to cry and hug her, the other half wanting to hug her and grab her ass, just to see what she'd do. And see what Will would do.

"Oh I'm so glad." She looked at her two friends. "Hey, put them in the family room for now, we'll move them later."

Heather introduced them to the room. Sabella and Heather went to college together and she was in town for a couple days to visit. She was engaged and her diamond was actually bigger than Heather's. She was a Heather clone, bubbly and outgoing, but with brown hair. Alexis knew Heather through Bella, and was much quieter. She had straight black hair to her shoulders and big brown eyes. Her eyes were not quiet however. From the moment introductions got tossed around the kitchen, her eyes stayed on Hunter. Bella noticed it immediately.

"Bella, here." Heather handed her a drink. "Try this for starters." They both drank. Heather then raised her glass to Hunter. "Bella, Hunter is engaged too. This April."

"Oh, spring wedding huh?" Bella held her glass in front of her with both hands. The rock of a diamond aimed at Hunter like a radiant tulip petal.

"Yes, we're hoping for some warm weather maybe?"

"Where at?"

"Outside Charlotte. How about you?" Hunter was on his third single-malt. It wasn't just his lips, but his whole face was tingling.

"New York, in May. May is beautiful in New York."

"Hunter was in our wedding, Will's best man." She looked at Bella then Hunter. "Will is returning the favor at theirs."

"That's so special, to…wait," Bella turned to Heather, then back to Hunter. A hand let go of her glass and reached out touching Hunter's arm. "That's right, that was you that gave that amazing toast."

Hunter nodded and loved feeling anyone touch him at that moment. He finished his drink. "Yes, my ten-minutes of fame."

"Thanks to him my own sister wouldn't give me a toast." Heather eyed him playfully.

"That's why Lainie never gave a speech?" Bella was surprised, just now realizing it.

"She was supposed to go after him, but didn't want to." Heather looked at Hunter. "Thanks."

"Anytime." They all laughed. Heather was then called over by someone in the living room. Bella took a step closer to Hunter.

"So that was a true story huh?" Her hand finally left Hunter's arm and returned to her glass in front of her. Her head was leaning towards Hunter with some hair slipping in the way.

"Yep. It happened." *When I looked up to him.* They continued talking and Hunter was trying to figure out if he should kick Will out from being his best man. His heart wanted to, but he would admit his brain said no. About this time, Alexis joined them and listened in, smiling at the story.

"Hunter, have you met Alexis?" Bella turned to her and moved some of Alexis's hair over her ear. She then grabbed Alexis's free hand. "Alexis, Hunter gave the best toast ever. He's known Will since they were," she looked at Hunter, "like 10 right?"

"Close enough." He reached out and shook Alexis's hand. "Hi Alexis."

"Hello." Alexis was not like either Heather or Sabella. She was younger, 24, and very quiet. She listened more than anything, and answered with her eyes. Big brown eyes that made the Balvenie go down faster.

Will refreshed all their drinks, and the three continued to talk about New York. Hunter had a cousin in the city.

Thirty minutes later Will, Jud, Hunter, and Mason, were playing spades with the Eastern cards at the table. Just behind them in the living room, Heather, Bella, Alexis, Lisa, and Bess, Mason's wife were scattered around talking and drinking. Everyone else was out back. John Mayer's, *Room for Squares* was blaring in the background and all sang to it. Hunter was getting drunker just smelling the scotch now. The fun atmosphere and his new cancer pushed away reason.

Hunter and Mason killed the neighbors in only 20 minutes. Everyone stood up to stretch to walk around. Bella and Lisa yelled from the couch that they wanted to play. Hunter waddled over to the bar area and began pouring more cancer treatment. Will joined him.

"How good is this shit?"

"It's awful."

"Everyone is hammered." Will then turned his back to the room and whispered to Hunter. "That Alexis girl is eyeing you big time."

"Yeah I noticed." He turned to casually look at the kitchen and noticed Alexis and Bella sitting next to each other on the couch talking. The two girls always seemed to be touching each other. Hunter then jumped in.

"Got any condoms?" His tone didn't match the context. It was asked as if it were nine hours ago.

Will laughed, nearly spitting out some drink. "Probably not."

Hunter pressed, the high school kid asking now, not the drunk card player. "What about the ones in your bag?" He turned to him. It was as if he was now sober for a minute.

"Oh those, yeah," Will laughed and turned around facing the counter. He fiddled with some bottles.

"That's a long story. We'll uh, talk tomorrow." Will's mannerism and calmness confirmed it for Hunter. He didn't blow it off or deny it; he just looked defeated for five-seconds and knew who was standing next to him. Hunter watched Will walk away to Heather and Lisa. They clinked glasses and jumped in singing "Back to You" with Bess and Mason and three others. He watched Heather, laughing, singing, and touching Will's arm. Her wavy thick hair swaying to the music. She then started dancing with Bess. Seeing Heather happy was awful. He couldn't explain why.

His now half-empty glass was taken out of his hand, snapping him out of his trance. He turned to see Alexis holding it and looking at him. She moved next to him.

"Hey, you okay?"

God no. "Sure."

She smiled and moved some hair over her ear. Hunter watched her, wondering where Bella was to do it for her. He looked down at his glass in her hand. She put it down and grabbed the Balvenie.

"I've never had this stuff. My father drinks scotch." She pulled the cork and smelled it.

"You may want to try it with ice."

"Nope." She filled his up with a smile, all the way to the top. "Let's share." She raised his, or their, glass and sipped. Hunter watched those brown eyes close and the rim of the glass touch her lips, tilting back. She sipped and licked her lips, then swallowed. Her hand came up to touch her upper chest, pressing down. Hunter just stared.

She opened her eyes. "It wasn't as bad as I thought it would be." She took another tiny sip. "Whoa, that's smooth."

Hunter just nodded, not knowing what to say.

"That's expensive isn't it?"

"Yep." He took the glass and sipped. She touched his sweater, plucking off a speck of lint or something. Her tan made her brown eyes stand out even more.

"You have an amazing tan." He looked her up and down.

"Thanks," came with a smile. And she grabbed his hand, held it up in the air, and twisted around once.

"My neighbor has a tanning bed in her flat. No tan lines." She continued holding his hand and turned to face the room. "Great Outdoors" was now being echoed and Bella called out for her spades partner.

"Oh, that's you Hunter." She shot a quick glance at him and pulled him over to the table. The sober high schooler talking to Will earlier was gone. The drunk card player with delicate, thin defenses and an aroused 24-year-old in his lap was back.

Hunter sat across from Bella, with Mason and Bess next to him. Alexis then sat in his lap, holding their drink on her leg. Heather was sitting in Will's lap in a pulled up chair to watch. Alexis was playfully swaying to the John Mayer song, enough to keep Hunter's spinning room full of potential energy.

Was this what Will felt like with Arianna? Or whomever else? Hunter knew to leave, wanted to get up and jump in the shower, but couldn't. His body wouldn't listen. It just succumbed to Alexis's body and eyes, and the mood of the bottom floor. The cancer treatment in the glass was helping with one thing, but hurting him in other areas. Ironic.

Four hands into the game, the crowd seemed to thin and slowly the house quieted. Soon after, Jud and Lisa left to head home next door. And the Balvenie bottle was empty, waiting for a model ship to be fitted into it. If Will pulled out another bottle, he'd be pouring liquid lobotomies.

Alexis would lean back into Hunter to see his hand. She even touched a jack of clubs as a hint to throw away. Hunter was impressed. Mason and his wife Bess won, by two points. Everyone hollered at the finally finished hand.

Before Hunter knew it, people started departing. Time was flying. He felt like it was just an hour ago that they had gotten back from the clubhouse. Mason and Bess were now gone to hugs and slaps on the back. Then Will and Heather just disappeared upstairs. Even Bella made a comment that the noise just vanished without a vote.

Hunter walked out to the back yard, half way down the pier. He spent 10 minutes with his own thoughts. Part of him didn't want to go inside, but the wobbly pier, thanks to a bottle, not engineering, sent him back in.

The stovetop light and a standing lamp in the living room, that's on a timer, were giving off just enough light to creep around. Hunter was rummaging through the fridge looking for some water, something safe and cleansing to try to convince his stomach to settle down. He was going to try to get into his room upstairs and lock the door. He knew the girls' bags were in smaller guest rooms on the first floor. Bella headed off in that way, stumbling into the smaller bathroom in her room to wash up.

Hunter found some water and guzzled it as if it was scooped up from an oasis. He grabbed another bottle and pulled the left door of the huge fridge closed. Even before it thumped shut, it made way for Alexis to take two more steps towards him. Hunter froze. She was wearing nothing, not even tan lines like she had said. The room may have still been spinning, but they weren't. It was like they were in the middle of the merry-go-round with people and galloping horses encircling them constantly.

He dropped the water bottle, rolling off somewhere. She wrapped her arms around his neck. Her big brown eyes said hi. Every inch of skin said yes. His whole body swelled and was on fire. She stood up on tiptoes and kissed him, then planted a kiss on his cheek.

"Can I see your room?"

Hunter couldn't speak. He was cursing Heather now, for leaving without a trace. She was his defense he thought. She would say something that his conscience would hear, while ignoring Will. He needed that big sister. He needed help.

Her hands let go behind his neck, a smooth palm touched his face and then slid down grabbing his hand. She guided him up the kitchen stairs. Hunter just gawked at the 24 year old's naked body up and down, as she strutted up the steps in front of him. The carpet upstairs was the most glorious he had ever felt.

They stepping into his room and she looked around. “Oh there is so much more room up here. I like it,” she whispered as she ran a fingernail across the smooth bedspread. Then turned to him and began unbuckling his belt, pulling it through the loops. Hunter played with her hair while trying to picture Cassandra.

He tried picturing Riley at the fridge, but couldn’t stop the merry-go-round. Heather, his father and mother weren’t able to be seen on the stairs either. The once proud stewardess was his last hope, but she must have been stuck in first class.

She was pulling off his sweater and then starting to untuck his t-shirt.

“So you ready to spend your whole life with one person in bed huh? The same body for life? Like Bella?”

Hunter sighed and gulped a breath. He had to get out of the room. His heart said to stop all this. His brain would say to simply pause it.

“I’ll be right back.” He stepped away, walking backwards not able to take his eyes off her. “Let me go to the bathroom real quick.”

“Well hurry.” She sat on the bed and leaned back on her straight arms, legs scissoring up and down slowly.

“We have a lot to do before sunrise.” She tilted her head to the left and opened her thighs slightly.

Hunter closed his eyes and bit his lip. Then he bumped into the doorframe while backing out, eyes still locked on her. He turned and headed to the bathroom down the hall. He used the balcony railing to guide him and glanced down into the dim living room. He found the bathroom and took what felt like a 20-minute piss. He splashed water on his face that didn’t help. He couldn’t bring himself to look in the mirror.

The only thing between him and his room of ecstasy was himself. He didn’t think it was going to be enough to stop him. There was no ring on his finger yet; could he pull off that argument with his conscience?

Hunter opened the bathroom door and closed it, but still steered by the scotch and mush for senses, he didn’t go back down the hall. Instead, he looked to his right and saw into an open bedroom of gray shadows. He staggered in that direction and found himself leaning against the doorframe of Colleen’s room, the youngest Ramsey. Butterflies were hanging down by fishing line. He bumped into one of them. A giant giraffe was in the corner, his ears tickling the glowing stars on the ceiling. And a dollhouse was to his left, the open side facing out with a table setting still set from Halloween.

Hunter looked around the child's room. The ringing was still in his head, but the merry-go-round had been shut off. The small bed was covered with stuffed animals. Every animal species in the Audubon book was represented. A teddy bear's head was sticking out between an otter and a penguin. Hunter then thought about Riley's teddy bear down in the garage, in a bag next to his golf bag. Didn't he swear to beat Will in something about five hours ago?

He shut his eyes and stood in the four year old's room, still swaying slightly from the scotch and Alexis's caresses and kiss. He knew deep down, no matter how righteous he is, no matter how much integrity he has, and how much he adores Riley, that he would look back and regret not going back into his room. This would never present itself to him again.

He closed the door and locked it. He took a deep breath and curled up on the floor under the window. With two pillows and a four-foot panda cushioning him, Hunter was out in 11 seconds.

About five-minutes later Alexis assumed Hunter passed out in the bathroom, especially with the bathroom door closed, and reluctantly headed downstairs. The night-lights lit her way along the balcony and down the stairs, as the naked 24-year-old found Bella's room, not her room, on the other side of the house.

The next morning, Hunter woke to a car horn blaring in his head. His eyes wouldn't even open all the way. He wanted out of the house, and his body, in a bad way. He didn't want to deal with Alexis, Will, Heather, and even his reflection in the mirror, microwave oven, and windows.

It was about 7am and no one would be up for another two hours. He didn't even bother changing, just splashed water on his face. His mouth tasted like wet fur. His eyebrows seemed to be swelling. He grabbed his stuff out of his room, and headed downstairs. He gulped some pulpy orange juice right out of the carton, then grabbed a water bottle. He closed the fridge door and glanced across the bottom floor to the far hallway. The girls' rooms were there and Hunter eyed the door, knowing what he had turned down on the other side. His eyes then rolled up to the ceiling and figuring the master bedroom was just above those guest rooms. Hunter also remembered the ninth hole.

While walking out, he hastily scooped up the Eastern cards and shoved them in the box, some forwards and backwards. They didn't deserve them. He loaded the clubs and bags in his car. He pushed the garage door button by the door, then pranced out, leaping over the invisible beam. The garage door and driver's door seem to close at the same time. Before heading home, he had a quick stop to make.

Even at 7:25 there were some early groups teeing off at the Ocean Course. He parked and headed into the main lobby. He was thinking about going into the pro shop when an older gentleman called out to him.

"May I help you?" The man's voice was calm and low, but to Hunter he was yodeling in the Alps. Hunter brought up a hand to his forehead.

"Yes, this deck of playing cards is for Henry, the caddie." Hunter held them out with the other hand. "I don't know if he's here, but I was going to leave them with him."

"Oh, no problem. I'll see that he gets them young man." His white stubble on his chin and face even looked weathered and salt stained.

"Thank you."

Hunter waddled down the curvy driveway from the clubhouse and found his car. A bank of clouds muffled the rising sun like a scarf, making it easy on the eyes for the moment. His old Volvo cranked up and left the Ocean Course, Governor's Drive, and Kiawah Island behind once and for all. Hiding behind his sunglasses, the sun would remain behind him driving home. The teddy bear riding in the passenger seat would keep him company. Whenever dirty thoughts of Alexis and the temptation of Bella caressed his principles, the bear just stared at him. Nothing needed to be said. A look was enough.

If his Trojan Horse cursed his past, the teddy bear honored his future.

"Cassandra. Cassandra Grace." Hunter announced to the car and looked over at the bear next to him.

"If it's a girl someday, that will be the name." The teddy bear rocked back and forth a little, as Hunter took a turn and hit some bumps over a bridge. He took it as an approving nod. He looked back out front.

"Yeah, Cassie for short."

Henry would get the cards the next day. He remembered them and smiled at them in his palm. For eight months, they would stay with the caddies in their lair downstairs. The cards pulled out some money from wallets, memories from the past, and laughs from the heart. Just before finding their way up to the bar, Henry took the cards home for two weeks. They even accompanied him on his buddy's Beneteau 57, while sailing to Bermuda and back.

Eventually, the clubhouse bar upstairs would call the cards home. For the next five years, they were for anyone to use and enjoy. Henry would call on them once in a while, fanning out history in his hands on every draw. The shifting and shuffling of the cards in his hands was like picking out different memories, golf shots, and jokes to share. At the end of the day, it was a privilege to walk these fairways. A privilege to meet so many people from so many places, and be the glue that binds new friendships made on the first tee. It's a privilege to feel sorry for people who worked in a cubicle. And it's a privilege to be able to walk off every single crumb, every single calorie, of every sumptuous dessert he had splurged on the evening before.

From November 2002 to April 2007……

19 games of Blackjack
2 games of Canasta
7 games of Cincinnati Poker
2 games of Contract Bridge
5 games of Crazy Eights
37 games of Five-Card Draw Poker
23 games of Gin
34 games of Hearts
12 games of Klondike Solitaire
6 games of Michigan
1 game of Oklahoma Gin
3 games of Pinochle
1 game of Pyramid Solitaire
46 games of Spades
4 games of Spit in the Ocean Poker

PART V

In Utero

Siamese Dream

Enter the Wu Tang

Vs

Pablo Honey

CHAPTER TWELVE

The high beams lit up the trees, walling up the road to the stars. The rental seemed to follow the runway of trees as much as the snowy pavement. The forest sliding by like a trench, seemed as lonely as the interior. The only other thing she saw on County Road 9 casted against the Balsam Firs, were deer like wooden props.

Ava eased off the pedal as a curve approached. The 21-year-old from Connecticut had never driven in mountains before, let alone slick with fresh snow. The turning SUV sent Perry leaning towards her slightly. He claimed to be too tired to drive, despite knowing the geography.

The forest thinned as they began rounding the lake and the town of Frisco approached. Glowing windows started dotting the hills here and there, as the lights flickered between the passing trees. Soon shops and rustic buildings popped up under the glow of streetlights, as the popular town began taking up the views. Blinking stoplights ultimately turned into changing ones. The town was more famous for what was around it than what was in it. With Vail, Copper Mountain, Breckenridge, Keystone, and Arapahoe Basin all within 45 minutes, the quaint town was a gathering spot for skiers and outdoor adventurers.

For the first time since leaving the airport, on the other side of Denver, a hand let go of the wheel as she softly slapped his left shoulder.

"Hey get up, we're there."

A second later, both hands were back on the wheel. Fingers wrapped around the leather. The SUV slowed to their first red light. Perry sat up rubbing his eyes and pulled on the seatbelt around the side of his neck. Ava slid a strand of her hair over her ear as she looked over at him.

"Do you have the directions? We have to be close, I remember Michelle saying it was close once it changed names to Summit Blvd."

"Why are we coming in this way? Did you get lost?"

"No, we had to come in a back way. Parts of I-70 were closed." She glared over at him. Then back out front as the green light lit up the frosty windshield.

"Oh that's right. Sorry." He looked over at her, then a building through her window. "Huh, that's new."

"When is the last time you all were here?"

"Two years ago. We went to Tahoe last spring."

Ava nodded, *oh yeah, when I actually wanted to come but wasn't invited.*

Perry sat up a little. "Make a left at the second light, the one that just turned red."

The house was three turns past the light, on a slight hill surrounded by trees. A small pond was between it and the neighbors. The 4,200 square foot, three-story house, was made of light colored stone and dark wood, with balconies on all sides, and bay windows. It could have been on the Frisco Chamber of Commerce pamphlet and *Architectural Digest.*

The driveway angled to the side of the house with three single car garages. Ava pulled up behind a Ford Explorer and parked, slushing to a stop. She exhaled and pushed the gearshift up into park. Something she had been looking forward to since turning the key at Hertz.

"Come on, we'll get the bags later." Perry wrapped his scarf around his neck and waited for her to come around the hood. They headed around to the front doors and the warmth of the glowing interior.

They were the last to arrive. The other four couples were already onto their third and fourth drinks. They all greeted them and the girls hugged Ava. Eric looked at Perry.

"How was the drive?"

Perry shook his head. "Long, but not too bad. Glad to be here."

Ava stopped in mid-sentence with Michelle, and slowly turned to Perry. She just stared at him.

"Ava it's so good to see you again." Lara came into the foyer. "We're so glad you could make it." They hugged.

Thanks to my goddamn driving. "Oh I wouldn't miss it," came the lie.

"Come on Perry, let's get your stuff." His cousin slapped him on the back as he pulled out his jacket from the coat closet.

Ava met everyone else and was lead into the kitchen. Some she had seen last week at school, some not since summer or even longer. *August and*

Everything After, was playing in the background. She nodded her head to the beat as she was handed her drink. While pretending to listen to most of the people, she wondered how she would make it through the week without a drink in her hand. 40 minutes later, she was unpacking before going to bed. The exhausted junior would sleep well, falling asleep immediately. As for the next five nights, she would stare at the ceiling when not looking at the digital clock. The best part of her day was around 6:00am, when no one else was up and she had her coffee in the kitchen nook all to herself. She looked forward to getting up early, which says a lot for a college junior who relished sleeping in.

The next day found them at Copper Mountain, slithering down green, blue, and for a couple, black runs. Ava had just picked up skiing a year ago and liked it. Within three days of that initial trip, she was navigating the blues with only one fall, if any. She was a natural.

Perry wouldn't know, he was racing down blacks with his cousin Kyle, and Eric. They played the macho role of handling the toughest runs. Over the holidays, Kyle took a job as a ski instructor at Stowe Mountain, near his hometown in Vermont. He played mouse to the cats that chased him down the hills. This mouse got away every time.

The only two kids sticking to the greens were Michelle and Ava. Ava was more than capable of handling the blues, but Michelle was one of the few she liked, and sacrificed a challenge for fun. She even fell at times on purpose to laugh and roll around with Michelle in powdery snow.

All 10 kids met up around 4:30 at the base of the lift, skies held vertically in one hand and gloves in the other. Like the day before, the sky was clear and bright, with pink, rosy faces claiming them all. Kyle, Lara, and Shane were the first ones there and got the first round of beers. As each skier made it down, they pulled out their bottle from the snow. The perfect cooler.

By 6pm, everyone was back in Frisco showering and slipping into jeans and sweats. Kyle was not only the best skier in the house, but the best cook, which got him the job as chef. It took four boxes of Barilla spaghetti, but Kyle was finally happy with the thickness in the boiling pot.

The huge kitchen's island had three bottles of red wine open, a bottle of scotch, and nine empty beer bottles. Half the household mingled in there, with the kitchen about the size of most of their apartments back at school. The other half was out in the living room in front of the massive floor to ceiling stone fireplace. A thick white rug covered most of the hard wood floor.

"Elderly Woman behind the Counter in a Small Town," was playing, piped into the room by Bose speakers mounted in the ceiling's corners. The stereo's five-disc CD carousel was playing Pearl Jam, Soul Asylum, Stone Temple Pilots, Eric Clapton, and REM.

Perry, Shane, and Michelle all attended Brown, with their significant others. Eric and his girlfriend, Lara, went to Amherst. Lara's sister, Emily, went to the University of Vermont with Kyle. If there was a family tree to organize college friends, they were all on the same branch, but different forking limbs. And the trunk of the tree came from rich soil.

None of the kids had worked a day in their lives, other than as a ski instructor or a lifeguard at a summer camp in northern Maine. Kyle and Lara at least could claim they had earned a paycheck at some point in their young lives. As far as the others, their checking accounts got deposits from their mother's driving through the teller in their Humvees and Range Rovers. In five days' time, it would make more sense to them to just leave and take a penalty fee, than clean up and gather all the sheets and towels for the cleaning crew between bookings.

By the time Kyle's meal was ready, two wine bottles were empty and everyone had gathered around the large oak dining table. Small conversations broke out between a larger one that had started off about the day's skiing. Soon it revolved around March Madness. Most concluded that Indiana was the best team, but even with their scary depth, could they win without hurt center Alan Henderson?

"I could watch Calbert Channey shoot a basketball all day." Shane said while raising his glass.

Finally, the recent election took over the room. Four of them voted for Bill Clinton, six for Bush. Most opinions and thoughts came from their parents and professors. Only Ava had an original point from her own brain. Michelle shot a glance over at her and her eyes darted everywhere as she thought about it. Just as it was making sense, her boyfriend Marcus spoke up and she looked over at him, grabbing his hand on the table.

The girls did the dishes and cleaned up while sipping more wine, as if programmed or practicing for their future roles within six or seven years. They all knew deep down inside their future lawyer and finance boyfriends were prepping for their roles too. Ava dropped a dish on purpose just to get a rise out of someone, but no one cared. Perry finally spoke to her, the first time since lunch.

"We need to cut you off?" Everyone laughed. Ava just tipped back her wine, appreciating the flavor of the $80 bottle.

Perry then headed into the living room as the fire simmered and popped occasionally. Kyle was searching a cabinet full of games. He pulled out Backgammon and Clue, both in weathered boxes with worn edges.

"There aren't any cards? They have to have some somewhere?" Kyle was squatting down looking in the back of the cabinet, which was under a shelf and bookcase. He closed the two doors and stood up, bringing Clue over. Perry found his seat again when he slapped the leather chair.

"Hey, I brought some." He leaned his head back as if that would help his voice get into the kitchen around the corner faster. "Hey babe, you packed cards in my bag, didn't you?"

Ava was pouring a new glass of wine and was about to stop half way. She then closed her eyes and bit her lip, and tilted the bottle down some more. Her glass was now full.

"Sure thing honey!" She said it with a huge smile and looked around the kitchen. No one got it. Two minutes later, she walked into the living room and tossed the deck of cards onto Perry's lap. He was in Birkenstocks, khaki shorts, and a flannel shirt unbuttoned showing his t-shirt, that was brand new, but made to look old and vintage. Apparently, the 3,800 square foot house also had a Gap in it.

"Thanks babe."

"Anytime sweetie," came with another sarcastic smile. Ava was already thinking about making the coffee and figuring out what time to set the timer for tomorrow morning.

Perry grabbed them off his leg, but then let his hand fall back down to the chair arm. He stared at the box. It appeared all the blood was sucked out of his face. His chest caved in. The excitement about having playing cards vanished, as it dawned on him these were it.

"Eastern? Pretty cool Perry." Eric snatched them out of his hand. He was looking at the box and flipped them to Kyle.

"Didn't they go under a couple of years ago? So how long have you had these?" Kyle caught them and joined the others in looking at Perry.

"Oh, uh I don't know, a while." Perry sipped his drink, trying to hide behind the glass.

"Nice." Kyle nodded and dropped Clue on the floor. He pushed it through the thick carpet like a field or savanna of reeds, sliding it under a chair. He then opened the box and pulled out the cards.

"What are we playing?"

The girls entered the room and everyone gathered around the huge coffee table. It was the cutout trunk of a massive tree, covered by glass. Between that and the fireplace, it was difficult to leave the living room without a wistful sigh.

By the time spades was the choice and teams were beginning to form, Perry's expression had turned to anger. His chest was now inflating, breathing in heavier puffs. He gritted his teeth at the empty box over on the floor now. He had managed to forget about it all, between the trip, skiing, and all his friends. But now it was coming back to him. He could still picture them scattered on his table back at the fraternity.

"Perry, you in or what?" Emily asked while sitting down next to Kyle, sipping her mudslide and resting her hand on his closest leg. Kyle looked up while shuffling.

Perry shook his head and got up to trudge into the kitchen.

"I'll sit this one out." He held up his empty glass for an excuse. All he wanted to do was throw the glass against the stone hearth.

Ava scrunched her eyes at him from the other side of the room, where she, Michelle, Marcus, and Carrie were sitting in front of the fire. She wondered what he was pouting about now.

Oh well, no telling. I think 5:55 sounds good for the coffee. Yeah, 5:55.

She then smiled and nodded at Carrie who was talking about something stupid. Perry came back and clicked the television on, finding a rerun of *Saved by the Bell.*

The 200-year-old, dead redwood supported three close games of spades, then a poker game among the boys. Emily and Lara then joined the other girls in front of the fire, giggling and laughing for the next hour. By one in the morning all were upstairs asleep or passed out.

Perry opened his eyes, lying on his side. He was facing the windows to the trees in the back of the house, still in their costumes of white. He pulled the comforter over his shoulder and into his neck. The warmth of the bed and view could keep most there until lunch. *I can't believe I'm in this goddamn place*, he thought, ignoring it.

He then flung the comforter down and kicked the sheets off. He snapped up out of bed. He walked to the window with his arms crossed, glaring between the shutters. He loved the ski trips over the years, usually once a year at either the holidays or spring break, and this one started out like all those others. Until last night. *Those goddamn cards!* Or was it two nights ago?

His view should be different, he felt. A view that comes with being several time zones away. From his perspective, a deserved view. And he doesn't have it.

His hands rubbed his face, pressing into his eyes. He reopened them on the view he'd been dealt and took a deep breath. He then looked up at the tip of a mountain between white branches, and thought about skiing today. They were going to Vail. He hadn't been to Vail in three years. The snow would be perfect.

He then turned to the clock on the far side of the bed and noticed Ava wasn't there. He blinked a couple of times, still waking up, and looked around the room while stepping into the bathroom. His bare feet were cold on the smooth wood floors.

Perry was downstairs two minutes later, checking the scene out front through the large, bay windows. It was only 6:45 and still somewhat dark outside. The clouds were just taking shape in the purpling sky. He then smelled the coffee and turned his head in that direction, puzzled. He was supposed to be having this cup of coffee at Cafe Verlet. Now it would be in this house, poured from an $80 Cuisinart.

He walked into the kitchen and stopped when he saw the silhouette at the table. He tilted his head to the right.

"Ava?" He continued around the marble island, leaning against the other side. "What are you doing up?"

Her elbows were on the table, holding the latte mug in front of her. She sipped as steam sailed up to the cast-iron chandelier. She turned to him, trying to hide irritation.

"Couldn't sleep. It's so quiet now." This was half fact, half in defense. Ava studied him for a second. It wasn't even seven o'clock yet, and he was in his Doc Martens, khakis, and a different flannel shirt. Gap must have earlier hours in Colorado.

"Yeah it is." He then looked around the kitchen. It appeared so different now, dim and even more vast without people mingling around. He leaned off the island and took three steps to the table. He pulled out the chair next to his girlfriend, four chair legs rubbing against hardwood.

"You okay?" He was glancing outside before settling on her.

"Yeah. Maybe it's the time change, you know? Just got up."

"Huh. Did you have fun yesterday?"

"I was rusty at first, but started getting back into the hang of it before lunch. Michelle and I had a blast actually."

"Good." He looked at her coffee cup and her hands cupped around it, thumb tapping. "Sorry for not skiing with you yesterday. I guess we got caught up with catching Kyle." He looked up at her, with her short black hair pulled back in a small clip high above her cheek. She looked adorable and it was before 7am.

"You want to ski together today? You will love Vail, the blues will be perfect."

"Sure. The-"

"-I haven't been to Vail in two years. Kyle and Eric…" Ava sipped her coffee and watched Perry transform. For about 30 seconds he was the cute guy she fell for sophomore year. She almost turned in the chair to face him and talk, when the new Perry emerged, masking the cute boyfriend. Once Vail came out of his mouth, she closed her eyes and brought up the coffee mug to her own. Now it was skiing, settings, cousins, his frat, an internship, and lots and lots of stuff. Some spoken, some in the background. She wasn't even on the totem pole anymore. She had always wanted to see Colorado and some of the ski locations they were going. Otherwise, she would have ended this back in Providence.

Now she sipped her coffee and listened to him ramble on, wondering how she could manage a long flight home. She could hide here, find her spots. Between the ski villages and the house, she could blend away and escape mentally. She can't on a plane. Colorado isn't worth all this.

She believed in reincarnation. She kept telling herself that he was going to come back as a garbage man or even a raccoon. It made her feel better, smile inside a little, knowing all this would come back to bite him. But if according to tales from India, and this bad karma was building up for another lifetime, what about her life now? Was it just a spectator to her revenge? She just hoped this wasn't punishment for her previous life.

She was thinking about leaving early, saying she didn't feel well and just buying a ticket at the airport. She was about to plant the seed, mention feeling funny and not sleeping well, when thumps echoed off the stairs and her private sanctuary was invaded. *Jesus, what are they all doing up so early?*

Perry popped up from his chair and joined the chorus that now took up the kitchen. The word 'Vail' came up every 45 seconds. She sat back and took in the whole scene. Perry was back to being one of them now. What did that make her?

I guess 5:15 tomorrow?

The tough girl inside knew to stick it out. After all, March in the Colorado mountains is a lot better than most places. Still, she decided to toss that seed into the ground just in case. She just wouldn't water it much.

She stepped out of the shower, body glistening, and stepped into the room. She toweled her hair more than normal, curious if Perry would even look at her body. He did, but talked about his ski boots. She mentioned taking a day to relax and adjust to the altitude and time. Tomorrow they were going to Breckenridge and then Keystone. She would cross those off on her "life ski trips' to do list. Vail was bigger and she could spend the day getting lost in it.

So, while the other nine headed up the Vista Bahn Express lift, Ava strolled the bridge leading into the main village. With the colorful three and four story buildings covered with bright shutters, full window pots, and peaked roofs, she felt like she was in Austria or Bavaria. Ava wandered into every shop, every store, and every cafe, soaking it all in.

By one in the afternoon, she found a coffee shop with a window begging for people watching. She ordered a $5 hot cocoa and sat back for her movie. A real script, with no telling how many characters.

By 2:30, she joined the plot.

She was resting her chin in her hand eyeing some grandparents walking by in ski gear, when the boy's voice brought her back inside.

"Excuse me, is anyone sitting here?"

Ava was startled and looked up. His voice was as soft as his face. His hair thick.

"Uh, no, no one is."

He smiled. "May I?" He grabbed the chair.

"Sure." She sat up more and grabbed the napkin her mug was on and dabbed her mouth. She watched him scoot up in his chair.

No one said anything for about 10 seconds, finally he looked over at her. "Hi, I'm Sean."

"Ava."

"Wow, what a pretty name. I've never known an Ava."

She smiled at him and messed with her hair a little, then sipped her hot cocoa looking out the window. *No one's every said than to me.*

"Is it short for something?" He turned in his chair interested.

She licked her lips, making sure there was no whip cream she hadn't swallowed, and looked at him. His eyes were dark blue. All of a sudden, he seemed embarrassed for asking and looked away.

She shook her head with a grin.

"Just Ava."

He nodded and looked back outside, as if he had never been this forward with someone before, and quickly realized it. She spun around checking out the coffee shop and was surprised to see no empty seats. With her mind occupied in the play performing out the window, the room had swelled. His was the only seat.

She cocked her head to the right looking at him.

"Where are you from?" She hooked a leg under her and faced him.

"Chicago, well just outside of it." He twisted in his chair as well, and soon both faced each other. Now in their own developing script. "How about you Ava?"

"New London, Connecticut. I was born in Danbury, about an hour out of New York, but we moved when I was six. I go to Brown."

"Very nice. What are you studying Ava?" He made sure to say her name every time he asked her something. He just loved the name. It seemed to match her face, as if her parents knew ahead of time what she would look like. It also made all this seem more real, like it was really happening in this random coffee shop, in a scenic ski town, 1,000 miles from home.

"English. And you?"

Sean nodded and swallowed his coffee. "I'm at Notre Dame. Chemistry major."

Ava was impressed. She knew two science guys at Brown, but they weren't like Sean. He didn't look like a scientist, he looked cute. She also knew Notre Dame was like an Ivy League school, but with better football.

"Do you like it there?" She brought up a foot on the chair and rested her chin on her knee.

"Yeah. I'm there on a scholarship; we could never afford it otherwise. Jeff Burris was my roommate freshman year."

She smiled, not knowing who Jeff Burris was, but knowing more and more who Sean was. "What year are you?"

"Senior."

"I'm a Junior. So it must be spring break there too, huh?"

"Yeah, most everyone here is into skiing big time. I just tried it Sunday for the first time."

"What do you think?"

"It's okay, I like it. I think I'll like it more as I get a little better. I was out this morning, but for some reason just wanted to take the afternoon off. It's kind of intimidating out there, like I'm in people's way and they'll get annoyed." He shrugged his shoulders. "And you Ava? Something tells me all Brown kids ski."

She laughed a little. "Just about I guess. I'm here with some friends from school and a couple from Dartmouth and Vermont." Just then, Perry entered her mind. Just saying the schools allowed them, and him, to creep into her head. She turned to the window scene, not sure where they were, but probably up the mountain. She felt connected to him even if he wasn't there with her.

Instead, she was here, 2,000 miles from home in a fake relationship prolonged by fate, sitting next to someone who grabbed the only seat in the place. Someone she felt so at ease with and could talk to. He had deadly cute eyes too. She wondered if he used those eyes to look at her with as much desire as he did a microscope. She turned to him. Turned to Sean, never thinking of Perry again. He was now a means to get home and move on with her life. A new life.

"I wish you could rent the entire mountain, and then just ski wherever. Not worried about pissing people off, or falling, or having to hang around snobby people."

"Oh absolutely." He laughed and pushed his coffee away from the edge of the table they were sitting at. "Then when you bust right off the chairlift, in the middle of everything, there is no one behind you cursing you and laughing, and having to ski around you."

Ava laughed and smiled, and gently touched his arm in front of her. She didn't realize she did it.

"Oh my god that's the worst part. I get so nervous when the lift gets to the end and you have to get off. That's worse than having to ski down the mountain."

Sean shook his head grinning. He reached for his coffee, "That's so funny."

They chatted in a relaxed fashion as if bored in class. Seats opened up, laptops were opened and closed, tables were pulled together, and for 30 minutes, the two strangers ignored it all. Radiohead's "High and Dry" was over, but her afternoon was just beginning.

Sean put his coffee back down. "You ice skate?"

She nodded, her chin back on her knee looking at him.

"So do I. You know there is an ice rink here, right?"

She picked up her head. "There is?"

Now he nodded, biting his lip. He started standing up.

"Come on Ava." He pulled his jacket off the chair and started putting it on. She just looked up at him, breathing harder. She was hoping for another cup of coffee and hot chocolate, now she was getting a skating date. She smiled and her body just started moving by itself. Her heartbeat drowned out her brain's voice. She was up and he helped her with her coat.

The outdoor rink was popular and even in March still perfect for the carving and swerving blades. Ava and Sean skated, losing track of time.

They talked, laughed, and made comments on bystanders. The only thing missing was the *Peanuts* piano song. Sean was staying in the village with his friends and leaving for Aspen tomorrow. Eventually they were standing along the boards, leaning over the edge looking up at the sky. The clouds were stained pink and purple to the west, just floating over the mountains like cotton candy.

"So what are you going to do next year? After graduation?" She started pulling off her mittens one finger at a time.

"Well, got a couple of things possibly lining up. One is in Boston actually."

Oh, hell that's close. "Boston's nice, you'd like it."

"That's pretty close to Brown isn't it Ava?" He asked the stupid question, knowing his geography, but couldn't directly say what he was thinking. It was an easy way into it.

"Uh, not too far." She squinted up at the mountain, knowing they were all up there. Up there so far away.

"There you are!" Both heads turned to a tall guy walking up to them. He had thick black hair curling out from a Notre Dame baseball cap.

"Go figure, we leave you alone for one afternoon and you're skating with Dorothy Hamill."

Ava smiled. She then looked at Sean.

"You guys done already?" Sean slapped him on the shoulder.

"Already? It's 5:15 dude."

Sean and Ava both looked at each other surprised. "Oh. Uh Zachary, this is Ava. Ava, Zachary."

He held out his hand, taking his hat off. "Hey Ava, Zachary. Nice to meet you." He flung his hat back on.

Ava smiled and shook his hand. "Likewise."

"She's a hell of a skater." Sean was looking at her, then turned to his roommate. "You're not going to believe this, she's from Danbury."

Zachary's eyes grew wide. "Really. My mother is from there. We lived near there before moving into the city. What's your last name?"

"Spence."

"Interesting. Where do you go to school?"

"Brown."

He nodded at her, then his eyes left Ava and found his roommate. Sean was stealing a glance at Ava.

"Hey we're headed back."

He looked back at Zachary, but not before Ava noticed him staring at her.

"Alright. I won't be long."

"Ava, awesome to meet you. Small world."

"Of all the gin joints in all the towns in all the world." She cocked her head to the left, moving some stubborn hair over her ear.

Sean looked over at her with a smile. He then looked back at Zachary walking away.

"He seems nice." She was squinting her right eye as the setting sun was just peaking over the mountain.

"Yeah, my roommate. Good guy. Scary smart. We had some classes together, but now he's a bio major. Going to med school at Vanderbilt next year."

"Oh wow." She turned around with her back to the boards and watched some kids race by. Across the rink someone fell, sliding and spinning to a stop with a grin. Some people up in a window were leaning out, pointing and smiling, overlooking the rink and street watching it all. Their movie playing out in front of them.

"So Ava, I need to probably get going." He reached into his pocket and still had a ski trails map. He pulled it out and looked at her, turning her head as well. "Would you mind if I got your number back at school? Maybe we can catch up or something?"

She got all warm inside, forgetting what it felt like to be asked out, to feel silly excitement for a phone call, and a chance meeting.

"Maybe?" She playfully pushed him in the chest, sliding him back some.

He grabbed the boards to stop and looked down at the ice, smiling.

"Okay, okay you got me." He then looked up at her. "Yeah I definitely want to call you. Just try not to flunk out of Brown in the next three months."

"I'll try." She smiled and then looked away at the action on the rink. *Oh my god. I'm so taking him sailing back home.*

They skated over to the ticket booth for the rink, and sat on the bench outside the door to change shoes. The rented skates dripping with ice shavings were put on a shelf against the rink. Sean turned to the guy at the booth.

"May I borrow that pen?" He pointed.

Sean unfolded the Vail ski map. He ripped off the top half with the mountain and ski trails full of blue, green, and black lines zig zagging all over it. He wrote his school and home number on it.

"Here's my number at school and back home" He handed it to her and then refolded the bottom portion a couple of times to make it more firm to write on.

"What's yours Ava?"

"401-555-3851. My number back home is 860-555-3309." She leaned over eyeing his handwriting. "Oh and it's Sean what?"

"Masterson."

They both smiled and tucked their treasure away into their jeans pockets. They said their goodbyes, and headed off in opposite directions.

Ava's head was spinning so much she forgot the time and where she was supposed to meet up with everyone. She didn't really care.

Ten minutes later she was walking down the street that led to the bridge, when Perry, Kyle, and Emily came walking up the other side.

Perry held up his arms. "Where have you been?"

They meet in the middle, people walking past them in all directions. Ava scratched her head and moved some hair out of the way. The breeze was picking up, swirling through the cavern of buildings and down the street.

"Oh, around."

"We missed you today sweetie. Did you have fun?" Emily put her hands on her hips.

You have no idea. "Yeah it was nice."

They walked back to the main garage where both SUV's were parked. She looked over at Emily from time to time and would miss her a little. As of the holidays a couple of months ago, they were probably going to be related, as Emily was engaged to Kyle, Perry's first cousin.

She would miss Michelle too, but that's it. Everyone else could disappear as far as she was concerned. Disappear down steep, black diamond trails in Vail, one by one. She hoped this chemist thing worked out. She already had a hypothesis brewing with her independent variable.

The rest of the week went smoothly and after her skating date, she couldn't wait for the flight home. The house felt different, her steps were lighter. The conversations became interesting from her perspective, as they would be the epilogue to their brief lives together.

The meals were delicious. The drinks refreshing. Even the hangover Thursday morning was greeted with a shrug. Keystone and Breckenridge were fun now; even skiing with Perry wasn't that bad anymore. It was like knowing ahead of time what you were getting for Christmas.

Friday night's dinner and card game would be the last she ever had with them. She would probably see Marcus and Michelle again around campus, which wouldn't be a big deal.

They were grilling hamburgers and starting to open some red wine. Kyle was still in charge in the kitchen, opening the double-door fridge. Marcus and Shane walked in, as the girls started pouring wine and making mudslides.

"Okay chef, what do you need?" Shane started rubbing Carrie's shoulders.

"A drink."

"I'm on it." Shane's hands left his girlfriends, grabbed a glass out of the cupboard, and moved over to the makeshift bar.

Kyle closed the fridge and put a huge plate of pre-made burgers on the marble countertop.

"Now I need the grill turned on."

"I'm on it." Now it was Marcus's turn, slapping Michelle's ass on the way to a holler and smile.

"We also need some tunes."

Eric was closest, and glad to oblige. "And I'm on that." He headed off. That left Perry, still in the living room.

"And let's get rid of these empty beer cans and wine bottles. I need some room. Perry!" Kyle shouted while peeling Saran wrap off the burgers.

He came around the corner. "What?"

"Hey, collect all these and get rid of them for me." Kyle's eyes swept around the island, then found his cousin's. Perry didn't say anything, just sighed and looked back in the living room.

"There are trash bags in the pantry I think." Kyle balled up the Saran wrap and tossed it in the garbage. He then pulled out rattling drawers until finding a spatula.

Perry put all the cans and bottles in a bag and walked it out to the garage, scanning around quickly. He dumped the bag in a trashcan, didn't bother with the lid, and walked back inside. The recycling bin was on the other side of the garage, too far away.

Perry came back in as 10,000 Maniac's, *Our Time in Eden* started playing. The girls started making a fire, which took longer than usual, but was fun. Ava was thinking she could pretend to pass out down on the couch, so she wouldn't have to sleep with Perry.

The burgers were perfect with three bags of tater tots. The highlight was a surprising snowfall during the grilling. The snow was light and soft, and disappeared into the ground and deck, already covered in white. Being from Vermont, it wasn't the first time Kyle had grilled in snow. Ava thought it was pretty cool. She could say she saw a snow globe with a grill in it. Kind of.

If Perry still scowled at the *Eastern* cards, Ava took them like candy. After games of Trivial Pursuit, Monopoly, Clue, and Pictionary all week, Ava joined a card game that last night. Perry was wearing a Nirvana t-shirt under his fourth different flannel, which Ava couldn't help but smirk at knowing he only knew two songs.

She hadn't noticed the name on the cards until then, and when she saw it, she thought about a compass. Her thumb ran over the name constantly, thinking about going east the next day. Flying east to a new life of happiness. She considered taking the cards with her on the plane, but decided not to. The cards found a cabinet with the other games. She would hold onto something else on the flight.

That night she did call the couch downstairs home, only on her own doing not the liquor. On her way up to bed around midnight, Michelle noticed Ava on the couch and covered her with a flannel blanket. A slight smile creased Ava's cheeks at the kindness, knowing Perry didn't even acknowledge her. She would mention it to her the next time she saw her on campus when deflecting shocked questions about Perry. As Shane and

Carrie were the last to thump their way up the stairs around 1:15, Ava slowly opened her eyes on the couch. The fire was down to just glowing embers and a black log, sprinkled with throbbing orange, seeping through cracks.

Ava clutched the thick, warm blanket with teepee prints on it under her neck, and stared at the dying fire for the next 20 minutes. The fading glow signaling the fading vacation and boyfriend.

On the flight the next day, she held the Vail ski trails map in her lap. She occasionally looked down at it, when not looking out the window at a sky full of future possibilities. Perry thought she was holding onto a memory of skiing and good times. He never noticed the phone numbers in blue ink near the side. She ran her thumb over the numbers, like the cards the night before, and couldn't wait to land east and start over. She couldn't wait for that phone call. She couldn't wait to throw away her scrapbook. She couldn't wait to buy a new one, that was empty, clean, and fresh.

Ava Elizabeth Spence couldn't wait to put this ski map on page one.

CHAPTER THIRTEEN

Nate pushed up the combination lock clicking it closed. His fingers then touched the black dial and spun it five times until stopping at 0. Then he spun it clockwise to 0. Then counterclockwise to 0. Then clockwise twice to 0. Another two counterclockwise spins to 0. Finally one more clockwise spin to 0 before continuing three more notches to 37. He then leaned in close to look at it. After eyeing it, Nate slung his backpack on his shoulder and left his beige locker.

The bell for fifth period had echoed in the hallway 10 minutes before. It's hard to believe that the hallway can be this calm, considering the movement and noise that's bounced around like a trampoline. The classroom doors were now the buffer, holding in the chaos like the dungeon door to a monster.

The common areas between lockers have tables, chairs, and computers with a sprinkling of kids. Some were at computers. Some were taking make-up tests. Some seemed to be doing nothing. Everyone seemed to be waiting. The whole school was a spring ready to uncoil.

Christmas break was two periods away.

Nate moved past his section of lockers and noticed Harper spinning her combination lock.

"Hey there Harper."

She spun around full of curiosity, then narrowed her eyes once seeing the source. She flashed a quick smile, but then scanned the area before returning to her lock. A few seconds later, the bell sounded and an announcement was made. Nate quickly brought up both hands covering his ears.

Twenty-seconds later, he entered another common area and saw another classmate at a computer.

"Hey Madison," came with a wave. She looked up from her computer screen and started to smile, then bit her lip closing her eyes. Unfortunately, unlike Harper, there were kids around.

"Whoa Madison, new boyfriend?"

"You two make such a cute couple."

"Madison, why didn't you tell us you hang out with Nate?"

She opened her eyes to glare at them, then returned to her screen trying to remember where she was. She suddenly felt heat on her back and shoulders and her head tingled. She yanked over the hood of her St. Louis Cardinals sweatshirt. Unfortunately, it didn't cover her whole head.

At the next section of lockers, Dylan didn't let Nate say hello, he beat him to it.

"Hey Nate, nice shoes."

Nate looked down and then started over towards them. "Oh yeah, thanks. My mom got these at-"

Half way to them, and half way through his explanation, Alex looked at Dylan as if he was crazy. Paul was on the other side of Dylan shaking his head.

"-so I think they make me fast, but the next pair will have shoelaces though."

"Yeah, shoelaces are tricky. I think I learned to tie shoes when I was in second grade." Dylan nodded.

Paul leaned forward at Nate. "Dude, what are you doing?"

"Well we're talking about shoes. See yours are-" Nate was cut off by Alex.

"He knows what shoes he has. He gets them at Foot Locker, not Buster Brown."

Dylan held up a hand. "Did mommy buy you that shirt too?"

"Yes, why?" Nate's eyes were skittering all over the place.

"Cause it's dorky!" Paul laughed.

Dylan leaned back against the locker. "Did you make your list for Santa yet?"

"Yeah I…" Nate continued on. And on. "…know there's no Santa of course. I-"

The three shared glances and smirks, and even had mini conversations while Nate continued. They were at least patient for him to finish.

"Next time we talk to you, that means don't come over." Alex informed Nate.

"Next time we ignore you, definitely don't come over." Paul piled on.

Dylan leaned forward inches from Nate. "Go away."

"Okay guys, see you next year. Get it?"

Dylan crossed his arms while looking dumbfounded.

"Why no I don't," came out oozing sarcasm.

"Oh, see technically it's the next calendar-"

"Is he really explaining this?" Alex turned to both his friends.

"Apparently." Paul answered for Dylan. All three then shook their heads and laughed as they moved on down the hall. Nate was almost finished.

"-though seventh grade will be more commonly known as next year." He watched them go and turn the corner. "Bye."

In Nate's world, there is no sarcasm, lies, nuances, or body language. It was too simple, that was one of the problems actually.

Nate then continued on, passing others and saying hello on his way to the office. The social affects of each comment were like dominos falling.

On his way through the office, he passed one of the assistant principals. Mike Wellington held up a palm for a high-five. He had just come inside from talking to Nate's mom in her car.

"Hey there Nate." He smiled, wanting Nate's last interaction at the school before break a positive one.

"Well, well hello Mr. Wellington. How, how are you, you today?" Nate was rocking back and forth more than normal, still excited about his chat back in the hallway.

"I'm good buddy. You ready for Christmas? The last one of the century?" Mr. Wellington was still holding up his hand, waiting for the return slap.

"Oh yes I am. Yes, I was just telling my buddy Dylan about my list. Those guys are so cool." Nate finally slapped his hand, either finally seeing it or finally figuring out what to do. His eyes then found the floor again.

"Well Nate, I-" Mr. Wellington then stopped and bent over slightly pointing to his own eyes with two fingers. Nate then looked up. "-I think your mom is waiting so no lallygagging now." He smiled at him.

"You got it." Nate headed down the hallway as the AP turned to watch him go.

A minute later, Nate pulled open the passenger door to his mom's Chevy Tahoe. The SUV seemed to swell when he got in. It was like the radio was turned on, but not a relaxing classical station or soothing voice on NPR. It was heavy metal or a talk show with five call-in's at once. Ten minutes later, they were at Challenger Grace High School, picking up his sister. Aspen was a freshman, two years older than Nate. The MacGregor's had a flight to Denver at 2:10, for Christmas in the Rockies.

Aspen slid into the backseat behind her mom. She had plenty to say, her mind full of thoughts. She couldn't wait to get away from this place and the kids in it for 12 days. The last period after lunch was the longest in her life. The only saving grace that kept her out of the clinic with a fake stomachache, was knowing the bus ride was not coming.

As the car door slammed closed shutting out the cold wind, Aspen plopped her backpack on the seat next to her. Her head came back into the headrest hoping her mom wouldn't ask how her day was. Instead, Nate's voice filled the interior like a recording stuck on play. She would argue she could hear it from outside.

Apparently, a fire drill threw off his entire day, causing two visits to the office courtesy of the AP and security guard, an untouched lunch box at lunch, and a keyboard key missing. Even his headphones he wore to dampen loud noises didn't help. Not to mention more dominoes falling, thanks to him, from across the classroom.

Nate was rocking back and forth in his seat, breathing fast enough to disrupt his speech. His voice, as usual was loud. He did not know how to whisper, at all, or use an inside voice. This continued for 12 minutes. Mom got in some sentences at times, more like thoughts that escaped her head.

"Why didn't they call me?"

"You didn't eat?"

"Did you go to your calm down corner?"

"They should have called me."

Aspen leaned over to make eye contact with her mother in the mirror, finally getting a glance from her. That was all. *I'm just great mom, thanks for asking,* came the usual thought.

That was the thought when she was nine, after telling all seven girls that came to her birthday party; they had to leave after just 20 minutes, because Nate lost a puzzle piece. 99 pieces wasn't enough and after yelling, throwing large household things, and scratching himself repeatedly until blood appeared. The police were called to Baker Act him. Thanks to Nate, the cake was ruined and the punch bowl was flipped onto the floor. She at least had the presents to open. Those were opened alone next door with a neighbor since mom was at the hospital with Nate until 11:30.

That was the thought when she was ten and finally jumped from the six-meter board at the city natatorium. She skipped across the pool deck, to the shouts and glares of two lifeguards along the way, to their towels and table with eyes as large as goggles. She never got even a glance. Problem was some boy cut in line at the slide where Nate was in line. This didn't go over well with Nate. Then his reaction, his shouting, and his tirade, didn't go over well with the other kids and lifeguards. Then some parents even got off the bleachers to see what was going on. More dominoes falling.

That was also the thought two years ago when she had to walk home from the mall by herself at night, and found her mom in the kitchen. It was bad enough that Natalie, Ashley, and Tori saw her alone at the mall, then passed her in Tara's mom's Mercedes walking home on the side of the road. It was bad enough this all happened after the week of bullying in three classes, the cafeteria, and hallways. The worst part was Ashley was supposed to go with her to the mall, but decided to make up an excuse to go shopping with the other girls. After walking home at dusk, since her mom couldn't come get her due to Nate's emergency therapy session after more self-injurious behavior, her mom's first comment was, "So we're upping his meds and going to try seeing this new therapist they recommended."

She turned her head looking out at the fields of Forest Park, with the St. Louis Zoo behind some bare trees and a hill. She wondered if he could keep this up all the way to the airport, but shook her head knowing the answer. Then she decided to answer one of her mom's questions. *Oh, and if they called you every time he flips out at school over something trivial, you'd be on the phone with them every 45 minutes.*

That's the thing that killed Aspen. The dominoes effect he caused; that shut down their lives and affected the setting they occupied, wasn't from a push, a fire, a fall, or a broken bone. It came from a gentle tap of a crayon breaking, someone borrowing his pencil for five-seconds and now it was encased in germs, batteries dying, someone looking at him, or an unexpected shortage of chocolate milk at a restaurant.

Aspen will never forgive their father for leaving. When Aspen was seven and Nate five, he left on a business trip to Wichita and never came back. When their mom noticed more clothing, personal items, and bags were missing than normal, she knew he had packed for more than a three-day trip.

But at the same time, deep down where the secrets she's complied in 15 years are filed, she doesn't blame him. On days like this, there was even some envy behind her eyes.

Nate came close to keeping it up all the way to the airport, but once he saw a 767 clear some buildings and bank left, he changed topics as quickly as the landing gear disappeared in it's belly.

"So, so, so we're getting on a, on a plane soon right? When do we get on the plane?" He was blinking rapidly when thinking. It was like his mind was taking pictures and was holding down the shutter button.

"Yes honey, get out your social story on flying and airports."

Nate opened the glove box and flipped through the laminated cards. Cards with silly pictures and childish phrases that would hopefully prepare Nate for anything that might happen from the ticket counter to baggage claim.

Thank god for the Rubik's Cube.

The MacGregor's keep a Rubik's Cube in every room of the house. Even the laundry room has one next to the fabric softener. One of the things Nancy MacGregor does every morning, is make sure they are all unmade, mixed up. If that gentle tap of the first dominoes piece was about to take place, this was one thing that could help.

They discovered it by chance in Aspen's room. A seven-year-old Nate was starting to melt down in her room while playing checkers. Aspen was half-mad, half-afraid, when she picked up her Rubik's Cube from her nightstand and threw it at him. He yelled at her, but then picked it up and began twisting and turning the colors. By the time one color was solid; his breathing was close to normal. By the time two colors were done, his eyes were better. By the time four colors were done, he was just rocking slightly back and forth. With all six sides done, Nate talked and could be redirected. His mom drove to the toy store the next morning just before it opened, and bought all they had. It was their version of Black Friday.

On the flight to Denver, it came out when the person in front of them leaned his seat back earlier than normally allowed. Otherwise, between the view out the window and his new Nintendo Gameboy Slim, Nate was fine. Nancy and Aspen MacGregor were able to enjoy a flight like normal people.

If only Aspen could turn off her brain when the seatbelt light dinged.

She still felt the locker at school, her hand gripping the cold metal causing her palm to turn pink. Feeling the warmth on the back of her neck, as the girls slow when passing her. The folded up notes passing under the desks down the next row. The same sandwich every day, at the same seat, at the same table, with the same people around her, all eyeing the people they really want to sit with. The soccer team's bench is still next to the field. Even approaching 16,000 feet going 180mph and St Louis getting farther and farther away, she still wasn't any further away.

They were last to arrive at the house in Frisco that evening. The other aunts, uncles, and cousins had sprinkled in throughout the day. Snowflakes seemed to spiral in different directions, not sure where to go. The fresh snowfall was deep. Their measured steps sunk down a couple of inches, disappearing. The porch was clean, planks of gray wood, as the snow couldn't get under the overhang. The MacGregor's stomped their feet, which acted like the doorbell.

Aunt Laura pulled open the door, ushering them inside the glowing foyer. Aspen and Nate were hugged by everyone, Nate leaning away from each squeeze. With the commotion inside, Nate was wearing his headphones. They were green John Deere ones his father had worn when working outside with tools or machines, like farmers wear on tractors. A fire was blazing after a fresh update of oak. Monopoly was spread out on the table. Colorful boxes and bags seemed to support the Christmas tree. The smell of Lasagna greeted anyone strolling into the kitchen. Apple and pumpkin pie might as well have been the air freshener. You would never know it was a rental house.

"Aspen sweetie, I love your hair longer." Aunt Susan's warm hands cleared her face of hair, her trailing thumbs caressing her cheeks. "How are you?"

"I'm good Aunt Susan," came her lie. It came out so easy it was like the truth. Aspen did like Aunt Susan the most. She treated everyone the same, her three kids were no different from the other five in the house.

"How was the flight Aspen?" Aunt Susan gave her a look, meaning she meant how was Nate. Aspen smiled and nodded her head.

"Fine actually."

"Good." She tousled her hair and her hand slid down to her shoulder, pulling her in for a hug. "I'm glad you're here honey." She let go of Aspen and took two steps to the counter. "Come here sweetie, will you help with the last pie?"

"Aunt Susan, can I go up and change real quick?"

"Oh, of course. Go, I'll wait."

Aspen smiled, a real smile, and hurried up the stairs with hope springing her up each step. She was sharing a room with Julie and looked forward to late night talks and hanging out with a cousin she sees too infrequently. Julie had already claimed the top bunk to Aspen's joy. She remembered Aspen didn't like being on top. She also had the top drawer to herself, as Julie took the lower one. Aspen didn't need the latest clothes or to know every song on The Verve's, *Urban Hymns,* she just wanted a hug and for someone to understand she still liked the crusts cut off her sandwiches.

Julie also didn't mind when Aspen would play her Tchaikovsky, Dvorak, or Mendelssohn. Aspen adored the violin. She was all set to join band, but never did in middle school. The teasing was worse. She would have added 'band geek' to her social resume. By the time high school started, it was too late to get into it. Their meanness was even able to drive her decisions. Her heart sank every time she saw a kid walking with the black box that held an instrument. She slowed while passing the music room, and peeked in the window at the stage to see who was in the first seat. She couldn't bring herself to listen to the Nutcracker. It was too depressing.

She washed up and slipped into a sweatshirt, then bounced down the stairs. Aunt Susan was waiting in a busy and packed kitchen, slicing apples.

"There you are. Grab some eggnog and help me cut these."

"Got it." Aspen slipped through the crowd and found the kitchen nook table. Two bowls were full of the creamy treat. Her cousin Miriam came over and nudged her in the shoulder.

"Hey there."

"Hey." She ladled a glass full in one pour. "What have you all been up too?" She took a sip, licked her creamy mustache clean, and turned to her.

"Oh just hanging out. Had a Monopoly game going, just relaxing the most I guess."

"Cool."

"So how is your brother doing?"

I'm great Miriam, thanks for asking. "Fine I guess. The flight was okay." She took another sip, as Miriam couldn't stop asking about Nate. The eggnog was different, it tasted really good. She swung her head around the kitchen, then found Miriam again to cut in.

"-Hey Aunt Susan needed me, I'll catch you later."

"Oh, right. For sure."

Half way to the apples, Miriam's dad, Uncle Terry, hugged Aspen.

"Aspen how are you?"

"Pretty good Uncle Terry," another lie came with a smile.

"How's Nate doing?"

"Oh well he's doing better, you know." She nodded, not able to fake a smile any longer. She looked off in the kitchen. Nate wasn't even in the room and he was still dominating it. She took another sip, licking her lips.

"Well that's good. I know your mom is working hard to figure things out." Uncle Terry's eyes then widened as he remembered something.

"Hey, how did the Rutledge Scholarship go?" He raised his eggnog for a sip.

"Oh I'm not doing it. I missed the deadline." The Rutledge was a music scholarship for a fine arts high school where Aspen could focus on the violin and her music. She didn't bother applying, thinking she would have no chance. The deadline is next February. Aspen then glanced at Aunt Susan, changing the subject.

"Well Aunt Susan needs me."

"Oh then you better get over there." He tapped her glass in cheers. "But you may want to get a refill."

Aspen looked down at her glass, empty except for the residue of nutmeg along the rim.

"Oh." She couldn't believe she drank an entire one that fast. She figured you don't have eggnog that often, it was a refreshing taste. She scooped up another glass full and poured. She gulped another swallow. *God, this is where nutmeg goes when it dies.*

She found her aunt again. "Hey there. Grab that bowl." Aspen noticed that Aunt Susan cut the apples with ease, like a stay at home mom who does nothing but study recipes would. It made sense. She took another sip of the eggnog and closed her eyes while licking her lips. It was so scrumptious.

The last aunt and another uncle stopped by to say hello and welcome her. Within 12 seconds, his name came up again. This time the lies were embellished and she started having fun with it.

"Aspen there you are!" Aunt Chris kissed her cheek and grabbed her softly by the shoulders. "You're getting tall honey, how are you?"

"Absolutely fantastic Aunt Chris. Deliriously happy. I'm almost dizzy." She raised up her eggnog in a toast and sipped more. "And how are you?" She leaned in as if begging for a response like a reporter, playfully elbowing her.

"Great, great, we…" she continued on about work and Terry's work, then something about her tennis team matches. Aspen zoned her out while sipping her eggnog. "…anyways, how is Nate doing? Any better."

"Boat loads," came with a smile.

Two minutes later, it was Uncle Austin, who found Aspen chewing on an apple wedge.

"Susan who is that helping you? If I had to guess, I'd say it was our little Aspen."

"She ain't little anymore Austin," came careening over her shoulder.

"I can see that." He smiled at her and hugged her. "Wow look at you Aspen, how is your year going? Last we talked was July Fourth."

"Uncle Austin, it's going insanely well, bordering on magical. Vice president of the Key Club, starting center forward for the soccer team, and the phone rings off the hook constantly. Drives mom crazy." She took a long sip, finishing her second eggnog. "I need a damn secretary to handle everything."

Her aunt's head turned slightly at the comment, but continued beating more eggs. Austin laughed and rolled with it.

"Uh, well sounds great. How is Nate doing?"

"Splendid. I'll cure him by Memorial Day."

She walked off for a refill and then continued helping her aunt. Her aunt worked the knife through the apples as if in sync with the grandfather clock's ticks in the hall. Ava tossed them into the bowl. Another eggnog sip was followed by another glance at the bowl of liquid heaven. She was pretty sure elves drank this stuff. Ava then focused on the pie duty, reaching for another whisk. She hit it against the mixer and it dropped to the floor. Some flour flung onto her jeans.

"Ugh, mother f-"

Just then, her mom came in the kitchen rubbing her forehead. "Aspen? Aspen dear, I need you a second."

Aspen chugged her eggnog and put the glass down.

"What the hell does she want?" It came out under her breath, but just loud enough. As she turned to walk off, Aunt Susan's eyes bugged out and she twisted watching her go.

Aspen found her mom just outside of the kitchen.

"What?"

"Have you seen the batteries? His Gameboy is about dead."

She sighed, "Well no. Are there any around here?"

"Must be, look in the cabinets where the games are or in the kitchen drawers for me dear. Uncle Rob is trying to talk to him." She took off. Aspen nodded. She tried the cabinets in the family room. Uncle Terry was adding a log and poking at the fire as Bethany, Macy, and Scott talked in front of it. There were seven or eight board games, a Twister mat, and two 500 piece puzzles. No batteries. She checked the kitchen. Aunt Susan pointed her gooey whisk at a drawer in the corner by the tiny television.

Aspen pulled it open. It had takeout menus from local places, a small phone book, lighters, an extra garage door opener, and a deck of playing cards. She was bending her head down, peering in, just as her mom came over behind her.

"Any luck?"

"No, but…" she squinted her eyes at the box of cards and picked them up. She turned them over and read *Eastern* on it. Then she flipped them in the air as if flipping a pancake. "Give him these." She handed them to her mom. "He likes numbers and can treat them like a puzzle or game."

"Okay, I guess he does play solitaire on the computer doesn't he." She walked off with the playing cards.

Uncle Austin was standing there watching it all and looked at Aspen. She winked at him clicking her tongue. "Memorial Day." She grabbed her empty glass and moved off to the eggnog, bumping into a stool on the way.

Her pour wasn't the best, and some missed her glass making a slight mess on the table. As she dipped in the ladle again, Macy came over.

"Hey, we're hanging out in front of the fire."

"Okay sounds good." She scooped up some more and this time found her glass. She attempted to put the ladle in the little glass holder, but it missed.

"Just had to fill up again. This shit's the bomb." Aspen took a sip while raising her eyebrows at her cousin and walked off.

Macy turned in shock. "Wait, what?"

Nate and Uncle Rob were in the family room, with frosty windows facing the front of the house. They played War, and then simply sorted and organized the cards in various piles and stacks. Aunt Chris and Laura eventually came over and the four played Rummy.

The other older cousins caught up in front of the glowing fire until dinner was ready. Aspen laughed at everything, even things that weren't funny.

Half way through dinner, Aspen couldn't keep her head up. Aunt Chris brought up her napkin to her mouth, then asked if she was okay from across the table?

"I feel a little light headed. I just need to go lie down I think."

Julie touched Aspen's hand. "Sweetie what's wrong?"

Aspen shook her head and grabbed the back of Bethany's chair for support. Her mom didn't notice she was gone for another six minutes. Nate was at the table.

Aspen was asleep on the couch facing the huge stone fireplace, wrapped in a brown flannel blanket with teepee prints on it. Her closed eyes lids joined her cheeks, flickering orange and red from the flames. The bourbon did her in.

In actuality, she was just ahead of the curve. Despite being the shortest day of the calendar year, it was a long one. And the high school freshman just unknowingly did what all adults do on days like that. Get drunk.

No one remembered to tell Aspen the bowl on the right was for the adults. Aunt Susan felt awful the next day, in tears. Her cousins thought it was funny and they were curious. Except for Julie, who asked to stay behind with her to be by her side. Aspen said no, and told her to go skiing.

At least it wasn't Christmas morning yet.

Aspen took Tylenol and curled up in bed until a little after 1pm. She couldn't believe that it took getting drunk to finally get some attention from her mother. Her mom also mentioned the cards worked with Nate, and thought it was a good idea of hers. Aspen smiled at that, but then closed her eyes knowing even when something good happens, his name has to come up. Dealing with Nate, while drinking, was definitely the way to go.

She missed out on Breckenridge that day, getting to spend the day hungover with her mother, Nate, and Aunt Chris, who no longer skied. Nate was upset with the change in plans of not skiing. Nate only sticks to the green slopes, but enjoys skiing and handles it fine. Between the movement, the sounds, nature, and all the constricting clothing, it is almost like therapy for him. Their mom would not leave Aspen alone and wouldn't let Nate go alone either. So, most of the morning was dealing with him. If she didn't feel bad enough, their mom even made it out like it was her fault they all had to stay home. Aspen's head was spinning from the rum night before, and now spinning from maternal guilt.

Her head and stomach improved as the day went. Aspen camped out in front of the gray stone fireplace that took up most of the wall. She messed with the Rubik's Cube, getting blue and yellow sides. She also played solitaire, which she never did with cards before. It was always on the computer. After five hands, she finally filled up the stacks of aces at the top, and won. She bit her lip smiling. It felt better, more real with cards than on their Packard Bell desktop at home.

While scooping up the cards and shuffling them, she looked at *Eastern* across the front of the cards. It made her think of heading that way back home. School was there too. The mall. The town street. The soccer fields. The treehouse behind the train museum most parents don't know about. It was all there. Waiting. Pushing and bullying its way into her short-term memory. She rubbed her forehead and massaged her closed eyes. Aspen tossed the cards on the stone hearth, spreading out into a long blue curvy shape.

Thirty minutes later seven-year-old Hannah, Julie's sister and youngest in the house, picked them up and mixed them all up. Uncle Terry joined her and they played War using multiplication facts. The second grader already knew up to her sixes. Uncle Terry would delay his answer a bit to give her a chance, but didn't need to give her too much. It was a shame looking forward, that he wouldn't be around in 30 years. Hannah would become an astronaut and fly into space. Knowing his sense of humor, he would claim his game of War was the reason.

Everyone came back and showered, the adults were gathered in the kitchen area before dinner. Come evening, Nate was in the forefront. Aunt Chris and Susan were making chicken parmesan. Until now, no one had heard about the death threat letter outcome, just his general struggles. In the first half of the year, there had been a steady decline in behavior and academics. Then earlier in the month, he wrote in a letter that he wanted to kill two kids. They had a meeting at the school the last week to address it, including their lawyer, three people from the school district, and the classroom teacher and ESE teacher.

Uncle Terry asked about the meeting. "So Nancy how did it go?" He was pouring Chambord liquor into tumblers 3/4 full of champagne.

"I don't know, there is still so much unresolved." She pulled out a stool at the kitchen's island. "They just aren't doing enough. I mean take Friday, they had a fire alarm. Fire alarms are awful for him, the sounds, it throws off the schedule. They didn't tell him beforehand." She sipped her drink and looked around the kitchen island.

"They are supposed to. It's in his IEP for god's sake. How hard is it to remember that?" She thought back to the meeting, then shook her head while others drank. "We never even got to this letter he wrote."

"Mrs. MacGregor, thank you for coming. Please sign in for me and they should be ready for you shortly."

"Thank you." Nancy MacGregor headed to the computer on the counter and 20 seconds later a name tag was printed for her. She sat in the office with her back to the windows facing the main hallway. Sixth, seventh, and eighth graders hustled back and forth behind her, noisy as usual, but the only noise in the office was a ringing phone and the thoughts in her head.

Their lawyer arrived five-minutes later. He wore $400 wing tips that never set foot in a classroom. He never got past the office. They quickly discussed some things before being called.

"Nate never got the hardcopy of his social studies notes this past Monday." She leaned over, nearly shoulder to shoulder. "I mean really, how hard is it to remember to give him notes. We're a month from the millennium, they can't figure out a way to remember? And Nate said she only came by his desk once all period. Seriously!" It was a whisper, but with effect.

Grady Nover nodded and scribbled in his notes. "Interesting."

Thirty feet down the hall, the principal, assistant principal, two teachers, and district personnel were having the same conversation, just from a different perspective. The phone buzzed and the principal pushed a button while two conversations around the table continued.

"Yes."

"Mrs. Tunks, Mrs. MacGregor is here."

"Okay. Will you show them to the conference room and offer them some coffee."

Betty Tunks released the button and closed her notebook. She sat back and listened to both conversations as if one, with a calm expression and fine-tuned ears.

"…have any idea I have 25 other students in the class, five of them ESE with IEP's themselves and the new ESOL kid? But I'm supposed to forget all them, and spend 45 minutes with Nate." The teacher spun her chair the other way. "I mean I've got material I have to cover by next Thursday." She shook her head in frustration and those at her end nodded and checked the far side of the table.

"Look, union is here, but if the lawyer starts asking direct questions to the teachers, they need to defer." The 26-year veteran teacher spoke to the table, then she looked over at a rookie teacher and nodded.

"Sasha, okay?"

Sasha nodded, thinking this was never covered in college.

That front office was a blueprint for the education system. It was a tug of war, with the knot in the middle of the rope never moving. It just shakes, getting tighter and tighter with tension in the middle, where the districts, states, politicians, and lawyers, make their moves and decisions.

Mike Wellington added. "He can only ask questions to gather information right now." The assistant principal then looked down the table and finally over to his boss.

Thumbs were clicking the tops of pens. Nails were tapping chair arms. A paper clip was being spun around and around and around. The AP's foot was pushing his knees up and down under the table like a piston. Then there was Mrs. Tunks. She looked calm and still, like a channel marker in a river of choppy waves and swirling currents. She looked around the table eyeing everyone while speaking. Her pulse matched her second hand.

"Okay, everyone get out your data and notes; get things in order before we go in. I'll introduce everyone." Her tone was Perry Como in December. It was like she was immune to the stress in the air, almost fogging up the windows in the two doors. She looked at the AP. "Where's Mr. Kinard?"

"Mr. Kinard?"

"Yes."

"I sent him to try to talk to a student."

On the other side of the office, team Nate was waiting in the conference room. It was the generic long wood table surrounded by school pictures, posters with inspirational quotes, and paw prints from the school mascot. The door was opened out to the hallway, where a teacher and student were sitting. They couldn't see them, but could hear them, or mostly her, as she was clearly upset. Nancy MacGregor and Grady Nover were sipping coffee in Styrofoam cups and waiting. After general chitchat, they were quiet, which allowed the conversation out in the hallway to seep in.

Alex Kinard loved kids like this. She had very poor grades and struggled in everything, but was sweet and respectful. In middle school, that's nearly unheard of. He'd take those kids over bright, smart-asses any day. A three-ring binder was open with papers scattered everywhere, and sticking out of the pockets at angles. There wasn't one paper with a sharp 90-degree corner. Her elbows were pressing down, crinkling other papers. They were supporting hands covering a damp face.

Mr. Kinard tilted his head a little eyeing her.

"Okay, okay, let's just start over. Let's just take a deep breath and take a look at your notebook Erin. I'm sure the notes are in here somewhere."

"They're not! And it doesn't matter, they won't help anyway." She ran her hand through her knotted hair and sat back in the chair. "I'm too dumb anyways."

She crossed her arms on her heaving chest. Sniffles echoing in the hallway. She had had enough. Mr. Kinard knew there wasn't much support at home. It was all on this girl. Maybe that was why he said what he was about to say, or he just knew sometimes kids needed to be slapped with some honesty. He also didn't know what else to try.

"You know what, you are. You aren't very smart. Nothing comes easy to you here. Every class probably seems the same; every teacher's voice the same."

Her mouth slowly started opening, her eyebrows beginning to arch.

"You'll hopefully get C's, probably D's. I doubt you'll go to college and graduating high school will be hard."

Alex and Grady both leaned forward in their chairs, on their own side of the hallway wall. Grady did to hear better, not believing what he was hearing from a teacher. He began mentally spraying lighter fluid all over the flame he wanted to engulf the school in.

Out in the hall, Alex leaned forward to make sure the girl was hearing him, and because he cared for his ex-student.

"But here's the thing, you're going to find your niche. You're going to discover something. I don't know when, I don't know how, you may not know, but at some point, you're going to find it. That one thing you do really well. No matter what it is, if it's drawing, cutting hair, baking, uh…typing, I don't know, you're going to find it and run with it. Just turn your back on all these things you're not good at, and only focus on that new passion. You will practice, get better and better, it will become second nature to you. You'll be so good at it you'll know it backwards."

Her face eased and she sat up a bit. The shock was being replaced with attentiveness.

"You'll do it better than anyone, you'll master it. No one will be as good as you. And that's when it will happen. People will come to you because of it, they'll need you."

Alex leaned completely forward resting his elbows on the table. He was now whispering as if she was the only student he had ever had in 17 years of teaching.

"I just know it, that one day I will read about Erin Tanvary in the paper, I will see Erin Tanvary on the 5:00 news, I will hear Erin Tanvary passing on the sidewalk, in a cafe, a store. You will find your niche in this world. Your world Erin, not a school's."

Erin's eyes were glistening, but not out of sadness, but hope. Alex sat back as the hallway immediately filled with people. The convoy approached as Mrs. Tunks led everyone into the room behind Erin.

"Okay, get this notebook organized tonight and I'll see you after the break." He stood up. "Merry Christmas Erin."

She nodded and wiped her eyes and cheeks.

"Merry Christmas to you too." She took a deep breath and clicked open her binder rings.

Mrs. Tunks took the seat next to Nancy MacGregor. Everyone else sat in the chairs in the order they came in. Mike Wellington was last, and just before closing the door, Mrs. Tunks reminded him about Alex.

Mike leaned out the door. "Mr. Kinard are you available right now? We are going to start the meeting."

Grady Nover eyed the door waiting to see the face to the voice he just eavesdropped on. He was grinding his teeth. Knute Rockne then entered the room.

Alex Kinard came in and sat next to his AP and across the table from the lawyer. He had no pen, no notes, no laptop.

Introductions took place, Nancy MacGregor stated her wishes, the lawyer addressed the social and academic issues, and Mrs. Tunks responded. The lawyer was rattling everyone in the room, except for two people. After ten minutes, everyone but Mr. Kinard had spoken. The lawyer was still trying to figure out why he was here, having worked with Nate for only five or six times. He taught in the room next to Nate's third period class and at times, was asked to come over and try to calm Nate down when he was upset. There was a reason he was next door for Nate's worst hour of the day. Mrs. Tunks didn't feel the need to defend anything.

After five minutes, icy stares replaced words, as the teachers had to take a back seat to Mr. Nover. Their held back yells and screams were muffled by job security. The representatives from the school district was useless.

They hadn't even gotten to Nate's death letter yet. Up until now, it was academics and a lack of effort in the classrooms to help him.

After ten minutes, Sasha was almost in tears. Mrs. Tunks was trying to take the role of Switzerland. Another teacher picked up her pen and flipped her legal pad to a fresh sheet. She started taking notes.

Hallmark. The Purple Frog. Talbots. Leopard Boutique. PNC Bank. Jobson's Fabrics.

Then the pen found her bottom lip, as she thought of all the places she'd seen "help wanted" signs on doors and windows, or hirings for non-administration positions. She'd make almost what she was making now, sleep more, not get migraines, enjoy Thanksgiving and Christmas breaks without grading papers, making copies, and writing up rubrics, be appreciated, and spend more time with family. Then the former Barnes & Noble cafe worker back in college, thought of two more.

Caribou. Boarders.

Mrs. Tunks spoke up after not knowing where the lawyer was headed. "So Mr. Nover, are you here as an advocate for Nate's academics or the letter he wrote last week? I'm confused, because up until now you are only mentioning things the IEP covers. Something you were not a part of and addressed last fall. I believe in September-"

"I'm Nate MacGregor's voice concerning both academics and the letter. I have no doubt that because of the poor academic and social support; he felt the need to write that letter." He looked around the table. "A boy who has Asperger's for crying out loud."

The room was silent. The only thing moving were eyes. And they moved down to the desk or laps. The walkie-talkie's weren't even squelching or beeping. Knute Rockne then addressed another locker room.

"That's a fantastic philosophy. That way he has an excuse and can blame a label for the rest of his life." Mr. Kinard looked around the room, stopping at the lawyer. "I mean let's not prepare him for life or anything."

Mr. Nover narrowed his eyes across the table at the teacher. "Excuse me, Mr. Kinard is it, I do-"

"That way when he misses a deadline in his job someday, he can just tell his boss, 'well I have Asperger's' and he'll say that's fine. Or even he injures somebody, kills somebody in an accident, a lawyer can just say, 'but your Honor, he has Asperger's' and the judge will say, 'well why didn't you say so, he's free of all charges'."

The teachers all stared at Mr. Kinard as if he had just invented the backbone. Some just looked down licking their lips in a silent victory. Others squinted their eyes knowing, thinking what was coming from across the table. Mrs. Tunks never flinched. The lawyer was furious, but also excited in that he had more ammunition against the school and the teacher from the hallway. He started speaking, but Alex Kinard ignored him and spoke to Mrs. MacGregor and everyone else.

"This kid needs social stories, role playing, and an isolated environment. You want him in a regular classroom for social reasons, to be like a normal kid, but he's not a normal kid. I'm sorry, but it's called the bell curve. Now no one wants to be around him or likes him, and he has even fewer friends. He isn't learning what a classroom is, he's becoming a leper." He pointed to the unfolded death threat letter with square creases throughout it by the assistant principal.

"He needs to take responsibility for his actions, in a more structured setting, with an immediate reinforcement or consequence. Get him out of general ed, put him in a self-contained. Teach him replacement behaviors, get him organized. He's very bright; the academics will be there when he's ready. Push his strengths, which is not being like most seventh grade boys."

Mr. Kinard leaned forward in his chair. "Mrs. MacGregor, we're the people actually in the classrooms with him."

He then addressed Mr. Nover. "You all need to be talking to the school board, not us."

No one spoke, or breathed. Nancy MacGregor's eyes were scattering everywhere and inhaled, about to say something, when the lawyer closed his notebook loudly. He shook his head at her and grabbed her arm, which closed her mouth. He stood up with a smirk.

"You'll be hearing from us."

CHAPTER FOURTEEN

The only better view from the tip of the Mountaintop Express, would be a hot air balloon. Maybe a satellite. Down the mountain was Mid Vail, ringed by tall trees with the Wildwood Express and Mountaintop Express lifts, pointed in different directions as if they were angry and ignoring each other. Dots of puffy ski jackets dripped down the mountain and curled around below them. They were so high; the bottom of Vail wasn't visible. With the trees up here dressed in new snow, the Avanti Express lift was hiding off to the left between them, barely visible.

The horizon was full of white mountains, like chunks of serrated ice. Pettingell Peak is 26 miles away and Longs Peak 60 miles away. That one is near Rocky Mountain National Park. It was a perspective you had to see to believe. Aspen thought the view from the Arch at home couldn't touch this one.

It was 3:45 on Christmas Eve. The arching sun was still yellow, but starting to set, now darker like an egg yolk as if losing power. In another hour, it would be resting on the trees off to their left. After four days of snow falling from grayness, the heavens pulled out its blue paintbrush for a few hours. More snow was on the way that night, but for now, it was bright and lovely above.

"The only thing missing is Aspen." Aspen's mom leaned over nudging her daughter. Aspen smiled and rested her chin on her arms, which were resting on her knees. They were sitting in snow with goggles pulled off and skis sticking out of the snow like telephone poles. With only one green run this high up on this side of Vail, and known as one of the tougher green descents, Nate never came up here.

"On a clear day, you can see Aspen from the top of Wildwood Express and Lost Boy."

Aspen peered around her mother off in that direction. Then looked in front of her to the north, guessing she could even see Wyoming. She adored the view and took a deep breath, inhaling the fresh and pure air. Pure air untouched by Nate. A setting that doesn't know what a Rubik's Cube is. A patch of snow never trampled in a tantrum of kicking of snow. A quietness without Nate's headphones. Just whistling wind, slushing snow being carved by skis, and her mother. Her mother, not Nate's mother.

"You know that's why your name is Aspen." She turned looking at her. "Your father and I went there for a vacation after the miscarriage, and nine months later you came along."

"Was dad happy?" Aspen asked while looking down at her ski boot latches, caked in frost.

"Yes of course. But that's when he was traveling so much. I know he was crazy about you." Aspen looked up at the ski lift carts almost directly above them. Half were empty, as they recycled above her up and back, up and back. Whenever she sees a ski lift cart, she sometimes thinks about the interstate. When she was little, if they were driving on I-70 or I-44, she would always ask her dad which car was on first? Who was in the lead? Seeing the lifts sway past each pole on their way around, now she sometimes wonders who was on the first lift in the morning.

Not crazy enough about me though.

Aspen had always felt a partial blame for him leaving. She knew the real reason, the dominoes game was just too much for him, but always wondered if she were better in some way, could she have been enough to keep him around.

The memory she remembers the most is going to the airport to greet him. They would walk right out to the gate and she would press her nose against the giant windows, watching his plane roll to a stop at the gate. If the angle was right, she would try to look in every circle window for his face. Usually he arrived at night and the cabin lights were on. If the angle was wrong, and the coned nose was aiming right at her, she'd look right in the cockpit at the two pilots. She would wave and smile at them, never knowing if they saw her, and mentally thanking them for bringing her daddy home.

Walking out to the gate was always tiring, but it didn't bother her because she knew she wouldn't have to walk back. She would have a ride. She still can picture the look on his face when he finally saw her and she had the 'okay' to run up to him. He carried her the whole way back telling her about his flight and trip.

Her favorite picture of him came from the airport. He was holding her and kissing her check 10 seconds after walking out of the tunnel, her favorite Care Bear, Snuggles, dangling from a hand. She was too young to remember it, she was two and her mother was pregnant with Nate. The picture is in her bedside table along with sheet music from Tchaikovsky.

By the time she was seven and Nate was five, and the dominoes game was already beginning to start, she remembers the look on his face was different. Aspen always thought his flight must have been bad. He stopped carrying her then too. His traveling was cut back as well, and even though he was around the house more, she still thinks about the airport visits the most.

Looking out now at Wyoming, or if not Wyoming at least miles and miles of boundless rough land, wondering where he was, she knew what he was thinking when walking off those airplanes back then. He knew who was waiting at the gate and the headache he brought, and most likely the nightmare it would become in the future. He was not thinking, *my precious little girl.*

She wasn't good enough for him. She's not good enough for the girls at school. She's not good enough for Coach Lisa. She's not good enough for Marcus or the sophomore she passes every day between third and fourth periods. She was lost. She might as well have been meandering on one of those mountains out there. At least she would be alone and no one judging her.

And as if right on cue, her mom chimed in.

"You know I think we have a plan for Nate. I really think things will get better. I've been thinking about the meeting..."

She continued on and Aspen pulled in her knees to her chest and rested her cheek on them. She stared at her mom talking, spewing out more hope for Nate. *Did you know I kissed a boy at a party two weeks ago? It was wonderful. But now he won't even look at me? Oh and I don't hold Snuggles in bed anymore.*

"...lawyer says. I've opened up an email account and we've started sending each other ideas and things that could happen."

Aspen closed her eyes. A few seconds later, her mother looked over. "You tired honey?"

All she could give was a nod.

"Come on, let's head back down. I'm sure everyone is about ready."

Aspen stood up, adjusted her knit hat, and grabbed her skis. She let them fall to the snow and stepped into them, clicking them on. She stood there and glanced out over her right shoulder at the vastness in front of her. Aspen took a deep cold breath, knowing she would see this view one more time. If only she could bring up some of that eggnog.

She stabbed the snow with her poles and twisted around 90 degrees, facing that view head on. She flexed her knees, leaned forward, and began sliding down the mountain.

The snow was thick and heavy Christmas morning. You could hear it tapping the cars, tree limbs, and the deck. There was no wind to steer it, so it just free fell like ripped parachutes. The kids were up early. Even Aspen, Macy, and Scott, the eighth and ninth graders, were first. The adults weren't up, so the three kids all crammed into the bay window watching nature's show outside. Macy and her brother were excited about the new snow for Copper Mountain tomorrow.

By 10am, the water under the tree was visible, as boxes and wrapping paper now covered the floor. Empty plastic cases that once held batteries took up an entire trash bag. Kids were comparing gifts; the adults were pouring more coffee. Except the MacGregor's who were upstairs.

It started when Cameron and Sydney, 13 year-old twins, got a Tickle Me Elmo. Nate made fun of it, calling it a baby gift, and questioned their parents' decision to get it for them. He couldn't understand it was just for fun and may be a collector's item years later. The problem was Julie's seven-year-old sister Hannah was in the room. The youngest in the house was still a believer. And Nate didn't understand what a lie was.

She stopped unwrapping a gift and froze, staring at Nate. Then turned to her parents, her face wilting like a dying flower. They knew what was coming, but didn't have time to say something or look nonchalant about it.

The tags read Santa.

"Mommy, what does he mean that you got the gift? That you're Santa?"

Everyone stared at Nate, who was still laughing at the red Sesame Street doll. Five minutes later, he was not laughing, but nearly screaming. Nate's gift, a Tamagotchi that was very hard to find, was the wrong color. Aspen was at a loss. The only positive for Aspen was now she wasn't the only one tired of Nate.

Her mom was with Nate, trying to calm him down as the dominoes were falling and his high-pitched voice was tipping them down the stairs. His mom and the Rubik's Cube finally calmed him down. Aspen was in the bay window looking at the snow again. She wondered what her father saw when he looked out the window this morning.

By noon, the power was out.

Monopoly, Pictionary, and checkers were the choice of games for the kids. Cameron bankrupted everyone within 90 minutes. Macy just knew she would go into banking someday. Hannah was rereading *Harry Potter and the Prisoner of Azkaban* for the third time.

The adults picked up the Eastern cards to play hearts. In the first hand, Susan purposely snagged up all 13 hearts and the queen of spades. Eyes rolled as Susan, who was also keeping score, more than happily jotted down 26 for everyone else. In the next hand, she couldn't get rid of a high 10 of diamonds. When having to follow suit, she grimaced at Terry's 4 of diamonds, laying the card down on top of his with a snap of the corner. And as if she knew what was coming, the queen of spades was eventually played off. She shook her head, *go figure.*

Nancy MacGregor didn't play once. When not with Nate, she just wanted to sit in peace and quiet and stare at the fire or snowy evergreens in the backyard. Her wine glass seemed glued to her lips, as if the mistletoe constantly followed her, floating above her.

By 6pm, the snow was now lighter and power was back. Everyone was downstairs for homemade pizza. No one was looking at Nate. Hannah was in a daze. Nancy was slurring her speech. Aspen was mentally not in the house.

Ho Ho Ho.

At 9pm that Christmas, the stars were winking down at the valley. The front went through and a cloudless sky seemed to let colder air swoop down from space. The temperature was in the lower teens. The fallen snow cloaked everything in perfect uniformed shapes. White or bright gray was everywhere, except on the underside of the tree branches.

The Sound of Music was on the television. Aspen, Macy, Sydney, and Scott were watching it by the fire, talking about music. Jake thought he was cooler since he actually downloaded two songs from Napster. Julie and Cameron joined them after being with Hannah in the kitchen. Macy said next time, he should get *Slide* by the Goo Goo Dolls or *Angel* by Sarah McLachlan. Aspen didn't bother asking if Mendelssohn or Vivaldi was available. With the clattering of dishes being pulled out of the dishwasher, the doorbell chimed.

Uncle Austin answered the door, swinging it open. "Hello, may I help you?"

"Yes, I'm sorry to bother you, but we are staying in the house next door and we're out of milk? We have a small child." The porch light made her blond hair lighter. She was wrapped in a flannel blanket, holding it closed and tight with crossed arms. She gave an embarrassed smile.

"Well of course, come in come in."

"Thank you." She stepped inside glancing at him.

She stood on the rug in the foyer, still wrapped up to stay warm. She looked around the foyer, dining room to the left, and formal living room to the right. Her thick ponytail swaying left and right. When Austin looked back at her, he stopped.

"No no come in it's okay. You don't have to stay there." He held up his hand gesturing her in.

"Oh, sure thank you." When they came into the kitchen, Susan and Terry were drying wine glasses by hand. Austin gave a quick explanation for the tall, stunning woman now in their kitchen.

Susan turned to her, twisting a towel inside the clear Bordeaux glass. "Oh no, how old?"

"Two. We got stuck inside today of course and well, you know how it is."

"Oh absolutely." Susan smiled, then tilted her head at her. "You have the most beautiful hair I've ever seen. My name is Susan by the way."

"Oh thank you. I'm Heather. It's nice to meet you, even in this embarrassing situation." She smiled at Susan, then scanned the kitchen area as Terry smiled and walked out into the family room. Heather took a deep breath, more relaxed.

Austin was leaning into the double door fridge. He spoke from behind the silver door.

"We have 2%, is that okay?"

"Oh yes. That's fine." Heather walked around the giant kitchen island as she noticed Susan turned her back to reach up onto a middle shelf. She put away two more glasses. Heather was biting her lip still scanning the area when Austin closed the door and smiled.

"How much do you need?"

"Oh just a cup," Heather shook her head at the whole jug.

"You sure."

"Yes."

"Heather where are you from?" Susan was still turned around putting away wine glasses. Austin turned to a cupboard for a cup or glass. Heather moved around to the other end of the island. Something blue snagged her eye.

"South Carolina." A tan arm emerged from under the blanket. Next to a basket of fruit and a pie covered in aluminum foil, was the box of Eastern cards. They vanished in her red nailed fingers.

"We wanted to give the kids a white Christmas. We sure got one."

Susan closed the cupboard door, came down from her toes, and turned around.

"You can say that again. Heather can we get you a drink or something?"

"Oh lord no, we have plenty of that over there." She started laughing and Susan joined her. Heather was rewrapping the blanket around her. Her speech was fine and she wasn't wobbling at all. Susan and Austin couldn't tell she had been drinking since 4:00 and the hard stuff about two hours ago, once the kids were down.

Austin screwed on the cap to the milk and put it in the fridge. He turned and handed Heather the cup of milk, in a plastic royal blue Denver Bronco's cup with the orange D on it.

"Here you go Heather. Don't worry about the cup, we can get it tomorrow."

"You're a life saver. Thank you so much." She smiled and took the cup, holding her wrapped blanket closed with the other hand.

Austin smiled, "Merry Christmas."

Susan grabbed her glass off the counter. "Here, let me walk you out." Susan opened the door and let Heather go out first. She followed her to the porch.

"Goodness it's cold."

"Yes it is. Well thanks again. Merry Christmas!" Heather turned and held up the milk, walking, but taking huge steps in the snow. Susan crossed her arms and squeezed herself. She leaned over looking to her right at the next house. Most of the lights were on downstairs, sending yellow rectangles and rhombuses down onto the gray snow. There was a car and two SUV's parked outside.

Susan looked upwards. The night sky was clear, and glued with stars. Orion. Ursa Major. Gemini. Perseus. With no light pollution, it was free admission for an observatory.

"Damn it's cold." Susan began rubbing her crossed arms and turned to head inside. The door closed, rattling the door knocker, leaving only the soft crunch of Heather's steps echoing in the cold night.

Next door, seven adults were celebrating Christmas and a rental house full of young children finally asleep upstairs. Considering the alcohol quickly disappearing out of the bottles, they were more happy about the quiet house than Christmas treats. The alcohol was fueling their conversations.

"We should do this in the spring." Jason pushed back from the table, crossing his leg.

"Ever been to Wyoming? Jackson Hole?" Noah asked.

Jason finished his drink and shook his head swallowing. "No, heard it was nice though."

"Oh it's so nice there. Kaylee you'd love it." Faith held her champagne flute up at her.

"Is it better than Aspen?" Kaylee had her doubts.

"Speaking of spring, did we get the rental in Augusta yet?" Jason addressed the table.

"Oh lord here we go." Arianna addressed the girls, knowing they would be left out of the following conversation. They all smiled and drank.

"Damn good question." Drew mentioned.

"Well I still need a badge." Will sipped his drink. No one bothered putting their drinks down on the table. Everyone just held them close in their laps or chair arms. The table was counterproductive.

"Between the three of us, we'll find one or know someone with an extra." Drew looked around the table.

"So we have the rental again, right?" Jason tried again.

"Yeah yeah, chill out. We're good." Drew calmed him down.

"More importantly is the Masters Y2K ready?" Will sipped. Everyone laughed. Noah, spit out some bourbon. Will continued.

"No, seriously, have they prepared?" Will started laughing himself, not able to keep a straight face.

"That's hilarious. So the azaleas bloom in October instead of March."

"Yeah and the ticket request list gets deleted."

"None of the member's jackets fit anymore. And McCord is welcomed back."

"Then on January 1st the WASP's are kicked out for only minority members."

"And Greg Norman shoots a 63 on Sunday to win."

All the guys busted out laughing. The chandelier seemed to shake. Jason was bending over in his chair holding his stomach. Drew and Jason were nearly crying.

Just then, the front door opened. Heather Ramsey entered the foyer with the Eastern cards tucked in the waist of her jeans. She closed the door and began shedding the blanket. She tossed it on a chair in the foyer, but missed. It fell crumpling up on the floor. She turned into the formal dining room just to the left. *Elegantly Wasted* by INXS was playing, which was fitting. The huge formal dining room table had been turned into a game room. All stopped when Heather arrived.

"Milk anyone?" She held up the cup and put it on the table. She started pulling out her chair.

"Nope, you couldn't take food or drink that was a rule." It came with an accusing finger pointing from Jason, who was still wiping tears from his eyes.

"Calm down that was my excuse." She sat down and scooted up, then put the playing cards on the table. Her husband Will and two others leaned forward at the other end of the table to take a look.

"Eastern? Wow, what were those doing over there?"

"You took a deck of cards?"

"Where were they?"

"What the fuck is Eastern?"

All attention was on Heather, as they gulped their drinks and listened to her tale of the journey next door, answering all their questions.

Heather, Kaylee, and Arianna had moved onto Black Russians from White Russians. Faith was still on champagne and all four men were gulping expensive, rare bourbon. Will was surprised she made it over there and back without wandering off to the wrong house holding a cup of milk.

Once the kids were down, ranging from 22 months to four years, the adult version of 'truth or dare' took on a completely new meaning. The alcohol surged it on as well.

Heather winked down at her husband and Will held up his bourbon in a toast.

"Your turn. Truth or dare Arianna?" Jason asked.

"Dare." Then Arianna took a card from the 'dare' pile and tried reading it through glazed eyes full of vodka and kahlua. Everyone quieted to hear her challenge. The grandfather clock around the corner was clicking. She cleared her throat.

"Go to a neighbor's house and steal something." She looked up. "Really, I have to go steal something?"

"Oh my god Arianna, that was Heather's card." Kaylee said, pointing to Heather.

"I just did that girlfriend!" Heather leaned towards her.

Drew started laughing, "You took from the wrong pile drunk!"

"Oh yeah!" Ariana said. Everyone screamed out laughing as she brought up her hand to her face. She then leaned over and fell out of her chair, thanks to no armrest. Three minutes later, everyone finally stopped laughing and stomachs were still sore.

Heather gave her the correct pile. Arianna's husband, Noah, looked over at Will next to him, shaking his head and held up his glass. Will smiled and nodded.

"No no, I want truth." Arianna held up a hand and put her drink down, changing her mind. She leaned forward and reached for the 'truth' pile. Faith slid them to her. Arianna read as if in a courtroom.

"When was the last time you had sex with someone other than your current partner. Who and where was it?"

Ooohs filled the dining room with exchanged glances. Most shot a glance at Noah, who was sitting back in his chair. Will looked over at his glass.

"Let me fill you up there Noah." Will grabbed his glass and headed into the kitchen area to some laughs behind him.

Faith and Heather clinked glasses curious where this would go. Arianna took a sip, still feeling like she was in court.

"Robert Tanner. Ad guy who was friends with Maria," she looked at Kaylee who knew Maria from back then.

"I guess it was," she sipped her Black Russian, until the ice slid to her lips, "a month before we met actually." She bit her lip looking at Noah. Will arrived right on time.

"Drink up."

Noah finally added to the conversation. In song.

"Was it in New York. Right in the very heart of it, New York, New Yooooork!"

Will looked over at him. "Nice Noah."

Noah's dare two turns before Heather, was to sing his conversations for the next 30 minutes. He decided on Frank Sinatra.

"No, Philly." Arianna added.

Forty-five minutes later Heather and Faith stumbled up to bed. Faith never changed, just passed out on the comforter. Heather just pulled off what she was wearing and slipped into bed. She was out in 15 seconds. Eventually Jason went up to join Faith. Then Drew kissed Kaylee and he headed up, followed by Noah who missed the first step at the stairs and nearly fell.

Everyone would curse themselves tomorrow morning, especially as the kids would wake up ready for action. Will, Arianna, and Kaylee were left standing in the kitchen finishing their drinks. The couples all knew each other from either childhood, college, or work. Arianna and Kaylee were the ones that were brought together by work. Will and Andrew went to school together at Wake Forest.

Arianna hopped up on the counter, swinging her legs back and forth. She started rambling on, which she did when she was drunk, as Will and

Kaylee laughed and started cleaning up a bit. By the time their glasses were empty, and no one honestly wanted another, Kaylee announced she was done. She waddled by Arianna and kissed her on the cheek. She then slapped Will on the shoulder.

"I better go make sure Drew made it to bed." She held up her hand and waved while walking off, not sure if anyone saw it or even cared. Her feet, covered in fleece socks, thumped up the steps.

Will flipped the light switch in the kitchen, leaving only the stove top light on. It glowed down on the gas stove's six grates. Some night-lights dimmed the hardwood floors in splotches. Arianna's legs stopped swinging and came to a rest. Will walked over to her, standing right in front of her. She spread her legs and her fingers dug into his sweatshirt, tugging him into her. Their lips pecked each other teasingly as they looked at one another.

"Let's go," Will whispered.

Arianna shook her head and licked his lips. "Right here."

"Are you crazy?"

"Everyone in this house is passed out, no one will know. They wouldn't believe it in the morning anyways."

"Jesus Aria." He pushed away from her, but she held him there, closing her legs on him like a vice.

"You know Robert called me Aria."

"That was true?" Will's hand roamed over her black tights, then under her over-the-shoulder sweater, sliding up her bare back.

"Partially. He just wasn't the most recent thanks to someone's business trips to Philly."

"This sweater is amazing on you."

"I know, it was worth putting up with the chill."

He then shoved his tongue in her mouth and they kissed hard for 10 seconds. He then pulled her off the counter and they walked into the garage. Thanks to the moon and the street lamps, the garage door windows tinted the inside gray. Jason's Ford Explorer was next to Will's three-week-old BMW.

Will rubbed his hands together. "Damn it's cold in here."

Arianna walked up to the German cars front bumper. "Then we better get busy." She turned around looking at him and slinked her way up onto the hood. "You'll never look at your hood the same way again."

After six years in the Rocky Mountains, and some 263 houseguests, the Eastern cards would travel in that direction, with Will and Heather Ramsey. An adolescent's spiced up game would take them back east. Heather looked at the deck, but didn't see cards. She saw a slideshow of their daughters first ever white Christmas, fun card games with friends as demanding children all lay asleep, and an adventurous trek to unknown neighbors in 12-degree weather. Will didn't see cards either. He saw the prelude to a wild ride on his BMW. He didn't even need the keys.

"Okay girls, I'll be back here in exactly two hours okay."

"Okay." Came in unison.

"Which one of you has a watch?"

Aspen and Macy were leaning down into the passenger window. They pulled back their sweaters answering him. "We do. Two hours."

"You got it. Have fun." The passenger window slid up, reflecting the lights and buildings of Vail behind them. Aspen, Macy, and Julie all put on their jackets, and giggled and laughed their way through the fairy-tale like village. It was Sunday, late afternoon, and relatively slow.

They skied Breckenridge, again, that day from sun up to lunch. The Christmas day snow brought perfect conditions for the next couple of days. After showering and packing up, the 14 & 15 year-olds headed off for one night together, away from everyone.

Just past the ice rink, they got out from the shelter of the buildings and stringed light bulbs criss crossing above. The sky opened up to them, with the burnt orange and peach clouds over the mountains as if a child displayed their messy finger painting. The orange sun was behind that mountain, and seemed to be pulling Aspen towards it. Towards a certain peak with a view.

They wandered around for 45 minutes. Aspen had just bought hot chocolates for all, and found Julie and Macy blowing their breaths at each other.

"Thanks Asp." Julie took hers and pulled the lid off. She started licking the whip cream.

"They make the best hot chocolate out here. I know it sounds stupid, but they just do." Macy's eyes widened as she too, pulled off the lid. She scooped a smear and dabbed it on Aspen's nose. They all laughed. Aspen loved when Julie called her Asp.

"Let's go back and hit the rink." Macy was putting the lid back on.

"Oh totally," replied Julie. They were both excellent skaters.

"Go ahead. I'm going to check out a couple of shops over there." Aspen nodded over her right shoulder.

Julie scrunched her eyes. "No Asp, come on it'll be fun. We'll help."

Aspen shook her head. "No, no really you two go show off. I'll meet up with you later. No worries."

"You sure?" Macy asked.

"Yeah." Aspen then looked at her roommate for the last six days. She was trying to figure out how to do this without Macy thinking something was weird.

"Alright, come on Juls." Macy turned and took two steps. Julie smiled at Aspen and turned to follow. That's when Aspen made her move.

Aspen took a giant step right behind Julie and wrapped her arms around her. She squeezed. Julie was mostly puffy jacket and thick sweater, but eventually found her arms and body under it all.

"Have fun Julie." *I love you. I'm going to miss you.* Her eyes were watery as she hugged her only true friend in the world. A cousin from Ohio, she sees maybe once a year. A tear plopped down on Julie's slick, North Face jacket.

Julie reached up and grabbed Aspen's gloved hands, and smiled.

"Okay okay goofball. I will." She laughed as Aspen let go and walked off. Julie turned, still smiling at the silliness, and watched Aspen go. Her smile faded away and tilted her head a little, as if it would help her see Aspen's face. She licked her lips as she started walking backwards, still watching Aspen walk away.

"Hey, you coming?"

"Yeah yeah." She turned and joined Macy. They grabbed hands and walked back down towards the rink. Just before turning the corner, Julie stopped and looked back behind her at the street scene. Aspen was gone, like a floating snowflake that finally disappeared into the white ground.

With five minutes before the lifts closed for those heading up the mountain, Aspen hopped on the Eagle Bahn Gondola, and soared 100 feet off the ground. Dressed like she was, she said she was going to catch up with family and find her little sister. The part-time lift operator, a junior at West Virginia spending his Christmas vacation away from home, didn't mind.

She put her hands in her pockets, crossed her dangling feet, and closed her eyes. The cold air made her lips tingle. She opened her eyes half way up and instinctually picked up her feet as she passed above a giant tree, even though she was 20 feet above it. Her hands felt the smooth water bottle in one pocket and metal in the other. Her dad had it easy she thought, he was able to use luggage. She used a bulky winter jacket.

Back at the house, she thought about him as she packed up her jacket with the things she would need. Was he excited when packing for that last business trip? Or nervous? Shameful? She felt at ease, her steps were light, shoulders void of tension, and there was no heaviness in her chest. She looked at her packed suitcase with pity. It was going to have to go back home. The Rubik's Cubes were too. She even thought of the Eastern cards, knowing her needle wouldn't point to 90 degrees.

With a bulkier jacket than Macy and Julie, she jumped in her uncle's car. Even leaving the house was easy, never even looking back for a final glimpse. She knew what was there. She knew what would be there tomorrow and the next.

This past summer she read *No Exit,* and the play named for it by Jean-Paul Sartre. For a 15 year old, she had a very unique view of hell. In the play, three people visit hell, but it's not full of flames, chains, and pitchforks. It was an elegant ballroom with velvet chairs and floor to ceiling windows paired with slender drapes. Real candles fit in the chandeliers and the doors reached up to the ceiling, 20 feet up. After a while, the three strangers bicker and can't stand each other. Aspen got it immediately; it has nothing to do with your setting.

Mary wakes up in a a tiny apartment that should be a walk in closet. A single bulb hangs in the middle of the two rooms. It swings with every elevated train rumbling by, sending dancing shadows slithering on the cracked walls. The good thing about getting up at 4:30, you can't see what's really there, crawling around. She tramps down to the bus stop to sit on a lonely bus at a lonely time of morning. She shuffles down to the subway to sit on a smelly train car. Then steps in her building of work through a back door, not because she's cool or knows the right crowd, but because they don't want her to be seen by people in the front.

Mary then cleans bathrooms, makes beds, scrubs toilets, wipes down showers, picks up dirty towels, and does the laundry for people who could care less who she is, or that she was once a little girl with dreams who still sleeps with her blanket. Her life is a baggage carousel, going around and around, seeing and doing the same thing every minute, day, week, year, decade, lifetime. She was the piece of luggage always on it going around, forgotten, lost, never getting off. Her hell isn't a roaring dark dungeon, but a five-star luxury hotel across from Central Park.

Kirstan was sitting in her chair, reclining back with her nine-month-old son sleeping on her chest. With his acid reflux, he won't sleep lying flat, something that made her sleep in a chair since he was born. She was averaging four hours of sleep a night. Her day job just paid the bills for the two-bedroom, 1,100 square foot apartment. Two hours earlier, she turned down another movie night with some girlfriends, just like last month, and the spring before for that matter, to save on money. Her husband was still traveling too much, but every little penny helped. Kirstan's eyeglasses were on the nursery table, missing the lens for the left eye.

After two miscarriages, a sister and sister-in-law each on their second child, and girlfriends whispering behind her back at why she didn't have a baby yet, the doorway, chipped and in need of paint, might as well have been the Pearly Gates.

Erik's Jura GIGA 5 was hissing behind him, brewing his morning coffee. With his hands in his pockets, he leaned against the doorframe that lead out to his marble deck and infinity pool. The pool encircled the entire first floor like a moat; crystal clear and inviting. His three-story house is in the small coastal town of Utjeha-Bušat, Montenegro. If resting your elbows on the edge of the pool, the rocky shore of the Adriatic is 50 feet below, and Bari, Italy 135 miles across. His blue Lamborghini Aventador Roadster parked in the driveway that leads into the second floor.

His 19-year-old son was flying to the office today. He would take over the business in seven years when Erik turns 50. His blond 6'1" wife, a former Miss Croatia, was up on the third floor in the gym. His life is not a merry-go-round, but a gleaming Eurostar train, zipping to endless possibilities and faraway places in no time. Whenever he desired. There is no question where Erik lived.

Aspen was in Disney World a couple of years ago. It was one of those moments she remembers as vividly as if it had happened two seconds ago. Two lines funneled by the cashier in the Crystal Palace, a popular eating venue at the Magic Kingdom near Main Street. She was dying to put the tray down on the metal railing shelf. With her food, along with Nate's, the two full drinks were wobbling it enough even without all the other food. Her forearms were killing her.

She would have passed the time by thinking about the rides she'd been on or trying to imagine what Space Mountain looks like with lights on, but they didn't go on any. According to Nate, if you don't ride the Tea Cups first, the others will not be worth it. It was closed for maintenance unexpectedly; something a social story couldn't cover. And with mom's rule of riding things together to be a family, and since he doesn't like Aspen doing things without him, the closest thing to a ride was watching the logs of Splash Mountain plummet down the track and sloshing through water.

Aspen looked over in the other line and noticed two kids, probably brother and sister. He appeared a little older. They were smiling, eating normal food kids eat, talking about the rides and their next Fast Pass. They debated on doing EPCOT, or Magic Kingdom again, tomorrow. She tried imagining their lives, their possible stresses then. The girl then mentioned other names of friends and classmates, and what they did at an eighth grade school dance.

At that moment, the only thing Aspen looked forward to in life, wasn't a trip tomorrow, a birthday, or a driver's license, but simply putting that damn tray down from her shaking arms. She didn't want anything spilling or dropping, making the afternoon worse. Her life was dominoes always teetering, waiting to fall at the slightest caress.

She looked up at the hanging signs above each line. Hers read *Hell*; the other line read *Heaven* pointing at the siblings. If a character dinner were taking place, Cinderella would get in that other line, while Maleficent would cut in front of Aspen.

Aspen understood Sartre's play better than others. It didn't matter where she was; she had a ball and chain dragging behind her and Nate poking her with a pitchfork. There was no heaven or hell, it was life on earth and everyone just moved through the two like convection.

By the time she leaned forward to get off the lift at Vail, her momentum making her trot down a small mound, she pulled out the water bottle and took a sip. She was thirsty, but it was more to wet her dry lips. The next lift was shorter than the last, almost by half. Aspen rode the Game Creek Express lift to the top of Wildwood.

Skiers were scarce, and the sunlight was joining them. It wasn't as clear as Christmas Eve, but still breathtaking. The far off trees were a darker green now, thanks to a dipped sun not able to pump life into them. The far off mountains, with snow like tile, had clumps of trees scattered around like stains.

Aspen trudged through the crunchy snow and stuck to the trees. She found a thick trunk with a gap in front of it. The trunks on either side making a stage for her show. She sat down with her back against it. The trunk was her velvet seat up in the balcony. She took a deep breath. *This will do.*

She brought two important things. One was a portable CD player with tiny headphones attached. She took off her gloves and threw them to her left. She turned it on, listening to it whine as the CD spun to life. It stopped and 14 was displayed in the box. She tapped the arrow button twice until three blinked, and then hit the repeat button. She wedged in the earpieces in each ear as Pyotr Ilyich Tchaikovsky's violin concerto began playing.

Her favorite violin piece filled her head as the mountain snow turned light gray in the dimming light. Specks of light, like twinkling diamonds, began popping up here and there down the valley. The sky to her left was still dark blue, but to the right, was dark purple.

She pulled out the water bottle and jabbed it down into the snow next to her. Then she pulled out the ziplock.

Aspen closed her eyes, as she couldn't bring herself to look, and pried open the clear bag. She shook it, like someone pulling out numbers in a drawing, and then reached in.

She grabbed a handful of pills and popped them in her mouth, as if yawning. She then gulped some water and squinted hard at swallowing so much that wasn't chewed. By the twelfth minute, she was picturing the violin under her cheek, with the rapid, jerky movements now over and the bow slowly, softly caressing the strings back and forth, back and forth. The melody was slowly moving her head and shoulders, as if conducted by her DNA.

The branches seemed to be listening to the Tchaikovsky as well, dipping and swaying to the ups and downs of the music in the breeze. It was like the violin and nature knew what was taking place, right or wrong, in Aspen's head.

Up until then she had swallowed 15 pills, mostly sleeping pills, but a few Oxycodones as well. By the time the song started over, the bag was empty, all 19 pills were gone.

A stinging pain grew roots in her chest, spreading all over, then went away. Then it came back again in a shock, only to peel away again. She gripped the water bottle tightly, crinkling it in fear. Then she released it, popping it back into place. She crossed her arms hugging herself. Her closed eyelids matched the darkening sky with purples and dark blues. Tchaikovsky lulled her to a deep sleep, still hearing the beautiful strings long after her eye were closed.

The last blurry vision behind those eyelids, was a little girl being scooped up by a father and hugged tightly in the air. She was swung around like a doll, with Snuggles mashed between them. The gleaming red and white striped TWA L-1011, just outside of the window at gate B8 of Lambert-St.Louis International airport, shut her engines down for the night. Four months before he left for good, they stopped allowing people to go out to the gates anymore, unless you were flying. She knew that was a bad omen.

Thirty-nine miles from where she was conceived, Aspen MacGregor left a world of mean kids, lost hope, and a disorder called autism.

From March 1993 to December 1999……

14 games of Aces Up Solitaire
27 games of Asshole
3 games of Auction Pitch
62 games of Black Jack
4 games of Black Lady Hearts
18 games of Canasta
15 games of Cincinnati Poker
7 games of Contract Bridge
5 games of Eleusis
10 games of Euchre
1 game of Faro
289 games of Five-Card Draw Poker
94 games of Five-Card Stud Poker
7 games of Five Hundred
79 games of Fish
110 games of Gin
6 games of Gut Poker
212 games of Hearts
148 games of Klondike Solitaire
4 games of Lowball Poker
51 games of Memory
13 games of Michigan
8 games of Palace
10 games of Pig
5 games of Railroad Euchre
309 games of Rummy
9 games of Seven-Card High-Low Stud Poker
58 games of Seven-Card Stud Poker
146 games of Spades
&
26 minutes of multiplication Facts

PART VI

Boston Celtics
Detroit Tigers
San Francisco 49ers
Edmonton Oilers
Sarajevo & Los Angeles

CHAPTER FIFTEEN

Addison Briggs was in seat 12A of Eastern Airlines flight 285, from Miami to Washington DC. It was the Tuesday of Thanksgiving week. He had the window seat on the left side, knowing it would pay off later. He'd been in the air for 70 minutes, just off the coast of Georgia, but it might as well have been 18 hours. That's when the 11 year old mentally boarded.

You could see it in his bag, organized the night before. Then his backpack, full of essentials in a kid's version of a briefcase. Both bags resting up against each other by the door. At dinner, his brussel sprouts were tolerable. He watched Peter Jennings give the news as if he could end up flying to any of those places. He remembered the stories in case he needed a conversation starter with someone next to him. In bed, his eyes ventured across his darkened walls at posters and pennants, then tried to follow a fan blade spinning too fast for 25 minutes. He finally drifted off to sleep at 10:40.

He was up at 6am, dressed by 6:15, and enjoying his maple syrup-drenched Eggo Waffle by 6:22. All complimented, and made more interesting, by the folded up Miami Herald sports page at the table. More conversation pieces, better ones. The flight that evening slowed the clock hands at Margaret Trammell Junior High that day. Every glance at the black rimmed, white-faced clock brought out confusion and sighs. He put up with a flannel shirt in 77 degree weather knowing it would be like a warm fire come 6:00 pm. Even when he was questioned for being 30 seconds late to fifth period science, he just looked at Mr. Graham and thought, *but I'm going to be on an airplane in four hours?*

Alone.

His father had to work late Wednesday and early Friday. His mother then offered to work some on Thanksgiving for the overtime. They could use the money with the holidays coming up. So Addison was being sent early to his aunt and uncle's in Virginia, just outside D.C. He floated down the school hallway and sidewalk to his mother's Oldsmobile Cutlass. They hugged him at the gate, waved at his plane from the giant terminal window, and looked up at the sky from the 836 Dolphin Expressway.

Being a school night made the flight even more epic. He and an elderly woman, already on board, were flagged for flying alone. They were given even more attention than usual. He strolled down the jetway like he was boarding Air Force One, walked down the 727's aisle as if a ring bearer, and found his seat like Han Solo.

Now, as they soared past Savannah, his portioned off dinner tray was taken away with a smile. The meatloaf and mashed potatoes were gone, only specks of gravy remained. The cooked carrots were still there. Addison didn't even need to hide them in the large, thick white napkin in his lap. He didn't need to wonder how many he had to eat to be considered 'good enough'. They just sat there, huddled together in a pile like fire logs. *Yes, those are my carrots. I did not eat them.*

"Honey, is there anything else I can get you?" She reached across the two empty seats taking his tray away. The passenger in 12C moved to the back to be near someone he had just met at the gate waiting to board. They would start a million dollar company within two years.

"May I get another Coke please?"

"Of course. How was your meal?" She really cared to know.

"Pretty good ma'am."

"But not the carrots huh?"

He looked up at her and shook his head cautiously. Her smile eased him. Then came a wink.

"I won't tell. Be right back with that Coke."

Addison grinned, a grin only made by someone ignoring carrots while going 400 mph, and reached into his backpack in the seat next to him. His *National Geographic* and *Sports Illustrated* had served their purpose. His hand dug around inside as his eyes scanned the glowing ceiling, as if he was looking inside. They weren't there. Next came the zipper compartment on the top. Only his Velcro *Ocean Pacific* wallet, pens, and Swiss Army knife were there.

So he reached back in the main compartment and pulled out a plastic case with some baseball cards. They would do until he got other cards.

He flipped through some random 1984 and 1983 Topps cards. His tray table was still down, making for a great baseball field. He laid out his hypothetical team by position. He was just about to decide the batting order when the stewardess came back with the Coke. She took his empty cup and handed him a new one, fizzing with bubbles, and the half-full can.

"Here's your Coke."

"Excuse me, do you have any playing cards?"

"Sure, let me check." She moved off behind him, stopping to chat with someone three rows back, then disappeared. He decided Sandberg should hit second and Brett third. Clean up was between Schmidt and Kittle, when she came back with the playing cards.

"Here you go. That was the last one, we'll have to stock up again once we land."

"Thank you." He scooped up his baseball cards and put them away safely in his backpack. Then Addison grabbed the deck of cards. The box was a rich blue with Eastern at the top and upside down at the bottom. The airline symbol, which Addison thought was a cross between a shark's fin or simply half a plane from above, was after the name.

They were wrapped in cellophane and Addison couldn't get the box opened. After two minutes of patience left his thumb and index finger red, the stewardess happened to be walking by.

"Oh here, let me help you honey." She sat down in the aisle seat and crossed her leg. The purple skirt and white blouse looked so fancy to Addison.

"These things are like cassette tapes to open aren't they?"

Addison laughed, "Yes they are." He watched her long, red fingernail slide under a folded down crease and pop it up. She crinkled it up into a ball in her hand and handed him the box. These cards were not card stock, but smooth, hard, thin, and crisp. Like all new decks, shuffling them at first was a pain. Eventually he began making his piles, all seven for Solitaire which was cramped on the seat back tray. The brunette stewardess was still there.

She never moved and just watched him. The man across the aisle in 12D asked her something, they laughed, volleying comments back and forth across the carpeted aisle, but she sat comfortably. Addison looked at her and knew she was obviously looking out for him, but also the relaxed calmness told him this was nothing new to her. She probably looked at empty seats like he looked at an unopened pack of baseball cards. He would have felt that way no matter what happened back at takeoff. Back when Han Solo was frozen in carbonite.

For all the confidence and thrill surging through his body the last 17 hours, he's still an 11-year-old boy who has never been away from his parents longer than a sleep over or four day marine biology camp out on Key Biscayne. It only took 15 seconds for it all to be sucked out of him. That's how long it took for them to push back the plane and turn it to taxi. The massive windows of the gate came into view out his tiny porthole window. Seeing his parents waving goodbye at him from behind five inches of glass, while he sat in a sealed tube about to fly 927 miles away, made him feel vulnerable, lonely, and unsure.

She saw it in his face, his rising chest, blinking eyes, and in his fingers entwined in the seat belt strap. To his unknown timidness, she plopped down in 12C and buckled up.

"May I join you Addison? Those cabin seats in the galley are so uncomfortable."

"Uh sure." He licked his lips and stole a glance at her.

She glanced down at his backpack on the seat between them. Only a fraction of the magazine was sticking out of the unzipped part, but the unmistakable yellow border gave it away.

"Oh, my niece reads *National Geographic.* Where do you live hon'?" They chatted and Addison found it easy to talk to her. She was pretty, he wondered what she looked like when she was in sixth grade, and had a gift to socialize. He had no idea they were now second in line for takeoff.

"Do you have a home? Uh, I mean of course you do, but, well where do you live?" It came out wrong and he looked embarrassed. She laughed, but not at him, with him.

"That's funny, I know what you mean. Yes, I'm from Atlanta, but based in Washington right now. There and Charlotte I guess. I just started so they send me anywhere."

"Did you always want to be a stewardess? I think you're good at it." Addison didn't know it, but he would trace this back to the first time he flirted.

"Not really, but I want to earn some money and can do it while traveling before going back to school in a couple years. I want to go to Optometry school."

"Is that an eye doctor?"

"Yep."

The nose of the 727 tilted up, leaning everyone back in their seats. Addison just assumed he was in a reclining chair, listening to an older sister or even on a shrink's couch for therapy.

"What's your name?"

"Darlene."

"Is your niece in Atlanta? He turned in his seat and hooked his right leg under him.

"Yep and Traveler."

"Who?"

"My dog."

She smiled and reached into her pocket, pulling out a bottle opener, then found a tiny leather booklet. She put the opener back. She unsnapped it and flipped through it showing him small pictures like his mom orders from school. They talked about themselves and what Addison and her niece were for Halloween last month. Eventually the fasten seat belt sign dinged off and she had to leave. Addison looked back out the window at the wing slicing through the clouds. Then suddenly they burst into a purple sky. The setting, dull sun seemed to be falling asleep, closing it's eye, on a dark cloud bank to the west.

Darlene leaned over resting her elbow on the chair arm and surveyed the cards. A red fingernail tapped a red five, then she sat back.

"Oh, yeah." Addison picked it up and moved it under a black six, then turned over an ace.

"Ahh, there you go. Nice. Honey I'll be back in a couple of minutes maybe, think of a game we can play." She stood up and grabbed something from a guy a couple rows up. Addison moved the ace up to the top and turned over a black ten. He lost badly in the two games of solitaire, but was trying to figure out what to play with his new girlfriend.

About 45 minutes before landing, it was slow in the cabin and Darlene came back. She had tiny pilot wings with her and pinned them to his flannel shirt. It might as well have been a Nobel Prize. She reached up and pressed a button, turning on an angled light above them.

"So what are we playing?" They played two games of rummy, that had to be paused every seven or eight draws for her to go do something, but that didn't matter. It was a fantastic first date. Darlene hadn't played cards since last spring in Athens at her sorority house. He had just played on Halloween with Asher and Edgar, in their usual Halloween ritual game.

Coming into National Airport was better from the left side of the plane. It was the one airport that the pilots didn't need a compass to land. Pilots followed the Potomac, winding its way north into the city and waiting runway hugging the river. Addison gazed out at the long gray wing dipping and raising, as the pilot followed his watery course. With about a mile to go, the nation's capital popped into view. First, it was the Lincoln Memorial and bridge of lights leading to it. Then Jefferson's domed tribute, with a copy mirrored on the water next to it. Finally behind it all, the towering Washington Monument.

From the view out the window, it seemed like the plane was landing in the water. The pilot distracted by the grand view out the port side. With the dark chop of the Potomac just feet from the plane, grass and blue lights raced by, just seconds before the runway slid under the plane like a conveyer belt.

He was told to let everyone else off first, then he and the elderly woman in the back would disembark. Addison zipped up everything on his backpack, and reorganized things in his smaller compartment. He double checked the fastener of the back of the pilot wings on his shirt, which he wore like a promise ring now, and unbuckled his seat belt. He headed down the aisle with the same thrill and confidence as when he boarded. Darlene and two other stewardesses were waiting in the galley. All were talking and laughing, then turned and smiled to him.

"Hey honey, you got everything?"

"Yes ma'am." Addison always gripped the one strap over his right shoulder.

"I'm going to walk you off and make sure your family is here okay?"

He nodded. Then he leaned to the left a little and peered into the dark cockpit ten feet away.

"But, unfortunately there's been a problem on board though. The captain needs to speak to you." She looked at him with the smile gone. Addison froze and swallowed. He thought they could hear his gulp down in baggage. It was as if the pretty stewardess turned into a teacher. Just then, the captain, all 6'4" of him, ducked out into the galley.

"Where is Addison Briggs?"

If someone as pretty as Darlene could worry him, the giant of a captain took away his saliva.

"Right here captain." Darlene crossed her arms and raised an eyebrow.

"Well well, so the problem young man is you can't step off this plane without a visit to the cockpit." He put his hands on his hips, making him menacing. Addison's shoulders eased down and he could swallow.

Darlene was now smiling at him. "Would you like to see the cockpit honey?"

Addison smiled and found his voice, and would have cussed if he dared.

"I'd love to."

"Well come on, you're too young to be hanging out with three beautiful stewardesses." The pilot put a huge hand out. Addison shook it, his hand disappearing.

"Captain Michael Tyler. Come on."

He was surprised that the seats didn't look very comfortable. The windows were narrower than he imagined. Otherwise, it was much much more than he had imagined. The dials and switches and buttons almost made him dizzy. It was a gray maze of circles, needles, and colored bulbs.

"How do you ever remember what they all do?" Addison stood behind the co-pilot's chair, eyes as big as the altimeter, sweeping left to right. He was very surprised at the control panels on the ceiling.

"Well they're grouped in a way, in common purposes. And some are the same. The co-pilot will have some," he pointed to both sides, "and I have the same ones. It really gets easier the more you practice with them."

"How fast did we go?"

"Once at cruising altitude, about 465 mph tonight."

Addison nodded and looked around as if in the Sistine Chapel.

Two minutes later, Darlene stepped inside. "Well, you about ready?"

"Sure. Thank you Captain."

"No, thank you, for allowing us to fly you up here. You have a happy Thanksgiving."

Darlene walked him up the jetway. His aunt, uncle, and three cousins were all standing in the gate. It was already half full with those ready for the return flight back to Miami. Some of their local friends also called the gate home, just to hang out. Four people standing next to a pillar by the Eastern desk were sipping champagne and wine in slender flutes. Laughter sailed to him from the right side, while a child trotted across his path holding up a toy plane as high as he could. 80,000 feet as far as he was concerned.

"There they are." He twisted while walking towards them, a little quicker than normal. His oldest cousin held up a white piece of paper with "DORK" written across it. Addison would roll his eyes at the 12 year old's greeting.

"Okay Addison, it was nice to meet you. Happy Thanksgiving." She waved at his aunt and uncle, smiling.

"You too!" Their first date was over way too fast.

She turned and reached up to retie some loose hair, and then strutted back down the jetway, her thumping heels slowly softening.

Baggage claim was busy and loud. The low ceiling pinched in all the conversations, announcements, and ringing & buzzing of the luggage stations coming to life. Praying heads framed the curvy metal tracks, as bulky suitcases paraded by under inspecting eyes. Eastern flight 285 was at baggage claim four. A giant light blue suitcase was first, playing pace car. Bryce, Ethan, and Toni asked all about his flight, and couldn't believe he was in the cockpit. Ethan kept sneaking glances down at Addison's pilot wings. Addison's bag was spit out the hole in the wall of hanging tarps midway through the race. His uncle heaved it off at turn three. When they all stepped outside through the sliding doors to the curb, the crispness of Virginia's autumn night slapped Addison's face. He even felt it on his neck between his open collar. It was sanitizing. He thought about never taking his flannel shirt off.

Uncle Trey drove and Aunt Sheila sat sideways to talk with Addison in the backseat. He sat between Ethan and his twin sister Toni, who were a year younger than Addison. Bryce was in the back of the station wagon, and a year older. 40 minutes later, they were home. Traffic around the airport and near Tyson Corner slowed them down. Addison noticed every license plate was a white Virginia, and it hit him that in just over two hours, he traveled almost the entire length of the east coast. By himself.

Along the way, he noticed highway billboards for local radio stations, Redskins players and ticket information, and grocery chains he had never heard of. There was also lots of traffic that was similar to Miami.

Once home, Aunt Sheila called her sister letting them know he had arrived. She handed Addison the phone, the long cord stretching across the kitchen to Addison, who quickly summed up the flight to his mom.

They had picked up two pizzas on the way home. The kitchen's island was their table, the stools their chairs. The box lids were flung open and anxious hands pulled out thick slices. Uncle Trey helped, rolling a pizza cutter through the gooey cheese to release the slices.

Bryce pulled open the fridge and shifted some things around.

"Hey mom, where's the parmesan?"

"Is it not there?"

More jars clinking, Tupperware sliding. "Nope."

"Huh, well go next door to the Wierda's. They may have some."

Bryce headed out. Addison leaned over to Toni while curling his slice for a bite.

"So they're weird?"

Toni laughed with a mouthful and waited to swallow.

"No that's their last name, but spelled differently. They're really cool."

Ethan didn't bother to stop chewing. "The dad has a Triumph motorcycle. It's awesome."

"She's a real good singer too." Toni turned to her mom, just before biting. "Does she still have the butterfly garden in the back?"

"I believe so, in the spring." Aunt Sheila added.

Both boys continued chewing. Toni tossed them napkins shaking her head. She was used to boys. Another slice later, Bryce came back. He twisted off the cap and sprinkled his slice. He passed it around.

"What's new with Betsy?" Aunt Sheila finished her first slice, tossing her crust in the box. Bryce and Toni reached in at the same time. Bryce smiled in victory, Toni sighed.

"Not much. She was going through some boxes of shoes."

A couple of seconds later, Ethan finished his second piece and, like a baton in a relay, passed it over to his sister. Ethan even pulled off the crust of his sandwiches.

"Ooh thanks," she said.

Around 10:15, all the kids had Oreos and milk before going bed. The 11:00 news said it would snow that night and into Wednesday morning. Addison had seen snow once, but it was an inch and gone the next day. The schools were out all week, unlike Dade County, and they all looked forward to tomorrow. They had a lot of catching up from two years of not seeing each other. Little did Addison know how much the geography would affect him.

He bought long flannel pajamas for the trip, something kids in Miami didn't know existed. His flannel shirt did come off after all, with a curl of his lips, but it wasn't the first thing he took off. That distinction went to the gold Eastern pilot wings from Darlene, resting on top of the box of playing cards.

Addison slept in Bryce's room, sleeping on the top bunk. There were no fans on the ceilings. Also the A/C vents were in the floor along the walls. Addison couldn't get used to that. A space shuttle and Concorde model hung from the ceiling. Invisible fishing line helping to defy gravity. The British Airways Concorde swayed a little above his feet as he just nudged it with a toe. He wondered if you could tell you were going Mach two from the inside looking out.

The 11:00 news was right about the snow, but off about the amount. It started slowly coming down around 11:30, hundreds of tiny white parachutes floating down aimlessly. Two hours later the winds whistled the snow sideways as the front approached the mid-Atlantic states. By the time the kids got up, it was thick confetti falling straight down from the gray sky.

Addison was the first up, a statue of flannel standing in front of the window next to Bryce's bunk bed. His hands were pressed against the glass, eyes opened to their widest aperture. He just stared. And stared.

Bryce rolled over, sighed, and peeked at Addison at his window.

"Did it snow?" He closed his eyes and wedged his face deeper into his pillow.

"Uh, you could say that." He finally blinked and turned to Bryce. "You live on Hoth."

Bryce opened his left eye at Addison and inhaled deeply. He swung his legs out and stood up, stretching. He shuffled over just behind Addison, peering past his shoulder.

"Yep it snowed alright." He scratched his head and turned. He walked out of his room into the bathroom directly across the hall. Addison watched him go, confused at his nonchalant cousin. *'Yep it snowed alright?' That's it?* He shook his head.

Addison stole another glance outside then walked over to Bryce's dresser. A John Riggins poster was on the wall. He hadn't noticed it last night. Addison looked at it, took a deep breath, and sighed. A bad taste in his mouth moved into his stomach, like swallowing something visually. Without closing his eyes, all he saw was Riggins running with Don McNeal hanging on for dear life, clinging to his stretched jersey. Then finally not able to hold on anymore, he let go, the jersey snapped back. Then Riggins, now free, lumbered down the sideline for the clinching touchdown against the Dolphins in the Super Bowl.

Addison closed his eyes and opened them down on the dresser. Bryce's view-master was next to his Rubik's Cube and Rubik's Snake. Some football cards were stacked neatly two inches high, right next to his Little Professor owl calculator. He peeked outside one last time, just to make sure he wasn't seeing things, and headed downstairs.

Within 20 minutes, all four kids were downstairs at the kitchen table. All were either blowing on their hot cocoa or kissing sips quickly. Aunt Sheila was making French toast with the thickest bread Addison had ever seen, and Addison loved bread. The kid, who once ordered a 'loaf of toast' with a straight face, was impressed. The smell of maple syrup, brewed coffee, and cinnamon, with the sight of so much snow outside the windows through the virgin winter eyes of someone growing up in Miami, made Addison simply delirious.

Breakfast was scrumptious, chased with hot cocoa lining his stomach like molasses. Powdered sugar coated the whole table. All in flannel pj's that could have been in an advertisement for LL Bean. He knew, still a day away from even touching Thursday's festive meal, this would be a hard Thanksgiving to top for the rest of his life.

That stayed true even when the power went out.

At 9:00, the radio station had reports of power outages west in

Petersburg and Moorefield, West Virginia. By 10:30, that would included Winchester. By 11, that included the Morris house.

Across the living room, Uncle Trey was kneeling next to the fireplace. He was pulling cut wood through a metal door in the brick hearth. Addison would later enquire about the door and hole. He saw there was a larger door at the other end, opening to the outside of the house. His uncle was building a fire before leaving, as if it were a puzzle he just took apart and now decided to put it together again.

His uncle owned a men's clothing shop outside of Washington. Once a week, some politician came in for a fitting or alteration. Joe Gibbs came in two summers ago. It was small, functional, and so simple it was fancy. They came for the dress clothes and Trey. He didn't even know how to work the register. There were people for that. The same one for 26 years. He roamed the back and fitting area, armed with with a measuring tape draped around his neck at all times. Aunt Sheila still will look at him some nights when he comes home and remind him to take it off. A stich, cuff, newspaper, or kindling, it was approached meticulously. In the spring and summer, the mowed lawn was a green checkerboard.

Addison shed his pj's and borrowed a thicker jacket from the coat closet. Between the coat closet, brick that is not seen south of Tallahassee, and the secret fire wood storage space behind a thick metal door like an oven, he was ready to move in. And he hadn't even seen the basement yet.

The Morris' lived on a cul-de-sac, with other brick and stone houses built between trees. Their backyard fanned out some 100 feet, angling up to more trees and a wooden fence. The maple tree's branches were bare now, like an elderly person's sickly arms and fingers reaching out. The evergreens past the fence were thick and straining under the snow's bulk. There were no clouds or even what appeared to be a sky. Just dripping grayness.

The four kids jumped and pranced in the new snow. Only their yells and Toni's shrieks could cover up the constant sound of crunching footsteps. Snowballs were kneaded. Snow angels were carved. Snowmen were built and risen from the snow like zombies from a graveyard, only happier and fatter. Addison's first ever one felt like Howard Roark's first house.

By noon, they were back inside, wet coats and boots in the laundry room. Addison was still amazed, from Bryce's remark at his bedroom window, to Ethan's about Addison's five snow angels. He was awestruck. Toni summed it up.

"Addison, do you remember when we first came down to visit you four years ago? That spring?"

"Uh, sure."

She leaned on the table. "And you made fun of us for our sand angels, sand castles, and comments at the beach?"

Addison was about to reply, when it hit him. He sighed and nodded. "Touché."

Uncle Trey came home early. His coat found the closet in the foyer. Two steps from his bedroom the burgundy scarf was untied under his chin and unwound. He still had one more things around his neck. At his bureau, he took off his Tank watch, then reached up and slid off the measuring tape over his right shoulder. They were both put down next to each other, the pair as old as the leather catchall they rested in.

The power remained out until 7:30. No one seemed to even care. Ethan pulled out Monopoly from a closet in his room. By the time the lights did come back on, the three hour game produced a square of hotels and houses ringing the board.

By 8:00, Addison's Eastern cards were downstairs for a game of Rummy. Bryce had three 8's and a run of 5,6,7 of spades. Toni had four 3's and a run of 9,10, jack of hearts. Ethan and Addison had nothing as the conversation of another possible Redskins - Dolphins Super Bowl got in the way of cards. After 15 minutes, Toni had enough, calling for a reverse from the playbook.

"Okay, no sports. So what was better, *Footloose* or *Sixteen Candles?"*

"Jake Ryan was way cooler than Ren McCormack." Ethan addressed the table.

"Jake Ryan was cooler than everyone. Period." Addison piled on.

Toni held up her Cherry 7Up. "Very true."

"Although Ren could dance better." Ethan offered.

"Who cares," Addison waved him off. "He dressed better and his 944 beats a VW Bug."

"Footloose." Bryce blurted it out while finally scoring some points, laying down four 3's in front of him. All three barely noticed, looking at him curiously. The oldest kid in the room, and a boy at that, gave his proof.

"Ariel blows Sam away." All nodded in thought, while Toni rolled her eyes.

"*Gremlins* or *Ghostbusters?* Worst monsters?" Ethan played along.

Toni laid down an eight, playing off Bryce's three, then discarded to end the game. "Ghostbusters, totally." She continued, seeing the other three were too busy counting points to discuss yet. "The gremlins were cute, but the rules were dumb. Was I the only one who had a problem with the, 'no feeding after midnight'?"

Ethan wrote down his sister's total and subtracted his numbers. "What do you mean?"

Addison turned to Ethan, "ten." Then to Toni, "That bugged me too, you mean about when it finally is okay to eat?"

Toni slapped the table like finally someone got it. "Yes! So you can't feed them after midnight, so when is breakfast? Can I feed them at 6:00, what if they get up early, how about 5:00? Is that too early?"

"Exactly." Addison tossed his cards to Bryce who was starting to shuffle. He shook his head.

"I think I see your point, a stretch, but it doesn't matter. Ghostbusters wins." Bryce began shuffling, arching the cards and fluttering together into a pile. Toni already was rolling her eyes again.

"Sigourney Weaver in that red dress on the roof." Bryce smiled.

"How about Phoebe Cates though?" Addison just realized Darlene looked a little like Phoebe Cates, but different eyes.

"Nah, you'll understand eventually." Bryce started tossing out the cards to everyone. Just then, the phone rang. Let the games begin.

The Olympics may have been in August, but if the decathlon needed an eleventh event, reaching the phone first in the fewest rings in the Morris house was it. If not the Olympics, it was the Kentucky Derby, and the ring sprang open the start gates. Toni's chair was the first to screech back. As custom, she was not alone.

"I got it!" *It's gotta be Jacqueline.*

"I got it!" *That's probably Aaron or Tyler.*

"Got it!" *Oh please just once.*

Addison sat back wide-eyed and took it all in. The closest phone, one of only two downstairs, was on the wall vertically just to the right of the fridge. It was a beige color and the long curly cord hung down to the floor.

Bryce pulled the front half off, buttons glowing, just as Toni bumped into him. She huffed. He grinned.

"Hello. Morris residence." There was a three-second pause. The grin slid off his face and his eyes found the ceiling. "Yeah hold on."

He held out the curved receiver to his sister. "It's for you."

I knew it! She snatched it out of his hand and hit him in the shoulder.

"Hello."

The boys headed back to the table, Addison still staring at them. It was one of those times he was glad to be an only child. They picked up their cards and Bryce began whispering his tutorial on why *Ghostbusters* wins. Toni returned a minute later and the boys all sat up straighter.

"Speaking of movies, I could use some popcorn right now." Ethan scooped up his cards, fanning them out in his hand.

"Good call," Toni playfully kicked him under the table.

Suddenly Bryce leaned forward with an excited expression fizzing up across his face. He slapped his cards down on the table; a little firmer seeing that weren't cooperating lately.

"Hey, can't we use that thing now?" He pointed to a large black box next to the coffee maker under the cabinets. Addison followed his aim, twisting in his chair to check it out.

"Oh yeah, it makes it faster." Toni leaned to her right to peer around Addison into the family room. "Mom, can we make popcorn the new way? Pleeeese."

Bryce chimed in. "Yeah in that thing," he was still pointing. "What is it again?" His extended hand and finger quivering, bouncing up and down as if that would help speed things up.

A calm voice came wafting into the kitchen from the couch. "A microwave."

"Yeah the microwave! Can we?" Bryce pleaded.

A minute later Ethan placed the flat, folded bag inside and shut the door. He pressed some buttons and hit 'start', lighting up the inside. As the microwave hummed to life, all four cousins gathered in front and stared in the door window. For three minutes & 30 seconds, they watched and listened to the sound of pure technological popcorn bliss. It was like four children standing in front of a toy store window in December.

After counting every single kernel, to make sure no one got more than the other, they sat back down with their pile of radioactive treasure. The card games continued, Spades taking over from Rummy, as did the comparisons for another succulent hour. Ethan started the next one.

"Yars' Revenge or Missile Command?"

The Thanksgiving turkey just tasted better when surrounded by the fall scene in the house. It was so foreign to Addison. He was flanked by snow, flannel, a fireplace, pumpkins, candles, and fall wreaths. They were out for decorations, yet felt like they weren't pulled from the attic or basement, but just grew a little at a time through October.

Uncle Trey deep-fried the turkey in the backyard. He shoveled out a square section that was basically a 10 foot by 10 foot ice rink, tiny boards and all. His uncle monitored the thermometer sticking out of the pot and his watch like a Swiss chemist. His uncle cooked by his second hand. Addison was slightly upset his measuring tape wasn't draped around his collar.

They never left the house all day, yet it felt to Addison like he was in a museum, or festive banquet hall. Every room, conversation, and activity became a painting frozen in time. And it was all unique for him. He figured if they were in Key West, the others would have the same thrilling feeling. His snow would be their clear blue water. His pumpkins were their shells. His pumpkin pie was their key lime pie. Addison realized his environment was shaping him. Miami, and South Florida, would push him towards things, and pull him away from things for the rest of his life.

If he needed any proof that the day was fantastic, the clock hands would help. If they seemed to slow Tuesday all day, they sped up Thursday. Before he knew it, it was 6:30 as he and Toni sneaked another piece of pie with an avalanche of whip cream. Then it was 10:00 and he was nudging the Concorde once again, giving it some turbulence.

Addison's parents arrived at Dulles International late Friday afternoon. Dulles was much closer and they were home in half the time. There wasn't a cloud in the sky from Cape Canaveral to Portland Head Lighthouse. His parents looked down at the east coast and watched it morph from greens, to light browns, to white from 32,000 feet.

That night after dinner, everyone was in the living room with a fire popping in the background. Every time a new log was placed on like latticework, it sounded like static electricity. The parents were comfy in chairs and the sofa, the kids sprawled out on the carpeted floor. The huge wooden television in the corner had the Miami - Boston College game on. If anything could distract Addison from the fire, it was the game, the first home game they missed in three years. By the 4th quarter, everyone, except Toni, watched with glued eyes. She was the only one who noticed the fire was dying.

She was laying on her stomach reading one of her mother's magazines. Her portable cassette player was next her, the cord curling up to her metal headphones. She was studying a Jordache ad, lipping some song, when Ethan threw a pretzel at her.

"Hey what was that for?" She said it very loudly.

"What are you listening to?"

She pulled away the fuzzy headphone from her right ear. "What?"

"What are you listening to?"

"Frankie Goes to Hollywood."

"I'm sick of them." Bryce chimed in while still watching the game.

"There's more than just "Relax" goof." She readjusted her headphones and went back to the jeans ad. A minute later, she rolled onto her side and pointed at the ad for her mom to see behind her.

"I like these jeans mom. Maybe for Christmas?" Again, she was loud.

Her mom waved her over. "Let me see."

Toni scooted up and walked on her knees to her mom on the sofa, showing her the ad.

"Addison, do they over-play that song down in Miami?" Bryce turned to him.

"Every second. That and 'Karma Chameleon'."

Ethan shook his head. "To the max."

The card game for the three boys resumed with 30 seconds left in the game, thinking Miami had won. Everyone froze 31 seconds later after the "Hail Mary". Bryce's cards were the first to fall to the carpet after that last play, like heavy leaves. Everyone just stared as if never seeing a television before.

"Oh my god," came drawn out from Bryce. He wasn't a huge Miami Hurricane fan, but a fan of football. It didn't matter your allegiance, the ending was historic in a Greek tragedy sort of way. Toni looked around not grasping it.

"So what's the big deal? Why is that Umpa Lumpa #22 running around the field going crazy?"

Addison and his father couldn't speak. Addison had only one card in his hand, the 10 of clubs, and he threw it to the ground as he kneeled up. He looked back at his dad as if trying to come up with an excuse for getting into trouble. His dad's head fell back into the sofa cushion, looking up to the ceiling. For the rest of the night, Addison played cards as if he had nothing to lose and he didn't care. Yeah, he wouldn't forget this Thanksgiving.

They went into D.C. on Saturday, surveying the Mall and attractions in clumps of snow. Addison was shocked how bright the sun can be reflecting off the snow like water. The only thing missing was the twinkling sparkles.

They went to the National Air & Space Museum first thing. Before leaving, Addison was sitting with his father, with coffee and hot cocoa posing as their humidifier. It was the first time they were really alone since his arrival the day before.

"So how was the flight? Mom said everything went pretty smoothly?" His father was blowing ripples across his black coffee.

"It was fine. I almost got nervous at takeoff for some reason, but I liked it." Addison's eyes roamed the great hallway, with a Gemini, North American X-15, and P-51 Mustang suspended above the crowd. He wondered if he could nudge it would they sway a little like in his cousin's room. His half-lie about almost getting nervous was easier with all the commotion around, getting lost in the shuffling people like a runaway piece of paper.

"The stewardess that met us at the gate seemed nice. They checked up on you enough didn't they?"

My girlfriend, Phoebe Cates? "Yeah everything was really cool. Her name was Darlene. I got to see the cockpit."

His father, who had been studying his face, smiled openly.

"Did they? Oh, that's fantastic. What did you think?"

Addison thought. "Well it was actually smaller than I expected."

His father nodded. "I guess that makes sense. I could see that."

A few seconds passed. "So I was wondering," Addison looked down at his hot cocoa. "Do the stewardesses ever sit with the passengers?"

"Well, I've seen them sit sometimes while talking or even helping with food."

"How about take-offs. Maybe landings?" Addison looked up at his dad.

"No I don't think so. I think there are regulations for them to sit in the galley. Why?"

"Oh no reason." Addison finally took a sip of his hot cocoa. It was the smoothest, richest he ever tasted. *Man, Traveler is a way cool name for a dog.*

Addison and his parents had a flight out of Washington National that Sunday. Uncle Trey drove the station wagon, with the Addison's dad up front and the two sisters in the back. The four cousins were swaying around in the far back, huddled around in a small circle.

Late Sunday afternoon was busy. It seemed half of Washington DC was trying to head home. Despite their wishes, they decided to drop them off at the curb rather than search for a parking spot. Hugs and kisses took place on the departure curb. With the overhang above, the whole place glowed red thanks to the brake lights. They checked in at the Eastern counter, full of zigzag lines like Disney World.

The huge, curved main lobby was one giant window. It seemed to echo every conversation, skipping the sounds off the concave glass. The Briggs family moved through the crowd to the far end of the airport. Their gate number was 37 on Terminal C.

They stopped in a newsstand with front pages for wallpaper. Every major newspaper within five states fit into slots like a quilt. His father walked over and scanned the headlines. While his mom picked out a magazine, Addison walked over and joined him.

He noticed the paper his father was checking out and moved next to him.

So the Soviets are performing nuclear tests in Semipalatinsk, wherever that is... His father read a few more and moved to the counter.

Dwight Gooden wins NL Rookie of the Year. Well that was a no brainer... Addison then followed his father to the counter.

"Honey why don't you get a magazine?" His mother was holding a *Cosmopolitan* and *Redbook.*

"Oh yeah, let me look around. I've got money." Addison thought spending his own money to buy something was as grown up as flying alone. Check, check.

"Okay buddy, we'll be right outside." His father patted him on the shoulder and headed out, side stepping a pilot walking in.

He had his Eastern cards and the case of baseball cards of course, but searched for something to look at. His eyes moved left and stopped at a *Sporting News Hockey*. He bit his lip in thought and reached for it. Someone named Paul Coffey was on the cover. If it was the snowball fight he had with his father, the constant shoveling of snow, or the whiteness that seemed to even be behind his eyelids, a hockey magazine made sense. Plus, he knew nothing about it.

"Hockey fan huh?" Addison's head jerked to his left as a pilot was standing next to him, looming above him. He was picking at the tops of a couple magazines unsatisfied, but kept searching. He looked back down at Addison.

"Well not really sir, hockey isn't very big in Miami."

"Very true. That's a football town. You must be a Dolphins fan then."

Addison nodded. "Are you a Redskins fan?"

"No, not from here. 49ers are my team. You headed home?"

Another nod. Not only was he a pilot, but the hat was close to a five star general's in Addison's eyes.

"Flown in there many times, beautiful city to fly into at night."

"Yes sir it is." Addison then checked the magazines he was picking at. He was curious what a pilot reads. "What are you going to get?"

He laughed and looked back down at Addison before surveying his options again. He picked a *Field & Stream*.

"I think this one will do." He tucked it under his arm and adjusted his hat. "Well young man, have a great flight down there."

"Where are you flying to?" Addison could never figure out why just before someone leaves, his confidence grows and he wants to talk more.

"Chicago. Going back in two hours. Enjoy your flight."

Addison watched him head off to the counter, then followed him quickly. He was behind the tall pilot paying for his magazine. The lady behind at the cash register smiled at him coming over, waiting to say hi when he got closer.

"Ah Captain Cavanaugh, long time no see."

"Judy, how was your Thanksgiving?"

"Not bad. Still full." She patted her stomach.

"Well that means everything went well then." He smiled and handed over two bucks. "Keep it." He picked up the magazine and tapped the counter with it. "Catch you next week."

She smiled, "You better!" She looked at Addison. "Good evening young man." She took the hockey magazine and read the price in the corner. "$1.75 sweetie."

Addison ripped open his Velcro OP wallet and handed her two dollars. He smiled up at her. "Keep it." It came out faster than he rehearsed. He got five steps away when he realized he forgot to tap the counter with the magazine. *Next time,* he thought.

Five more steps later, he found his parents outside, spotting them through criss crossing people. He worked his way over to them like a game of Frogger. He looked off to the left and right, but couldn't see the pilot.

"All set sport?" His dad's wrist came down from checking his watch.

Addison nodded.

They took up seats D, E, and F in row 19, just off the back of the wing. The flaps were right under Addison's nose as he looked out. He and another boy five rows up were given small toy planes. It was a newer Boeing 767 that Eastern just started flying in the last year. It was like opening a pack of baseball cards and getting a rookie card. Even his dad was impressed and checked it out for a second. Addison had never seen one before. His dad saw one once taking off while driving on 836 into downtown Miami. The model plane brightened his mood after he noticed Darlene wasn't part of the flight crew.

Once allowed, he pulled down the tray table and put the model on it right next to his deck of cards. Then he pulled out the hockey magazine. He found it interesting, not knowing a lot about hockey. From November to March, hockey was actually in the papers in Miami. The local news would show scores occasionally. Once the "snowbirds" leave around Easter, zooming off to Canada and the Northeast, hockey vanishes as well. The Stanley Cup finals score may be on the last page in the bottom corner.

He took in the stats, which he compared to baseball's, and the pictures. He liked the Hartford, Minnesota, and Detroit logos, thinking they were pretty cool. He didn't like any of the Canadian teams. He noticed a couple things. One was that hockey players tend to have funny names unlike other sports. Gretzky, Coffey, Lemieux, and Bourque wouldn't seem right in football or baseball. He also wondered where all the Russian players were. They kicked serious butt in the Olympics, especially last February in Sarajevo, but he didn't read or see one of them in the magazine. Then there were the names of the divisions. Adams & Patrick were in the Prince of Wales conference, and the Norris & Smythe were in the Clarence Campbell conference. They didn't get their names from a compass heading or geography book like other sports.

Half way down the East coast, the magazine was slipped into his backpack and his father and he played cards. He wasn't looking forward to going to school tomorrow, but the holidays coming up muffled the sound of the first period late bell. Also, the Dolphins would have home-field advantage in the playoffs and he knew he'd go to at least one of them. He didn't know which playoff game, but he did know that if they got to the super bowl, they would probably play the pilot's team or his cousin's.

Eventually the 727 banked right off the Atlantic, and flew over Fort Lauderdale. The flaps just outside his window grinding a bit lower each couple of minutes. They flew to the center of the state, before banking left for a U-turn. The pilot aimed the black nose of the plane at Miami, due east. No one looking out the windows needed a map or questioned where they were. The darkness below was all alligators, snakes, brackish water, and Mangroves of the Everglades. Then like a switch, literally on the other side of a 12-foot canal, dull yellowish lights dotted the ground, as civilization took over the land. You didn't even need a ruler to trace over the line.

Once they crossed US27, with the Everglades behind, it was like a million bright yellow push pins were sticking out of the streets and neighborhoods in straight, geometric lines as far as the eye could see. He figured his Uncle Trey would appreciate the exactness of it. The flaps were hanging down as far as they could go, looking like they would fall off with the slightest shake of turbulence. The roofs of the cars on the Palmetto Expressway raced by as the plane glided down under 100 feet. The dull streetlights of Dade County were replaced with the small blue ones of the tarmac.

Armed with visions of Darlene, drifts and mounds of snow, a deck of new playing cards, and Paul Coffey, Addison Briggs was back home.

It was the Refrigerator's fault. At least that's what Addison would say.

A little over a year after watching the pilot from the newsstand's team beat the Dolphins in Super Bowl XIX, Addison biked down to Asher's house for Super Bowl XX. Asher Gibson was Addison's best friend, and lived 3/4 of a mile around the corner.

For all intents and purposes, the game was over by halftime. Their only question was would New England score a touchdown? After commenting for the 23rd time, paired with flailing arms, shaking heads, and eye rolling, that the Dolphins would make this a closer, better game, they now hoped that Walter Payton would score. They felt he deserved it. It was the only reason to keep watching.

Not only did he not score, but when inside the two yard line late in the third period, had to watch Jim McMahon hand the ball off to William Perry. The 350 pound "Refrigerator" steamrolled into the end zone instead of "Sweetness". Just as the Bears celebrated in the back of the end zone, Addison had a sneeze attack, then needed to blow his nose. *Where'd that come from?*

He peddled home at the start of the fourth quarter, as it was a school night, sniffling the whole way. He went to school that Monday, but had no appetite at lunch. By sixth period he was breathing through his mouth. He came home without going to tennis practice. That's when his parents knew he wasn't feeling well. Addison doesn't miss tennis practice. And he hated being sick.

"You need to feed a cold Addison. There's plenty of chicken salad and roast beef, ok?" He nodded as his mother felt his forehead for the fifth time in five minutes. "Call if you need something." She kissed his forehead and went off to work holding her coffee.

Addison is #8 in the state in the 12&under boys' tennis rankings. The 12-month tennis weather and international travels brought a cavernous tennis depth to the state. His father saw the stunning hand-eye coordination when the four-year-old picked up some ping-pong paddles in the neighbor's garage. His mother saw the determination when she toted him along to her adult team matches, and he hit against a racquetball wall over and over and over for hours. The rhythmic sounds of the ball off the strings and wall never varied, like a metronome. Mats Wilander did the rest.

He first saw the Swede when he won the French Open in 1982 as a teenager. He loved his name. He loved his hair. He loved his backhand. He loved the colorful, striped cord bracelet he wore. He loved his game. He wore Sergio Tacchini shirts for his matches, which were not easy to find. A Swedish flag hung vertically behind his door, with Mats in black tape down the middle yellow cross. The Swede and tennis were Addison's passion. Not many 10 year-olds ask Santa for a racket-stringing machine.

Addison saw the last two hours of his classic, six and a half hour match against John McEnroe in the 1982 Davis Cup quarterfinal. Many consider it the greatest Davis Cup match ever. Mats, just 17, not only hung in there against the best player in the world on American soil, but pushed McEnroe 9-7,6-2,15-17,3-6,8-6. A year later, Addison cried and didn't leave his room for five hours, after Wilander lost to hometown hero Yannick Noah in the French Open finals in straight sets.

The last time he was home sick was two Decembers ago, which just happened to be the same day as the opening singles matches in the Davis Cup. He watched his hero beat Jimmy Connors in straight sets on clay in Gothenburg. Now, on a Tuesday in January, he wondered if he'd get lucky and have something worth watching. Thanks to cable, there were 32 choices.

He took a hot bath mid-morning, trying to inhale the steam. He scrambled some eggs and mashed them between two pieces of toast. He wished he had an airplane model to make, something to keep his mind occupied. He'd love to go to Asher's or Tara's, they have an Atari. Around 11:00 he flipped the television on, and checked all 32 channels. Nothing. He left it on MTV and grabbed the Eastern cards. He plopped down at the end of the couch Indian-style and shuffled. His seven piles of cards just fit on the middle, leather cushion.

He nearly won his second game. His four piles of aces above were stacked up to eights and nines, but one card was still face down under a stubborn red queen. He blew his nose for what felt like the hundredth time.

The pile of balled up, heavier tissues littered the carpet by the couch like igloos. Just another thing kids do when parents are away at work.

The video for "Let's Hear it for the Boy" started, with the kid in the dunce cap tapping his feet. Addison rolled his eyes and leaned over to grab the remote box. He moved the switch down to one, then clicked his way back up, stopping at 19. CNN was showing the launch pad at Kennedy Space Center, as *Challenger* was poised for take-off. Steam and smoke seeped out as it waited to be unleashed to the heavens.

Addison noticed there was about two minutes to lift off and shuffled into the kitchen for more juice. He came back into the living room and found his position again, just as the announcer relayed the countdown.

"T-minus one minute, forty-two seconds."

He scooped up the cards and started shuffling again. They quickly showed the official crew photo, all six astronauts and one teacher in their light blue outfits holding their helmets. The flag was in the background and a model of the shuttle was on the table.

Addison thought it was pretty cool that a teacher was going to go into space. He thought a teacher from every county in the state should go up. Design a huge shuttle that could carry 100 people into space. Then come back with the knowledge of space travel filling their lessons and stories, which would fill the student's minds and dreams.

"T-minus one minute, nineteen-seconds."

He wondered when that would happen. See a huge ship like that go into space. If *2001: A Space Odyssey* was correct, and everyone said it was brilliant, then NASA needed to get a move on. He figured movies are just early, like books. According to Orwell's *1984,* there should be cameras everywhere and Big Brother constantly watching over us, according to his parents. *Like that's going to happen anytime soon!* He finished shuffling.

"T-minus fifty-one seconds."

Another seven stacks of cards. He moved over a black seven under a red eight. Then turned over a black two. He wondered if all this would ever come true. Would these shuttles go up into space daily, weekly, hourly eventually? Reagan mentioned a Star Wars missile program, apparently to protect us from the Soviets or people in the Middle East, but was it just a reference to the movie? He wondered if it really would happen. He picked up a black five and red four and moved them under a red six.

"T-minus twenty-seven seconds."

He overturned a black king and moved it over into a blank space, then turned over the four of diamonds. He thumbed over three cards and flipped it over. *Nothing.* He thumbed over another three cards, flipped it. Nothing. Another three, then flipped it over. *Finally!* Addison snapped down a red jack under a black queen.

"T-minus ten, nine, eight…" Three more cards counted, then flipped. A nod approved of an ace, the first one, and placed it above two kings. "… four, three, two, one, lift off…"

Addison froze as he watched the engines and boosters burst to life. Slowly the shuttle cleared the tower and started twisting. He all of a sudden felt real upset for being sick. He wanted to be at school today for this, to watch it in the classroom. He wondered if Mr. Klein, Mrs. Richardson, and Mrs. Jarrell, his favorite teachers, would want to go up. He didn't think Jarrell would.

One minute after leaving launch pad 39B, Addison looked down and reviewed his piles again. He reached the bottom of his playable cards and turned them back over to start again. He needed black cards. He checked the television again and then reached for the tissue box on the floor between igloos. He pulled out two and brought them up to his face. And blew, again.

2,257 feet per second. *Holy Crap.*

The Mission Control announcer just said that was the velocity. Addison shook his head. He tried to comprehend how fast that was, but after thinking about a car on I-95, a Formula One car in Belgium, or a 727 going to the nation's capital, just couldn't wrap his head around it. It's like lightyears, something you just can't grasp.

What he did grasp was something yanked his vision to the screen. Something wrong.

It was an explosion of white clouds with orange shooting stars coming out of it. Then two white puffy jet trails forking off in different directions. Addison, knowing full well he was alone, looked around the living room for a second, as if someone was playing a trick, or wanting to know if he was the only one seeing this?

The weird thing was as this was happening; the Mission Control guy continued talking with more statistics, as if nothing was wrong.

"One minute, fifteen seconds. Velocity 2900 feet per second. Altitude, nine nautical miles, downrange distance, seven nautical miles."

Why is he still talking? Everything must be okay...right?

Addison's eyes told him something terrible just happened. His ears continued to tug the rope the other way. Addison dropped the cards on the couch and moved in front of the television. He kneeled right in front of it, almost inches from it, and like the little girl in *Poltergeist,* started talking to the screen.

"What's going on? What happened?" Then there was the silence.

Fifteen-seconds of it. Eerie silence.

Fifteen-seconds on Christmas morning, at your birthday party, or your wedding will go by in a breath, or a lightyear for that matter. 15 seconds in the dentist chair, principal's office, or watching the Space Shuttle blow up in front of your eyes like real life Star Wars, is an eternity.

Still nothing. Just his heart beat in his ears.

Then the camera zoomed in on one of the loose rocket boosters. Between streams of white, spreading out of the initial burst cloud like roots, was a rocket curling away, as if finally loose from its restraints with no thought of direction.

At last a voice crackled through a microphone.

"Flight Controllers looking very carefully at the situation... obviously a major malfunction."

Malfunction? That's what you call it? Addison all day would remember that word. Not explosion, problem, catastrophe, but simply 'malfunction'. It was odd, yet perfect in the situation.

He moved back to the couch, unknowingly sitting on some of the playing cards, and watched his young generation's "Oswald Moment" play out all afternoon. His mother was in a salon getting her hair done when JFK was shot. His father was in the bar at the Biltmore in Coral Gables, having a beer after 18 holes when Apollo 11 landed on the moon. And now he had his moment of location: The couch at home, playing Solitaire, when the Challenger exploded.

Later in the Fall, Addison and his parents drove over to Naples to see his grandfather. He had moved there two years ago with a desire to feel warmth from the sun, not the furnace, and to never pick up his snow shovel again. The old house outside Madison, Wisconsin also felt lonely once his wife of 53 years died.

Addison missed his grandmother and their place. Much like his cousins in Virginia, he enjoyed visiting a place polar opposite from Miami. On the flip side, Naples was closer which meant more visits. His grandfather was only two hours away. The problem was 90 minutes of it was driving through uninhabited, exposed swamp.

Alligator Alley is the skinny road between Fort Lauderdale and Naples. Once past the toll plaza, it was a straight, two-lane runway for 80 miles. There is no shoulder, no rest stops, no lights, no passing lanes, no security. It is just paint on pavement through the middle of the Everglades, full of everything in the Florida Audubon Society book from alligators, to snakes, to ibises. They wouldn't even put up a fence along the sides for another three years. Addison thought it was the closest he'd get to driving on a safari in Africa. It looked almost the same other than the lack of giraffe heads bobbing around. All that was missing was the open Range Rover and binoculars.

It was no Range Rover, but his mother's Oldsmobile Cutlass. His dad was driving and his mom was knitting a blanket for her father, whenever a Naples winter is too chilly. Addison was in the back listening to his tape player and looking at his tennis magazines. *Tennis Today* was over on the seat next to him and *Tennis* was open on his lap. He liked the cover, how the lowercase letters of tennis were all connected at the bottom, kind of like cursive. Ivan Lendl was on the cover. Addison hated Lendl. He was curious if anyone liked him. The Czech was constantly in finals and the nemesis for, well, everyone.

The only good thing was he wasn't in the Davis Cup much, if at all. Addison thought he was an evil machine from behind the iron curtain. Built in some cyborg factory on the outskirts of Prague; with smoke stacks sending plumes of thick ash into the sky, darkening it like some other planet. And out came Ivan. They gave him sawdust in his pockets, which he used to rub on his grip, but Addison knew it was to try to pretend he was natural, from the earth like some tall majestic Redwood tree the factory cuts down to burn up inside.

But while driving across the Alley that day, he thought of something. Something he never had before. Maybe it was the strangeness of the view.

Maybe it was just maturity, being 13 now. But deep down, covered in layer upon layer of his engraved righteousness and virtues, was a simple fact: He was so good.

If had to pick one player to win a match on any surface, grass to clay, for some hypothetical match to save mankind, or simply a bet with his signed 1984 Donruss Don Mattingly card at stake, he would pick Lendl. He closed his eyes as if that would keep the vision from surfacing. Edberg had the backhand and volley, McEnroe had the grit, Mats the counterpunch from the baseline, Connors the return, but Lendl just had that 'something' that powered him into every Friday and Sunday of tournaments. There was no question.

Addison opened his eyes and shook the thought away. He turned the page and refocused. Soon "I'm on Fire" ended and side one of *Born in the USA* was complete. Addison flipped it over to side B, and "No Surrender" soared out of his foam earpieces. He finished his tennis magazines and was about to pull out his *National Geographic*, when he realized he had the real thing out his window.

The dry season brought out a brownness to the Everglades, that being so flat looked like a savanna from the backseat. After a couple of seconds and a few lyrics, it was then the Belgium countryside, maybe parts of France. And then small green helmets like peas in the distance, started methodically moving their way through the brush.

"*Like soldiers in the winter's night, with a vow to defend. No retreat, baby, no surrender.*" It was inevitable, but if it was a dreamer's mind making a tedious drive go fast, or knowing his grandfather was an hour away, he always thought of the war. His grandfather survived the Battle of the Bulge, pushed over the bridge at Remagen, and got to the Danube. The war was unofficially over by the time they got to that river, but not the Rhine. It was never talked about or discussed, no matter how much Addison wanted to know. But after his grandmother passed, it seemed right. Last summer the interview took place.

His parents drove him over for a week; it'd be just the two of them. They played cards, watched baseball, cooked, and one night, talked about the war. Addison brought a map and questions he had thought of for about four months. The only thing missing was the stopwatch ticking for 60 minutes. He wrote down facts, drew arrows on the map, and remembered feelings. He came away dumbfounded. There was the first live combat and firing of weapons. The first casualty in the unit. The first hand-to-hand combat. Even the first shower.

That's the thing he remembers, which sounds funny. It wasn't that the other things weren't more dramatic, they most certainly were, but he'd seen movies, read books, and looked at pictures of the war. It was the little things you don't think about or realize that make the others more extraordinary in their perspective.

No shower for four months. He couldn't comprehend that. It was light years. It was 2,257 feet per second. From landing in France, crossing into Belgium, and finally getting to a rest point, it was four months. Showering, shaving, going to the bathroom, sleeping, napping, eating rations, and then oh yeah, dodging bullets, land mines, and knives. Addison couldn't sleep that night, June 28, 1986. He stared at the ceiling.

The next morning everything was different in a way. His grandfather still wore his long pajamas despite it being 85 degrees at 8:30. His coffee was still jet black and thick like oil. The cereal and danish were the same. The setting was the same but the characters were different. He would never complain about using a coaster again. He didn't mind not being able to put his feet up on the coffee table.

On that trip, his grandfather also taught him how to play Euchre. The four-player game of winning tricks while only using a third of the deck, is very popular in the Midwest. He immediately taught Asher, Edgar and Corey when he got back home. It became their new foursome game.

You only play with face cards, tens, and nines. Once trump was picked, the favored suit, the jack was the high card. The other jack of the same color was the second best card. Then ace down to the nine.

He remembers the first time he played with his grandfather and his buddies. He wasn't the cute grandson or bright tennis player. He was a card player at a table with a blank slate for a reputation. They would write the results on it in magic marker that wouldn't come off, no matter what Addison did from then on. It was as interrogation with cards and note pads. He couldn't crack. Cards were more than a game in his grandfather's house. It was sacred ritual.

He and his grandfather were down five to four. The cards were dealt.

Everyone passed to Oliver, the dealer. He took the top card, a queen of diamonds.

"Let's do queens boys." He then looked across to his partner. "Karl, I'm going alone on this one." Karl sat back in surprise and put his cards down. He was out of it. It was Oliver against Addison and his grandfather. Oliver felt his hand was so good, he could go alone and get all five tricks. He would get four points and that would put them at nine to four. This was huge. The lamp over the table just got brighter, or was it hotter?

Oliver led with the ace of diamonds. Addison was wondering what trump card his grandfather would play. His grandfather threw off a ten of clubs.

Oh crap, grandpa doesn't even have trump? Addison followed suit and dumped his king of diamonds. The jack of diamonds pulled out more cards. Then the jack of hearts did the same. Three tricks. Two to go. Oliver had the lead, and put the queen of diamonds down. Team Briggs had nothing. Four tricks. One to go. Addison had one card left, he saved it not seeing any clubs. Oliver threw a king of clubs down. His grandfather shook his head, and tossed a jack of spades. Nothing. Oliver was already smiling; however, the middle schooler wasn't done yet.

He laid the ace of clubs down. Karl sat back and slapped his hands together. Oliver picked up the pencil and bounced it of the table playfully. His grandfather winked. Addison held them to just one point. That wink was a memory no slide photo album could match.

He popped open his cassette deck and pulled out the tape to flip over. Then pressed rewind and waited.

"Born in the USA" started. Years later, he would laugh that he thought of his grandfather's actions and the war when listening to this song. The lyrics and ironic message didn't hit home yet. Punching clocks with a timecard was the daily highlight, if you were lucky.

But for now, it was anger. It was passion. It was the throbbing beat of God & country. The song was made to be heard on a two-lane highway or dusty road in the country. The only skyscraper was a water tower, maybe in Portis, Kansas, or barn & seed silo outside Poseville, Indiana. Addison felt there was nothing subtle about it, nothing soothing. Springsteen didn't sing it, he shouted it, yelled it from the torch on the Statue of Liberty. The drums were pounded. He wondered how the drummer's glasses didn't fall off. The organ keys struck, pressed down until finger tips were red. There were electric guitars, not acoustic. The song throbbed and screamed imagination.

Last year at a tennis tournament, they played the song over the PA system on the courts during warm-ups. Addison never hit the ball harder in his life. He went for a winner every time, despite trying to simply get loose. For four minutes and forty seconds, tennis was a Formula One race.

Soon the toll plaza on the eastbound lanes zipped by next to them, which was the finish line. The race across the Alley was over. It was a race no one cared to win, just finish. Another 20 minutes and they were in his driveway. It was a typical fall day in Naples, which meant 81 degrees. His grandfather still wore his cardigan. That always killed Addison, making him sweat more in his shorts and *Prince Racquet* t-shirt.

The house was small and simple, all that he needed. Addison use to complain a bit at the size, especially when compared to their old house in Wisconsin. Not anymore. They went out for seafood that night and played cards until bed. Addison wasn't a son or grandson, but a partner and despite age was to produce results like anyone else.

Cards were a way of life in the Midwest, part of a winter survival guide when the snow swept against the house in drifts. His father, growing up in the mid-Atlantic states, knew of cards, but it wasn't engrained. He quickly learned while dating Addison's mother and visiting her at her parents. Addison learned early on that even at eight years old, "Ahh shucks" wouldn't cut it. Playing with his friends became as easy as coloring inside the lines.

Down eight to six, two points away from defeat, his father was dealing to his left. His grandfather and partner was across from him. 20 cards were tossed out, getting scooped up. His father put down the four remaining and turned over the top card. Trump was hearts. The ten.

Addison fanned his out. King & Jack of hearts. Jack of diamonds. King & queen of clubs. *Whoa. Breath, look calm. You have nines and tens as far as mom and dad are concerned.* It wasn't a loner, but good enough for a point, maybe two if he played it right. At the same time, if he didn't play it right and they got set, it would be two points for his parents and game over.

His grandfather across from him passed. His mother passed. It was his turn. *Where's the ace of hearts?*

That was the one card that could stop him from getting two points. Also, he didn't have any ace off-suits. That could hurt. He licked his lips and took a slow breath. He could hear his pulse in his ears.

Over the next 90 seconds, Addison would do two things his grandfather, and card master, swore to never, ever do.

"Pick it up Dad." His grandfather's eyes slowly slid up from his hand to Addison across from him. He just watched his grandson give trump to the other team. If he didn't pull this off, there may be only three bowls on the table for breakfast tomorrow.

His father took a deep breath and picked up the ten of hearts. He discarded something, probably a nine or ten, and looked at his wife across from him. His grandfather didn't move, not even rearrange cards. *Oh man…*

His grandfather put down a king of spades. His mother followed suit with the queen. Addison's turn. He looked at his father. *Do you have the Ace?*

It was the one card that could trump his grandfather's king. He could throw off his queen of clubs, but what if dad had the ace? Could he take that chance? If he lost the lead, even with both right and left bowers, he could lose. So, he did the second thing his grandfather said to never do. He trumped his partner.

Addison threw down the king of hearts. His grandfather had to adjust in his seat. Even his mother looked over at Addison. Not only was it trumping him, but with a high king. If this didn't work out, forget cereal, he may not have a bed tonight.

His father shook his head as he laid down the ace of spades.

Addison took a deep breath. *Oh my god he did have it. I've got 'em. I think…*

His grandfather then took the cards from the middle and stacked them next to him. One trick. He then looked at his grandson, still with curiosity. He was flicking the corner of a card in his hand like a principal tapping a paddle. Addison couldn't look over at him.

Addison had the lead, and led with the Jack of hearts. He needed to pull out the other ace, the trump ace.

His partner sighed at the highest card being played so soon. His father put down the ten of hearts. His grandfather a king of diamonds. *Oh man, my partner doesn't have any trump!*

His mother put down a queen of hearts. Two tricks. But no ace, where was the ace?

His grandfather grabbed the cards and stacked them crisscross over the first stack. Addison then laid down the other bower, the jack of diamonds. Everyone rolled their eyes and shook their heads.

"Really Addison?" His father joked as out came the ace of hearts. His grandfather finally breathed and threw an off-suit card. His mother tossed out the ace of spades. Three tricks.

They had their point, but now could he take all five tricks for two points and tie the match at eight? There was one trump out there. The nine. Were his parents saving it or was it in the dealer pile?

He flicked the king of clubs down. His father held out his card, face down in the middle of the table. He then eyed his son. Addison looked at the card, *Eastern* facing the ceiling, waiting to be flipped over. It might as well have been a math timed-test that Addison would flip over the nanosecond a teacher yelled, "go". He leaned forward, tapping his foot. *Come on come on come, what is it?!* His hands were shaking.

His father flipped over the card. Queen of diamonds. Addison sat back in his chair and gulped a breath. Everyone laughed. No trump.

"Oh come on, I had to tease you a little." His father's gamesmanship was not appreciated by Addison's pulse. No trumps came out; the ten must have been in the dealer pile. His off-suit king won. Four tricks.

It was a foregone conclusion with Addison still having the lead, and everyone having to follow. He put down the queen of clubs. His mother threw down the ace of clubs earlier, the only card that could take him, and everyone's last card came fluttering down with distaste, joy, and relief, depending on who was watching them come down like leaves on a picnic table.

Five tricks. Two points. Game tied at eight.

A nod from his grandfather was like getting a trophy.

They lost 10-9, but Addison took away more from the game than the score. He had a bed that night, a cereal bowl in the morning, and a confident memory under his skin. Addison went to sleep that night without a problem.

They left Sunday night and the only thing worse than Alligator Alley during the day is Alligator Alley at night. With a cloudy sky hiding the moon like a teasing magician's cape, the only lights were from the oncoming cars that hopefully stayed in their lane. Addison wondered if his grandfather would be alive long enough to see Addison drive up to his driveway. Would the drive across go faster knowing you have to pay so much attention to the task at hand, or was his music-filled head with closed eyes more like a fast forward button? He couldn't wait to find out.

Once home that night, Addison put the cards back in the wooden box on his dresser. They joined his Swiss Army knife his father had given him, a pin from his grandfather's army jacket, his wallet, Darlene's pilot's wings, and his old ticket to the 1986 Lipton International Tennis Championships. That's when he watched Mats Wilander play in person for the first time.

CHAPTER SIXTEEN

The trade winds ushered in Halloween to South Florida with 80-degree temperatures. The only pumpkin patches were down in Homestead. No one wears flannel. There are no colorful leaves. No crisp breeze. No haystacks. Everyone wore two things each Halloween in South Florida. A costume and a film of humidity.

"Why is Halloween always on a school night? It should be the last Saturday in October. Period." Corey Evans was sipping his apple juice and eyeing his cards. He had nothing and showed it on his face.

Addison nodded while rolling up his sleeves. "Good point. Let's pass a bill."

Asher stood up and walked over to turn the ceiling fan higher. He sat back down and picked up his cards. Everyone still waiting on Corey.

Cards became a ritual for the boys. On Friday evenings, they found themselves at one of their house's to watch *Miami Vice* and play cards.

It wasn't Friday night, but Addison, Asher, Corey, and Edgar had a Halloween tradition called, "Cards for Costumes". Someone had to select the Halloween themed costumes. Tonight's game would decide who picked out the costumes for next year. This year was taken care of, thanks to Edgar Garbey.

He had won last year and decided Magnum PI would be the theme. He wanted to be Higgins, dressed in tan safari clothes and leashed his two Golden Retrievers. They were Zeus and Apollo. Asher was TC, suspenders and all, and Corey was Rick. Addison was Magnum. He wasn't happy.

It wasn't the character, which was awesome, it wasn't the toy gun in the back of his jeans, the fake mustache, or the Hawaiian shirt tucked in. It was the hat. Addison slipped on the borrowed Detroit Tiger hat with scorn. Not only were they in the same division with the Yankees, but the better team. He made the other three swear to never tell Don Mattingly if they should ever run into him at Publix, Swenson's, or the arcade.

With apple juice in glass tumblers as if scotch, or something they saw in the movies, the cards were leaning towards Asher and Edgar tonight. Corey asked for four cards with a shake of his head.

The tape player clicked off. Addison looked at Edgar. "Your turn."

Edgar rolled his eyes and got up, ejected Van Halen's *1984,* and flipped it over to side B. He pushed play and came back to the card table. "Hot for Teacher" began. All the boys would agree, it was the most superb guitar playing of the decade.

"God this is a good tape." Asher then put up two fingers. Two cards were spun in front of him. The agreeing was about to end.

Corey changed the subject. He nodded to the Don Mattingly poster next to Addison's closet. "What the hell is that doing up?" Soft cursing was the coolest thing to do when alone. It came with the card games.

Edgar and Asher rolled their eyes at the same time, hearing this argument for years. The poster had Hitman written at the top and Mattingly was in a white pinstripe suit like Al Capone or some mobster from he 20's would wear. He had a black bat for a machine gun. Bullet holes were sprayed across the poster. Like the flags around town, that Addison seemed to obsess over, his Mats Wilander poster was an inch higher on the other side of the room to show its importance.

Corey was a Baltimore Orioles fan. Much like Addison, he clung onto his team thanks to Spring Training. They were in Miami every March and their minor league team played in downtown Miami. Corey was seven years old when he went to a game one summer with his father, who was from Annapolis. It was the only game they went to that year, and was the last time Cal Ripken Jr played in the stadium. He was called up late in the year to head up to Baltimore to play third base at the time, and the rest was history. Whenever Addison was over at Corey's house, he always made fun of the Ripken poster on his wall. It's a vicious, teasing circle for the 13 year olds.

"You mean the Hit Man, who out hit a certain shortstop?"

"Whose rookie card is more expensive?"

"You mean the 82 Topps rookie right? Then Mattingly's is."

"No I mean the 82 Topps Traded rookie card. The greatest card of the decade."

"It's not a real card."

Edgar and Asher eyed each other and shook their heads, hearing this for the 70th time and wondering how long this debate would go. Edgar asked Asher for three cards.

"How the hell is it not a real card?"

"If you can't get it in a pack at a 7-11 for 75 cents, it isn't a real card."

"Whatever, every store has it and it is the most expensive card by far."

Edgar looked over at Addison. "Why can't you get it in a pack?" Asher turned to Edgar with an icy stare for encouraging them. He held it for 30 seconds. Edgar did a double take when seeing Asher, and shrugged shoulders defending himself.

"It's only in the traded set that comes out mid-year. You have to buy the whole set, then pull out the Ripken, which breaks up the set. It's the only way to get it."

"Or just go to a card store or show and buy it like every other card in the world. Of course, you have to have $75-$80 to get it. Or you could just get two Mattingly rookies for the same price." Corey spoke to the table.

"Whatever, you can't find it for under $50." Addison's rebuttal.

The two then spat out statistics from the '87 season that rivaled a financial report. Asher knew better than to question the accuracy. They did this once last year and in the middle of the argument, Asher got up and pulled the *Baseball Encyclopedia* off Corey's shelf to confirm. He shook his head as he read what they were saying, verbatim, to the decimal. *How the hell is he only getting B's in Algebra*, Asher thought back then.

"Who's won a world series recently?"

"That's a team thing. Whose stats are bold or have an asterisk next to it more?"

"Junior would have more if he had a short right field porch like your boy."

"Whatever. Ripkin's got Murray hitting behind him for protection."

"And what do you call Winfield?"

Asher then summed the whole conversation up, and ended the revolving argument.

"Duck Season. Wabbit Season. Duck Season. Wabbit Season."

Apparently, the defense rested and all made their bets with colored poker chips. Asher thought his two pairs, fives and kings would win. Edgar's three of a kind, sixes, came with a smile. He scooped up the chips in the middle. Asher was pissed, and decided to change subjects and change his mind from the cards.

"More importantly Dennis Connor, how are we doing with the raft?" Asher stole a glance at Addison, then both looked at Corey, the resident helmsman. Edgar was busy kneading his chips like bread, enjoying the clinking sounds they made.

Corey took a sip of his apple juice cocktail, then held it out to the table. Ice rattling over Edgar's chips. "We're on!"

Corey was a sailor. He had learned to sail after walking. He had a Laser sailboat that he raced at times. The boys thought it was so cool he owned a boat. They all had been out on it at some point, or his father's that was almost 40 feet. He raced and found the sounds of the rushing water more thrilling than trophies. The others didn't see him much on the weekends; he was in Coconut Grove where the sailing club was. He played tennis too, but not up to Addison's level. Corey got three games once. Addison had a fever.

The New River Raft Race was a two-decade long tradition. It was held in Fort Lauderdale, snaking through downtown under four bridges until reaching the inner coastal. The only rule was a raft couldn't have a motor. It was propelled by muscle and sweat. The crowd and other boats were armed with water balloons. As far as the goal of the race, that depended on whom you asked.

The boring said it was to reach Tarpon Bend first. Some swashbucklers said to fall overboard less than five times. The daring said to get the hundreds lining the river and those leaning over the bridge railings like balcony seats, as soaked as them. The legends said 17th Street Causeway by dusk or when the booze finally ran out. The kids wanted to make it to Tarpon Bend in one piece, hopefully without running out of water balloons. Last year they got their first taste of it, their first soaking. They were absolutely hooked, as only kids would be, doing an almost adults-exclusive activity.

Corey brought his glass back from his announcement toast. "It rocks."

"So what was that we painted in your backyard last month?" Addison just remembered the last time he was over at Corey's house.

"That was varnish, not paint. Two coats worth. It will be like the transom."

All three crew members looked at their captain confused. It did drive them nuts when Corey talked in nautical terms foreign to them. Corey shook his head and sat up.

"It's basically the back of the boat. That way no one falls off." Corey was glad his father wasn't around, or he'd get yelled at for not saying stern. He then kept it simple.

"I took two sunfishes and connected them with the transom and a netting from the mast holes. It's like a Hobie Cat, kind of. I'm working on a pole sticking up like the letter Y that will be our sling shot."

"Now you're talking!" Asher raised his glass.

Addison raised his chin to Corey. "Wait, tell them the best part." His eyes then found Asher and Edgar with a grin.

"I named it." Corey finished his apple juice and eyed them over the rim of his glass. Asher and Edgar froze as if their batteries died. Five awesome seconds passed.

"The Wonkatania."

Asher leaned forward, not blinking. "You named it the Wonkatania."

Corey nodded. "Painted the name on last weekend." Another couple of silent seconds.

"That's awesomely brilliant!" Asher looked at Edgar.

"I love it!" Edgar slapped Corey on the shoulder.

"Ok, so who's in this year?" Asher sat up a little more.

"Us four," Corey looked at Addison. "How about Tara?"

"Yep. She even asked me last week about it."

"Perfect."

Pretty much. "Gaby is in too." Addison mentioned out loud.

"Who?" Asher's head shot around to his best friend.

"Gaby. You know…" Addison looked at him, then picked up the cards Edgar dealt.

"Gabrielle Hernandez. Sits behind me in 2nd period." Edgar said in assistance. Then surveyed his cards in his hand.

Asher narrowed his eyes, then pictured her. His face eased, eyes opened wide.

"The one with the awesome legs."

"God yes," was echoed over the cards by all.

"She's an unbelievable soccer player." Addison added.

Asher looked around the table. "Really?"

"Totally. Incredible player." Addison eyed Asher.

Edgar then tapped the table to bring order and minds off the tan, smooth legs of Gabrielle wearing Esprit jean shorts from Civics, and back to poker in Robin's Nest.

Corey won with a straight, but it wasn't enough to erode Edgar's mountain of chips. While Addison was fitting his Eastern cards into the box, Edgar rubbed his chin like Confucius.

"Hmmm, what to dress up as next year? So many choices, so many choices.

The holidays came and went fast. Addison got a new tennis bag and another year's subscription to *Sports Illustrated* and *Tennis.* He and Asher went out on Corey's father's sailboat for a day. And most of the kids were in the Orange Bowl, New Year's, for Miami's second national championship, beating Oklahoma for the third straight year.

Addison also reached the fourth round in his age group at the Rolex Junior Orange Bowl tennis tournament. Junior players from all over the world made the pilgrimage to Miami for it. Addison beat two players ranked higher than him, and found home court advantage in tennis was no different from football, baseball, and basketball. He always wondered how a football team or basketball team could lose badly coming out of the visitor's locker room, then turn around three days later and on their home court or field, win easily, looking like a totally different team.

It wasn't that he played on the courts a lot, he did at times, but it was just the whole setting. Waking up in his bed, with his homemade breakfast versus a hotel buffet. The roads, the weather, the sports section in the paper, his parent's car versus a rental, and a few friends as well. It all made everything more normal. He played out of his mind in the second round; beating a kid he had no business beating from Bradenton, Florida.

He came back to win the last two sets against a kid from Marietta, outside Atlanta. Then came the kid from South America. He showed Addison, sometimes no matter where you are, the better team or player just wins.

The Argentinian schooled Addison 6-2 6-2, 4,406 miles from home. The importance and stage of the moment got to Addison before even the first serve. There were 78 people around the court. Addison didn't see the dark green fence along the sides of the court, just people and eyes like owls trained on him. The hometown boy. During warm-ups, he didn't even feel comfortable, putting his first three backhands into the net. Not into the tape, making that popping sound that at least sounds cool, but into that empty, nothingness of a black hole that was the mesh net. After he lost his serve to go down 0-2, he just knew he was in trouble. Going into set two, he just didn't want to get a bagel.

His parents sat with Asher's and Tara's parents. Asher and Tara joined Edgar, Gaby, Vanessa, Gary, and Chris on the bleachers. At first, their heads went back and forth following the Penn 2 tennis ball. After 20 minutes, they moved back and forth while looking down with closed eyes, knowing he had no chance.

They greeted him once off the court. Tara hugged him after his mom. A half hour later he was in those same bleachers watching a match from the under 18 bracket, between a kid from California and one from Spain. Asher nudged him in the shoulder. "Dude, he was a year older than you. You have any idea how incredible it is that you got this far?"

"Yeah." He knew he was right, but it didn't help. It was like getting the box of raisins in your Halloween bag. *Gee thanks.*

Tara was sitting on the other side of him.

"Hey," she knocked his knee with hers, "you'll be out there with these guys in a couple years. You watch." She finally looked over at him. A soft face meant to soften another. Addison looked over to meet eyes, then looked back out on the court at the Spaniard. His backhand was like Becker's.

Addison played gin that night with his dad on the back screened-in patio. The night was cold for Miami in January, and crisp. The thermometer read 46. Their breaths puffed out in front of them, then got lost in the patio's screen. A little steam was floating away from the pool, like a pond in a dense forest. His dad never brought up the tennis match, allowing his son to share those feelings with his breathes if he wanted. Maybe it would carry them away to a forgotten place.

The raft race was a hit in February, on the New River, in the living rooms of the six kids, and even the halls of the junior high. Water balloons rained down on them like a meteor shower, but the Wonkatania held together and paddled on. Their slingshot even sent a few soaring, wobbly bombs into the crowd as well, a couple reaching the Andrew's Avenue bridge tower.

But something was missing in Addison that month.

Baseball cards.

He wasn't sure if it had happened over night, wasn't sure if it took place when his eighth grade schedule arrived in the mail, or when the 1986 baseball season ended, slipping through Bill Buckner's legs. He still looked at them at times, but not as often. The kid in him that breathed faster when opening a pack, now took quicker breaths for other reasons. At the same time, something took over. When he looked at money in his wallet, he didn't think of which packs to buy. He thought of movie tickets, ice cream afterwards, clothes, and a future jeep he dreamed of. Even his Eastern cards looked different now. He never wanted to play solitaire anymore, just poker, Euchre, or spades with the guys while discussing sports, MTV, and girls.

Or it could have been Tara Brookens's birthday.

He'd known her since they were in kindergarten together. He thinks he started collecting baseball cards a little after that, so he told himself he was just replacing a long time desire with a new one. She lived six houses down, and was passed on his way to Asher's house. The 22 square slabs of sidewalk out front of her house became his theater. He didn't ride slower or faster, or do something silly or pop wheelies. In his mind, he was on stage just walking or riding his bike, performing for the briefest of chances that she was looking out her window, and would see him. This "new" him.

He and Asher were sitting in Tara's kitchen talking with her dad about the news of Joe Robbie Stadium, which they hated, and high school just on the horizon. They were the only boys she 'unofficially' invited to her party. Tara and the other eight girls, the 'official' invites, were outside in the pool singing, jumping, and splashing to squeals in bikinis as the Beastie Boys *Licensed to Ill* played in the background. Looking out the kitchen's bay window, Tara was not the cute friend since kindergarten anymore. She was a pretty teenager who danced to REM and wore Benetton clothing well. The freckles around her smile were gone. Tiny hints of makeup replaced it on weekends. Their parents knew each other well. They had been in each other's rooms more times than anyone else. But Addison found himself not just thinking about her, but eyeing her more and more.

It started at the raft race, soaked. Her jean shorts and t-shirt, plastered to her one-piece bathing suit, kept tugging his eyes. The one thing he remembers most from that afternoon, wasn't the Wonkatania, wasn't the guys, wasn't being the youngest kids to finish, or arching water balloons like balled up paper into the trash can from across the room. It was Tara's hug she gave him when they finished and all celebrated. His heart pumped in bursts and stomach crumpled. He was afraid the others heard it, or felt him tremble.

He thought of both hugs, in the bleachers and the embrace aboard the Wonkatania. It was warm, despite being soaked. It was thrilling while melancholy. It was the smell of lilacs among sweat. She was steady while they floated. The tingling sensation from the hugs was suffocating.

When they were 8, they made a cute pact while watching *It's a Wonderful Life* one warm December. If neither were married by the age of 30, they would tie the knot wherever they were. It was never brought up again, and Addison was now wondering if she still would honor it. It wasn't that he wanted to get married at the time, or even knew for sure he wanted to marry her in 15 or so years. It was fact that they had this little treat tucked away in their past that no one knew about, and he prayed she thought about it at times. Occasionally, he would stare at his ceiling fan at night, wondering if it would come true and if Tara was doing the same in her bed down the street. As years past, deep down he felt as he was thinking of it, she was thinking of ice cream, Sting, or Cover Girl commercials instead.

March was Addison's favorite month. The weather was perfect. Spring training brought 18 teams to the state, most south of Orlando and within a three hour drive. The calendar page brought the beginning of the exodus of snowbirds from South Florida. I-95 tilted to the northbound side as all the Canadian, New York, and Jersey plates funneled home.

The boys' card games continued, with more discussions involving girls, movies, music, and this new thing called pop culture. Poker was slowly becoming his favorite game, obviously not bound to the number of players. They still played Euchre, hearts, spades, and gin, but poker was more like the movies. The cards were going with him to more and more places. And maybe most importantly, Key Biscayne held the fifth biggest tennis tournament in the world. The Lipton Championships was the only two-week tournament that wasn't a major. It was a fortnight of warm days, cool breezy nights, and 256 of the best tennis players in the world. Crandon Park turned into its own little village, main street, and hub that swelled tennis. With 128 men and women players, on 19 courts, from 10am to 11pm, there were a lot of tennis balls to be picked up.

Through some connections from coaches, most young tennis players in Dade and Broward County were able to be ballboys and ballgirls. Even if you didn't play tennis, kids wanted to be part of it. Asher was sick during the two-day orientation sessions, and would miss out this year. Gabrielle would be the rookie this year, with Tara, Corey, and Addison.

There was also the thrill of missing school. All four had good enough grades to miss three days each week. With the weekend between, the four kids would be crossing over the Rickenbacker Causeway to Key Biscayne eight times. Going to bed Sunday night, knowing you will not go to school Monday, is wonderful.

At 8:15 on a Monday morning, Addison flung his backpack over his right shoulder and headed down to Tara's. Gabrielle and Corey would be over soon, as Tara's mom would be driving them today. He hoped to get there before the others and be alone with Tara. There was nothing he planned on doing other than hanging out. There was nothing he planned on discussing with her other than whatever came up. He just wanted her to himself in this setting, so he could look back and dream up a glorious plot later on.

Her mom answered the door. "Addison, come in come in. How are you?" She hadn't seen him since the Junior Orange Bowl. She patted him on the shoulder with one hand. The other had a large oven mitt clawing a wooden spoon smeared with chocolate, or something dark and gooey.

"I'm good, thanks." He scanned the foyer and formal living room to the right, his senses on alert for her daughter. Addison followed her into the kitchen, his nose taking over in case he didn't know his way.

"Whoa that smells good Mrs. Brookens."

"Thanks hun. I was hoping they'd be ready for you all to take today for a treat later, but I didn't get them in the oven soon enough." Her mom wore an apron like it was a heavyweight championship belt. The whole block anticipated every creation she came up with, every chance to sample something.

She stood in front of the sink and turned on the water.

"Gabrielle is here, they're in Tara's room."

Oh, great. "Cool." His lungs collapsed. He looked down at the counter and flicked a crumb.

Mrs. Brookens turned while scrubbing her hands. "Go on back honey, they're expecting you."

Addison sat his backpack on the floor, up against the wall with the phone. Its long beige cord hanging limp to the carpet. He turned the corner accepting he wouldn't be alone with Tara. Then, just down the hall from her room, one of the greatest sounds of the decade greeted him in thumping bursts. It quickened his steps, even stretching his stride a few inches. His head cocked to the right as he heard it. He smiled.

One could argue the greatest sound is the crunching noise of the game cartridge when it was shoved into the slot of an Atari 2600. Followed by the tapping of the red button on the corner of the controller, along with every single beep, blurb, and tweak sound from television.

Or possibly, it could be argued that it is the thick plucking bass chords of "Every Breath You Take". It was muffled by her closed door, but still seeped through out to Addison. It was absorbed by the walls. He felt better, alive with a desire to get into Tara's room with Gaby. Even the black-framed pictures lining the hallway become much more interesting, like the wing of a museum. When hearing it, you instantly were in your own music video no matter where you were.

He knocked twice, an announcement more than a request. Then he pushed open the door. The song and beat reached him with no wall or door to buffer it. The whole room vibrated with bass, glorious English bass. His head just started nodding. For a few minutes, the bedroom became the Sistine Chapel or Centre Court Wimbledon. Gabrielle was on Tara's bed, bobbing her own head to the rhythm, while flipping the pages of a magazine. She looked up and smiled.

"Hey Adds." Gabrielle had been called Gaby or Gab for so long, she now called everyone else by their first syllable. Asher was Ash, Vanessa was Van, Edgar was Ed, which he hated, and even Tara became Tar.

"Hey Gabs." Addison pulled out Tara's desk chair, turned it around, and sat down. The small television on the dresser was muted on MTV, as Till Tuesday's video "Voices Carry" was on. A Duran Duran poster was over her desk and a Madonna poster was by her closet. When he closed the door, he noticed on the back was a poster for Guess jeans. There's a guy and girl on it wearing jeans only. Their bare backs were showing as they hug and give a look at the camera. She used to have an E.T. Movie poster there. Addison wondered if her mom knew. Like his baseball cards, Tara was moving on from cute, kids' stuff.

Tara came out of her bathroom. "Addison Briggs. What's up?" She was re-tying her side ponytail.

He shrugged. "Our absences. We should be in World History right now." He picked up the *Synchronicity* cassette case and read the back. "What a shame."

Gaby then got up on her knees and pointed to Addison, as if he was in the first row of the audience. She began singing with Sting, like auditioning for drama class.

"I feel so cold and I long for your embrace. I keep crying, baby, baby, please!" She then brought both hands to her chest, pressed over her heart, pleading at Addison. He began clapping.

Tara laughed and threw a stuffed animal at her. "Nice." Tara moved over to her dresser and picked up five or six cassette tapes. She shuffled through them, sliding them from one hand to the other, and picked out four. She stuffed them in her backpack.

"I can't wait to get out there. It's so nice out."

"Are you guys taking a jacket?" Gaby had refocused on the teen magazine, but tossed it on the pillow behind her.

"Nah, only for the night sessions." Tara looked at Addison, "How many night sessions did we get assigned?"

"Four. Wednesday, Thursday, Saturday, and next Wednesday."

The night sessions were popular and hard to get. First timers couldn't do night matches. With only four lit courts, there weren't as many matches as the day session. At night, almost every court had a big name on it. Gaby couldn't do it, being her first time, but had other plans.

"I wish you could do nights, it's so much fun." Tara sat on the bed next to Gaby, both bounced a little.

"Yeah, next year you can though." Addison leaned back, still holding the tape case. He glanced over at the television, as his favorite Pat Benatar video was now playing. If anything could pull his eyes off Tara's smile and giggles and Gaby's legs, it was someone in the cockpit of a P51 Mustang soaring over occupied France, dodging bomb bursts and enemy fire, while "Shadows in the Night," blared over the intercom from headquarters. It doesn't get any better than that.

"It's okay," she pulled a piece of lint or something off Tara's shirt, "it works out real well being spring break next week. I have that soccer camp to go to."

"Oh yeah, that's right. Where is it again?" Addison unconsciously started tapping his finger on the chair to "King of Pain".

"Chapel Hill. You have to get invited to this one, and I did. I'll be the youngest one there, I can't wait. We stay in dorms on campus!"

"Oh my god, really?" Tara shot a glance at Addison and both were impressed.

"So you get a roommate?" Addison asked, eyes still on Tara even thought she looked back to Gaby.

"Yeah, I found out who she was last weekend. She's older than me. Our parents talked on the phone."

Tara and Addison exchanged looks again, nodding. Addison then looked down at the tape case.

"So I still have yet to listen to side A on this? I think I've only listened to seven, eight, and nine."

The three kids talked and laughed for the next 10 minutes waiting for Corey to arrive. The whole time, Addison kept stealing glances at Tara like a spy camera. Once "Wrapped Around Your Finger" ended, they pressed rewind.

The four eighth-graders squeezed into the back of Mrs. Brooken's station wagon for the ride to Key Biscayne. Instead of sitting in rows of uncomfortable chairs and listening to Mr. Bryson's math lesson, they listened to both sides of *Synchronicity.* Instead of looking at equations and variables on a dusty chalkboard, they saw the hustle of morning rush hour on I-95 and downtown Miami work life. All new to them. Between that, spring break next week, and thanks to Lipton, only a two-day school week this week, the four kids' pulses reached vacation levels. Their eyes were jittery, surveying everything out the windows.

A helicopter lifted off from Jackson Memorial. The bridge on the river just off the Miami Avenue exit was opening. The downtown monorails were sliding into the city. Tara spoke to the windshield.

"I don't think I've ever seen Miami at 9:20 on a Monday?"

After paying the toll on the Rickenbacker, Corey looked out south on Biscayne Bay. A huge flat aqua gem shimmering to the horizon with only one lonely white sail. "I've never seen the bay this empty." His sailing club, the Coconut Grove Sailing Club, was just off to the right in front of the group of taller condos on Bayshore Drive.

Addison glanced to his left, north. The art deco buildings of Brickell stuck up on the shore like Crayola markers of different shapes. The famous one with a section in the middle missing, pulled out like some giant Lego piece, was there, palm tree and all. It brought out a smile on Addison's face. Like every kid who grows up in Miami, it's put on their young resume.

"Where do you live kid?"

"Miami sir. You know, where that water front building has a palm tree growing in the middle of it."

He then noticed an Eastern 757 bank left and disappear into the clouds over Dodge Island. He wondered if Darlene was on board. The trips out to the tennis center were almost as exciting as tossing a ball to Chris Evert.

The ball kids' tent was behind the stadium court. Rows of chairs faced the front, like a motivational conference in Vegas, but were only used as the initial greeting to pass out court numbers. After that, it became a holding tank and shady rest spot for 13-18 year olds. There was a soda machine, snacks, and refreshing fans in the corners.

Kids were randomly assigned courts, with a premium on stadium and court two. There, you were almost guaranteed to be in the background of television cameras and get top players. The kids figured out that first year, if you sit way in the back, they would run out of courts by the time they get to you. After groups of six are assigned to all 16 courts, the left overs were the second wave of ball kids, replacing the first group in shifts. Usually they got stadium or court two right away. On their second day this year, it finally paid off.

Gaby and Tara handed towels and bounced tennis balls, always new and fuzzy, to Chris Evert, Boris Becker, Yannick Noah, and Jimmy Connors on grandstand. The highlight of the boys in stadium was Steffi Graf, Mikael Pernfors, and two Czechs that apparently hated each other.

Ivan Lendl was playing Miloslav Mecir. If anyone besides Addison needed another reason to hate Lendl, they were awarded with a bucket of ammunition firing like a tennis ball machine. Lendl got mad when some towels were left out on the court off to the side. One was draped over a clock in the corner. Another on the ground by a line's persons box seat. Corey had to grab it and hide it behind a fake plant.

Then Mecir, known as The Cat, started throwing sarcasm like volleys to all the other lines people and ball kids, having them pick up every towel, leaf, water bottle, and imaginary speck of dust on the court. The crowd loved it, roaring in approval. Lendl, who always looked mad to begin with, was absolutely livid. Steam was coming out of his cyborg ears. Addison really thought laser beams would shoot out of his eyes that the evil communists had implanted. He then said a word that would get Addison in detention at school and a beating from his dad.

Two points later, Lendl looked back at Addison for a ball. Addison was so nervous he was shaking while holding up the two balls. He prayed when he tossed one to him, hoping the bounce was acceptable, and sparing him from dodging a thrown racket. Addison would always comment on that moment when talking about the day, but inside, he came away with something else. The clear fact that Ivan Lendl absolutely pounds his groundstrokes.

The kids would admit that the time in the tent, walking around with a badge getting them into places normally off-limits, and just hanging out was maybe the best part. It was a social aspect that none would consider three years ago. While waiting in the tent, they sat in groups listening to their Walkman's, playing card games thanks to Addison's Eastern deck, and talking about videos, clothes, and movies. The endless soda machine wasn't too shabby either.

The weekend brought the biggest crowds. The sidewalks and concrete paths between tents, vendors, courts, and palm trees were impossible to see. From the blimp above, it looked like pipes of people flowing like water at right angles and straight lines throughout the tennis village. The field had been cut in half by Saturday as the third round finished up and some fourth round matches began.

All four kids were in the ball kid's tent ready for their court assignments. As the days and week came, the number of kids needed had dwindled. Their plan of sitting in the back and being the second wave onto the courts would not work anymore. Most of the kids knew who was scheduled on the courts. Graf and Edberg were scheduled for Stadium in 30 minutes after the morning session. Mats Wilander and Andres Gomez were court two later on.

Addison was able to watch Wilander practice on one of the outer courts a couple of times over the last few days. Addison stood and stared at his idol hitting balls for 45 minutes. It was a lesson no teacher could match in class that day, and a memory no VHS tape could equal. But watching him play a live match from behind him, with crowd noise and pressure shots ricocheting off his Rossignol racket was something totally different.

They sat in the chairs all biting their lips, a heel tapping the floor in quick anxious bursts. They leaned to the left, then right peering between the heads in front of them trying to steal a glimpse at the numbers. Addison took deep breaths. Tara, without knowing, reached over and grabbed Addison's forearm with a squeeze as the official approached. The tingles spreading through Addison were almost melting. He forgot all about tennis, and his eyes just slanted down to her hand. He wanted to slide his hand up and grab hers. The Lipton official reached them, passing out the court numbers. He didn't even notice.

Gaby court three.

Corey court six.

Tara court seven.

Addison court two.

"Oh my god," Corey nudged Addison with his shoulder. "Mats will be on court two dude!"

He heard him, and the tent seemed to raise off the ground for a moment as if floating up on his goosebumps, still swelling. What he couldn't figure out, which was shocking, was if Mats or Tara was inflating the goosebumps?

"Okay kids, remember your badges and hats. Check the map for your court location and be ready in 10 minutes."

All the kids got up and mingled. Chattering voices filled the tent. Some went over to the fountain drink machine, some searched the donut boxes for one last treat, and the rest checked the court maps. Addison had his first class ticket in his hand, but a desire to be with Tara was sending him towards the back of the plane. Even a seat next to Mats Wilander wasn't enough right now. He wanted a seat next to Tara Brookens.

After 30 seconds of fretful searching, he found a kid with court number seven.

"Hey, do you want to trade?" Addison held out his card.

If someone wanted to trade, it usually wasn't good. The kid glanced down skeptically, then his eyes widened and lips parted.

"What? You do know Sabatini is out there now and Wilander is due up next?"

Addison just nodded. He couldn't speak; afraid hearing the word *yes* would snap him back to his senses that were still woozy from Tara's touch.

The kid shook his head. "Whatever dude, here you go." They exchanged court numbers. Groups began forming and heading off in packs to the courts. Addison looked down at his number seven, rubbing his thumb over it. He realized he just gave up Mats Wilander.

Who knows if he had not seen him practice earlier in the week, if he would do the same thing. But just being by Tara made his heart twitch. He looked down at this forearm and smiled.

Tara came by and bumped him with her shoulder. "Hey, have fun."

Addison looked at her, "Yeah for sure. It's-" His mouth stayed open and he looked around for a second. "What do you mean?"

"Out on court seven. I'll tell you all about Mats later, I promise, okay?" She smiled at him.

The tent that was floating a minute ago, was sucked down into a spinning drain. The arousing tingling sensations melted, turning into sweat. Addison was sick to his stomach.

"Wait, you're on court two? I thought you had seven?" His eyes shot down at her court number. He felt like a heating pad was dropped over his neck and shoulders.

Either he had looked at it wrong, maybe it was upside down, or her finger was covering up the bottom of the 2, or he was still dizzy from her touch, but Tara had a two written in marker, not seven. He swallowed, making his face turn pale. Tara looked at him, thinking he was upset about her seeing his idol.

"Hey do you want to switch?" She touched his arm, "Here I know you love that guy."

No I love you, since sixth grade and eating ice cream at 31 Flavors after we all saw 'Real Genius'.

"No, no that's okay."

"Whoa, dude what happened?" Corey came over, standing next to them looking at his court number. "You had court two, you had Wilander! Why did you trade?" He looked up at Addison.

That last sentence hung between them for what seemed like a minute. Corey was shocked. Addison just wanted to leave, start walking home right then. Tara was confused too, but then looked down at her number, and then Addison's. Something clicked inside her. She looked up at Addison.

"You had two? You…" She stopped and her mouth opened slightly. Addison looked at her, his eyes were almost watery and just walked away. His head was down. His arms didn't even sway.

Gaby and Corey headed off with their groups. Tara just stood there, staring off at Addison until he was swallowed up by the moving crowd and gone, lost in a sea of red Adidas shirts. She glanced down at her number one more time, then back up in his direction, getting it.

Oh my god. He likes me, I mean like, really likes me.

Court Seven was like winning the NIT. He was able to watch the hard hitting, serve and volleyer Kevin Curren, Russian base liner Andrei Chesnokov, and Amy Frazier. Curren and Chesnokov were both in the top 30, but had no idea about the American Frazier. He'd never heard of her. He actually learned a lot from Curren's game, and the Russian's groundstrokes were very impressive.

The thing he remembered about Amy Frazier, was no matter what had just happened, a double fault, a let court that dribbled over onto her side, or getting her serve broken to lose the second set, she smiled and said, 'thank you' every time Addison or the girl in the other corner tossed her a ball. Every single time, she actually said it. That stuck with Corey the most, and he found himself pulling for her. She lost and Addison thought she deserved to win just on being nice, but knew nice people rarely finish first.

But the problem was about 500 yards behind him was Tara, with her tan legs, pretty smile, and bouncy ponytail sticking out the hole in the back of her hat. She was throwing tennis balls to a guy born in Vaxjo, Sweden who was up on Addison's wall above his desk. The same fingers that gripped his forearm, enough to feel his skin, veins, and blood getting aroused, was feeling the furry Wilson tennis balls that Mats Wilander would catch to either serve or slip into his pockets.

He really did want to walk home. He did not want to go back to the tent. What would it be like with her there now, in front of Gabrielle and Corey? He wandered around for a while, checking out the souvenir tents, outer courts with players practicing and acting more loose and informal, but gave in and headed back. There was a desire to get it over with, like a test in science class.

"Hey buddy, we grabbed your playing cards if that's okay?" They were sitting in a circle near the back of the tent. All three were as sweaty as him form the warm, Miami spring day. The girls had their shirt sleeves bunched up over their shoulders showing off glistening arms. Addison went to the drink machine, and pushed his cup into the Sunkist lever. He joined them and watched the card game. They all shared stories from their courts. Addison found himself incapable of looking at Tara. It wasn't jealously of being within arm's reach of Mats Wilander, but the awkwardness of being within arm's reach of her. All of a sudden, he felt exposed, naked, and not the close friend since kindergarten from down the street whose moms exchange books and favorite wines. *She must have figured it out…*

Gabrielle's mom came to pick her up. She wasn't staying for the night session and would pack tomorrow morning for her flight to Raleigh-Durham. Her soccer camp was waiting. Tara, Corey, and Addison hung out together and played cards with two other kids from Coral Springs. Eventually they went to court two for the last set of a Jimmy Connor's match and first five games of Zina Garrison vs Mary Joe Fernandez fourth round match. It seemed Fernandez's entire high school was in the stands, the local teenager turned the match into a Davis Cup affair. Poor Garrison had a whole four people pulling for her. Her coach, trainer, and two friends.

They used their meal coupons and got burgers and fries. They sat under a Lipton Tea umbrella in the main courtyard, where 50 other tables were scattered around. Tiny white picket fences edged all the grassy areas. It really was like a miniature city for two weeks. Along the edges, where their table was, several huge trees hung over everyone. You could tell they weren't planted, but here as they built things around them, maybe even here when they, not the condos on the other side of the street, were the tallest thing on the Key. Halfway through the meal, Corey got up to go to the bathroom. Addison and Tara were alone. He immediately took a bit of his burger, thinking if he was chewing, he couldn't talk and she wouldn't ask him something.

"I can't believe Gaby is going to that soccer camp. That's so awesome." Tara slurped her Pepsi.

Oh, thank god. "Yeah, she told me Thursday that the high school coach already invited her to talk about things. She is skipping JV and starting on varsity next year."

Tara put her drink down and shook her head while reaching for a napkin.

"Can you believe we'll be in high school next year?"

"No." Addison finally shot a glance at her. "I still remember Mrs. Miller in kindergarten."

The conversation was normal, but their eyes gave everything away. There actually was an awkwardness between them now. Addison found comfort that they only had the Tuesday afternoon together here. Wednesday night was just he and Corey. He wondered how things at school and at their lockers would be from now on.

She ripped open another ketchup packet and squeezed some out in her basket. She started dipping some fries into it. Addison took a bite of his burger. There was silence for the next 20 seconds. *Where the hell is Corey? Come on.*

He looked up at the huge tree next to them, dangling over their umbrella. He wondered how many stories it has heard and how many memories were shared under it. Addison imagined the tree storing them all like sap, or holding it there in each ring of its trunk like songs on a record album. Just then, a gust came up, and he hoped it would blow and float one of those stories to him, maybe peeling away from a branch or being sucked out of a leaf, and drift into him, giving him an idea of what to say to her. Better yet, drift into Tara, allowing her to say something.

Corey finally came back and the three finished up eating before discussing where to get dessert. Tara's mom baked treats for them all week, but they did not last long enough. They found a Haagen Dazs vendor in front of the stadium and got ice creams. They meandered back to the ball kids' tent.

He and Corey began a game of gin while Tara laid on her stomach and watched. She was listening to Crowded House on her Walkman with her chin in her hands. Corey won, reaching 100 first. Addison was battling the cards, Corey, and the presence of Tara lying there. His mind couldn't keep track of any discarded cards.

Tara's mom pulled into the back parking lot an hour later. The three piled in and were tired, with more window watching than talking taking place. The bright lights of Miami filled his window, a movie strip of colors and flashes. The city looked different now. Addison was different now. Tara was different now. More importantly, they were different now. Was he thinking into this too much like girls tend to do?

It was the longest 35-minute drive in his life.

Wednesday night found Addison and Corey at Lipton for the men's quarterfinals. Addison's mom dropped them off and they found the ball kids' tent at 6:10. The breeze was stronger than usual tonight. It wasn't the common 10mph breeze off the Atlantic, but pushing 20mph out of the northeast. The palm fronds weren't swaying like normal, they were bent and flapping like an old stiff flag. The stadium seating swirled the winds like a funnel making ball tosses for serves a nightmare.

Two quarterfinals would be on stadium back to back, the other two were played earlier. Men's and women's doubles semifinals were on courts two and three. Only 45 kids were in the tent that night. Most weren't worried about getting a good match, which was more likely the farther into the week they got. What was on their minds was the weekend. Usually those that were selected for the men's and women's final Saturday and Sunday came from the second week.

With most kids out on courts, Addison and Corey remained with the second group for stadium. Another six kids remained for court two. Most kids bunched up with friends, some were alone. Addison and Corey were with Justin again, from Coral Springs. He mentioned he wasn't a huge tennis fan, but liked to play it occasionally and it was a great excuse to miss school. They were playing poker on the ground comparing schools and movies. Justin was impressed that Addison and Corey were in the New River Raft race, as he had been there before as a spectator throwing water balloons.

Addison was looking down at his hand. The seven of clubs was on the end, where he put cards he could discard. He slid his thumb over the black seven, back and forth, thinking about court seven written in marker. He thought back to Saturday night when they were eating hamburgers and were alone for a minute or two. He wanted to ask her about that marriage pact they made years ago, but wouldn't dare now. Was he still the friend from down the street or a cute boy who could crush her heart if he wanted. Judging by the poster on the back of her door, something told him he was just an old friend six houses away.

Just then, two guys walked in the tent. They stopped at the entrance as if not sure how to proceed. They each had three brown pizza boxes. Corey looked up too, and Addison was about to tell Justin to check out the scene, when Addison froze. His chest was the only thing moving, swelling a little more every second.

"Guys…that's Aaron Krickstein." The other looked familiar too. He mentally flipped through his old *Tennis* magazines and tennis highlights on television.

"Who?" Justin looked around, then back at the two guys.

Corey recognized him after a second. "Whoa, you're right. Who's the other guy?" They were both sitting up much straighter.

Addison shook his head and watched them walk in about half way before the Lipton officials recognized them. Two ladies walked up to them with shocked smiles and talked to them.

"So what's going on? Someone ordered a pizza?" Justin looked back at Addison.

"I think that other guy is Jay Berger."

Corey's head snapped over to his friend. "Really?"

Addison nodded slowly. "He lives down here." He peered over at Corey.

Addison and Corey exchanged looks as two of America's youngest, future stars stood in the ball kids' tent holding pizza. After a couple of seconds, they were introduced and turned to address the tent. All 13 or so kids staring with eyes as round as tennis balls.

"We want to thank you for all you do. We used to ballboy, and hope that maybe a couple of you will someday return the favor if you ever turn pro. So, anyone like pizza?"

The stupid question was greeted with roars and looks at those sitting next to them thinking, *is this really happening?* No one stayed where they were, even if they weren't hungry. The two young Americans even passed out the slices, which could have had anchovies and roaches on it, it didn't matter.

Two minutes later the three boys found their old spot, this time with paper plates of pizza from a local place out on Key Biscayne. Addison and Corey exchanged another look while taking their first bite, thinking the same thing: *Aaron Krickstein, the 24th ranked player in the world, just handed me this slice of pepperoni. Holy crap!*

Before they knew it, Krickstein walked over to them, standing behind Justin. He peered down eating a slice as well. "What's the game boys?"

Addison and Corey couldn't speak. Just stared. Justin answered for the group, as he didn't truly grasp what was going on.

"Uh, poker."

"Can I join you?"

"Sure." Justin moved over and looked at Addison and Corey. They were hypnotized.

Krickstein held out a hand to Justin. "Aaron."

"I'm Justin."

After a couple seconds, Addison blinked and sat up, locating his voice. It was as if he was plugged back in.

"Addison." They shook hands. Corey then rounded out the intros.

Addison took the cards and started shuffling.

"So who did you guys see today?"

The boys filled Aaron Krickstein in on their matches today and the last week, including Lendl's towel fiasco with The Cat.

"I was a ballboy once, some ATP indoor event up in Detroit. Did McEnroe once." Krickstein nodded over his shoulder. "Jay used to ballboy this tournament when it was up in Boca."

Addison leaned to his left and found Jay Berger, sitting with some other kids enjoying their pizza. He then looked at the 20 year old. "Are you going to play Davis Cup?" He started flipping cards to everyone.

"Yes, I definitely hope to. That would be an honor."

All four fanned out their cards, tossing a quarter into the middle. Aaron scanned the kids. "Sorry, no change guys."

"I think it'll be okay." Corey mentioned and they all laughed.

Addison pressed the Davis Cup again. "That's good, cause we need you. Mac and Fleming can't do it all anymore."

They talked college football, tennis, and pizza while working on a second slice of pepperoni. Justin won the pot; swelling up to $2.75, with a diamond flush over Krickstein's three of a kind. Krickstein and Berger left a couple minutes later, leaving a buzz in the tent that remained until all the kids headed out to their courts. The buzz went with them, teasing the first group of kids.

"No way!"

"What?"

"You're kidding!"

"Get out!"

"Shut up!"

"Are you serious?"

"What kind of pizza?"

CHAPTER SEVENTEEN

Lisette Herndon always had the coolest Trapper Keeper back in junior high. Her hair was a blond waterfall, a photo snapped with a slow shutter speed. Her Edwin or Guess jeans were pegged perfectly. It was as if the cuffs were hemmed by her fingers each morning. Her locker was always in the prefect location. She wore the band's t-shirt the morning after the concert. The white Reeboks were never dirty and the Ray-Bans never smudged. Her three Swatches had colorful Swatch guards no one else had seen at Burdines. The deadly sin of envy followed her like the shadow of an eclipse, coating over everything in her setting, and seeping into everyone's bloodstream. Boys stared with wide eyes, yet turned into childish mutes if she approached. Girls stared with narrow eyes, but bubbled over gushing if she requested them. It was said a few seniors came to her sweet sixteenth birthday party.

She was going to be a problem.

Asher's locker slammed. "God, I'm starving."

"Me too." Corey added while opening his lock.

"Well tell Edgar to hurry the hell up." Addison was leaning back against his locker and crossing his arms. His eyes focused on the scene directly across the bustling hallway. Lisette was there, along with her entourage. They were mostly boys who just gawked at her; laughed at anything she did, and assumed they had armor just from being close to her. Addison, Asher, Corey, and Edgar referred to them as Cleopatra's bodyguards.

The only boy that seemed worthy was Jeremy, who could control the other boys. He was the only boy Lisette really paid attention too. The others were puppies at the girls' heels. He was the starting pitcher for the high school's baseball team, ranked #7 in the state. He was going to either stay locally at UM, or head off to Mississippi State, LSU, or Arizona

State. Unless he was drafted in the first round of the major league draft, which this week was the rumor. Addison and Asher saw him at the beach once and the movies. He seemed to have a collection of little nymphs surrounding him at all times.

Sophia Castillo was in the mist, who acted as if the silver spoon was actually in the womb with her. Her father owned five of the largest car dealerships in South Florida, from Palm Beach to Monroe counties. She had her own car in the driveway three days before her learner's permit. The day she actually got her learner's permit, its replacement was dropped off after Sophia complained about the color. Addison, Asher, and Edgar dreamed of saying to her what they said in their heads. She was reapplying lipstick, thanks to the mirror on the inside of her locker. She dabbed the corner of her mouth and closed the metal door, spinning the lock. She turned and playfully punched one of the boys in the chest after some comment. All the boys laughed, because, well it was just that funny. Lisette and Sophia then turned to a third girl, still stuffing a book into her locker. Addison was observing her too.

The homecoming queen then closed her locker and turned around, flashing her green eyes while pushing her pink wallet into the back pocket of her jeans. The three girls, Jeremy, and two of the other puppies then moved down the hall, through the corridor of paparazzi. Everyone else studied them, eyed them, and leaned to the person next to them for whispers. Asher was no different.

"She looks hot in that off the shoulder thing."

Addison took a deep breath and leaned forward off the locker. He knew Asher wasn't talking about Lisette, who Asher liked, but the third girl. Addison's crush.

Addison ignored his best friend's comment and nodded past Asher's shoulder to Edgar, finally arriving. "Here he is."

Asher turned. "Dude, what took you?"

"Chill out, give me a second." Edgar started spinning his combination lock. Addison stole another peek down the hallway. The celebrities were now disappearing into the stairwell. *How the hell am I going to get to her?* It wasn't the first time he thought that.

Kadence Whitaker was everything Lisette was, but different. Maybe more, as far as Addison was concerned. She didn't brag. She was brunette.

She was quiet. She was smart. The senior was voted homecoming queen last month. She played center midfield for the high school's soccer team. Her sweat was glitter.

When Kadence was in a room, it was like walking into a room with a Christmas tree. It didn't even need to be a Victorian bed & breakfast in New England, or a log cabin chiseled out of redwoods in Montana. Wherever the room, it was full of warmth and promise, and you couldn't help but take a deep breath and smile.

He has one class with her, knows a mutual friend, but unfortunately friends and clicks dictated what you did. And the caste system of the high school shunned on junior boys even looking at senior girls. And there was Lisette.

Going up to Kadence would be like approaching Ronald Reagan with his secret service detail surrounding him. This protection didn't have a submachine gun, 9mm, or hidden knives. They had demeaning glances, snide comments, painful ignores, and meanness fostered from last period, last week, last month, and last year. In other words, much much worse.

The boys, like everyone in first lunch, had 40 minutes to get back for fifth period. Within five minutes, the fenced in parking lot would only be 2/3 full, with senior and juniors, and those sophomores that had siblings or knew someone, racing off as if a green flag was waved.

"Where we going?" Addison pushed his hands into his Levi's pockets.

"I'm in the mood for a breakfast lunch actually. How about Latin America?" Corey said while watching Sophia pull out of her parking spot without looking.

"Damn, good call." Asher agreed. Latin America restaurants, for a chain, had the best Cuban breakfast around. It was cheap, good, fast, and washed down with Cuban coffee. Maybe two.

"Ooh, I could use a café con leche actually. I think it's our turn to get Mr. Kael's anyways." Corey said.

Sophia's Ford Bronco pulled away, rolling through the stop sign.

"Hey, she actually slowed a little." Asher said. *God she's a bitch.*

"Well why on earth would she stop?" Edger added. *Bitch.* "When did they get her that thing?"

"Over Halloween. I mean who wants their daughter driving around in a two year old Audi 5000 for god's sake." The Bronco slipped into the line of cars exiting the back gate. Addison shook his head.

"I think a house fell on her sister."

Fifth period AP European History was always crowded. It was actually interesting in a romantic-type way and was an AP credit. It was also open to juniors and seniors. And Mr. Kael was the teacher. Mr. Kael was the coolest teacher in school and had a cult following. He had taught for 30 years. Lived on three continents, spoke two languages, feet touched the Great Wall, and was the 38th American to top the Scotland Munros list. He spoke in a monotone voice and dragged out the last syllable in every sentence. His bow ties were never straight. Addison thought if he and his Uncle Trey ever met, they would close down the bar or cafe they were in.

Two weeks ago, some seniors strolled in five minutes late. It wasn't from a flat tire or long lines at Burger King. A senior tradition of "liquid lunches" took place at whoever's house was vacant during the day. Beer was easily found. The three came in, and before they found their seats, Mr. Kael asked why they didn't bring him any.

They laughed it off, and played dumb sitting down. He then asked them what kind it was. Two of the boys exchanged looks and found him staring at them. He was leaning against the lectern spinning his glasses in one hand. It dawned on the kids that he really wanted to know. At times, he was the cool neighbor you went over to hang out with when your parents were driving you nuts. Any other teacher, they lie and move on, but this was Mr. Kael. Eric shook his head at what he was about to do and came out with it.

"Heineken."

"Green lizards huh?"

Silence. Wondrous eyes. The term was new to the seniors. Age trumped youth.

"How about Amstel?" Mr. Kael tilted his head, curious.

The one senior turned to his buddy, who shrugged his shoulders at him. *Are we really discussing this?* Again, it was Mr. Kael.

"Sure, anything really, but usually cheaper stuff." They, like everyone else, were sitting up a little straighter.

"Smart."

Mr. Kael then spent the next five minutes discussing the difference between Dutch and Belgian beers, relating it to the political philosophies of each country, the reason the '74 Dutch lost the World Cup final to Germany and how they are more famous for it, and the choice of suits of King Baudouin. Two juniors took notes.

"Okay enough Low Countries rhetoric. Books out, notebooks open, pencils ready. We're going to get pure crazy today on The Age of Discovery, Reconnaissance, and Expansion. Chapter three everyone." Kael then eyed the three senior boys, waiting for them to see him. 10 seconds later, they looked up at him.

"Don't be late again." He held the stare for another five seconds, then addressed the class. "Okay, so Gaspard de Coligny, he was a partier who sure liked his wine."

The four friends came back from lunch on time, with a treat. Corey delivered the café con leche, and found his seat. It started as a joke one day in September. Marie caught Stanley Kael in the hallway before lunch, looking tired with heavy eyes, and decided to bring one back for him. The next week another appeared, then another, and another on the fourth week. Or was it second? No one knew. No one cared. Every week after, someone continued it. There was no schedule, no class roster with penciled checks in the margin. Someone, at some point, just did it. It wasn't about bribery or favoritism, more like thanks. It became a ritual, tradition, something no yearbook could show. It also tended to relax him, holding an unexpected present, and led to better things.

Corey's seat is next to Addison's, as they were among the eight juniors in the class. Kadence was against the far wall, with Sophia behind her. One of Cleopatra's guards was in the room, but she never bothered with him. Kael didn't have an alphabetic seating chart, and the kids respected it.

Twenty minutes into class, the Cuban coffee was gone, as was the lesson plan. Kael loved discussions, especially about topics that the kids showed interests in that were not in a textbook. They had quizzes on the news that required them to check out a newspaper at least three times a week. Whatever hot topic was in the news was brought into the classroom.

The last discussion was two weeks ago concerning Salmon Rushdie and his *Satanic Verses.* Today's was flag burning, which was in the news lately. Three schools allowed the burning protests and two schools in New England didn't raise the flag over the weekend. Addison had plenty of ammunition for this topic, but needed an enemy to put up a challenge. The ammunition came from the city of Miami, snowbirds, and a grandfather's stories. The target was placed out in the firing range by someone on the far side of the classroom.

So many thought the Soviets were the great villain of America, but Addison thought they were much closer. This enemy invaded the country daily, in droves come October, using the holiday of Halloween to begin their scary, evil masquerade. They would retreat come Easter, and begin plotting their next invasion. They were the Canadians.

Addison would admit there were probably plenty of nice ones, just like not every American was Ben Franklin. As he got older, more and more lazy American's pissed him off. And there was the crime issue in this country, specifically Miami. But the cars with Quebec and Ontario plates that Addison saw the most, were tanks driven by mooching, disrespectful soldiers from north of the border.

They drive as fast as they want. They drive as slow as they want. Any lane was theirs to drive in. Any parking spot was theirs to use. They did what they wanted, without any consequence knowing that come Easter, the Canadian Snowbird Army would retreat into their homeland unpunished. Tickets were ripped up, warnings laughed at. The only thing they brought back was a tan, plenty of Sweet & Low, and condiments.

Instead of going to Publix like everyone else to stock up their condos, Addison had been to restaurants on the beaches and seen them steal everything from salt & pepper shakers to silverware. They take sweetener packets like mints. Owners lose more money off that, than vacant rooms in the off-season. Then there was the flag issue.

The hotels, condominiums, and apartments they call home for five months will fly the Canadian flag, to be nice, but is the same height as the U.S. flag. Addison noticed that it is the same case with Cuban flags. Addison just takes a deep breath, and chews on his lip.

Between that, living in a city that thinks immigration should have the security of EPCOT's World Showcase, and a Badger fan in Naples, Sophia Castillo never had a chance.

"That's a good point. So which amendment are we discussing, first or fifth?" Mr. Kael had his feet up on his desk, curious to see where they would take this new point.

"But it's not property."

"Yes it is."

"Your house or car is your property; you can burn them down if you want."

"It's not the burning. It's the-"

"No no it's the action, freedom of speech. You can burn books, why not the flag."

"What if someone burns a Bible?"

Mr. Kael nodded at that point. Five minutes later, it almost ended.

"Oh my god, come on guys, someone invent fireproof flags and this point is mute."

Most laughed, the kid did have a point. The debate would have probably stopped there. Sophia didn't whisper softly enough though.

"Jesus give me a break it's a piece of cloth."

Addison's head slowly turned to the right. He put his first round in the chamber.

"Don't you have to be a citizen of this country to contribute?" Silence. Not a sound.

"Excuse me?" Sophia wasn't whispering now. The whole classroom tilted towards Addison.

"Excuse what? What don't you understand? It's English." Addison's fiery glare was lit by a lantern from the North Church and coastline of Florida. Addison's voice was amplified by an entire, fed up student body. Mr. Kael's feet uncrossed and swung off his desk.

Sophia was red. "Who do-"

"Would you burn your parents? Well you might, but I don't think anyone else would." Stanley Kael's classroom turned into Mrs. Hillcock's art class. Edvard Munch's famous painting, *The Scream,* was in every desk facing Sophia.

"I'm sorry, I didn't come here on some stupid raft that-"

"That's debatable, oh and for the flags not being raised up North; I say we tell two guards from the Tomb of the Unknown Soldier. I guarantee you, they will walk the 700 miles through the snow and rain with no food or drink, to raise that flag and stand guard. The whole thing would be an honor. Let's see someone try to bring it down or burn it then."

Four senior boys exchanged glances thinking that was pretty cool. Everyone knew Addison was a big time tennis player, but now they were seeing him with different balls.

"See that's what the cloth is, blood. Yours, your families, colonists, a prisoner in a rock cell half way around the world, and everyone else who came here not because it was close or easy, but because you wanted to respect virtues. That flag might as well be the same one from Iwo Jima or Bunker Hill, even though we didn't have a flag-"

"Don't you have some dorky tennis game to go play?"

"Don't you have a freshman to tease?" Corey jumped in, not able to stand it anymore. The common citizens were revolting.

"Alright that's enough. This is no longer a debate. And we only debate in here, plus I'm out of coffee." Kael stood up, announcing it was over in the calmest manner only he could pull off.

Sophia was shaking her head, stunned, nostrils pulsing. She looked at Kadence, then one of the puppies. She mouthed something that Addison couldn't make out completely, but knew one of the words was *asshole.* The puppy, who was only in the class because Sophia and Kadence were in it, glared at Corey, then at Addison. He was mouthing something too.

Addison was closing his notebook when he did a double take at him. "What are you looking at!" It was no question.

"Mr. Briggs, I said enough." Kael changed the subject, knowing there were two minutes left before the bell. "Make sure your homework is copied down. You may get started on it if you choose."

Addison pulled out his book from the rack under his chair, plopping it down on his notebook. He just stared at the front of the class. The three Dutch beer drinkers, all seniors, seemed to rotate their glances at Addison. All either grinned, nodded, or tapped their pencil in thought.

The bell startled the class. Everyone snapped to, getting up, gathering items. Voices emerged. Kadence was the last to stand, finally getting up after Sophia bumped her shoulder.

"Come on." The senior finally took her green eyes off Addison.

Thanksgiving arrived and Wednesday was as easy as you get in high school. A quarter of the students were gone, the rest mentally gone. Even the teachers were running recipes, families' flight arrival times, and sleeping arrangements for the holiday in their heads. Addison brought in the Eastern cards and finally pulled them out in European History class. After turning in a paper and watching a history video the last two days, the class broke up into pockets of kids. Addison, Corey, and two of the Dutch beer drinkers were playing poker. Loser had to carry all the books to their lockers.

Sean, a baseball player, teased Addison. "These cards are old, how long have you had them?"

"Awhile." Addison put three cards down and Manny slid him three more.

Sean nodded in thought. "So can I burn these if I lose?"

Addison didn't hesitate, leaning forward. "Of course, but I'd fight you over it." He sat back, "I think I'll have you just carry my books instead, senior."

They laughed and Mr. Kael came over. He was behind Manny, and bent down to get a better look at his hand.

"Didn't get that jack on the river, huh?"

Manny rolled his eyes and looked behind him. Then slapped his cards down. He knew he was done. Smiles spread for everyone else. Kael pulled up a chair.

"You boys ever played Roll Your Own Poker?"

All their raised eyebrows answered him. Leave it to Mr. Kael to know some cool, unknown game. They played for the remainder of fifth period. Kael won of course and Manny carried the books.

Addison and Sean were talking about Jeeps when Manny pushed in Addison's book. The two seniors left, Sean gave Addison a high-five. Manny gave him a playful push.

"Okay junior. Hope you enjoyed it."

Addison is well liked. He's not the most popular by any means, but he's no loner. Everyone knows he's a tennis player, and a good one who would go far. He wasn't just out there to get a letter on his jacket and have fun. He was the only non-football, baseball, basketball or soccer player to get Varsity Sports for seventh period. It was basically PE for jocks, when they would train, practice, or travel for events. He was very fit and could outrun several of the soccer and football players. That's how the seniors knew him. He was the Jeremy version of tennis and some seniors spoke of him in their circles. Addison's been in the school paper and *Miami Hearld* for tennis. The only thing is tennis was not as sexy as football, baseball, or soccer in high school.

Across the hall, the celebrities and Cleopatra's guards eyed Addison. For the past three weeks since the flag debate, Addison became a hero to every underclassman, and public enemy number one to Sophia, even Lisette a little, and the puppies. Craig was one of them, from Kael's class. Not only was he a puppy, but he played a certain sport. He also called himself an athlete.

Addison hated golf. Despised it. Golf was beneath him. He and a lot of tennis players routinely made fun of it. He felt it wasn't a sport, but a hobby up there with shuffleboard and darts. It was for mostly fat people and non-athletes, he thought. "There's a reason every pro athlete retires from baseball, football, tennis, hockey, or basketball and then plays golf," he once argued with Edgar. "It's for when you're not in peak form anymore, washed up, and need a relaxing hobby to take up time."

He felt they were as tough as professional soccer players when they're touched by a fingertip or breathed on hard. The only good thing about golf was you could play in rain, unlike tennis. But then when it does, "All golfers do is complain and wuss out while heading into the clubhouse. Tennis players would play in rain," he had argued.

Craig was over at the lockers, but Addison rarely looked across the hall when at his locker. So, he also never saw the peeks Kadence was stealing.

For the first time Kadence saw things through someone else's eyes. For years, especially the last semester of junior year up until now, she felt jealous, envious, and curious eyes on her, and her group of friends. But that day in Kael's classroom changed things. The thing she took away was not Addison, not Sophia, the puppy next to them, but the hateful eyes of everyone else on Sophia, that was finally loving what was happening. She eyed Addison walking out that day, wondering if the feeling was for her too.

It was now not just in Kael's class or the lockers, but everywhere, from the hallways, the parking lot, to the fields. Rome was burning. Kadence knew Lisette and Sophia were Romulus. *Does that include me too then?*

The last thing she did after spinning her lock and walking off to her next class, was glance over across the hall. Addison always seemed to peer over at her, then look away just as fast. It wasn't the scornful glares shooting past her to the others, but shy ones.

The Friday of Thanksgiving was cloudy, with lazy weather for a lazy turkey hangover. The low clouds seemed to trap in the heat. The city was on fire. It was as if everyone had a fever, simmering since last October 15th. The Orange Bowl was the future inferno.

The Notre Dame - Miami game was all that mattered in South Florida. Even if you hated both teams, this became the last episode of M.A.S.H. That's if you weren't going. Everyone was antsy. Everyone was in their corner, bouncing and pounding their fists, about to put the mouthpiece in at the bell. Everyone sped through yellow lights. Everyone's body was already beginning to yell and scream on the inside. Addison was reading the sports section, again, and his foot was tapping the floor. He had already been on the phone with Asher, Corey, Edgar, and his cousins in Virginia discussing Thanksgiving and Catholics vs Convicts II.

Tara came by around 2:30, dropping off a soft cover book her mom wanted to give to his. They talked since it had been a while, then joined Addison at the kitchen's eating nook. It was the first time they were alone in a while, and they caught up with news. Addison had moved on from the crush of junior high. He still found her beyond cute, but there was a foundation built since kindergarten that was stronger than anything they could redo now. He felt it would possibly get in the way if they dated. If she asked him to date, he wouldn't say no, but he was not going to pursue anything. Also, in a weird way, that Lipton ballboy tent issue was in the background, like a tickle in your throat, just waiting to turn into a cough at any second.

"Hey, Christi and I are going to go see *Back to the Future II* tonight. Wanna come? Isn't Asher in town?"

"Yeah, we played cards last night at Corey's. We can call him, I'm sure he'd be in." He closed the paper, folded it over, and tossed it on the far side. He picked up his foot and rested it on the chair, chin on his knee.

"What'd you get on the math test?"

"92. You?"

"90. How was the Depeche Mode concert last week?"

They chatted for a couple minutes, catching up with each other. They had classes together, saw each other in the hallways, and playing fields, but sometimes there was no substitute for a quiet table on a Friday afternoon during a holiday.

"Where's Gaby?" Addison asked.

"I don't know? I know she's in town. Edgar is gone isn't he?"

Addison nodded. Edgar kept up with Gaby more these days.

"Went to Tampa."

Just then, the phone rang. After two rings, Addison was half out of his chair, it stopped. He figured his mom got it. Five seconds later, a door opened and footsteps approached.

"Addison!"

Both kids turned their heads. "What mom?" Addison then yawned.

She came into the kitchen. "Hey hon, that was Mrs. Hernandez. Gaby called her collect. She's stuck out on the beach and needs a ride."

He and Tara exchanged looks, half out of coincidence, half out of confusion.

"What's going on?"

"Long story short, they have one car right now and her dad has it in Palm Beach until tonight. Cousins left town, Edgar is gone, and she is hoping you can help out."

"Of course, is she okay?" He started standing up.

"Yeah, I guess she is out there with soccer friends at Penrod's, and their ride left?"

"Left?" Tara asked it, beating Addison.

His mom shrugged her shoulders. "Tara sweetie, are you busy? Do you want to head out there too?"

"Sure." She looked at Addison, who nodded and ran to his room for his shoes. Tara would ordinarily hit the bathroom to check her hair before going somewhere, but knew it would be pointless in three minutes.

Addison's navy blue Jeep CJ7 was in the garage. He didn't drive it to school. There is no telling what would happen to it in the school parking lot. It never crossed his mind to even try it. There are no doors, just a little bimini top if it rained.

Twenty minutes later, they were on MacArthur Causeway heading east to Miami Beach. Plenty of cabin cruisers and go fast boats were in the main channel, but Dodge Island was virtually empty. The cruise ships, including the blue-hulled *Norway*, the longest in the world, were out to sea for the holidays. Tara was holding her hair back off her face, looking off at Government's Cut and Fisher Island. REM's *Green* was in the tape deck. "Pop Song 89" was blaring. Addison lipping the lyrics, Tara nodding her head.

"Do you know where she is?" Tara turned to Addison. You didn't have to scream in the jeep, but it helped to face the person.

"No, we'll park as close as we can and then just find her I guess."

Addison turned left onto Alton Road, then right on First Avenue. No luck. They made a couple of lefts and found a spot on Second Avenue & Washington. Addison and Tara walked down to Ocean Drive and crossed the street. South Beach was like Brazil's "Carnival" every day. In November, with snowbirds and holiday tourists, it was Times Square New Year's.

The sky was a puffy patchwork quilt of black, gray, and silver, with threads of white seeping through. It was the type of sky that didn't threaten rain, despite the dimness, it was just cloudy. It seemed like 6:00 not 3:00.

"How the hell are we going to find her?" Addison was scanning the street. Penrod's Beach Club was three blocks away. A group of Notre Dame fans came out of a hotel, skin whiter than most, but daring wearing the sweatshirts around town. Addison felt like handing them a copy of Poe to read *Fall of the House of Usher*, just to mentally prepare themselves.

They crossed two more streets, heads scanning in all directions. Penrod's was close.

Tara patted his back, then pointed. "We go over there." Addison followed her extended arm and saw three girls walking through a parking lot of a hotel. Gaby was one of them.

"Oh, that's how." He laughed and looked at Tara. Addison was flipping his keys around in his hands and refocused on the girls. Then his keys swung to a stop. His stride slowed. His heart did the opposite.

Kadence Whitaker was next to Gaby. Another girl was on Gaby's right, but Addison didn't even look. They had tight jean shorts over the bathing suits and loose t-shirts on. He looked down at his feet and steps.

He licked his lips. *Holy shit. Kadence Whitaker is going to ride in my Jeep. Breath. Breath, relax.*

"Gab!"

"Tar! I didn't know you were coming." Ten more steps later, they hugged.

"I was over at Addison's when your mom called his," eyes moved to Addison, except Kadence who was already checking him out. Her eyes flashed between he and Tara in thought.

"We're lucky we found you so quickly."

"Totally."

"Are you okay?"

"Yeah, there was just a mix up and our ride pulled away. We went back to the volleyball courts to get something and when we came back out, they were gone."

The sand courts behind Penrod's was a gathering spot for people watching and showing off as much skin as possible, while getting sweaty. The courts were always full. The beach club pumped music back to the courts that floated to the high and low tides as well. When in Rome's "The Promise" was back there now for everyone, seeping through between buildings. Seven of the girls' soccer team was there most of the day. Gabby and two seniors, Kadence and Isabella, were left.

Everyone knew of each other, even if they didn't hang out or talk. Kadence had her arms wrapped around her towel and small bag.

"Hey." She smiled at Addison, who returned the favor. Isabella knew Addison, like most everyone now, after the great flag debate.

The kids reached his Jeep, with looks of surprise and excitement. Tara hopped in the front; Gaby stepped up on the tire to get up into the back seat, which was one long seat. It was a repeated action; she was a veteran of the Jeep rides. Kadence and Isabella didn't know quite what to do.

Addison looked at them both just as Gaby said what he was thinking.

"Come on, hop in. There is no wrong way." Gaby sat behind Addison, Addison's dream in the middle, and Isabella took the fourth wheel on the right.

"Addison, how long have you had this? I've never seen it at school?" Isabella looked over the Jeep like a private jet.

"He won't bring it to school, will you?" Gaby leaned forward; reaching around the seat and teasingly shook his shoulders, "Despite my urges that he should." She sat back and smiled.

Isabella was looking around her seat. "Are there seat belts?"

"Yeah, around your waist." He turned around looking in the back. "Like an airplane." His eyes were down in their laps, making sure they could buckle up. He watched Kadence click hers, and looked up. She was studying the simple dash and stick shift sticking out of the floorboard like a small Tiki torch. She then found Addison and tilted her head a little. He took a deep breath, turned back around, and inserted the keys into the ignition. *Oh my God. Oh my God.* He pulled out onto Second Avenue.

Gaby faced the two seniors. "I remember when this was in his garage as he and his dad rebuilt the engine."

"That's how I got it so cheap." He spoke to the mirror.

"Hey, what did I do that day when my dad and I came over?" Tara tried remembering back.

"You tightened a head gasket with a wrench." He laughed.

"Oh yeah, see, if not for that we'd be in a cab right now." Everyone laughed, even Addison, thinking back to that spring.

Kadence didn't say much, more taking it all in like normal. Her eyes said the most. The Jeep was like some taboo ride. She tried to remember the last time she rode in a car with the windows down. She saw not a shy junior who eyed her like a lot of students. She saw a boy who could be on the homecoming court next year, with a Jeep, and rooted friends that was not the book cover she thought he was.

The navy blue Jeep made its way to Alton Road. They stopped at the light.

"Okay, your hair goes forward?" Isabella looked at the others surprised. "Shouldn't it blow back?" They laughed again.

"It's not a movie set Is." Gaby reached up and touched Tars's arm. "Hey Tar, are you home this weekend?"

"Yep."

"I need to come over, it's been too long."

"Absolutely."

Cars at the light gawked at the Jeep. Addison was used to glances, but these were stares from heads leaning around something in the way to see. Jeremy had nothing on him right now. Addison bit his lip as the situation inflated on him. He hadn't had this many pairs of amazing legs and great asses in his Jeep ever, not to mention two seniors and someone who had a crown and flowers given to her at the 50 yard line. He liked REM, but this called for something more.

Addison pushed the eject button and pulled out the tape. "Hey, look in there and pull out *Wide Awake in America.*" Tara pulled down the glove compartment and took the REM tape. She then handed Addison a white tape. He pushed it in, side A facing up, and pressed rewind. There are only two songs on each side, so it rewound quickly. One of the greatest eight-minute songs would be in the background for their cruise through Miami.

The light turned green and Addison sped the Jeep though the light and back onto MacArthur Causeway. Palm trees zipped by in rhythm down the middle. The mansions and boat docks of Star Island and eventually Hibiscus Island floated by to the right. A Chalks seaplane bounced and sloshed to a landing to their left in Government's Cut. He couldn't dream this up. Addison sighed, thinking this is what Sunny Crocket feels like. By the time they reached the bridge in front of the Miami News building, the live version of "Bad" was half over.

"...In temptation...Isolation...Let it go...and so fade...fade...fade away."

Edge, Adam, and Larry took over for the last three minutes. The song reached legendary status with the smiles and laughter of the girls in his Jeep, and would be associated with this drive forever. Next spring, at college, when he is 40, the song will be his drug to escape reality. When heard somewhere surprisingly, it will be God's way of saying, *Here you go, remember that ride when you were 17?*

By the time Addison pulled onto I-95, "A Sort of Homecoming" was playing and Addison was thinking about the homecoming that would take place in the next few minutes. He needed to cheat Rand McNally.

It would make sense to drop off the seniors first, then Gaby, and finally Tara just a couple houses down from him. However, there was no way Kadence was getting out of his Jeep first. He was handed an unexpected gift. He needed to be man enough to open it. Carefully.

He blamed some Canadians for driving slow and not letting him over into the turn lane in time. Addison pulled off at the next exit and came in from the other direction. It turned out no one noticed or would have cared. The girls were so busy chatting over the wonderful sound of wind, and looking out from the "faster, bigger go-cart" as Isabella called it. They didn't noticed the house they were at until Addison stopped in Isabelle's driveway. Even though she seemed nice, although he was pretty sure it was because he drove a Jeep, he almost wanted to kick her out of the Jeep to speed things up. Tara decided to go to Gaby's and hang out a little. Three minutes later, they hopped out. Before getting out, Gaby hugged Addison from behind saying thank you. And then at 4:37 pm, on a cloudy Friday afternoon, Kadence Whitaker sat in the passenger seat next to Addison Briggs.

Somewhere in the world, where it never rains and the humidity never reaches 50%, with doves from the Seoul Olympic Games ceremony soaring overhead, Mats Wilander and Don Mattingly ate ice cream together and watched U2 and Bruce Springsteen videos while shining a US Open and MVP trophy.

He wanted things to slow down, despite what his chest was doing. He turned off the radio as she buckled up. She then untied her ponytail and let her hair fall to her shoulders, framing her face. She watched him shift, and pedal the clutch and accelerator while backing out. He felt her green eyes on him. She moved some hair over her left ear. Then things went too slow.

He stalled the Jeep.

He sighed and grinned to himself. She continued to watch him.

"I can walk."

He rolled his eyes and looked over at her. A sly grin greeted him.

"Funny." He started it up again, and the Jeep rumbled down the street.

"I don't blame you for not taking this to school."

"Really?" His right hand left the stick and joined his other at the bottom of the wheel. He didn't need anything above third gear for the next eight blocks.

"Absolutely. Those assholes would definitely do something to it." Her eyes were closed, feeling the wind against her cheeks, her eyelashes. He peeked over at her, his eyes wouldn't leave her face. He then quickly looked back out front as he wandered into the middle of the quiet street.

"Yeah, daddy wouldn't be able to just get me another."

Kadence didn't open her eyes, but smiled at the comment, knowing whom he was talking about. Part of him felt bad, knowing Sophia was her friend. Another part didn't, hinting at her the question of why she hung out with her. Deep down, everyone knew that answer.

"So are you dating Tara?"

Addison's chest stopped for a second or two. She then finally opened her eyes and turned to him.

"No. Why?"

She studied him. "Just wondering." Kadence looked back out front, seeing the trees, parked cars, houses, and streetlights differently from the open Jeep. "You two are cute together."

"We've known each other since kindergarten."

"Really? I guess that makes sense. Take the next left. How long have you known Gaby?"

"Sixth grade."

"She mentions Edgar a lot."

Addison slid his left hand to the top of the wheel, as his right helped shift down into second for the turn.

"Yeah, there's something going on there for sure. He's liked her for a while."

"Yep." She nodded with her chin ahead of them, knowing he was stealing looks over at her. "I'm that one, with the blue and yellow palm tree."

Colored floodlights painted the palm trees in the driveway's island blue and yellow. The Whitaker's two-story house was bigger than most around, and stood out. Not in size, but texture. The house was all white, with smooth curves and curling balconies. There seemed to be no edges, and other than the front doors, garage doors, and windows, not a 90-degree angle to be found. On the right, a two-car garage curled out from the house, rounded and making an *L*. More palms and gumbo-limbo trees edged the sides. Addison pushed it up into neutral and let the Jeep coast to a stop in her circular driveway. He checked out her house, noticing no lights seemed to be on. There were no cars in the driveway.

"Is someone home?"

"Uh, I think so." She unbuckled and played with her hair. Addison's chest heaved more and more. This was ending way too fast. Being this close to her, with no one around, was like having the entire floor of an art museum to himself as he stood in front of a Georges Seurat. She was lovely from a distance, but the closer he got to her, he could pick out all the little details and specks that made up her whole masterpiece.

She swung her legs out and reached into the back. She pulled out her bag and towel, then came around to the side again. She was standing next to the Jeep, her hand up on the windshield frame.

"Well thank you Addison. It was a fun ride."

"Yeah sure." He took a deep breath, everything still rushing. He bit his lip and looked at her. *God you're beautiful.* He knew he had to take advantage of her alone, with no secret service detail surrounding her.

She smiled at him and her hand let go of the windshield frame, beginning to take her first step away. He closed his eyes and just came out with it. Eventually, at some point, you have to stop bouncing the ball, and serve for the match.

"Hey…" he opened his eyes as she took that step, but stopped and turned her head to him. "Do you want to go out next weekend?"

The comment hung in the humid evening air. She didn't budge, didn't even flinch. He wondered if she heard him or if he said it in his head, in those dreams that she was in. She then grabbed the mirror right in front of her and tilted her head to her left. His eyes started darting around until finding her again.

She looked at him, not the book cover from the hallways, and suddenly she wanted to see more inside. She also had never been asked out before. She'd been asked to the movies, the beach, parties being part of a group, and eventually broke off with someone or another couple. Most times she found out through someone, telling her what to do and where to go and when. It was like some kids, the popular ones, had publicists to handle this for them. But this was new, never this direct before. The cute tennis boy, who narrated a 60-second documentary trailer for Arlington National Cemetery in fifth period, just asked her out the real, official way. An old-fashioned way. A grown up way.

"Yes."

It sounded weird, too official, and not natural. He even quickly wondered what she meant. But she felt like it was the only way to answer him. She decided to play with it, supporting her response.

"My parents would have to come along to chaperone. Is that okay?"

His lips parted a fraction and he looked up at the house for a second, expecting them to be in a window watching through binoculars.

"Uh…sure," he turned back to her, thinking she was worth it. "I-"

Kadence leaned forward over the passenger seat and whispered, "I'm kidding." She smiled and stood back up straight, gripping her bag a little tighter. He immediately eased and sat back a little in his seat.

"Thank god."

The Saturday of Thanksgiving was like waking up in a dream. Addison was fairly certain he slept with a smile on his face throughout the night. His mom's omelet was the best ever. He tried his father's coffee and it was only bad this time, not disgusting. Taking the trash out was thrilling, even when the bag ripped. And they hadn't even gotten to the Orange Bowl yet.

They arrived around 11:00. Asher and Corey were already there, with all their parents. Others came by too.

"Dude I couldn't sleep last night."

"No joke, do we win by 50?"

"Check it out, I'm wearing my dad's golf shoes. Metal spikes."

"We should have gotten here for a breakfast tailgate."

"Does UM even go out for the coin toss?"

"I'm going on a date with Kadence Whitaker next weekend."

A flag flapped. A cooler closed. Silence. Crickets in the Everglades were probably chirping.

By 11:15, the charcoal grills were lined up and ready. The dousing of lighter fluid was like the scissors cutting the ribbon to begin groundbreaking. By 12:30, the burgers and hot dogs were devoured. Soon after that, the first touch football game was started between cars and pitched tents. The square, red and black hurricane warning flags were not put up at the beach by lifeguards, but by alumni on their vans, tents, and motorhomes. The historic Goodyear blimp was circling overhead, like a giant crow or vulture to the Notre Dame fans. To the kids playing touch football, it was filming them with the voice of John Facenda narrating it for NFL Films.

Their long TV timeouts found them playing cards with Addison's deck. For the first time, and only time in his life, he witnessed a real life royal flush hand. Victor Parrish's dad, a friend from North Miami had that honor. He was given the king, jack, & ten of clubs. He then discarded two and got the ace and queen.

By 5:00, the huge stadium lights flickered on, followed by the ghostly orangish-yellow ones in the walkways and concourses underneath. The old girl was coming alive. The stadium was like a Saturn V on the launch pad; breathing, swelling, just waiting to explode.

At 6:00, the kids entered the stadium to get their seats in general admission. They were with the crazies in the closed end zone. The long, simple scoreboard and palm trees in the open end faced them across the stadium, with the lights of downtown in the background. Despite the numbers painted on the benches, no one paid attention to them. You found a space and stood. Their parents would come in an hour later with assigned seats, better yet square markings on the bleachers, under the press box.

It turns out Sun Tzu wrote the playbook for the Hurricanes. It was over before the kickoff. It was over before the coin toss. It was over on the bus ride into Little Havana. The Miami players didn't even need to resort to coin toss antics like the Oklahoma game in '86, when the Hurricane captains refused to shake hands and told the referees, "Just give them the ball at the 50, we're going to kick their ass anyways."

Instead, they cemented the tombstone when they sprinted through the tunnel, emerging from the smoke like a pack of wild animals; their muscles fueled by 12 months of revenge, and pranced straight to the Notre Dame sideline. The officials had to push the home team back to their side, but not before taunts and expletives were hosed down on the visitors like a squall. That included a verbal rape of a former Notre Dame President. Father Theodore Hesburgh was standing on the sideline, with his cross dangling under the white collar. Game, set, match. Craig Erickson's bomb to Randall Hill on 3rd and 45 late in the third quarter, simply planted the flowers on top of the grave.

The only Fighting Irish player trying to show some life and emotion, was Ricky Watters. Every time he was on the sideline, he twirled the white towel around trying to whip up some emotion. It might as well have been a flag. It was so loud, quarterback Tony Rice could not be heard at the line of scrimmage. He even had to scream in the huddle. If the formation and play called back in the huddle wouldn't work, he couldn't audible, it couldn't be changed. Half the play calls were doomed to fail at the snap. The stadium literally won the game.

Notre Dame may have had the better team on paper, and may be more of what college football is supposed to be and represent, but this was a street fight. The two toughest kids on the block squared off, and Miami knew to take the gloves off. It's all they know. It was as if Notre Dame marched to the center of a battlefield in the 1400's, their band pounding the drums, blowing into their bagpipes, and sent coach Holtz out to meet Coach Erickson. Erickson never showed. Miami, being unconventional, surrounded them and came at them like Indians or a gang.

Addison scanned the stadium, wondering if he had this home field advantage a couple years ago, would he have beaten that Argentinian kid? He thought he knew the answer, but now wondered.

Sunday no one had a voice, just raspy wheezes. Addison slept in until 11, read the paper until 12, and then hit the courts at 1:15. It was without question the worst practice of his life. His coach shook his head 15 minutes into it, telling him to get his head on the court and focus. He tried and tried. All he heard was the Orange Bowl's roar, a ringing between his ears. All he saw was Kadence's brunette hair blowing about, those tan legs next to him, and her green eyes watching him stall his Jeep nervously. This was going to be a long, long week, making Christmas Eve seem like child's play.

That night Addison went into the living room and found his dad. He was in his favorite chair, with stapled papers folded over in his lap. A crystal tumbler with exact etches and carvings like graph paper, held three large ice cubes and his beverage. He was chewing on the end of his pen, a habit Addison's mom gave up trying to break years ago. Addison plopped down on the couch next to him. The late afternoon football game was on CBS, Bears at Redskins. The volume was off, so instead of Pat Summerall and John Madden, it was Tony Bennett's voice playing on the family record player. Art Monk had just scored, helping the 'Skins pull away 31-14 with eight minutes left. Addison waited for his dad to turn a page or flip one back. Two minute later he finally did.

"Hey dad, I need to ask a favor?" He was still looking at the game.

His dad swallowed his sip and put his glass down on the coaster.

"Sure buddy." The pen was now tapping the chair's arm.

"I need to borrow some money." He stole one last glance at the game, then turned to him. His dad was looking at him, waiting.

Addison swallowed, his cocktail not smooth scotch from the Scotland Highlands, but saliva soaked in trepidation.

"I need $80."

His dad raised an eyebrow. "What for?"

Addison turned and tucked his leg under him.

"This came out of nowhere, really. I need Nutcracker tickets."

His dad unfolded the papers, now nice and flat in his lap. "Nutcracker? What is this about?" He crossed his leg.

"I have a date next weekend dad, but the show is so soon there are no cheap seats left. I called, promise, but the only thing available is expensive ones up front." Another swallow. "I would have gotten cheaper ones, but this happened so quickly and I didn't know the show was so soon in December."

His dad reached for his glass and took a sip while checking out the game. "Man, Nutcracker. I saw that for the first time up in DC." His slow sip and swish in his mouth told Addison his father remembered that show, however long ago it was. He put the drink down a couple seconds later.

"Well how much are the seats, the ones available?"

"$75." Addison bit his lip for at least the 20th time. This rivaled watching the fifth set of the Lendl-Wilander US Open final on this very couch last year.

His dad left the game and looked at his only son.

"Who is she?" He was expecting Tara.

"Kadence Whitaker."

His dad shook his head, his lip sticking out a little.

"She's a senior. Plays soccer and is friends with Gabrielle."

"A senior?"

Addison nodded. "She was homecoming queen last month."

His dad bent his head down a little, the weight of that news heavy. He looked up at him through his eyelashes almost.

"Homecoming queen…"

Addison nodded twice and then a wonderful smile took over his face. "Yes."

"Well how much do you have?" His dad tilted his head a little.

Addison switched legs under him. "I have $120." He wasn't going to switch seats, like he would during the football game or tennis match if things weren't going well, but felt like a little change may help.

"What about food? Are you going to go to dinner too?"

Addison's swayed his head back and forth. "Well, I'd like too, but we can grab pizza someplace close. That one, Franco Giovanni's-"

"No." His dad brought up the scotch, which was resting on his pants leg. He kissed a sip. He sighed at the lingering burn, now moving down his throat.

"My son is not taking the homecoming queen out for just pizza."

Addison inhaled slowly. He inhaled love, he inhaled victory. It appeared Addison didn't even exhale, just held that breath in, forever. He sat back in the chair more relaxed.

"Where is it at?"

"The Olympia, downtown. Apparently this is the last event before they close for major renovations."

"You want to take the car?"

Addison shook his head.

"I didn't think so." His dad smiled. "We'll take care of this. Don't worry."

Addison looked away at the game, then back to his dad.

"Thanks Dad."

His father nodded. "Did you finish with the pool?"

"Not yet." He stood up and bounded out towards the patio, to a half clean pool glowing aqua, and a clear night sky fit for an ocean explorer. His dad watched him leave the room, and could tell excitement, not muscles, moved his legs.

He then looked back at the game. Now it was his turn to bite his lip in thought. "She's Funny That Way" was playing on the record player. The needle releasing a voice and sound that filled the room with softness. His father smirked, raised his crystal tumbler at the record player, ice clinking in a toast.

"Did you hear that Tony, the homecoming queen." He tipped back his glass to finish it, sucking in an ice cube to crunch. *That's my boy.*

Friday night found Addison running errands. First, he stopped by Eckerd's to pick up a prescription for his mom, followed by Publix in the same shopping center. Next, was over to Asher's to drop off a book, *The Joy Luck Club* for his mom. He then took a book Asher's mom had and deliver that to Tara's mom, who of course had a movie rental for Addison's mom. Ordinarily he would have rolled his eyes at something a homing pigeon should be doing, but then again, his mind was occupied and influencing his senses. Before heading to the Brookens' house, he used the trip to Asher's for an excuse to hang out a bit. He finally left for Tara's with Anne Rice's, *The Vampire Lestat.*

"Hey Add's, come on in." Gabrielle's influence wasn't limited to just the kids. Mrs. Brookens tousled his hair as he came in the foyer. He handed her the Rice novel and followed her into the kitchen.

"Would you like something to drink?" She put the book over next to the answering machine. Then rummaged through some bills and papers looking for something.

"No no I'm fine thanks."

"You sure?"

Addison nodded and took a seat at a stool at the island.

"I've got a movie for your mom around here somewhere," she walked over to the far counter and desk built into the wall. She turned around, "Honey I'll be right back, it must be around here someplace?"

Addison smiled at her, "No problem."

Tara was in family room on the phone. She leaned to the right, stretching the curly phone cord over the couch and end table. She smiled at Addison with the phone pressed against her cheek, waving at him.

"What did she say…huh…huh…for sure…okay, catch you later." She hung the phone up on the wall and playfully punched him in the shoulder.

"Hey."

"Hey. Who was that?" Addison picked up a post card from Jamaica that was on the counter. He brought it up close to look at the picture.

"Christi."

"You all doing something tonight?"

"I think so, going to someone's house. She's picking Gaby and I up later."

Addison flipped the card over, checked the stamp on the back, then put it back down. He picked up another one, this one from the Grace Bay on Turks and Caicos.

"Sounds good."

Tara eyed Addison and moved around to the other side of the island. She picked up the Anne Rice novel along the way. She looked at the cover.

"So you're going out with Kadence tomorrow, huh?" It sounded like a question, but her body language and tone said it wasn't. She began flipping through the pages.

Addison, again brought this postcard up closer.

"Yep." He tilted his head inspecting something.

"Where you going?" She licked her lips. Her eyes never leaving the fluttering pages.

"Nutcracker."

A couple of seconds passed. She nodded, while the pages continued. Her eyes shot up to him for a second. She then put the book down and looked at the postcard he was holding. He flipped this one over and checked the stamp. He took a deep breath and put it down, while glancing around the kitchen. Tara picked it up and looked at. It was something to do with her hands while her thoughts were traveling. She looked up at Addison. He was staring at the card she was holding, then looked up to her.

"Here you go honey. It was in the machine in the bedroom." Tara's mom curled in around the corner and took off her glasses. "It's rewound so no worries."

Addison read the binding and rolled his eyes. Mrs. Brookens' laughed. He stood up and grabbed his keys. Tara flipped the postcard over, staring at nothing, and then let it fall to the counter. She picked up the other one from Jamaica.

Three minutes later, Addison and *Steel Magnolias* were in his Jeep and backing out of the driveway. He left Tara's house, and in a way, the umbrella table at Lipton where they had hamburgers, as well. That day was long gone now. He couldn't even tell you the outer court he was stuck on anymore.

CHAPTER EIGHTEEN

Nutcracker confirmation number. *Check.*

Paco Rabanne cologne. *Check.*

Jeep washed, vacuumed. *Check.*

The Cure's *Disintegration* forwarded to song two. *Check.*

Wallet with cash. *Check*

Cary Grant like confidence. *Oh, hell yes.*

Addison studied himself in the mirror again. His blue blazer was dapper and comfortable. The white button-down was smooth and ironed. His father's black wingtips were snug. After three redo's, the blue paisley tie was now finally at his belt buckle. He had on dark jeans, which he knew isn't what his *Official Preppy Handbook* would say is proper attire for a 7pm Nutcracker show, but then there also isn't a page on taking out a senior homecoming queen who is way above your pay scale.

He lifted up the hinged lid to his wooden box. He pulled out the Swiss Army knife and put it in his pocket. It just felt grown up. He then scrunched his eyebrows, as the Eastern cards weren't in there. He didn't need them, but they should be in here. He scanned the room, twisting about, but figured they were around here somewhere.

He pulled back the cuff of his blazer and checked his watch. 4:00. *Here we go……*

Addison looked both ways seven times before pulling out of the driveway. He drove 22mph. The speed limit is 30. He stopped at stop signs long enough to watch four clouds overhead move an inch from his perspective. The only thing he didn't do was signal with his arm when turning. It took him six minutes to pull into Kadence's driveway. It usually takes him six minutes to get to the light at US 1.

There were no cars in the driveway. Only rustling palm trees and a UPS package by the door that greeted him. He looked at a spot on the front door, with his fist inches away, and couldn't believe he was going to tap it. Part of him wanted to get a cut on his knuckle from knocking. Just to have it. He would proudly reply in the school hallway, *Oh this, yeah I got that knocking on Kadence Whitaker's front door when I picked her up.*

He knocked.

He knocked again.

The package worried him. It brought out drops of dew seeping out from his forehead. A baby snake hatched in his stomach. *Why hasn't someone gotten this?*

On the way over here, he was nervous about meeting her parents, more importantly her father at the door, and going through the usual interrogation while waiting on her. Right now, he would gladly have to meet the entire family tree, even if the mafia. He did a double take when he noticed the intercom panel and doorbell. Addison took a deep breath staring at the button. He just knew he would end up pressing it and pressing it, over and over and over…

He closed his eyes and reached for the button. Just then, deep clicking sounds came from behind the door. Deadbolts were unlocking. The door opened.

"Hi." Kadence peeked around the door swinging inward and smiled. She stepped from behind it and swiped some hair off her face. She was stunning and backed up to let him in. The snake was gone. Addison's stomach was now a jar of fluttering fireflies.

"Hey Kadence." She was in a beige dress with black heels. A black belt hugged her waist and white pearls circled her tan neck. Her lips were soft red and she had some make-up on, but not too much. The fireflies escaped out the holes in the lid, and were now glowing down his legs and up his throat.

"You look incredible."

The forwardness caught her unexpectedly. "Thank you. You look good yourself."

They stared at each other for a couple of seconds.

"You know you have a package?" He pointed off to the side.

"Really?" She leaned forward and peered around the doorframe. "Huh, I guess I didn't hear it. I was here all day."

Addison picked it up and brought it inside.

"Thanks," she swept her hand around to her left, "just put it…

anywhere." She closed the door and he placed it on a glass table in the foyer. Music was coming from upstairs, choked by a closed door.

"Come in, make yourself comfortable okay. I'll just be a second." She walked off, disappearing behind a fake fern. She then appeared up on the second floor behind white pipes for a railing, which looked down into the living room. She opened her bedroom door, and Duran Duran's "Union of the Snake" off *Seven and the Ragged Tiger* spilled out. The door thumped closed, softening the band. Addison put his hands in his pockets and wandered around.

Getting comfortable was going to be tricky.

Everything was white, black, or silver and the surfaces were hard, smooth, and shiny. The tables were huge slabs of geometric glass. The floor was tile. Counters were marble. There wasn't a lamp anywhere. It was all track lighting and lights were embedded in the ceiling. A Christmas tree towered in the corner, fake and tall, at least 20 feet. It had a frosted tint to it. It was covered in silver balls and wrapped in light blue tinsel. Addison didn't even know they made tinsel in that color.

The interior reminded him of Clay's house from *Less Than Zero*, but on a smaller scale. He half expected to see Rip come from around a corner and threaten to beat him up if Kadence wasn't brought back home on time. He wanted to throw down a soft bath mat somewhere.

The dining room table was one giant rectangle of glass. He checked out pictures and anything to learn more about her. He wished he could get into her room. Seeing someone's room was like reading a resume through props.

The music was turned off upstairs, followed by her door opening. With all the hard, squeaky smooth surfaces, breathing was echoed. She came down stairs, now holding a tiny black purse. Her heels clanking.

"So you're alone?"

"Yeah," she snatched some keys off a counter, "my mom is a real-estate agent. She's rarely home on the weekends. I think she's showing two houses in Cocoplum." The way she said it, gave the impression it was a common reply and second nature. She turned to look at the huge round clock on the wall over a couch. It was at least seven feet in diameter with lit up, neon hands. It was the centerpiece of the living room, which made sense seeing there are rarely fireplaces south of Orlando.

"My dad's probably playing cards by now with his lawyer friends. He's part of some big card games after golf out on the beach."

Addison nodded and looked around. The kitchen cabinets were glass and chrome spaced around. He then came back to Kadence. He wondered how someone so soft and beautiful could come from a house like this. It wasn't that the house was ugly, it was actually very cool. Visiting and hanging out would be amazing, but he wasn't sure if he could live here. There was no place to put your feet up while watching a movie or tennis that wasn't awkward.

They headed out and got into his Jeep. Without a door, he buckled her up. She thought it was cute and smiled at him. He thought it was erotic and tried not to stare at her legs inching out a little more with the dress sliding up to her knees.

"Are you hungry?"

"Yep." She pulled up her hair, exposing her neck, and twisted it until letting it fall to her shoulders.

"I thought we'd go to McDonald's." Addison keyed the Jeep to life.

"Well, can I at least get two happy meals?"

"Sure."

She glared over at him with a grin, then opened the glove compartment out of curiosity.

"Do you like seafood?" He pushed the shift up into first.

"Oh, god yes." She shut it and looked up at the sky through the ultimate sunroof. Three days of rain gave way that morning to a clear December sky. It was just beginning to get dimmer out, as the lowering sun was spraying the clouds purple, orange, and gray.

"Cool." Addison eased the clutch out and circled around the huge palm trees in the middle of the driveway.

"Good job not stalling." She looked away to hide her smile. He looked over and gave her a look.

"Whatever."

The Jeep sped up and Kadence listened to the unique, rubbery, whining sound of the large tires. She wasn't sure if it was them being larger than normal, or that they were two feet away from her with nothing between her and the asphalt, but it was thrilling. Addison pushed the play button on the stereo, and drowned out the tire sound with the rolling, twirling guitar chords of "Pictures of You." After two minutes of glorious guitar sounds, Robert Smith's voice finally arrived. Addison peeked over, watching her lip the lyrics. He was going to, but decided she looked way better doing it.

They reached 79th Street Causeway as Kadence kept the hair away from her face and out of her eyes. She took in the bay with the mirage of lights from Miami Beach skipping off the dark waves. The clouds were now brighter pink and peach.

Dinner was at Mike Gordon's, the legendary powerboat racer turned restaurant owner. Something odd happened that he couldn't wait to tell his dad someday. While standing and waiting to get a table at the front, for the first time ever, Addison didn't stare and fantasize at the hundreds of black-framed photos of speedboats, Marine Stadium, Miss Budweiser, and boat race scenes covering the walls. Something, or someone else, had his full attention.

Their table was across the aisle from the windows, but still a soothing view. After just five minutes, it dawned on Addison that they could be at the top of Pier 66 in Fort Lauderdale, eating in their revolving restaurant at the top, and his eyes still would have remained at the table.

The two kids talked and asked each other curious question after question, smiling and nodding their heads in approval. School never came up. Everything else did. Addison devoured his grouper. Kadence finished off New Zealand white fish. This coming after they shared lump crab cakes. The bill was paid and Kadence headed off to the bathroom. Addison then quickly tried tucking his wallet in his inner jacket pocket for now, until he could slide it into his jeans later. There was something already in there. He pulled out the lapel and reached inside. He found the Eastern cards.

He laughed to himself as he tried figuring out what they were doing there. He figured they were hastily put there after a card game with the boys. They will sometimes have a "jackets required" game just to sound snobby and preppy. The cards must have been in the jacket for a couple of weeks. He put them back in his jacket and stood up, noticing Kadence returning. The wallet then found his front jeans pocket.

"So how was your happy meal?" Addison asked her while buckling her seat belt.

"Okay. I didn't get a toy though?"

Addison couldn't think of anything quick enough, and just smiled at her as he walked around the hood to his side. He climbed in and noticed she was looking at him the whole time.

"Don't stall."

He didn't.

With dinner over, and an hour worth of conversation absorbed, both kids felt like they could move on, relax with each other knowing they were now comfortable. They unconsciously loosened up, unwound, and their body language hinted the date was officially beginning.

To get to downtown, with the beautiful night and the homecoming queen in a Jeep, Addison took the scenic route. That meant over to the beach and down Ocean Drive and Washington Avenue. He made sure to pass the Delano Hotel, the Clevelander, Amnesia, and Club Nu. Addison then swung by the Versace Mansion. He slowed and stopped out front to look. They were not the only ones. A couple of people were taking pictures through the gates. Others were posing out front for group photos.

"I've never been by it and not seen people out front." Addison said while leaning on the steering wheel to see around Kadence.

"I've never seen anyone inside." Kadence mentioned, while unbuckling and standing up, resting an elbow on the windshield. "Have you?"

"Now that you mention it, I'm not sure. I must have though." Addison's seat belt clicked and he joined her standing. "Can you imagine the stories in that place?"

"No." She shook her head, "I mean, just the people alone that have gone in there."

Just then, three Ferrari 308 GT's drove up and stopped. The first two were black and the third white. Addison and Kadence sat back down. The guys driving them were young, and dressed in linen suits as their arms rested on the door. They stopped with the white one right next to the Jeep. The guy was wearing sunglasses. While the kids buckled back up, they watched two prostitutes come out of the black ones, cross the street, and start mingling in front of the gates. That distinct Ferrari engine sound exploded from the rear of the Italian machines, and they sped off, leaving tire tracks. A family of tourists with kids joined the endless photo shoot at the gates, asking one of the high-class hookers to take a photo. The one smiled and snapped away, flashing them up twice with the Nikon's flash. Then she handed it back with a smile.

"Only in Miami." Addison said while starting to pull away.

"Exactly." Kadence added.

Addison found himself crossing MacArthur Causeway once again. Last time was with a Jeep full of gorgeous legs. Now with a vision in beige, her gorgeous legs crossed at the knee, heel tapping to "Fascination Street".

Kadence looked over at him. "I love how their songs are half instrumental."

"Yeah that's true."

They reached the bridge to the mainland. It appeared there was a lighthouse back at Fisher Island, as a full moon was released by the Atlantic. This glow didn't sweep around every 20 seconds, but constantly warned the city to pay attention to the blinding colors. The Centrust building was lit up in aqua blue, with its customary holiday snowflakes. Even the underside of the few low, lingering puffy clouds were lit up by the lights, reflecting oranges, yellows, and whites.

"God it's a beautiful city." Kadence's eyes recorded it all.

Addison nodded, then looked over eyeing his date, from heels to hair. *Yes, beautiful.*

The last song of *Disintegration*, "Untitled" began just as they passed by the Olympia Theater on Second Avenue. After 30 seconds of an accordion, slow tumbling guitar notes took over. Addison turned it up. He got lucky and found a spot on the curb three blocks away. He sat there, waiting to turn the Jeep off. Kadence flipped down the sun visor and checked her face in the tiny, smudged mirror. Addison turned and watched her.

Robert Smith hit the second verse. "*Never quite said what I wanted to say to you, never quite managed the words to explain to you, never quite knew how to make them believable, and now the time has gone, another time undone.*"

Addison's eyes moved from Kadence to the stereo. *Not anymore, not tonight,* he thought.

He turned the keys killing the four cylinder. He checked the street, then stepped out. Kadence didn't move, just sat their uncrossing her legs and looking at him slyly. Her green eyes waiting.

"You okay?" He put his right hand on the roll bar behind his seat.

"Aren't you going to get the door for me?"

Addison snorted out a laugh and smiled as he made his way around to her. She looked down watching him unclasp the metal buckle, then she reached in for her purse on the floorboard.

"You ready?" He asked her green eyes. His legs were wobbly.

She nodded.

In a city vomiting neon, curves, and trend, seeing the old-fashioned theater marquee above the sidewalk, was grounding and refreshing. It was timeless, disrespecting the art deco flashiness all around like a stubborn grandfather.

"Have you been here before?" Addison thought he knew the answer. She verified it by shaking her head, as her eyes roamed over the marquee. *Nutcracker* was in big red letters, like the tiny magnetic ones on her fridge growing up. Then her eyes found the old ticket booth, framed in big white light bulbs.

"Have you?" She touched his arm.

"Nope."

Their tickets were at will call. Their red velvet seats were 11 rows from the stage. Their escort down the aisle wore a tux with white gloves. Their eyes were wide. Their veins throbbed. At first they gazed behind them, at row upon row, level stacked upon level of plush seats. They twisted left and right to see full balconies flanking them on both sides like elaborately carved bookends. Then up at a decorated ceiling that could have belonged in some 300-year-old church in Europe, spared from Allied bombing. Finally, there was the massive burgundy curtain hanging in front of them, thick and rumpled. Teasing shadows were escaping under the bottom, slithering on the slick stage as the performers prepared.

The two kids would lean toward each other, kissing shoulders whenever they talked. The theater, despite the hum of voices before the start, brought out whispers like a library. Whenever they stood to let someone pass, he placed his hand in her back. After the fourth time, it stopped quivering. Each time they stood, he imagined people behind him, maybe up in those balconies looking down at them thinking, 'Huh I wonder who that couple is'?

"So you've seen this before?" Kadence asked, while tilting her head to see his eyes.

He nodded. "Two years ago in DC. We went up visiting family for Christmas and saw it there. I liked it, but it's something you need to see more than once to understand what's going on. Unless you've read it. I will admit, I wanted to take my Walkman thinking I'd get bored, but I wasn't." He was looking up at the stage and curtain, then turned to her. She was studying his face, her eyes a microscope. He just wanted to kiss her. Just then they were both saved by the blinking of the lights, then the theater darkened for good. Voices hushed. Someone coughed. The audience took a deep breath.

The opening number began, the "Overture", which pushed Kadence's head back a little in surprise. *I didn't know this song was from the Nutcracker?*

A minute later that huge curtain slowly rose, unwrapping a festive street scene from New England, or was it Austria, or maybe some children's book? Wherever it was, it was everyone's Main Street from their dreams, that they know is too good to be real. She leaned forward; her back came off the chair slightly, taking it all in. Addison realized he would have a struggle throughout the play. Half of him gawking at the stage, while the other half wanted to steal glimpses of Kadence.

A few minutes later a second curtain like a thin vail, was pulled up, and the interior of the Stahlbaum's living room dominated the stage. "March" started playing and again, Kadence was taken aback. *Wait, this too?*

She leaned over. "Okay, I didn't know this was from the Nutcracker either. I thought they just played it in malls during Christmas?"

Addison smiled, remembering he had thought something similar two Decembers ago.

For most of the first Act, from the gathering and frolicking, Drosselmeyer's grand entrance, the presents, Clara's smile, the colorful poofy dresses and long hair ribbons, to the toy nutcracker. Kadence inched closer and closer and closer towards it all. It was like the whole scene and atmosphere was pulling her from the back of her seat, tugging at her emotions and heart. By the time the Christmas tree began stretching and growing to the rafters, and the Mouse King made his grand entrance, her back was straight, her pupils completely dilated. The mice threw cheese. The soldiers would parry swords. The nutcracker held up the mouse king's crown in victory. At some point, every adult in the audience thought back to their fourth grade yearbook photo.

It dawned on Addison that it was a perfect storm, so to speak. He thought about the house Kadence came from, the tree that was up, the eerie quietness of a Saturday, even the echoes ricocheting about. That the warmth and spectacle on the stage was completely foreign to her. It was like nothing she had ever experienced, yet knew deep down, was out there somewhere from a post card or magazine cover. A doctor's drops didn't widen Kadence's eyes and make them wet, it was a flooding of Hoffmann's childhood fantasy with Tchaikovsky's soaring melody.

The first act ended and both kids found their way to the lobby. Addison put his hand on her lower back again while squeezing through gaps in the throng of people. It was like touching a priceless museum piece without the alarm going off. They found a spot on the paisley carpet under one of the sparkling chandeliers. He looked down at the carpet, wondering who had stood here before.

"I had no idea all those songs were from the Nutcracker?" Kadence touched the smaller tail of his tie and moved it behind the other until hidden.

"Yeah, it's like *Casablanca*. Have you seen that?" *My god, do that again.*

"No." She was curious.

"You say the same thing when you first see that movie, but for the lines. Every famous quote you've ever heard comes from that."

She nodded and looked around at the mass of people. The crowds and lack of space pushed them closer together an inch at a time, as people passed and moved about. It was noisy, yet soothing. It was busy, but organized. Addison's hands were in his pockets, and he rubbed his fingers together, trying to bring back the feeling of her dress and flesh just through the fabric. They each got a ginger ale just before the dimming of the lobby lights sent them to their seats. After the surprising treat of the first act, Kadence had no idea what to expect in the second.

Make-believe would give away to grace. Chivalry would step aside for treats. Clara would bow in respect to the Sugar Plum Fairy. Chocolate. Coffee. Tea. Delicacies, mixed with movement that Kadence couldn't fathom. She would swear the Arabian dancer was made of rubber. Addison thought she was like an old action figure of his, with limbs bending and angled in impossible ways. The two male dancers in the Russian scene danced with a pace stuck on fast forward, appearing to move as if wearing the burning coals. After "Trepak" played for the scene, once again Kadence shook her head. *Seriously, this song too?*

Soon the playful scene with Mother Ginger ended. Nine little ones in dresses that appeared bigger than them, scurrying under her circus tent-like dress, leaving the stage. It was time for "Waltz of the Flowers."

Maybe it was the strumming of the harp that put everyone in a trance. Maybe it was the stage dimming for the first time since Act II began. Maybe it was the characters not being from a land of sweets. But there was a profound sense that something different and wonderful was about to happen.

The horns gently began. The Snow Queen was in place, with 18 dancers around her on toenails awaiting her command. Never swaying, never teetering, not moving a muscle. Nineteen elegant mannequins in the largest, most enchanting holiday window display ever. Snow cascaded down all around them, like tumbling stars. Soon the violins took over, activating the dancers, bringing them to life.

Up until then, Kadence showed surprise, joy, awe, and envy through every muscle and nerve of her body. Her head would tilt, lean over, and follow a dancer. In her lap, a finger would point up and twirl as if commanding one of the girls. She would even point to something while leaning over into Addison. She looked everywhere, almost worried she'd miss something. That would change.

Two minutes into the song, it was her turn to be a mannequin. She didn't blink, her lips parted and mouth opened, and her whole body tingled. She just stared in wonder and shock. She couldn't believe what she was watching. It was the most beautiful thing she'd ever seen.

It was as if one dancer, the most superb dancer of all, was cut up into little pieces in a cruel way. Maybe the jealous villain thought he was ridding the world of her talent, her body parts littered all over the stage. But then all the pieces, as if still connected by the same heart, and hearing the ups and downs of the music, all began moving as one. Slowly, the parts morphed into a new body, eventually a new dancer, and moved in a unison not from this world. They circled. They leaped. They crossed each other, twirled, and danced as one. The soaring melody was the ballerina's pulses, their source of energy. The violins swished their skirts. The horns swayed their heads. Smiles never cracking.

Four minutes into the song, stronger violins and horns made the song seem darker, a more somber mood. That's when they pictured the villain on the stage at the dramatic part. He was off in a corner, slumped on his knees in tears of rage. His fists balled up shaking them at the heavens that his plan had backfired. And off in a dense forest in Bavaria, Siberia, maybe some snowy planet across the Milky Way, he watched not one, but now 18 works of art tease him in a snowy dance from the gods.

Towards the end, as the Snow Queen pranced though her dancers, Addison looked over at Kadence. With the music floating into his ears, his eyes weren't fixated on the Snow Queen, but the Homecoming Queen. She was now that perfect, pristine model or mannequin in a store window. Her chest was breathing in and out, the top of her dress puffing out. Her eyes moved in that trance all over the stage. Addison slid his hand over the armrest, into her lap, and found her warm hand. She turned hers over to accept his prying fingers and they held hands for the remainder of the play. Addison's chest now heaved, as he let Tchaikovsky continue to take him away in a dream. His dream, not Clara's.

The scene ended as the music was silenced. The crowd erupted, with all 19 dancers posing perfectly on the stage. A forest snow globe from your dreams.

Addison snuck another peek at Kadence.

We'll always have Paris.

The kids let go hands, but only to clap and stand with everyone else at the encore. Eventually Kadence stopped clapping, and just clasped her hands together and brought them into her chest. Her ears heard the roars and claps. Her eyes soaking in every dancer bowing on stage. The lights came on; they interlocked fingers, and held hands up the aisle.

Kadence then dragged him over to a round table draped in lace. She slipped a program off and then stood with many others just mingling. She flipped through it, allowing Addison to lean in for a peek as well.

"They're all Cuban." She turned back to the sixth page with the principal dancers.

"Well, we are in Miami."

"I know, I know, but the main characters, the main dancers, all trained in Cuba before coming here." She flipped back a couple pages. She looked at Addison. "I had no idea there was a ballet factory down there pushing out these dancers. They were incredible."

"Baseball and Ballet I guess. What were their names?"

"Suarez, Abella, Garcia." She pointed to one of them. "She was in Minneapolis last year."

A few minutes later, they moved out with clumps of suits and dresses towards the exit. Kadence held his hand in one hand, the program in another. It was something she would keep for a long time. Addison dreamed that it would be her version of his Eastern pilot wings. Three blocks later, Addison buckled her up and she flipped down the visor again.

"We need to get you a better mirror." She rubbed her thumb over it, only making it worse.

"You don't need a mirror. You're gorgeous." He hopped in as a finger started digging into the half Windsor at his neck. She grinned and looked over at him, then flipped back up the visor.

"Now where junior?" She pulled open the glove box.

He rolled his eyes, "You thirsty?"

She nodded. "Yes." She bent her head down looking inside. "You don't worry about anyone stealing anything?"

"Not really, it's not worth getting worked up about. I just don't leave anything irreplaceable in here." He pulled the tie though his collar and started folding it up.

"I mean if they want to be a loser and steal a cassette tape or tic tacs, oh well." He handed her the folded tie and nodded at the compartment. She took and fit it in, while pulling out a tape.

He was going to mention Springsteen's *Born to Run*, really wanting to hear "Jungleland". The senior had other ideas.

She ejected one Cure tape, for another. She pushed *Kiss Me, Kiss Me, Kiss Me* into the slot and played the buttons back and forth until finding song two. The playful "Catch" started and Kadence immediately started singing and swaying to one of her favorite songs. Addison turned the corner, and made his way down Brickell Avenue, watching her. He could tell she probably played this loudly in her room and danced as if on a stage, with only old forgotten stuffed animals as her audience.

She stretched her arms up above her, feeling the wind slap her palms and wrists, as she looked up trying to grab the occasional puffy clouds lit up from the city. She joined Robert Smith, singing loudly over the roaring wind.

"You know I even think that she stared like you, she use to just stand there and stare, and roll her eyes right up to heaven, and make like I just wasn't there!"

They continued down tree lined Brickle Avenue. Addison only ventured into the other lane twice thanks to the show next to him. Eventually they turned and pulled into a Mobil station on SW Third Ave.

"Getting gas?"

Addison killed the engine as he pulled up to the minimart, not a pump. "Not exactly. Be right back."

This and another gas station on Coral Way were two he knew that served to minors if you played the part. Wearing a blazer and button down, he could get a case if he wanted. He reached into the back of a freezer, pulling out the coldest one he felt, and closed the glass door with a thump. He plopped down the 6-pack of Mickey's pull-tabs on the counter, then handed over a $5 bill.

"$3.25."

Addison nodded and walked out, leaving the bill on the counter next to a display of Marlboros. He scanned the station, put the six-pack behind his seat, and hopped back in.

She leaned back and peered behind his seat. "Mickey's?"

Addison laughed. "Heard of it?"

She shook her head, then sat back up straight.

"Oh it's the cat's ass. Opening them is the best part."

Ten minutes later, Addison dropped four quarters in the toll plaza basket at Rickenbacker Causeway. The moon was behind them now, resting on some clouds over the Everglades maybe. The lights of downtown could probably be seen in space. They came down from the drawbridge portion, with Miami Seaquarium straight ahead. Rusty Pelican was to the left.

"Have you eaten there?" Addison looked at Kadence.

"No." She looked over, checking it out.

"That was my backup plan for tonight."

"Really?"

"Yeah, there or Monty Trainers"

"Ooh, I like Monty's."

Addison nodded in approval as they pulled off the road. The Jeep tires crunched gravel for a bit, then found the paved parking lot for the beach. It wasn't a massive beach, but just a thin layer of sand from the end of the bridge to the Miami Seaquarium. With its limited size, it was routinely crowded during the day. At night, only half, with most camping out on the beach in front of fires, or just a towel between them and the sand. Five beached Hobie Cats sat on the beach to the left. Biscayne Bay stretched out in front of them, with smeared colors on the far side under Coconut Grove.

Several cars were already there, a radio was playing somewhere to the right, and a fire glowed the faces of seven to eight people in a circle down on the sand. Addison parked the Jeep and turned off the ignition.

"Wow, nice view." Kadence unbuckled and stood up, leaning on the windshield.

Addison pulled out two bottles and handed one to her. He showed her how to open it, the pull-tab taking some getting used to. With the steering wheel in the way, he couldn't stand next to her, so Addison moved behind his seat and rested his forearms on the roll bar. They sipped their beer and talked about the city and water displayed on front of them. Eventually she moved behind her seat and stood next to him, with the roll bar becoming their bar. By the time the second round was ordered, the cool December breeze was coming over their backs. She shivered, and as much as he loved seeing her in that dress, knew she needed his jacket.

"Here, put this on. You'll definitely need it for the ride home." He shrugged it off and draped it over her shoulders like a cape.

"Thank you Addison." She flung her hair out from the collar. "Ooh that feels better."

An hour later, despite being only 11:30, which in Miami time is like 7:00 everywhere else, other than maybe New York, the kids reluctantly knew they needed to head home. The bottles were empty and all evidence was in the trash can on the beach. For the ride back, neither talked much, as their minds played out the unfolding scene. The ride home presented

Addison with one of very few things that bugged him about the Jeep. The annoying gap.

The front seats were far apart with just the floorboard between them and the gearshift up between their knees. There was no console to rest arms on, or to lean over onto while holding hands. It was awkward to hold hands in the Jeep. For now, he thought about touching her back at intermission, holding hands during Act II, and rubbing shoulders and arms while standing at the bar of the Jeep. He did like seeing his blazer covering her like a warm blanket. In a way, part of him was all over her.

Twenty-five minutes later, the Jeep pulled into her driveway. The palm trees were aglow again, and this time two windows were lit up, one in the living room and one upstairs. He unbuckled her and they walked up to the door, his hand finding her lower back again. A hanging lantern's light filled the porch light yellow.

"You're not going to be in trouble are you, being late or anything?" Addison stopped at the front entryway and looked her over. He was trying to figure out how to delay this for as long as he could. He also was dying to kiss her and see what she would do. There was part of him that thought they would go out again, yet another part on the surface said this was it.

"No, no I'm good. Here, thank you so much." She pulled off his blazer and handed it back to him. He slipped his arms in and welcomed the warmth. The night was getting cooler. He tugged his sleeves down an arm at a time, and took a deep breath. There she was again in that dress, hair perfectly messed up thanks to the Jeep, and those green eyes locked onto his.

After a couple of seconds, they both caught each other saying, "Well", interrupting each other's sentence. They laughed at the silliness, and not knowing what to say. He then just made up his mind to end this. Just get it over with, once and for all. How often are you standing on the homecoming queen's front porch after a date? Addison began shaking his head slightly, half for how beautiful she looked and half for just saying, *ahh, enough is enough…*

"Addison, I..." she stopped in mid phoneme as he slowly moved towards her, his eyes roaming all over her face before jumping into her green eyes. His right hand came up, touching her cheek, cupping it. She blew out what breath she had and sucked in a new deep breath that seemed to suck him in closer. She tilted her head back a little and those green eyes peered down at his mouth an inch away.

Addison kept his eyes open, focusing in on her inches away. Kadence then brought up a hand and planted it on his pounding chest, and pushed him back. She looked down at her purse in her other hand.

"I, uh, need my keys."

Addison closed his eyes for a second in defeat, and backed away.

"Oh, right." He then watched her take a few steps back.

Kadence pulled out her keys and spun around. She slid the key in each slot, then pushed the front door open. She stepped through the tiny gap she made and disappeared inside, peaking out at him one last time. Addison peered up, as the porch light was then turned off. Left in the darkness of the front porch, he blew out a long breath and turned. *That's it I guess.*

He knew he shouldn't have tried to kiss her. His hands found his pockets and took a step when suddenly, a noise behind him brought him to a halt. He twisted around.

The door was opening again. Kadence stepped out, this time with no purse, and pulled the door closed behind her. She clasped her fingers together in front of her and stood on the doormat. Kadence's eyes then shot a glance up at the black lantern hanging above them, that was now off. She then stared at Addison.

Addison turned around completely and gave her a funny look. The two just stood in the darkness for a second or two, before Addison's curious grin disappeared as quickly as the light. She was still staring at him, waiting. He sighed as he finally got it.

Addison's hands came out of his jeans and he took two steps towards Kadence. She bit her lip. Her hands parted, arms now at her sides.

Addison's arm reached for hers and grabbing her hands. His fingers gently curled into hers and carefully squeezed them. He leaned into her, their noses touching, as he looked into her eyes. He tilted to the right a bit, and his mouth found hers.

They kissed in the darkness, holding hands at their sides for a while. Soon her arms came up around his neck and opened her mouth for more. Addison sighed and wrapped his arms around her waist, pulling her body into his. They tilted their heads while breathing strongly through their noses. She felt glorious up against him, her chest into his.

They stood for a minute, kissing. The Eastern cards were even there for it all, inadvertently in his jacket pocket and now mashed between him and her chest.

After that minute was up, which felt like five minutes, she pulled her lips off his and buried her head in his chest. They held the embrace, she feeling his pounding heart in her cheek. She loved it.

"Thank you for tonight Addison. It was wonderful."

"Yes, you are." He played with her hair under his chin.

She swallowed hard and turned. She opened the door and stepped inside. At the last second, just before the door closed, her head peeked around it. She smiled at him and whispered.

"Call me." The door closed.

Addison stood there, floating on the mat. It was a magic carpet. He then heard those two deep clicking sounds of the deadbolts, and remembered hearing them earlier when he was worried she wasn't home. He shook his head and headed back to the Jeep as if he lost 50 pounds.

On the other side of the door, Kadence pressed her forehead into the door and closed her eyes. She smiled. Her hand came up and flattened against the door, as if still trying to feel him.

She whispered. "Oh my God."

She opened those green eyes and leaned back, staring at the door inches away as if trying to look through it.

"Oh my God," she whispered again as her hand left the door and found her mouth, covering most of her face. She turned and grabbed her purse on the small table and her heels echoed in the house as she moved towards the stairs.

Addison sat in his jeep gazing up at the house, as the window downstairs went dark. He then looked up to the second floor and pictured her walking, no skipping, no better yet twirling up the stairs on her toes, along the railing, and into her room.

His Jeep cranked to life and he pushed rewind on the stereo. Eventually he swung the Jeep around the towering palms and headed home, with The Cure's "Catch" filling the late night air once again.

Addison looked up at the sky, framed by the silhouettes of trees lining the street. It was a runway of stars and cloud puffs, but his open Jeep never landed. He was still on the magic carpet from her porch.

"And she use to fall down a lot, that girl was always falling again and again, and I used to sometimes try to catch her, but never even caught her name."

His eyes found the road again, white with headlight beams. He spoke to the stereo.

"Her name is Kadence, Robert. Kadence Whitaker."

The next day he was over at her house around lunch. He met her parents, although the mom left within 10 minutes to show another house. This one in No Name Harbor on Key Biscayne. She seemed nice, but flaky. Her dad came across as very cool. He asked Addison to show him the Jeep, and Kadence had to come out and almost close the hood herself to get them back inside. They also talked cards and her dad was impressed he knew how to play Euchre. Between the Jeep, playing cards, and seeing joy on his daughter's face, Addison could have asked for his blessing in marriage and he would have slept on it.

She showed him her room, they listened to tapes, and he checked out some of her old pictures. At one point, she was standing near her closet, fixing her hair. She was in short khaki shorts and a navy Esprit sweatshirt. He just wanted to walk up to her and hug her. He didn't even need a kiss, just wrap his arms around her and hold her, as if she had just walked off a plane from a weeklong trip and he was there at the gate. An embrace that squeezed out loneliness and said, *there you are, I can't stand being away from you.*

They went back to his place to hang out a little and Addison's mom thought she was, of course, adorable. Turns out Kadence is a tea drinker and she and his mom had a cup of Fortnum & Mason Countess Grey, his mom's favorite for special occasions.

They spent the rest of the afternoon hitting the tennis ball. She had never played before and his patience showed just how crazy he was for her. He actually hit pretty poorly for his standards. She was very distracting on the court. He realized she could never be his doubles partner.

They went to The Big Cheese for dinner, picking up Gabrielle on the way. Asher and Edgar met them there. Tara said she was busy. Addison ordered his usual, lasagna and orange soda, the same thing he had gotten since he was seven. Asher had to remind Addison three times about the Dolphins - Patriots game that night at 8pm.

Later that month she would come to watch his Junior Orange Bowl matches. On Christmas night, she came down for a visit, bringing him two gifts. One was a new visor with a mirror, and the second was the Cure's *Head in the Door* tape he didn't have. He gave her his present, a new Guess jean jacket for those chilly rides in the Jeep. New Year's found him and the boys playing cards and watching Miami beat Alabama in the Sugar Bowl. At the same time, Notre Dame killed then #1 Colorado in the Orange Bowl, giving Miami another title. New Year's bowl games could be tricky on allegiances, as the boys found themselves pulling for Notre Dame to help in the whole New Year's traditional scenario.

In March, they went to the Lipton Championships, taking in the action from the stands, not the back of the court holding tennis balls. He loved seeing the players, and Mats of course, but found his memories of hanging out and strolling around with Kadence stronger. They went on the Middle Friday afternoon session into the evening session, and he realized while driving home that night he only watched tennis half the time. The other half was walking around and sitting with her.

In April, she came to his Easter Bowl tennis matches. They also watched *Casablanca* at her house, with now the quotes surprising her. They had to stop the movie three times to make out on her couch.

In June, they went to prom. They sat at the same table with Sophia and her date, and Lisette and Jeremy. The awkwardness at the table was priceless and as thick as the humidity outside. Even the initial hug between Kadence and Sophia, reminded Addison of the fake hugs gymnasts give each other at the Olympics. It had all the sincerity of a Lendl-McEnroe handshake.

Jeremy was actually not bad to talk to. He was envious of Addison's Jeep. They talked baseball and about the new Stone Roses album. It all seemed fake to Addison though, knowing if not for Kadence, he wouldn't be allowed to breathe his same air.

That night, they were among a group of 14 kids that had three adjoining rooms at the Fontainebleau Hotel on Miami Beach. They partied hard until well past midnight. That night Addison and Kadence slipped away to their own room no one knew about, and had sex. It took two times to get the hang of it, and then rolled from there.

On the way home the next morning, Addison put in *Wide Awake in America* and played "Bad" one more time. He remembered it was the first song he played in the Jeep with Kadence. This was the first time he had played it since that surprising day Thanksgiving weekend. It seemed like yesterday, and yet could have been a lifetime ago.

CHAPTER NINETEEN

The next time Addison played "Bad" in the Jeep, was four years later. It was a time and drive that required reflection. Addison needed some truth serum. The song was his needle.

He didn't have the Jeep for freshman and sophomore year. Then last August, the blue CJ7 boarded a train car and headed up the east coast, as far as it could go. He had just passed Whitin Reservoir and was rolling through Douglas, Massachusetts. With the whole day at his disposal and the Jeep, he took the back roads without a care for time. He also did all he could to avoid the outskirts of Boston traffic and his distaste for interstates. Thanks to growing up in South Florida, and I-95 as its backbone, he stayed off them whenever he could. Even his choice of college reflects this geography lesson.

It wasn't just that ten-lane artery starting in South Florida, but most of the city that pushed him away for school. He longed for hills, even mountains. After being blinded by the artificial colors of South Beach, downtown, and even the old Claude & Christo Pink Islands, he needed to be soothed by the warmth of natural fall colors. Come Halloween his boots, not flip-flops, would trounce and crunch through them on the ground. Grainy sand would be sucked away, like a low tide's backwash, allowing snow to drift and twirl its way down all around him.

UM wanted him, but it was never an option. Going to school at Miami would feel like going away to tennis camp, while taking classes. Their men's team was usually ranked high, but he wanted a college experience.

This would explain the magnets holding up two admittance letters on the fridge. There for him to see, scrutinize, and compare. Colorado or Mississippi? Boulder or Oxford? Southern charm or Rocky Mountains? SEC tennis or Big 8 tennis. As opposite of Miami as you could get. Cal, LSU, Texas, and two other schools made the list, but not his final cut. In the end, Dartmouth would trump both, unexpectedly. He didn't think the Ivy League would call him. Brown didn't take him, but the small Vermont school, with historically one of the better tennis programs in the Ivy League, did. He couldn't turn it down.

But did he sacrifice tennis though? That was the question seeping into his head, spreading like roots. The question turning into a choppy sea, rolling him left and right in bed some nights. He played just as much thanks to the indoor facility, but it was different. Where would he be if he was at Oxford, Boulder, or one of the other schools that wanted him? Or would there be no difference?

The CD was on repeat, and started again as he crossed into Rhode Island. Up until now, school and tennis were in his thoughts. Like the landscape whizzing by that was more green and fresh, a new thought sprang up. Family. Providence was only 16 miles away, which meant he'd be on Brown's campus before dinner. Bryce Morris was there, and Addison turned down spring break trips with friends to hang out with his cousin and his own thoughts. He would stay with him for the weekend. The last time he saw his cousin, was last month at his grandfather's funeral.

After the weekend, he thought about meandering around New England for the week. Bryce was heading home to Virginia, Monday. The senior had some leads and interviews to start getting ready for. He almost demanded Addison come with him, not to be alone, but Addison needed a week to himself. Alone with his thoughts, a map, and an open Jeep, he would spend the week curling through the New England landscape. There was no agenda or timetable pressing over him. Addison wasn't sure where exactly he would drive, but felt his grandfather would help in a way. Maybe he'd see a sign, town, or road that just struck a nerve inside. He figured his environment, mixed with his thoughts would steer him. Sometimes the death of someone close will make you reevaluate your life.

There was no warning, no deteriorating health signs, no cause for concern other than just being old. One second he was watching the Wisconsin basketball game, the next he wasn't. A neighbor noticed the television was on all night, which was odd. Then there were the two-bagged newspapers in the driveway. Mr. Aaron Briggs didn't forget his morning newspaper.

He was buried at the National Veteran's Memorial Cemetery in Union

Gove, Wisconsin. Addison cried at the end, holding it together longer than most. It may have been that the moment finally hit him, or it was the sight of all the white tombstones in perfect geometric lines no matter the compass heading, and knowing his grandfather was now among them.

He now looked out at the Rhode Island landscape on the other side of the Jeep. He wondered if the countryside of Belgium or France looked like this. Did his grandfather ever notice the land, trees, or birds? Or were his senses for staying alive too strong? He hoped he was maybe there now. He couldn't just be another tombstone, not his grandfather. He pictured him walking around Mons, France, holding a guidebook, not his M1 Garand rifle. He can't believe how huge the La Collégiale Sainte-Waudru appears. Maybe he walks in, gets lost, and eventually finds a seat, just memorized by a scene in one of the stained glass windows.

Then Addison checked out his side of the Jeep. Maybe now he's in Cologne, looking at the Cathedral from across the river, amazed at its bulk and mass. Its spires aimed at the heavens so high, they would shear off passing clouds. Then he was shaking his head, knowing it wasn't there the last time he was standing at the river. He almost felt like apologizing.

The last time Addison saw his grandfather was a weekend in August. With windows fogged up with humidity, they watched baseball and played cards inside. He had replayed the entire weekend in his mind, wondering what he could have done differently, what he could have asked him that he hadn't, and what he could have studied while he had the chance.

The song ended, again, as his Jeep turned into campus. He arrived at Bryce's frat house and parked across the street. He detached the faceplate to the stereo and tucked it in his backpack. The CD stayed in, with no way of ejecting it now. Like Dartmouth, Brown's spring break was next week, but the Friday before found most people already gone. Of the 18 kids that live in the house, only five were around. Bryce answered the door and hugged his cousin. Bryce picked up his duffle; Addison slung his backpack over his shoulder.

"How was the drive?"

"Not bad. Saw a UFO outside Millbury." Addison looked around the living room and peered up the stairs to his left, as a pair of jeans disappeared up the top.

"Sweet. Are you hungry?"

"Very."

The boys had a habit, more like a tradition, of lying to each other when they first met. It started at a second cousin's wedding in D.C. years ago.

Addison and his parents drove straight to the church from Dulles International.

"Hey what's up?" Addison was tucking in the back of his shirt under his jacket.

"Hey, not much."

"Where are we sitting?"

Bryce nodded off to his right. "On the right side, Tip O'Neil and Ronald Reagan are next to us. Echo & The Bunnymen are playing at the reception you know."

The next time was in Miami as the Morris family came down the Monday of Thanksgiving week. Addison finally walked in after being at the dentist.

"Hey it's about time you show up. So what's new?"

"I have two months to live."

And so on and so on…

Addison changed and ten minutes later, they were sitting in the Wild Colonial Tavern. Addison had turned 21 five days ago. They drank, ate, and caught up on their lives. They paid their bill, flirted with the waitress, and were waiting for change.

Addison was watching the waitress walk away, tapping his finger to a pretty bad song playing over speakers from somewhere in a back room. His head swaying ever so slightly, just for a second.

Bryce put his beer down. "Are you moving to the beat of Color Me Badd?"

Addison's head turned quickly, coming out of his trance. "Huh, what?"

"Are you tapping your finger and head to Color Me Badd?" Bryce said it slowly, accusingly.

"Color…no, no, I'm-"

"You so are. You're into-"

"No I don't-"

"Yes, I just watched you."

"No-"

"Dude, do you have their CD?"

"Oh my god, I-"

"Cause I wouldn't leave it in the Jeep, it may get stolen."

"No…" He shook his head looking up, laughing.

"Do you stroke one to their video "I Wanna Sex You Up"? I bet you-"

"Oh, for God's sake shut up."

Bryce continued to smile and laugh out his nose. He changed subjects.

"So where you going to head Monday?" Bryce crossed his leg.

Addison grabbed his beer. "I think Newport." He finished it, subs sliding down the inside. "Never been there actually. The hall of fame is there too."

Bryce reached for his mug. "Oh, perfect." He finished his as well. She came back with the change, smiling while dropping off the bill folder.

They headed back to his frat in Bryce's car.

"So what's the plan tonight?" Addison was eyeing the buildings and campus, thinking he would have gone here if they had accepted him.

"Well there's a usual Friday card game at another frat. We hang out at times, party with them here and there. With everyone leaving or gone, it should be low key."

"Can I get in?" Addison leaned forward checking out something passing.

"Well it's above your clearance level, but you'll be with me. I'm sure it will be okay." He eyed his cousin quickly. "Again, not many people around."

"Am I going to be making fun of them?"

"I'd be pissed if you didn't. Hayes is actually pretty cool. I know he's still here."

Addison nodded, looking out front, at where they were going.

"I need to shower."

"No problem. I can play Color Me Badd or Wilson Phillips over the stereo if you want."

Addison closed his eyes. "Just drive."

"Chet Wilcox."

"Addison Briggs." They shook hands in Bryce's doorway.

Bryce's neighbor from down the hall had just gotten back from the library. "So, you're down from Dartmouth?"

"Yeah, just for the weekend."

"Very cool." He grabbed a CD, *Automatic for the People,* from Bryce's desk, and held it up to Bryce at his computer. "I'm borrowing this." He headed out and slapped Addison's shoulder. "You're playing cards with us tonight right?" He started heading down the hallway.

"Yeah."

"Excellent. Let me clean up."

Bryce was clicking his mouse, following it on the screen with his eyes.

"Hey, do you have cards?"

"Yeah, why?"

"I figured you would. We started taking our own over there. The one guy, we think, used a marked deck one night." He pulled out a 3 1/4 floppy and tossed it in his backpack.

"So why do you go over there?" Addison sat on the bed.

Bryce shrugged his shoulders. "It's just this one guy you gotta watch. Rich prick."

Addison's fraternity was tennis, if he had one. The guys' and girls' team were a family. He had plenty of other friends as well, arriving on campus a tennis rock star. He was the two seed as a freshman and most were curious about the tennis stud from Miami. He knew three frat guys at Dartmouth, and hung out with them a little, but never wanted to join.

These composites could make a guy change his mind.

He noticed them at Bryce's frat, going back 27 years, but this frat had been around forever. The second floor had a huge, open room at the top of the stairs, with two hallways branching off in opposite directions. The whole wall was taken up by these black framed composites, about 4' x 2', taken each year with everyone's headshot. The first frame was from the first class, 1932, up until last years. Exactly 60 years of history and brotherhood. Addison thought it was pretty cool. A guy on the last two, walked by noticing Addison studying them.

"Hey, you came with Chet and Bryce right?"

"Yeah. Addison."

"Perry. Welcome." He kept his left hand in his pocket, the other holding a Rolling Rock. Addison inched his arm forward to shake, but could tell Perry didn't want to, and awkwardly drew it back. He turned back to the composites, hoping Bryce and Chet would hurry up. The seven brothers he saw here all acted as if they were on the first one from 1932. And on the one from 1957. 1971 too. Even on one in five or six years when they would be long gone and graduated.

Bryce introduced Addison as his brother, and allowed for vague interpretations to float in the air. With 64 brothers in this house during a normal day, and another 38 at Bryce's, no one could remember and know everyone. Hayes was walking up the stairs with Bryce and Chet now. He seemed okay, and was the warmest guys in the place. He actually smiled at Addison and shook his hand.

"Hi, Hayes Petry. Welcome."

"Addison, thanks so much."

Addison could feel Perry behind him, like a guard on post. If it were cold enough inside, he'd see his breath float over his shoulder in puffs.

"Pretty old huh? They've been around forever here." Bryce said it casually to Addison, who nodded at all the frames. Bryce then did a double take and leaned forward to inspect one face up close. He pointed to one from two years ago, and turned. "Hayes, were you trying to grow a beard?"

Hayes laughed. "No, I can't remember why, no wait; it was the rugby team's hell week. We didn't shave the whole week." He matched leans and peered over Bryce's shoulder. "I guess this was taken mid-week?"

He laughed and moved down the hallway. Everyone followed. Perry brought up the rear, eyeing Addison with Bryce's "old" comment weighing on his eyelids. He stared him down. There was something about Addison he didn't like, and now Bryce's comment added to his suspicion. Why would he say that to him. He should know about us. *This is my brother, Addison.* Yeah, bull shit.

The card game was in the game room, in the corner of the house. It was one of the bigger rooms, with a billiards table and two foosball tables. There was a real card table, green felt and slots of chips. Addison sat next to Bryce, with Chet on the other side of Bryce. Hayes was next to Addison, with Perry and Matthew across the table.

Dr. Dre's *Chronic*, was playing in the room. Money was laid out on the table. The game was five-card draw. Matthew actually liked the Eastern cards. He's from New York, and flies them often out of JFK.

Perry shook his head. “Why the hell are we playing with those?”

Bryce and Chet exchanged a look.

“Well I’m sure you have house rules, which is fine. So we can bring the cards.” Addison eyed Perry. Bryce shot a glance over at Addison, surprised at the angle.

“Perry they’re fine, look at them. Besides, he has a point. Come on, let’s do this.” Hayes slapped the table once, then sipped his beer. Perry nodded and acted cool, but was furious inside. Addison picked up on his little body language instantly. Cash was handed over as chips were passed out accordingly.

Three games in, everyone talked as the beer flowed and cards flipped. At one point, Addison turned to Hayes. “So you’re sticking around for spring break?”

“Yeah, at least the beginning. I may head home to Philly for a couple of days at the end of next week.”

Matthew started shuffling. “When do you and Marcus leave for Colorado?” He gave Perry a quick look.

Hayes turned to Perry, surprised. “Nice, I didn’t know you were heading out there.”

Perry sat up. “Keep it down. I’m not now.” He eyed the carpet leading to the door. “I’m actually going to Paris for the week. Girl I know is over there studying abroad for the year. We’re going to hang out for the week.”

“What about Ava?” Matthew stopped shuffling and looked at him, hands still smothering the cards.

Nothing.

“What does Ava know?” Hayes asked it with a touch on concern.

“I’m going to tell her tomorrow something has come up, and I need to go home. I just won’t use the ticket to Denver.”

“Does Marcus know?” Matthew asked, then finished arching the cards into one stack. He continued shuffling.

“No he doesn’t.”

Hayes and Matthew exchanged glances.

The table was quiet. The cards and Dr. Dre were the only sounds heard. The cards were dealt. Hayes was in the lead, with everyone else jumbled up together behind him. Chet was already down half.

Perry won the hand with two pairs, but botched up the bet and could have gotten far more in the pot. He was stacking his chips again when the door opened. Two girls walked in. The boys all sat up straight, and heads turned. They were holding beers and holding hands. The one was laughing at something, acting like it was just said at the door.

"Ava, you need to knock." Perry's voice was like a judge handing down the verdict.

"Sorry, damn, didn't think it mattered. Here." She handed him a beer and then a second to Hayes. Hayes actually said thanks, then did a double take at Ava behind him. His eyes then glanced over at Perry before looking on the table for the bottle opener.

The second girl, a blond, started nodding her head to the music. She was scanning the table, her eyes moving from chip pile to chip pile.

"Hey, has anyone seen Marcus?"

Heads shook. Eyes looked around. "Nope."

"Did you try the basement?" Hayes offered.

"I ain't going down there, it's still disgusting from last weekend." She made a ghastly face and looked at Hayes.

"It's disgusting from last year." Ava bumped her with her shoulder and looked at the three new guys at the table.

"If I see him, I'll send him your way." Matthew bounced the comment off the table to them.

"Come on." Ava pulled her out of the room. The door closed.

Chet continued looking at the door, as if he could still see the blond through it. Bryce kicked him under the table. He laughed.

"Hot huh?" Matthew looked at Chet. Everyone nodded.

"That's Michelle." Matthew said while taking his cards.

"Marcus is a lucky guy." Bryce added. More nods. Except from the left of the table. Addison was eyeing Perry. Addison then began curling his toes.

His grandfather told Addison to never show anything to a player at the table. No facial expression. No itchy fingers. Addison would grab the chair with his hand and squeeze, channeling any anger or nerves into the wood or plastic. His grandfather pointed to his hand, now red with marks from the chairs hard edge.

"You need both hands on the table Addison," his Grandfather said. "Players will see your hand like that."

Addison nodded, looking at the evidence, holding a glass of lemonade.

He had to figure out a way to release tension no one could see. And it came from watching Ivan Lendl.

Lendl was playing Wilander in the 87 US Open final. Addison was watching on the couch. This was after moving there from the chair, where he went after the bean bag, all preceded by originally lying on the floor looking up at the television, as Pat Summerall and Tony Trabert welcomed everyone to Flushing Meadows. Nothing was working.

Mats was down two sets to one and in trouble. Lendl rifled a forehand winner to break Wilander. Lendl could hold serve twice and he'd win. His mom looked at Addison, knowing he wasn't liking the outcome. She joked, "Aren't you going to throw something? You look better than I thought you would."

He shook his head and turned it off, not wanting to watch the inevitable. Anyone else, he watches to the end, seeing Mats shake hands like the gentleman he is. But this was Ivan from the iron curtain. He stood up and then nearly fell down, as if both his legs were asleep. It wasn't his legs. It was his toes. He had curled them up, bunched them up in his shoes so tight in anger, that he couldn't straighten them. They were sore for the next hour. He inadvertently, had his trick.

Sitting in the corner room of that frat, they curled at Perry. He watched Perry never look at his girlfriend. He felt his breath on him out in the hall. He knew he was the one using a marked deck. Then Addison thought of Ava, walking out. It could have been Kadence or Tara for that matter.

An hour later Chet was a spectator and Bryce was about out. Hayes was one hand away from bowing out, leaving Addison with Matthew and Perry. There were also others watching. It was like the walls were too thin, and they leaked to the guys on the composite pictures, who passed it down from one to the next, one decade to the next, finally to the few kids downstairs. People had showed up in the room.

Addison and Perry had the most chips, with Matthew hanging in there. The hands continued, and the room swelled with people and edginess. There was no question who were the main characters. The issue that bugged Bryce was the supporting cast. A supporting cast on those walls outside.

Addison was dealing this hand. His flicking wrist sent the cards out as if casting a fishing line, hitting his spot every time. Perry was sitting back in his chair, tapping his finger.

"Where do you go to school?"

"Dartmouth."

Some heads turned to Addison. Bryce closed his eyes. Perry raised an eyebrow and chuckled. Addison did nothing. He just finished his deal and picked up his cards.

Perry thought he knew this answer, he just wanted to see Addison's reaction to the next question.

"Do we have a chapter there?"

"No clue." He tossed in his ante and looked up at Perry and Matthew. Perry was madder at the carefree attitude than the answer.

For the next five hands, Addison melted Perry's chips. Four stacks, became three. Three tall ones, became three small ones. Then two stacks. Perry's face was clay. Something changed on it every five-seconds. His shoulders were pushed together. And his eyes were absolutely everywhere. Then there was Addison. Addison was a monument.

What Perry and his brothers didn't know, was Addison grew up playing cards with a guy that treated card games like he treated the war. Total focus, there was no second place, no fun & games, anticipate your opponent, and if need be, run out into that field and kill those two Germans with only your bare hands and a small knife, before they get a clear shot. This frat schmuck across the table would be child's play.

The one thing that did perk his defenses, like his cousin, was the crowd. He, Bryce, and Chet were basically all alone. This made him long for the high school hallway, and having to deal with Cleopatra's Guard. This room really made them like puppies.

The next hand found Matthew giving up, cutting his loses. The cards were dealt. Addison needed to try to end this. The chip piles were agreeing with him.

Perry's jaw and more importantly, his betting gave away his hand. It was probably good. Addison's wasn't. But as far as Perry was concerned, it didn't matter. Calls were followed by raises. Addison really wanted to get rid of four cards, but house rules said he couldn't. Three would have been smart, but not when bluffing. He asked for one.

Perry looked at him surprised, wondering how good his hand could be. Perry had three nines. Addison had a pair of fours.

The raises were piling up on the calls, the chips were piling on chips in the middle, the pulses were throbbing into thuds.

Addison raised again. It was up to Perry, who looked at his money remaining. If it was less than 30 minutes ago, it was much less than four raises ago. He couldn't take a chance. He took a deep breath and threw his cards down. "God damn fold!" Everyone came down off their heels, the room lowered.

Addison smiled at him and reached forward, swiping the money towards him. Bryce wondered what Addison had, and was going to ask him later after leaving. He was shocked to find out within five-seconds.

It was an unwritten rule to not show folded hands. Addison never did it. His grandfather never did it. His grandfather's friends in Madison and Naples wouldn't even mention it. But Addison sensed Perry was at a breaking point, mentally and chips-wise. The next hand could snap him.

It was Perry's deal and Addison picked up his five cards, and turned them over as he tossed them. "Here you go. By the way, that pair of fours was mighty weak huh?"

Perry's eyes were the size of a poker chip. He spewed out a ten-second cursing rant, followed by a thrown bottle cap at Addison. He held up a hand to block it. It felt like a potato chip hitting him. Matthew stood up at his chair, his game done long ago, crossing his arms. Two brothers with hands on their hips moved closer to Addison's chair, almost standing on the arm rests. Bryce almost pissed in his pants. Ava and Michelle came in hearing Perry from down the hall, then left.

Hayes tried controlling the table and told Perry to deal. Hayes was struggling, along with one of the brothers hovering behind Addison. A fellow brother was losing, bad, and getting taunted by a GDI from another Ivy League. At the same time, there was a struggle with honor. The brother in need was the one brother that half the fraternity was sick and tired of dealing with. After two years, if the fraternity was sinking, and there was one seat left in the lifeboat, some wouldn't go out of their way to search for Perry.

Addison swallowed, knowing he didn't need to do that, but his toes were killing him. Addison looked at the Eastern cards shuffling and thought of his first game of solitaire when he was 11. He thought of the games with his grandfather. The game with Aaron Krickstein. The games with Asher, Corey, and Edgar. The strip poker game with Kadence two weeks before she left for Northwestern. The games at Dartmouth. He just needed an average hand. Just three solid cards out of five one more time.

Perry dealt, snapping them down on the table with his thumb. Addison grabbed his, but looked at Perry, waiting for him to look at his hand. When he did, his chest barely came out. His eyes zipped left and right, back and forth across the tops of his cards. Addison reached for his knowing he had nothing. Perry was searching his cards for something that wasn't there, searching for the best two or three to hang onto.

Addison moved his down to his lap. *Show nothing, show nothing, look at each card for two seconds. Toes, toes, toes. Count…* He turned the edges of the cards up.

Three red and two black cards. Two spades, a club, a diamond, and a heart. Not exactly good news. However what made his toes nearly break, were the red and black numbers.

6, 5, 8, 9, 7. He had a straight.

Not only would he bet high, mimicking the last hand where he bluffed, but now, wouldn't even ask for a discard. There was no way Perry would think he wasn't bluffing again.

No one, the six at the table, to the seven standing, could remember the last time they saw someone ask for no discards. Perry asked for two, which surprised Addison, but felt like he was trying to show a brave front. The bets came, the raises followed. Then Perry didn't have much left. *He's trying to bluff me dry,* Perry thought.

No one was looking at Perry. All eyes were on an emotionless Addison, and the lack of chips in between Perry's arms. He turned and looked up at Taylor.

"Go get my Ritual Book." Taylor returned 30 seconds later and handed Perry his Ritual Book. Every brother is given the black book at initiation. Perry looked at the coat of arms on the cover, then opened it. He pulled out something rectangular. It was white, with slanting blue lines fading to red ones. He held it over the table and dropped it on the pile of chips.

It was an Air France boarding pass booklet. CONCORDE was written at the top. No one said anything for several seconds. No one could see the ticket, no one knew where it lead to, but it didn't matter. It could have gone to Siberia. It was a seat on the Mach two rocket, costing at least $10,000.

"I call and raise." Perry smirked at him, dripping in attitude and cockiness. It wasn't so much the amount that he wanted to enforce; it was the principle that he can buy a ticket on the Concorde and was good enough to risk it.

Everyone turned to Addison. Bryce covered half his face with his fingers and sweaty palm. The ticket was a little more than half the table value. Addison reached into his jeans and pulled out his Jeep keys. They jingled as he tossed them on the cash.

"Call."

A chair squeaked. Swallows were heard and felt in the room. Dr. Dre was even silent. Even Addison had to take a deep breath and blow out. No one blinked and everyone's eyes got watery because of it.

Addison looked at the keys and thought of his engine, and that summer he spent with his father rebuilding it. The Jeep was the hub of the neighborhood. People would pop in to check on it, chat, and just hang out. How many times did Asher, Corey, Edgar, Tara, and Gabrielle come over? How many new songs did they hear on the radio while leaning over into it, twisting a wrench? How many stories did his father share with him in the garage that may not have come out if not for the Jeep and tools? How many times did he drive it to Naples? The last time he saw his grandfather, he sat in the passenger seat on two occasions. He even took off his faded, red Wisconsin hat so the wind could blow his hair. "You know, in the war, the windows were pushed down on these things…"

Now, he saw his engine on the middle of the card table. They weren't keys, but a Jeep that was no longer his. Just like that, it was gone. It was for sale, and instead of being surrounded by shimmering streamers and colorful balloons on a used car lot, it was fenced in by colorful chips, and green and brown beer bottles. *Oh my god, what have I done…*

Perry laid down his cards, just as everyone leaned forward over the table.

He managed a two pairs, two 5's and two 9's, thanks to the discard. Perry leaned forward ready to take the pile, then he would see if he and his brothers would beat the hell out of Addison.

Addison closed his eyes and slowed his breathing. His heart was in his throat and no matter what his toes did, he was now fighting the emotions.

He won. He would keep his Jeep most importantly, and had a ticket on the Concorde. He beat this prick, but he was on the second floor of a fraternity house with seven brothers who would be beyond pissed, at a GDI no less. *How the hell do we get out of here?*

Addison leaned forward and laid his cards down.

Jaws dropped and eyes exploded open, then shifted to Perry. Some stared at the middle of the table, considering what was there.

Bryce ran his hands through his hair and pushed back form the table. "Let's go," came in a shaking voice, a seismograph needed to check his pulse.

Addison stood up and grabbed the keys first. He then looked around at the cave of people surrounding the table, expecting something to happen, and was surprised. No one did anything. No one said anything. It was a mixture of shock, anger, and justice.

Perry finally stood up and threw a beer bottle across the room. It somersaulted between Addison and Bryce like a boomerang, smashing against the wall. Crystals of glass raining down on the Papasan chair and floor.

"You're so dead!" Perry's teeth were mashed. His fist a hammer.

Bryce pointed at him. "Look douchebag, you're-"

"Don't." Addison grabbed his cousin's hand and brought it back down.

Addison's hands were shaking as he picked up the ticket folder and started scooping up some of the cash that found its way on the table, when chips were running out. He didn't bother with the chips. He felt a leg up against his side, and someone stepped into the chair, pushing it into his hip. Bryce started grabbing cash too, and wide eyes met Chet's.

"That's cards, fair and square. We're leaving." Addison looked up at Perry and Matthew next to him. Chips were still scattered on the table. Addison didn't care. He looked down at his cards, as Bryce clenched his upper arm, pulling him out. He started backing away, moving towards the door. They didn't bother with the chips, they just wanted out of there. Fast.

No one moved, a layer of trees in his way. Addison looked all of them in the face as he walked through and by them, leaning into them like wading through waist deep water. Bryce and Chet were right behind him. Hayes and Taylor's look said it all, the last two to feel Addison slide through towards the door. *You're lucky it was him. Get out of here, before we do something we all should do, but don't want to do.*

A minute later Ava walked into the room.

"Damn they were in a hurry." Perry had his hands to his face, walking away. As usual, she picked up the mess. She started pulling chairs out and grabbing two cards that fell onto the floor. She snatched two beer bottles as well, putting them upright on the table.

Michelle came into the room as some moved out. "Good lord what happened in here?" Marcus was right behind her, sneaking up, and picked her up like a rag doll. She kicked and screamed as if being kidnapped.

"Marcus! What are you doing?" A playful tone now swirled in the room that three minutes ago would have blown up if a match were lit.

Ava laughed from her knees, between the table and a fallen chair on its side. She stood up and started clearing the table. All 52 blue cards, and two jokers, found the snug box. She grabbed Perry's Ritual Book and put the deck of cards on top.

Five minutes later, the Ritual Book was slid into its place on the bookshelf. Then Ava glanced around Perry's room, tapping the Eastern box on her thigh, before deciding to toss the deck of cards into a suitcase. She figured they would get used next week. She also assumed they belonged to someone at the frat. The Eastern cards were now scheduled for their own flight. A flight west, much slower than their original owner's would be.

"Jesus Christ! Don't ever do that again, you hear me!" Bryce hugged his cousin as they reached the far side of the street. They squeezed and eventually pulled away from the embrace.

"Holy hell what did I just do." Addison brought his hand up to his forehead. The adrenaline the surged through his body at the table was now sucked out of him. His legs felt like they were asleep. His head airy.

"Next time you come down, can we just get drunk and chase girls?" Chet put his hand on Addison's shoulder, bending over slightly catching his breath.

Addison turned and looked up at the house; through bare trees just beginning to come back to life with a few leaves.

"My cards are in there."

Bryce gave him a look. "You wanna go back in there? Help yourself."

Addison actually thought about it, but just took a deep breath as they all started breathing normally. Addison was only shaking on the inside now.

"Come on." Chet pushed everyone forward towards Bryce's parked car. Bryce was the last one in after fumbling with his keys. He turned the ignition.

"Wow," Chet looked at Bryce and then Addison in the backseat, "it started up."

"Did you expect us to blow up?" Addison laughed.

"Actually I did."

Bryce peered up in the mirror at the back seat. "You ever going to tell your dad about this?"

"My dad?" Addison leaned over towards the middle of the back seat. "I'm telling him and yours this summer."

Bryce smiled as he pulled out into the street. He looked up in the rearview mirror once again. "So I guess you need to pack."

Addison Briggs was in seat 19D of Air France flight AF001, from New York's JFK to Charles de Gaulle International, outside Paris. It was the Monday morning of Spring Break. He had the window seat on the right side, having absolutely no clue what to expect.

Two days earlier, Addison left one Ivy League campus for another. He packed and drove to New York on Sunday. He would still spend the week meandering around, but via train not Jeep. And it wouldn't be New England, but France, Belgium, and hopefully Germany. Just possibly, he'd run into a certain ghost as well. The cobblestones of Paris would be first, however. He'd always wanted to call Paris home for a couple of days.

His backpack had two Michelin Green Guides, one France and the other Germany. There was also his folder of notes and maps from his grandfather. He figured he'd soak in Paris for two days, then head up to Normandy. From there maybe Metz, and into the Ardennes of Belgium. He could put his bags in a locker and follow his maps to find places. He then hoped to get into Germany and the Rhine. He couldn't wait to stand on a certain bridge and try not to cry.

With the trip of a lifetime suddenly thrown at him in one sleepless night, the only itinerary was a hotel wakeup call near JFK. There were no preparation or tour guide markings to possibly follow. He figured he'd use the flight to go over details. Problem was, and it was an absolutely marvelous problem, there wouldn't be much time.

3 1/2 hours.

An extra-inning baseball game. The drive from Miami to Orlando. *The Godfather*, with a break in the middle to make a sandwich and pop popcorn. The length of his winning, four set match at Yale last month. That's all it took to cover six time zones.

He of course knew about the speed. Everything else was, well, shocking. For as big and wide as the plane looks, with its bat-like wings, the Concorde is actually very tiny. Inside is like a 727, maybe smaller. The cockpit was nothing but gray switches and gauges, everywhere. He couldn't even see a dash or panel. He thought only a surgeon's hands could turn something on or off without bumping others by accident. The menu was the fanciest he'd ever seen, thick and heavy, with a tasseled string down the middle. It's loud. It was the first time he couldn't hear his heart pounding in his ears since turning off his Jeep. It was noisier at times thanks to the afterburners, and when first ignited, there was a burning, gas smell. And then there was the speed and elevation. It might as well have been light years.

All the flight information was displayed on the bulkhead between the first and second cabin. Mach. Feet. Temperature. Speed. After just 20 minutes, they were supersonic at Mach 1, 660 mph. Wispy clouds probably 50 miles away sailed by like tissue paper in a breeze.

Then 820 mph.

970 mph

1130 mph.

1320 mph. Mach two.

Ninety minutes into the flight, they were at 53,000 feet. He could actually see the curvature of the earth. They were flying above the cirrus clouds. With only outer space above him, he wondered how many humans could say they had seen the top of the highest clouds on Earth? It was like seeing the other side of the moon. It was -56 degrees Celsius outside, yet the window was hot to the touch. If he needed any reassurance of how fast they were going, by the time he did some quick mental math, figuring out that was the same as -70 degrees Fahrenheit, they had traveled 100 miles.

He peered down at his jeans, his blue blazer. He looked at his hand in his lap, then turned it over to see the creases of his palm. He didn't feel any different, didn't feel like he was going two times the speed of sound. And all this had nothing to do with what was going on inside Addison. That was a whole other story.

He just knew his grandfather had something to do with that last poker hand. There's no question in his mind. He parked his Jeep in long-term parking and just sat in it for ten minutes. He touched and rubbed the hood before picking up his bags and walking away. It was like he was apologizing and making up from two nights ago. His coffee was black and strong in the main concourse, like his father's and grandfather's. His bag was carried, not rolled like the new lazy norm. He handed over his passport at the Air France ticket counter with all the panache of a spy. His thank you to the lady before leaving, was a wink.

He paused in front of the departures screen, the size of a tennis court suspended over the waxed, tile floor. His eyes roamed down the list of cities. Austin wasn't there, but Dallas was close enough. He found Denver, down the mountains from Boulder. Miami. No Baton Rouge, or Oxford, but New Orleans was the best he could do. Eventually his eyes found San Francisco with Berkley a neighbor. He felt a connection to all of them. Between visits, phone calls, brochures, magazines, coaches calls, and most importantly dreams, he was at all of them despite choosing Hanover, New Hampshire.

That's when it hit him, with a feeling like inventing something revolutionary. The plane ticket was his patent. His burning question from Friday, that he originally hoped to answer this week in New England, could be answered now. And it laid in those computer graphic, city names up on the schedule board. Each of those cities are a written introduction, but no body, no conclusion. There never will be. They'll always be unfinished pieces of work, only prologues.

Because for whatever page, verse, and chapter of his Dartmouth memoirs he is in now, it brought him here. He stood there, holding that plane ticket, feeling the joy like one of those seven year olds in the Stahlbaum living room, because of his choice three years ago to go to

Dartmouth. This page would not have been turned at any of those other campuses. Pretty soon, Dartmouth's would be complete as well. Addison couldn't wait to pen more cherished achievements and memories.

Only Miami had a story complete to tell. It told him of the last time he flew somewhere alone, without being completely sure of what to expect. And the character from that tale, was an 11-year-old boy.

He passed a newsstand. He wondered who was on the cover of *The Hockey News* this week. Pavel Bure? Mario Lemieux? What articles were in *National Geographic*? What did the 1993 Topps baseball cards look like? He sat at the gate as if next to the umpire's chair, waiting to be called to get the championship trophy. He stepped on board as if the space shuttle. He strolled down the aisle like heading to the stage with an acceptance speech. Finally, he sunk into the black, molded leather seat like something from an Italian race car, ready for his space ride.

At 8:02, flight AF001 lifted off runway 31L. Fifteen-seconds later, it banked hard left to take its noise away from civilization. It climbed quickly. It accelerated just as quickly. A 1979 Champagne was served to everyone, with a lobster appetizer. The champagne's flute felt thin, yet heavy, and unique. He ordered the grilled sea bass with caviar cream sauce, Swiss chard, and wild rice. Addison had no idea what Swiss chard was, but it sounded really cool. His voice was low, his tone confident, like he ordered this as often as he ordered his black coffee and blueberry muffin each morning at the coffee shop, three blocks away from his bed. The 21-year-old then looked in his backpack for something.

He finally found what he was after and pulled it out. He held it and looked at it through the eyes of a gemologist. The gold wings were not as shiny. The blue and white Eastern logo was a smidgen duller. But Darlene's Eastern Airlines pilot wings, better known as his promise ring, still felt the same. He put it on the tray table next to his champagne flute. They would be like his dog tags for the week. They were him.

Addison looked at the wings next to the champagne, going at the time, 700 mph. He shook his head. The wings didn't vibrate and the champagne was still and level, as if on a table at the equator. He wondered where Darlene was. Up here somewhere, below him a few cloud levels? Was she heading into the eye doctor's office wondering how full her schedule was? Was she playing fetch or walking her dog? Addison couldn't remember the dog's name, and felt ashamed. He thought back to that first flight alone to DC, and sleeping under Bryce's model Concorde.

Ten years. He turned looking out his window, as if he could see it all being left behind in the exhaust. Was Kadence sleeping in? What was on the back of Tara's bedroom door now? Who was the youngest to finish this year's raft race? Will a player bring pizza for the ball kids at Lipton this month? Did someone get Mr. Kael his café con leche last week? Does Asher also grin every time a card game comes up around Halloween?

Where did it go? Thinking back he couldn't complain. It was superb. A decade-long lavish party. He wondered what he would do in the next ten. The supersonic speed of his real life Concorde was taking him to a galaxy of possibilities.

The stewardess came by, with a puffy thick scarf you'd only see for special occasions. Her hair up in a perfect, circular bun. Addison held up his left hand.

"Yes sir?" She clasped her hands together.

"I was wondering. Do you have any playing cards?"

She smiled. "Well of course."

From November 1984 to March 1993……

19 games of Black Jack
106 games of Euchre
5 games of Fish
252 games of Five-Card Draw Poker
61 games of Gin
286 games of Klondike Solitaire
14 games of Memory
2 games of Roll Your Own Poker
117 games of Rummy
73 games of Spades
1 game of Strip Poker
6 games of War

EPILOGUE

Some years later, on the same calendar day Misty Carmichael shared her stories of Riley Grace, formally Riley Cobb, to her husband of six days, Benton Elliot strutted into the antique store in Manhattan. Benton and two other friends continued their search for a gift. They were down to six hours.

"So what do you have in mind?"

"I don't know," Benton spoke to Evan, but eyed three grandfather clocks near the entrance, "but I will once I see it."

"Awesome that narrows it down." Allison sipped her latte as she turned the corner looking at a rack of fur coats. "I didn't know they have clothes here?"

"Yeah they have real old stuff too." Evan glared at Benton.

"Oh come on, we'll find like, the Maltese Falcon, or something really cool and everyone will be jealous." Benton put down a cigar cutter made of gold.

Allison slid over three coats on the rack before pulling one off. She slipped it on and swiped her long hair out from under the collar with both hands.

"Ally that's got your name all over it." Benton looked at her while picking up a teakettle with the England coat of arms from King Richard II's time period on it.

She spun around as if on a runway. "I think it does. I should wear this to work on casual Fridays."

Benton was looking inside the teakettle. "You guys still do that?"

"Yeah, it's more of a joke actually. My boss wore a robe once."

Evan walked by looking down at his phone thumbing a message.

"Sports fans, we need to find something."

"Okay okay." Benton touched nearly everything on his way around the store, both floors, leaving a print to stamp it wasn't good enough. 15 minutes later, they gathered in the front of the double doors and exited onto the busy street. A yellow cab pulled up as the man's arm came down. He pulled open the door with the same hand, tossing a brief case on the far seat. The cab pulled away, as did the school of cars as if following it.

"What now?" Evan asked. He nodded across the street. "How about a kid's meal prize?"

Benton smiled as they headed down the shady side of the sidewalk, with lines of people moving about in opposite directions like flat escalators side by side. He fished his hand into his coat pocket, wiggling until he found them. He pulled out a deck of playing cards. He slipped open the top and pinched the cards, sliding them out.

"You got them playing cards? Seriously?" Evan shot a glance at Allison.

She leaned over, looking around Evan.

"Cause nothing says, congratulations on your wedding day from your longtime friend, like playing cards."

"Chill out guys, these are for me." He flipped through them before sliding them back into the box, and closing the lid flap.

"These are old, my father use to fly Eastern way back in the day. I think to Washington." He twisted them around checking both sides of the box.

"Never heard of Eastern." Allison reached for them and checked out the box herself.

Evan followed the cards over to Allison. "So how much were they?"

"Don't know, stole them."

"What?" Allison looked up, throwing the box at an unprepared Benton.

"You took them?" Evan was now staring at Benton picking them up after bumping into a passing couple. They were all now stopped on the sidewalk. Evan again looked at Allison shaking his head. The same guy that restored a 1987 Alfa Romeo Spider convertible for fun, couldn't pay $2.50 for a deck of cards. It was so Benton.

Allison pulled out her phone after it buzzed. She read it while talking.

"I'd pay money to see you at the cafeteria in prison. While everyone tells what they're in for, and after hearing two for murder, grand theft, and kidnapping, you could say for lifting grandma's bridge cards."

Benton looked over at Allison with a grin.

"Good one."

He slipped them into his inner jacket pocket and began walking. His hands buttoned his tweed jacket, then found his jean pockets. He glanced up at the sky, squinting with the sun gleaming off the Empire State Building at the end of the canyon of metal they were navigating.

"They're just old playing cards for god's sake." Then his eyes found the much softer sidewalk view again. He stopped at the curb with everyone else.

"Now there's an interesting story to go with them."

CPSIA information can be obtained
at www.ICGtesting.com
Printed in the USA
LVHW040012030922
727460LV00002B/283

9 781948 928069